INCARNATION, PAIN, THEOLOGY

Northwestern University
Studies in Phenomenology
and
Existential Philosophy

General Editor Anthony J. Steinbock

INCARNATION, PAIN, THEOLOGY

A Phenomenology of the Body

Espen Dahl

Northwestern University Press
Evanston, Illinois

Northwestern University Press
www.nupress.northwestern.edu

Copyright © 2024 by Northwestern University. Published 2024 by Northwestern
University Press. All rights reserved.

Printed in the United States of America

10   9   8   7   6   5   4   3   2   1

ISBN 978-0-8101-4701-0 (paper)
ISBN 978-0-8101-4702-7 (cloth)
ISBN 978-0-8101-4703-4 (ebook)

Library of Congress Cataloging-in-Publication Data

Names: Dahl, Espen, 1974– author.
Title: Incarnation, pain, theology : a phenomenology of the body /
    Espen Dahl.
Other titles: Northwestern University studies in phenomenology & existential
    philosophy.
Description: Evanston, Illinois : Northwestern University Press, 2024. |
    Series: Northwestern University studies in phenomenology and existential
    philosophy | Includes bibliographical references and index.
Identifiers: LCCN 2023051327 | ISBN 9780810147010 (paperback) |
    ISBN 9780810147027 (cloth) | ISBN 9780810147034 (ebook)
Subjects: LCSH: Phenomenology. | Mind and body. | Incarnation. | Pain—
    Religious aspects. | Theology.
Classification: LCC B829.5 | DDC 142/.7—dc23/eng/20240305
LC record available at https://lccn.loc.gov/2023051327

To Helge and Åse

Contents

	Acknowledgments	ix
	Introduction	3
1	Phenomenology and Incarnation	12
2	The Body between Matter and Form	46
3	"I Cannot"—The Passivity of the Body	67
4.	Touch and Skin	88
5	The Inner Contradictions of Pain	109
6	Communicating Pain	129
7	Incarnation and the Cross	154
8	Embodied Hope	176
	Coda	200
	Notes	209
	Bibliography	235
	Index	247

Acknowledgments

It has taken me many years to write this book, but it was not completed without help. I would like to express my gratitude to those who have read and responded to drafts of my chapters: Thor Eirik Eriksen, Ola Sigurdson, Alejandro Alvelais, and Mathias Sollie. I also extend my thanks to Michael T. Heneise, Theodor S. Rolfsen, and Istvan Czachesz for their help, support, and stimulating conversations. Furthermore, I have profited from discussions with my colleagues in the research group Interdisciplinary Phenomenology at UiT—the Arctic University of Norway.

I am grateful to the publishers that have granted me permission to reproduce a handful of pages from already published articles: "Weakness and Passivity: Phenomenology of the Body after Paul," in *Phenomenology of the Broken Body*, edited by E. Dahl, C. Falke, and T. E. Eriksen (London: Routledge, 2019), 13–28, reproduced by permission of Taylor & Francis Group; and "Job and the Problem of Physical Pain: A Phenomenological Reading," *Modern Theology* 32 (2016): 45–59, reproduced with the permission of John Wiley and Sons. I have also drawn on general perspectives and ideas from previously published material. Chapter 3: "Mottageligheten og kroppens fenomenologi," in *Skapelsesnåde: Festskrift for Svein Aage Christoffersen*, edited by S. Holte, M. T. Mjaaland, and R. Jensen (Oslo: Novus, 2017), 37–54; chapter 5: "The Inner Tension of Pain and the Phenomenology of Evil," *International Journal of Philosophy and Theology* 78 (2017): 396–406; and chapter 7: "Inkarnasjon, kors og smertens fenomenologi," *Teologisk Tidsskrift* 4 (2015): 148–63.

INCARNATION, PAIN, THEOLOGY

Introduction

This book intends to present a phenomenological approach to the body. There is no scarcity of phenomenological literature on the body, since it has occupied phenomenology almost from its beginning. Already in 1907, Edmund Husserl gave lectures in which the body was given lengthy treatment, which he expanded and revised in his later writings. Edith Stein, who started as Husserl's assistant, developed the phenomenology of the body further. Helmuth Plessner and Gabriel Marcel also elaborated on phenomenological perspectives on the body from early on. However, the theme of the phenomenology of the body has, for good reasons, been attached to the name of Maurice Merleau-Ponty. While Merleau-Ponty did not intend to provide a phenomenology of the body as such, but rather a phenomenology of the appearance of the world through the body, his persistent return to the body throughout his authorship warrants his status. In recent decades phenomenological perspectives on the body have spread to different fields, such as environmental thinking, theology, pedagogics, cognitive science, medical humanities, disability studies, and gender studies. Most recently, a new "carnal turn" in Continental philosophy has even been heralded.[1] Whether we will witness a significant philosophical shift is too early to say, but it will anyway not be completely new, since valuable works in the field have been produced for more than a hundred years already.

There might be many reasons for the spread and the vitality of the phenomenology of the body, but it is safe to say that the body is central to phenomenology as such. If the source of all knowledge is the experience of the world in its originary, intuitive givenness, then the body becomes pivotal, both as the closest of "things" given to us, and also as the "place" from which we direct ourselves to the world. If we can only open up toward the world from the body, the body must play a constitutive role for us: I can undergo my own bodily sensations of pleasure, fatigue, desire, or pain as lived from the inside. But the body also allows me to turn outside myself, for it is because we are embodied that we can see, hear, and touch, in short, perceive the world. Moreover, an experienced, spatial world with various shapes and dimensions presupposes a body that can spontaneously move about. Indeed, our orientation in space must start from a center that is not itself a geometrical point. It is rather the lived body that makes up the zero point from which we can distinguish between left and right, up and down, far and near. Unlike any other points in space, we cannot move toward or away from this zero point. This does not so much suggest limitation or imprisonment, but attests to the importance of our body as the indispensable transcendental condition for having a spatial orientation, along with self-experience and perceptual access to the world.

What is peculiar to the body, seen from the phenomenological perspective, is that it is not only the condition for experiences, but it can also be regarded as an object in the world: as a biological organism, a thing subjected to physical laws, or endowed with qualities observable from outside itself. At once, the body opens us to the world and belongs to the world. I can inspect others' objective bodies in this way, but also my own. Although I can feel the inner resistance in my moving fingers and the tactile sensation as they touch a table, I can also just watch my fingers, the folds of the skin, their joints, and their nails, just as I watch my clock. There must therefore be at least two ways to regard the body, both as lived from the subjective perspective, and as an object among other objects as seen from a detached perspective. Both of these perspectives seem to have a solid phenomenological foundation, as both are given to experience in distinct ways, as two perspectives on one and the same body. While I do not contest this in the following book, I want to question whether these two perspectives are exhaustive. The objective body appears to me as if already abstracted from the way it is experienced from the inside, and the lived body is certainly experienced but strangely disentangled from its material dimension and inner workings. But is this all, or are there dimensions still unaccounted for? Do we not also have lived experiences of our body that attest to its inner opacity, resistance, or materiality without turning it into an object among objects? Perhaps there are even experiences that cross the borders of the lived and the objective body, perhaps they point beneath, to a more hidden sense of the body?

These are among the questions this book seeks to explore. As its title suggests, I will focus on three notions, namely incarnation, pain, and theology. The first notion, incarnation, is meant to capture the full sense of being a body, body and mind, flesh and blood, from head to toe. The obvious negative motivation for revisiting incarnation stems from the historical and contemporary tendency to neglect it. There is a current flowing from Platonist and Gnostic impulses in antiquity, to the modern detached ego, paradigmatically pronounced by Descartes, and on to the ambiguous body culture and media technology of the present day. In various ways, these all attest to what Charles Taylor has called "excarnation."[2] Phenomenology seems particularly suited to remind us of the indispensability and significance of our bodies. The term "incarnation," as it is used in phenomenological literature, is taken as synonymous with being embodied; that is, not just that we have bodies, but that we *are* our bodies. In my inflection, however, "incarnation" means something more, suggesting that the body also entails what I will call flesh and blood.[3] To think incarnation all the way down, from head to toe, from lived experience to its material foundation, is one of my concerns.

While phenomenology has no problems describing the subjective givenness of the body, its perceptions, movements, and affections, it seems less clear that it has the same ability to account for the dense and opaque stuff that comprises our bodies without turning it into an object. That we have bones, muscles, and organs is undeniable, yet we are hardly aware of them the way we usually live our body, being engaged in the world. If there somehow is an inner experience of otherwise hidden aspects of my embodiment, what is it like? Such a dimension of our body, such flesh and blood, cannot be identical to the familiar lived body, but can we say that there is something foreign to it? Does it perhaps appear as essentially ambiguous, where mineness and foreignness, activity and passivity, and interior and exterior cross each other? To think incarnation means, in my account, to open up for such questions.

It is one thing to invoke a notion like flesh and blood, but another thing to show that it is phenomenologically accessible. We can inspect an objective body and reflect on the lived body. But if phenomenology starts from the givenness of experience, we must ask where and how flesh and blood give themselves to our experience. If flesh and blood are withdrawn from my lived body, it is also true that the lived body has an inherent tendency to escape my attention and to withdraw into the background as I am absorbed in my various engagements. But when I encounter an obstacle or I am too exhausted to accomplish my aim, the lived body can make itself remarkably present. However, when it comes to the hidden workings of my organs, the complex movements of my muscles, or the solidity of my bones, we are no longer dealing with a background that we can at any time bring forth in an act of reflection. Still, there are also occasions where all my awareness is redirected toward that region of my body, and one important occasion concerns the second notion of my book's title, namely pain.

"There is nothing that reminds us of our embodiment (our vulnerability and mortality) as much as pain."[4] Although written almost in passing, Shaun Gallagher and Dan Zahavi here give a very precise and condensed expression of my ambition, namely, to investigate the intimate tie between embodiment and pain. Pain reminds us of our body by forcing our attention toward it, making it concrete and impossible to flee. Pain seems to remind us of the matter we consist of, and the biblical myth of forming man from the dust suggests the link between the creation, and after the fall, to live through pain, and eventually our destiny to return to dust. According to Joel Michael Reynolds's reading: "God's punishment links the creation of the human as an *atsab* [pain] to its first experience of *atsab* [being formed]. That is to say, the human comes to experience itself in relation to its materiality through pain."[5] But even if pain reminds us of our material conditions, do we not still treat the body in pain as a lived body? Is pain not the most vital feeling of living my body in its inescapable presence? My contention is that the mode in which the body in pain appears discloses the lived body, for sure, but along with it another dimension of our body also appears: not the objective body as inspected from the outside, but the body as experienced from the inside in its density, materiality, or what the creation story calls dust. The body in pain seems to be shot through with various tensions and contradictions—between lived experience and materiality, between being intimately mine and yet over against me, of being my body and my urge to escape it. If this is so, pain reveals some deep ambiguities of our incarnation.

Additionally, the quote from Gallagher and Zahavi suggests that pain reminds us of our "vulnerability and mortality." Our body usually makes us capable of pursuing our tasks; the body works as what Husserl calls the organ of my will, of my "I can." But that makes us easily forget that the body is also vulnerable in its inner as well as outer nature. The organ of my will can also refuse to obey, which becomes clear in the case of illness. I am forced to accept my "I cannot," and another side of the body appears: the same body turns from activity to passivity. I remain incarnate in the state of severe illness, but the illness also has the power to disclose, because it makes the body's otherwise overlooked passivity come to the fore. Perhaps, as I will later explore, this also indicates that bodily passivity is never completely cut off from our activity, but in a fundamental sense makes it possible.

There is also another central sense of vulnerability, the vulnerability of being exposed to externality. Such vulnerability is not so much a mark of failure or limitation, but should be seen as the flip side of our ability to have a world, experience things and others, and relate to our own selves. To have a world means that my body is open for more than itself, but the more open it is, the more vulnerable it will be to what I am exposed to. The human skin is particularly important in this regard, since it is at once the line that protects and gathers my interiority and at the same time the medium by which the world can be reached and touched. Externality can inscribe itself as a gentle touch, perhaps a caress, or as a violent intrusion, as the knife cuts into the flesh. The inherent ambiguity

INTRODUCTION

of being open toward and vulnerable to the world stems from the same skin, like two sides of the same coin.

Both illness and the nudity of the skin can occasion pain. Pain remains, moreover, particularly important for my phenomenological approach to incarnation, since it seems to come with a particular power to disclose the dimension of our body called flesh and blood. As I will claim, the analysis of the body in pain will shed light on one specific mode of bodily givenness, one that arguably challenges some of the established phenomenological distinctions, such as those between objective body and lived body, form and matter, activity and passivity, auto-affection and hetero-affection. What makes the body in pain both challenging and fruitful to phenomenology is that it is inherently ambiguous and thus crosses those dichotomous structures. The phenomenological task then becomes, as I take it, not to resolve but to preserve the ambiguity in fidelity to "the things themselves."

"Incarnation changes everything."[6] This quotation is taken from Merleau-Ponty, whose principal occupation is to place the mind back into the body and install the body in the perceptual world. This particular quotation, however, refers to incarnation in the Christian sense, for in the quoted passage, Merleau-Ponty is not talking about embodiment in general, but about the idea of God becoming man. This is where theology, the third notion of my title, becomes relevant. The figure of God becoming man, as Merleau-Ponty takes it, subverts central distinctions, such as those between God above and the world below, Creator and creation, eternity and time. But if God becoming flesh transforms the conception of God, does it not also transform what it means for us to be human, or at least raise the question of humanity in a radical manner? Merleau-Ponty argues that the incarnation "reopens the question of the distinction between body and spirit, between interior and exterior."[7] In reopening the question, the incarnation also points in certain directions. For the Word to become *sarx* (John 1:14) literally means becoming meat, flesh and blood. The Christian idea of incarnation does not only suggest that God assumed a lived body, but also a body rooted in the material and organic world, or more biblically, a body that bears the stigma of the dust of the ground (Gen. 2:7). If Christ, according to Christian belief, is at once fully God and fully human, this representative human body suggests that all human bodies are dust and breath, matter and life, flesh and blood. The idea of the incarnation does not invoke a biological body open for objective inspection, but suggests a manner of living and experiencing the body, as from the inside. For this book's purpose, the important thing is how the specific incarnation of Christ can reopen phenomenology to the question of what it means for humans to be incarnate in general.

INTRODUCTION

It is far from new to bring phenomenology into conversation with theology. It has done so from its inception and in recent decades more than ever, but not without stirring debate. As Dominique Janicaud famously claimed, the theological turn of French phenomenology—having Emmanuel Levinas, Jean-Luc Marion, Jean-Louis Chrétien, and Michel Henry in mind—has betrayed Husserl's most important principles. Such phenomenology, Janicaud argues, fails to observe that speculative metaphysics is beyond the reach of phenomenological description; it fails to accept the phenomenon as autonomous and essentially finite; and ultimately, it fails to draw a strict line between theology and phenomenology.[8] But the defenders of the theological turn suggest that Janicaud operates with too confined a conception of phenomenology, and, more radically, that theological questions are necessary in order to inspire revisions of phenomenology itself.[9]

While I think there are good reasons to broaden the phenomenological approach beyond Janicaud's restrictions, I will not attempt to provide a theological revision of phenomenology. More modestly, this book will draw on and engage with traditions outside phenomenology, and since Christianity is one such tradition with particular relevance for my topic, it also finds its natural place in my investigation. I see no reason why phenomenology should not listen to the tradition of Christianity, and particularly to theology, which is its self-reflective articulation. Still, theology will be approached from philosophical phenomenology, which means that the distinction between theology and philosophy will not be collapsed. To my mind, Paul Ricoeur captures this relation with precision: "The philosopher is not a preacher. He may listen to preaching, as I do; but insofar as he is a professional and responsible thinker, he remains a beginner, and his discourse always remains a preparatory discourse."[10] Unlike Janicaud, Ricoeur has no problem listening to theology, especially because it gives something to thought and thus potentially expands the horizon of his philosophy. But the listener as philosopher cannot simply assume the faith in God that theology presumes. Engaging in conversation with theology does not mean assuming the role of a preacher, as Ricoeur puts it, but that of a listener. The philosopher as a listener is an eternal beginner who hears the message as if for the first time, where nothing is taken for granted and everything is still open for exploration.

In the chapters to follow, I will engage in critical conversations with many texts, primarily from the phenomenological tradition, where Husserl's second volume of *Ideas*, Merleau-Ponty's *Phenomenology of Perception*, and Henry's *Incarnation* will play a prominent role. As for the dialogue with theology, apart from biblical texts, contributions from the patristic era, notably Irenaeus and Tertullian, will be given special attention. This is partly due to their intense occupation with the nature of the body of Christ, which has direct relevance to the topic at hand, and it is partly due to the fact that they have already been appropriated by phenomenology and thus invite further phenomenological discussions. The structure of the book is meant to reflect my evolving exploration of incarnation. The first four chapters explore its phenomenological implications, discussing incarnation in terms of the lived and objective body, form and matter, activity and passivity, touch, and skin. While I will refer to the phenomenology of pain in these chapters, the substantial treatment of it is fleshed out in chapters 5 through 8, focusing on its inner tension, the problem of communicating it, the relevance of the cross, and the way it is related to hope.

Chapter 1 announces the overarching theme of the book: incarnation, both in the generic sense of the general human embodied condition and in the specific sense of God becoming flesh. Starting with an exposition of the general human incarnation, as found in Husserl, Merleau-Ponty, and Henry, it also becomes possible to discern how such thinkers pave the way for different approaches to incarnation in the specific Christian sense. But also the other way around: the idea of God becoming flesh can also inspire intensified reflections on human embodiment in general. To make an adequate account of our incarnate state, I will propose that, in addition to the objective body (*Körper*) and the lived body (*Leib*), we need a third dimension, not least to capture the body in pain. This dimension is what I call flesh and blood, which is at once material and lived.

Chapter 2 deepens the analysis of flesh and blood by way of exploring how the Aristotelian notions of form and matter have been applied in recent constructivist and realist accounts of the body. But do we have to choose between material realism or constructivism in order to account for our incarnation? In steering between those options, I argue that Husserl's notions of form (*morphe*) and, particularly, matter (*hyle*) still prove fruitful. *Hyle* is at once given to me as impressions of my lived body, and yet has a certain autonomy that suggests the density of the body's materiality.

In chapter 3, the book argues that the mainstream phenomenological tradition has taken the active, well-functioning body as its paradigm. Such "phenomenological activism" primarily regards the body as the organ of "I can." Even though Husserl and Merleau-Ponty occasionally pay heed to paralysis, delusion, phantom limbs, and various forms of illness, these instances tend to be treated as abnormalities, whose phenomenological function is to shed light on the normal body. I suggest, in contrast, that the basic structure of the phenomenology of incarnation looks differently if we start from the broken body in its own right, from its state of "I cannot." The upshot of such a perspective is that the relation between activity and passivity must be revised, giving priority to passivity as the basis on which any activity can be actualized.

Touch and the skin are the topics of chapter 4. From Aristotle to Husserl and after, touch has occupied an exceptional place with regard to bodily self-awareness. Touching inextricably involves the one touching, which means that one cannot touch from a detached perspective. The apparent immediate presence of touch needs to be further explored, with regard to the alterity inscribed in touch and the alterity within the touching body itself. The skin is not only the medium of touch, but also harbors a double structure that outlines the limits of the interiority of the body along with its exposure to the exteriority of the world. Both touch and skin, I will claim, shed light on the ambiguity of mineness and alterity, interiority and exteriority.

Chapter 5 is devoted to the phenomenology of pain, gathering findings from the previous chapters and pushing forward to a more detailed analysis. The contention is that pain is essentially shot through with inner contradictions. First, it gives itself as impressions (matter), and yet pain refuses to be fully integrated into any stable synthesis or intentional function (form); secondly, pain unfolds in the lived body, and yet it retains some form of foreignness to that body (flesh and blood); and thirdly, the suffering self is at once strongly identified with pain, and at the same time, pain seems to stand over against the self as an unwelcome stranger.

For the one suffering pain, there is a similar tension concerning the experience of isolation and at the same time a longing for intimate community, which is the focus of chapter 6. I will address the problem of communication, or more specifically, the difficulty of bringing experiences of pain into common words. I take Elaine Scarry and Ludwig Wittgenstein to provide helpful analyses of this tension, a tension which is strikingly dramatized in the broken dialogue of Job and his friends in the book of Job. Any satisfying account of the problem of communicating pain must, I will assert, pay heed to the delicate and difficult tension between separateness and relatedness.

As the first chapters approach the body and pain phenomenologically, only suggesting their theological relevance, the last two chapters (chapters 7 and 8) will engage more substantially with theological voices. Chapter 7 addresses the cross. If one understands incarnation in the specific sense of God becoming flesh, then arguably the crucified Christ should be regarded as its fulfillment, because the trials of pain make the incarnation concrete and manifest. The cross, as I take it, explicates the phenomenology of pain with graphic clarity: the embodied pain cannot be escaped; being in pain, Christ is riveted as much to the cross as to his human flesh and blood.

In the face of the hopelessness of pain and death, chapter 8 introduces the notion of hope. Initially, pain seems to be the very antidote of hope: it exposes us to something we had never hoped for, and it unfolds in a time that is fixed to the present. However, precisely because pain fixes us to the present, pain's aversive "it should not be" motivates the counterfactual imperative of hope, something hoped for that "must come," beyond the temporal horizon of pain. The topic of hope leads to an exploration of its relation to promise and along with it, how past, present, and future are conceived according to hope. But what future does such bodily motivated hope entail for the body itself? I will finally address the question of whether it makes phenomenological sense to hope for some form of bodily resurrection in a life after death.

1

Phenomenology and Incarnation

The notion of incarnation easily leads either to the traditional idea of a soul entering the material body or, in a more modern version, of a mind put into the biological organism that we are. In either case, the idea entails an essential separation between entities that are somehow paradoxically united in the human person. But it is also possible to approach incarnation by starting from a perspective where the body is not originally foreign to the soul or mind. The body is both what impresses as well as expresses the mind, and as such, the body is the very shape that human existence takes. We grow with our bodies, we discover the world and become self-aware through it, and the body is essential to the content of life, its pleasures as well as pains.

In the Western tradition, the most influential symbol of incarnation remains that of Christ, coined by the formulation from the Gospel of John: "And the Word became flesh" (John 1:14). Whatever further theological implications the formulation implies, it is at least clear that the Christian idea of incarnation means that God identifies Himself with the human condition, with its intellectual, emotional, affective, and spiritual dimension, but emphatically also with human flesh and blood (*sarx*). From the formative period of Christianity, the major theological challenge has been to understand incarnation in such a way that it fully preserved the integrity of our notions both of God and of humanity as they come together in Christ. But such a theological enterprise like this only makes sense if the incarnation of Christ is already taken to reveal the deep structure of both God and humanity. Without entering further into this theological territory, I will only note that this sense of incarnation may be relevant to the phenomenology of the body in a twofold sense: on the one hand, does not the idea of God becoming flesh call for a phenomenological explication of what that flesh philosophically entails? And on the other, could it not be that the phenomenology of the body still has something to learn from the Christian notion of incarnation?

As a first response to these questions, this chapter will be an exposition of some of the most influential, and to the present concern, most relevant accounts of the body, namely those of Husserl, Merleau-Ponty, and Michel Henry. I will distinguish between two senses of incarnation. On the one hand, the "specific incarnation" denotes the Christian sense of the Word becoming flesh; on the other hand, "general incarnation" refers to the human embodiment as such, comprising how our experiences, affections, acts, sensations, and intentionality are inherently interwoven with our bodies. Both Merleau-Ponty and Henry have provided significant perspectives that bear on human embodiment in general, along with its implications for the incarnation of Christ. In the latter half of the chapter, I will assess Husserl's and especially Merleau-Ponty's and Henry's accounts, arguing that they do not adequately include what I call flesh and blood and thus leave out a central dimension of the incarnation in both senses.

Husserl on Embodiment

In order to pave the way for a phenomenological treatment of incarnation, it will be helpful to start with some fundamental notions and conceptions found in Husserl's works. Although Husserl showed little interest in the question of the incarnation of Christ, his phenomenology of the body has been so influential in the ensuing tradition that it indirectly bears on that question.

Hardly any later accounts of the phenomenology of the body have completely ignored one distinction Husserl made central, namely that between the objective body (*Körper*) and the lived body (*Leib*). This distinction sheds light on the difference between how I experience my own body and the way other bodies, physical things, and other persons show themselves to me. My own body is given along with my self-awareness prior to any explicit attention to it. However, it is possible to turn toward my own body in another way, observing my body with a particular physical makeup and as subject to causal laws. In the latter case, I adopt the same attitude I take toward other things and bodies around me that are not lived as immediately mine. The distinction between the lived and objective body implies several aspects, and the phenomenological tradition has spawned various articulations of the distinction, thereby highlighting different aspects of it. For instance, there is a distinction drawn between having a body versus being a body (indicating different relations to the ego),[1] the body in-itself versus the body for-itself (separating the two forms of being),[2] the constituting versus the constituted body (pointing out their different transcendental functions), the unthematized and thematized body (which relates the body to intentionality in different ways),[3] and the body seen from a first-person versus a third-person perspective (highlighting the epistemic positions from which the body is perceived).[4]

Clearly, the distinction between the lived and objective body in all its inflections comes with a package of concepts and problems that are central to the phenomenological enterprise, such as subjectivity, constitution, and the stratification of the intentional analyses. There are also developed further notions of the body that focus on delimited aspects between the lived and objective body.

Without discussing further the impact and richness contained in the lived/objective distinction, my point here is merely that phenomenology seems to be compelled to draw such a distinction in order to prevent a fundamental category mistake between the givenness of the lived body implied in all my perceptions and actions, and the objective body given as a correlate to my intentionality. However, the distinction signifies two perspectives and should not be reified by making the two bodies into an ontological duality.[5] Since the body remains one body, we must either say with Helmuth Plessner that we are, ontologically, irreducibly ambiguous creatures, at once lived and objective body; or more modestly, as I take Husserl to propose, that there are two irreducible ways in which the same body can be given according to a subjectively lived or a detached perspective.[6]

Husserl arrives at the distinction along different paths, for instance by analyzing how my body is given in the sphere of ownness vis-a-vis other bodies, or by investigating the function and appearance of the body in relation to the life-world.[7] The most elaborate account of the distinction, however, is carried out in the second volume of *Ideas*, in which Husserl attempts to provide an account of the phenomenological basis of the natural sciences (physics and zoology in the broad sense) and the humanities or what Husserl calls "spiritual" sciences.[8] Husserl's goal is to clarify the complex founding relation between what is given according to the different attitudes operative in the natural and human sciences. According to the naturalist attitude, nature can legitimately be treated as the totality of spatiotemporal things. Under this view, Husserl explores what it means for the human body to be made up of matter and subjected to the laws of nature (the laws are phenomenologically given as a sense of interdependence on the surroundings).[9] The soul is taken here as a psychological stratum of the objective body and, in analogy to physical nature, with its own psychological structures and laws. When approached according to the naturalist attitude, the physical substratum founds the psychological stratum, but as soon as the attitude is changed to the personal attitude, the founding order is reversed: now the concrete embodied person is given prior to any detached view of a physical body. With an increasing emphasis in his later writings, Husserl claims that the objective body relies on abstraction, an abstraction that presupposes that we are able to objectify an aspect that belongs to the unity of me as a person. Such abstraction cannot, however, be accomplished solipsistically, but must be mediated by the other, or more generally, by intersubjectivity. In this sense, intersubjective objectivity constitutes the sense that things are there for everyone, which again makes it possible for me to relate to my own body as objective.[10]

All experiences of other material bodies presuppose the lived body—both as co-given in any perceptions, and as constitutive for the way the world appears. Seen from one perspective, the objective body I have is a thing among other things; yet, as my lived body, it is not one among others, for it is the only body given as *mine*. "Thus, purely in terms of perception, physical body and living body [*Körper und Leib*] are essentially different; living body, that is, as the only one which is actually given in perception: my own living body."[11] Only my lived body has a field of sensation, kinesthesis, and can be freely moved according to my command.[12] Since the lived body is inalienably mine, Husserl asserts that there is an unbridgeable gap between the experience of my body and all others.

Although the distinction between the lived and objective body involves a certain perspectival dualism, it is not meant to pick out two distinct ontological entities, as if my lived body were an entity detached from my material body. The ontological unity of the body is not an ontological dogma, but a unity rooted in the way the objective body is constituted as a higher stratum starting from the lived body. Granted the objective body, Husserl claims it is evident that "what is most proper to the Ego is something experienced in or at the Body [the lived body], that it is something unified with the Body in the manner of a constituted stratum within a constituted Objectivity." Corresponding to the way the lived and objective body is one, the other person also appears, not as a mind and a body but as a unity: "What we have here is not two things intertwined with each other extrinsically. Rather, what we find here is intrinsically one."[13] Despite this unity, Husserl differentiates between different senses of the body which correlate with different attitudes (naturalist or personal) or perspectives (subjective or detached). According to Husserl's constitutive investigation, the lived and objective body must be analytically discerned and assigned different transcendental functions: the lived body as constitutive and the objective body as constituted.[14]

Clearly, the objective body is insufficient to account for what we mean by incarnated subjectivity, simply because such an objective body contains no experiences and it is not lived as mine. Even if the lived body is not a spatial object, it still serves an indispensable spatial function. While I can inspect things from various sides, move further away or closer to them, to the left or the right, my perspective with respect to my own lived body remains the same, since I can never remove myself from it. If I move, the center that I am, moves along. While I can walk around a table, Husserl points out that "we cannot walk around our hand or around our own Body, and we cannot approach or recede from ourselves at will."[15] Before things are placed within the coordinates of objective space, we already inhabit a space, oriented around our own body. Material things are never seen from "everywhere" or "nowhere," but are oriented relative to the lived body, that is, as left or right, over or under, far or near. In a more general way, Husserl can say that the lived body occupies a "here," and it is from this "here" that we can locate the thing "over there."[16] From such an absolute point, space is spread out in its meaningful dimensions. By alluding to the metaphor of coordinates, Husserl speaks of the "here" of my lived body as the zero point: "The Body then has, for its particular Ego, the unique distinction of bearing in itself the *zero point* of all these orientations."[17]

Yet the lived body is not only the zero point of orientation, but also the field of sensations. My world is opened to me through various sensations, such as vision and hearing. While I can spatially localize an object in vision and detect the source of a sound in hearing, they appear at a distance from the sense organ, which is why I do not see my seeing or hear my hearing. In touching, however, there is no such distance. The tactile body must be immediately present, since we only sense the touched object when we also sense the body touching.[18] Because touch is always given along with the lived body that touches, it comes to play a central role for Husserl in mapping the difference between the objective and lived body. Tactility indeed involves a double sensation—both touching and being touched—which is why my lived body is immediately given to me in the touch. Along with touching, and as a subcategory thereof, there are so-called "sensuous feelings," such as pleasure and pain, that share touch's self-referentiality as bodily manifestations.[19] I will return to this in chapter 4.

Although such sensuous feelings lack intentionality, they appear localized in the body, sometimes at very specific locations. Furthermore, there is yet another type of sensation that is vital to the lived body, namely the inner sensation of movement. This is phenomenologically given in the feeling of movement, or kinesthesis, and refers back to my fundamental ability as a willing subject, encapsulated in the phrase "I move." Kinesthesis does not denote the objective body's movement in space but registers the immediate sense of movement according to the totality of the lived body. Through the mutually constitutive functions of sensations and kinesthesis, we can constitute objects as three-dimensional.[20] For if the hidden sides of an object seen from a vantage perspective must be taken to refer to sides available from another perspective to which I can move, the unitary thing draws on horizons made possible by "I move."[21]

Kinesthesis is part of a broader notion of our lived body as a functional organ. As a functional organ, we do not merely experience a series of streaming appearances of external objects, but appearances that are internally related by a system made possible by our kinesthesis. If kinesthesis links the appearances together in accordance with possible movements, sensations and kinesthesis can together form a unitary system that gives content and profile to all phenomena oriented around the lived body. The body as a functional organ highlights a further difference between the objective and lived body, for not only is the lived body the only one of the two that is given as mine, but it is also the only one that I can enact. I have control over the acting body, it is the organ of the general "I can" and therefore the organ of my will.[22] The meaningful movements I perform are not effects of causes or reactions to stimuli, but are subject to me and my capabilities and always sanctioned by the subject. In this sense, Husserl writes that my body "is an *organ of the will*, the *one and only Object* which, for the will of my pure Ego, is *moveable immediately and spontaneously*."[23]

This initial outline of the most significant aspects of Husserl's analysis of the lived body demonstrates that we are far removed from the excarnate body, but on the way to an understanding of the incarnate subject. While the distinction between the objective and lived body is important, Husserl emphasizes that there is an intimate relationship between them because they both account for the numerically same body and because the lived body always accompanies the objective body. I can regard my own body both as lived and objective, and I can bracket the objective body and reduce my body to my pure sphere of ownness. However, the opposite does not hold: my body can never be solely an objective body. My primordial ownership, pre-spatial zero point, and the immediate givenness of my sensations, along with my bodily agency, strongly suggest an incarnate subjectivity. Nevertheless, it is not clear that Husserl will allow for the full sense of incarnate subjectivity. It seems that his commitment to transcendental philosophy prevents him from relinquishing some sense of a pure ego independent of the body. Yet, when viewed as a concrete person, "I the man," immersed in a surrounding world, Husserl does not believe that we are confronted with a physical body with some sense of the soul added on to it. The embodied person appears as a unity:

> Man in his movements, in his action, in his speaking and writing, etc.,
> is not a mere connection or linking up of one thing, called a soul,
> with another thing, the Body. The Body is, as Body, filled with the soul
> through and through. Each movement of the Body is full of soul.[24]

CHAPTER 1

Every bodily gesture is expressive of the incarnated soul—what more could be implied by incarnation?

Now, Husserl is careful to distinguish between different senses of the ego. The notion of the person implies an empirical ego that perceives and acts with its lived as well as objective body in its surrounding world. However, such an empirical ego is not itself the ultimate transcendental condition that makes consciousness possible; rather, the latter presupposes, on the one hand, a pre-reflected consciousness—a streaming manifold—which, on the other hand, must be unified by one identical pole, namely the pure ego.[25] This ego is not itself part of the conscious content but its very condition of possibility. The constitutive difference between the empirical and pure ego can, according to Husserl, be demonstrated. We can bracket off physical nature, including others' bodies: "But my consciousness, regardless of how the components of consciousness were altered, would remain an absolute stream of experience with its own essence."[26] When all physical reality is bracketed off, we are led back to the transcendental field where the pure ego resides. Since it belongs to my temporal stream of consciousness, the ego is immanent, but since it is not identical with the stream, the ego is transcendent. Thus, it is paradoxically given as a *"transcendence in immanence."*[27]

No doubt, the pure ego we are left with is an impoverished ego; it is not a self with its body or immersed in a world, but is a formal pole.[28] Although such an impoverished notion of the ego does not undermine the fruitful analyses of the lived body, it is clear that such an ego cannot be entirely identical to its lived body. In searching for a fruitful phenomenological account of incarnation, this might be disappointing. But before concluding too hastily, we should consider the benefits of Husserl's position. Given that we think of ourselves as incarnate beings, is there not a sense in which we would regard our subjectivity, our very ego, as something more than our lived and objective body? If my body breaks down, for instance in illness or paralysis, as I will discuss in chapter 3, is it not important to cling to a sense in which the ego is not therefore impaired? When confronted with pain, doesn't Husserl have a point when he says that the sensations we undergo do "not belong to the realm of what properly pertains to the Ego"? He continues: "Just as the Body in general is over against the Ego, so [is] everything '*non-I.*'"[29] Bodily sensations, such as pain, do appear to the ego, but still in the mode of "over against it." Husserl's ego as transcendence in immanence might show its strength here, since the pure ego preserves our transcendental identity as something more than our bodies.[30] According to an alternative approach, the fact that the other appears as a body from which I can conduct an analogical appresentation in order to experience the other as an alter ego has been criticized for reducing the other to the same. Yet, as Derrida has argued, it is precisely because Husserl only allows for a mediated access to the other, making the other accessible in its inaccessibility, that he truly respects the other as other.[31]

Husserl conducts several analyses of God, primarily as some form of a teleological idea, but he never expounds on the implications his analysis of the body would have for the incarnation of Christ. He leaves the elaboration of such implications to posterity—a task, as we will see, taken up by Merleau-Ponty and Henry in their own ways. However, Husserl does at least on one occasion propose that an idea of communication with divinity, or as he calls it, the absolute, necessitates the notion of incarnation: "Obviously, the absolute spirit would also have to have a Body for there to be mutual understanding."[32]

Merleau-Ponty on the General Incarnation

Merleau-Ponty does not presuppose a pure ego as the transcendental pole that secures the identity through the various constitutive achievements of consciousness. In his commentary on Merleau-Ponty, Taylor Carman argues that it is not sufficient to appeal, as Husserl does, to touch and its double sensation for establishing my bodily self-awareness. In touching my own body, I must presuppose that the touched part of the body is granted as mine. Hence, touch is not a privileged sensation that attests to my ownership, for the sense of ownership of my body must already be presupposed all along. For this reason, Merleau-Ponty is dissatisfied with the sense of a pure ego that needs to connect to its own body when there is no connection to be made. The basic fact, Carman writes, is that "the body just *is* the self."[33]

Merleau-Ponty's incarnated subject is thus a unity, but not a self-subsistent unity since it cannot be cut off from its environment. Subject, body, and the world make up an original whole from which we can later discern its components by means of reflection:

> In so far as, when I reflect on the essence of subjectivity, I find it bound up with that of the body and that of the world, this is because my existence as subjectivity is merely one with my existence as a body and with the existence of the world, and because that subject that I am, when taken concretely, is inseparable from this body and this world.[34]

This strong sense of the unity of subjectivity, body, and the world implies that it is my own lived body that is under scrutiny. While Husserl elaborates on the distinction between the lived and objective body in many ways, Merleau-Ponty takes this for granted but does not provide further analyses of the objective body. The reason is probably due to the orientation of his investigation, where another distinction plays a more vital role, namely that between our lived primordial, pre-reflective body on the one hand and reflections on the body on the other. In giving priority to the primordial body, Merleau-Ponty nonetheless notes how philosophy tends to neglect it to focus on representations of the body. But these two senses of the body do not coincide because they are given in essentially different manners: the former as part of my perspective of the world, the latter as given over against me as an object in front of me. In Merleau-Ponty's words: "To say that it [the body] is always near me, always there for me, is to say that it is never really in front of me, that I cannot array it before my eyes, that it remains marginal to all my perceptions, that it is *with* me."[35] To grasp my own body as an objective body would require another body to perceive it.

If we focus on the lived body, there is a solid sense of incarnation operative here: subjectivity is given along with the body and within its world. In a retrospective overview of his project, Merleau-Ponty actually emphasizes incarnation as his main theme. He explains that "the perceiving mind is an incarnated mind. I have sought, first of all, to re-establish the roots of the mind in the body and in its world."[36] Hence, the incarnation of which Merleau-Ponty speaks is conceived as the incarnated mind or the general human condition. To understand the centrality of the idea of incarnation as a phenomenological topic, it is helpful to look at the historical context. Merleau-Ponty recounts that in his formative years of the 1930s, a broad stream of phenomenology and existentialism became prevalent in France. French existentialism occurred as a reaction against idealist philosophy, and it did so, he recalls, by emphasizing a new theme, that of incarnation.[37] Husserl had undertaken significant analyses of such incarnation, but they were not publicly available until much later. (Merleau-Ponty, we know, consulted what later became known as the second volume of *Ideas* in Leuven.) It was Gabriel Marcel who brought the theme of incarnation to the fore in France. Marcel claimed that my body cannot be conceived as a scientific object among others: I do not even *have* a body, he famously said, I *am* my body.[38] Merleau-Ponty confirms that it was the impulse from Marcel that inspired him to aspire to a phenomenological account of "our conditions as incarnated beings."[39]

It was not only the main theme of Merleau-Ponty's thinking that Marcel initiated, but equally important, a particular style of philosophizing: "Gabriel Marcel said that philosophy presents a particularity which differentiates it from all other sorts of disciplines: it deals with mysteries, not problems."[40] In Merleau-Ponty's rendering, problems are questions that can be solved without involving myself, whereas mysteries have no clear solution at all because we are not external to them, but caught up in them. This holds for the body as well. To work out the precise relation between me and my body, Marcel again pointed out that thought by necessity encounters something opaque and mysterious.[41] The theme of mystery, wonder, enigmas, depths, opacity, along with a particular style of philosophizing, became central to Merleau-Ponty's phenomenology to its end.[42] Accepting Marcel's sense of the mystery of the body, Merleau-Ponty sees no way in which it can be interrogated, except through a reflection of what is already lived unreflectively. This reflective interrogation turns both on perception anchored in the mystery of the incarnate subject, and, at the same time, on a similarly mysterious world in which perception is always involved.[43] As Merleau-Ponty proposes, the presence of the world to our perception is so intimate that it comes close to a sacramental communion:

> Just as the sacrament not only symbolizes, in sensible species, an operation of Grace, but is also the real presence of God, which it causes to occupy a fragment of space and communication to those who eat of the consecrated bread . . . so that sensation is literally a form of communion.[44]

The sensible things of perception are actually there, in their real presence—according to their *leibhaften Wirklichkeit,* as Husserl puts it— just as the incarnated subject is there, communicating with the things of the world.

To Merleau-Ponty, it is the bodily perception that weaves world and subjectivity together. Perception is neither isolated sense data, the mind's capacity to associate such data, nor an intellectual inference from me to the outer world. Perception is our primordial bond to the world as already pregnant with meaning. This means that Merleau-Ponty does not take our relation to the world to be an epistemological gap that needs to be bridged. Naturally, we can distinguish between subject and object, me and the world, but in order to do so, the mutual relation between them must already have been established on a pre-reflective level. The subjective body plays the key role here: "At the same time as the body withdraws from the objective world, and forms between the pure subject and the object a third genus of being, the subject loses its purity and its transparency."[45]

Merleau-Ponty's subject is already interlaced with its bodily involvement with the perceived world. My own body is not reducible to pure subjectivity or objectivity, which means that Merleau-Ponty gestures toward a less pure and deeper notion. He introduces a third genus of being that predates any reflective dichotomy, and which gives rise to such dichotomies because it is inherently ambiguous—a "subject-object."[46] This ambiguity is already operative in Husserl's example of bodily reflexivity that occurs when my right hand is touching my left hand. In this instance, I not only touch my own "objective" left hand, since I simultaneously feel the right hand touching. For Merleau-Ponty, this means that both touching and being touched, subject and object, are part of my singular body.

I will return to this fruitful idea later, but for now, we need a more detailed description of our perceptual bonds to the world. When Merleau-Ponty speaks of sensation he is presupposing the richer notion of perception, wherein sensations possess meaning, albeit vague. Perception is never without meaning; we are, indeed, "condemned to meaning."[47] Merleau-Ponty is therefore critical of any attempts to isolate sensation, as found in empiricism and Husserl's sense data or *hyle*. In perception, we do not encounter sensual content devoid of meaning that we must then intellectually synthesize or interpret. Rather, Merleau-Ponty, following Gestalt psychology, posits that even at the primordial level, things are given as meaningful unities outlined against a horizon.[48] The whole has primacy, and it cannot be reduced to its parts.[49] The empiricist model of atomistic sense data associated with psychological laws fails on two counts, according to Merleau-Ponty. First, if the association or synthesis of sense data is not to be arbitrarily imposed, the field of sensation must initially imply some inherent structure or gestalt that orients the association. In other words, sensations must be delineated as meaningful against a horizon.[50] Second, the way such an empiricist model accounts for sensation is an abstraction from the lived experience it is part of, turning it into some strange self-subsistent atoms that no one has ever perceived. Consequently, the model removes sensations from what they are supposed to explain, namely being in a human world.[51] The intellectualist alternative, according to Merleau-Ponty's typology, fares no better. If the intellect possesses ideas or judgments, sensation cannot provide us with anything new or alter our knowledge, but is simply subsumed under the workings of the judgments.[52] In this intellectualist account, we are left with an impoverished, functional notion of sensation, which is nothing more than a dead letter at the disposal of the intellect's activity.

Things change dramatically once we realize that perceptions have meaning prior to syntheses and judgments. At this primordial level, Merleau-Ponty refers not to posited things with a predicative identity, but to phenomena imbued with a physiognomy, that is, with a familiar gestalt. Prior to reflection, we live in a world filled with meaning. The reflecting subject cannot constitute this world, but must hark back to its pre-given, pre-reflective homeland: "Sense experience is that vital communication with the world which makes it present as a familiar setting of our life. It is to it that the perceived object and the perceiving subject owe their thickness."[53] This thickness is not a boundary to overcome, but belongs to the very soil from which both the perceived object and perceiving subject emerge and yet cannot exhaust.

Where Husserl speaks of the body as the field of sensations, Merleau-Ponty broadens the field to include the interplay of subjectivity, body, and the familiar world. While there is no pure ego uncontaminated by embodiment, Merleau-Ponty still speaks of subjectivity, neither as a sovereign instance in the order of constitution, nor as an absolute pole of identity to the manifold appearances, but as an incarnated subjectivity that finds itself participating in the world. Since the incarnate subject is caught up in the thickness of the perception spread out in its fields, philosophy is deprived of any place outside or above it. Philosophy starts in medias res; it can only be carried out as a reflection that turns back on what is given, namely the pre-reflected.[54] Phenomenology's slogan of returning to the things themselves means for Merleau-Ponty to reach into these pre-reflective and primordial layers that reflective knowledge has grown out of but still tends to neglect: "To return to things themselves is to return to that world which precedes knowledge."[55]

The subjective, lived body actively explores the world through movements and actions. Thanks to what Merleau-Ponty calls the body schema (sometimes misleadingly translated as "body image"), I do not need to check the spatial coordinates of my moving limbs—I have an immediate sense of the limbs' movements along with my whole posture. The body schema is not derived knowledge from empirical content, it is not an image of my objective body or intentional object, but a pre-reflective, "total awareness of my posture in the intersensory world, a 'form' in the sense used by Gestalt psychology."[56] Such a form indicates the holistic organization of body and world. By means of my body schema, I can immediately move my body in its milieu, or better, pursue my tasks in various situations. While the body schema works anonymously, independently of my conscious ownership, it is nonetheless integral to my acting and perceiving body. In this sense, we are led back to the subjectivity of the body. I not primarily hold sway *over* my body, as Husserl has it, but I *am* my body. "We do not merely behold as spectators the relations between the parts of our body, and the correlations between the visual and tactile body: we are ourselves the unifier of these arms and legs, the person who both sees and touches them."[57]

Having sketched out his view of the body in terms of sensation, movements, and ownership, Merleau-Ponty provides an interesting use of what Husserl called the zero point of orientation. For Merleau-Ponty, the zero point has implications for his view of human finitude.[58] He agrees with Husserl that we orient things in relation to that zero point of our lived body. The zero point cannot be a static and theoretical gaze, since it is anchored in an active body and its engagement: "The word 'here' applied to my body does not refer to a determinate position in relation to other positions or to external co-ordinates, but the laying down of the first co-ordinate, the anchoring of the active body in an object, the situation of the body in face of its task."[59] The emphasis on the practical situation, "in face of its task," is indicative of Merleau-Ponty's practical or existential orientations, which are not predominant in Husserl. To understand the meaning of pre-objective space, one needs to consider the constellation of the demands of the situation, along with the way the body responds to it.

The bodily "here" evokes a sense of finitude, since it delineates the only perspective that is available to me. While this may first appear as a limitation, it does not debar me from space; rather, it is the finite position that opens up the possibility of inhabiting space in the first place. The alternative is a space lived by no one. Such finitude implies a perspective that strongly opposes any metaphysical dream of a God's-eye view—the total gaze that transcends any limitation. When Husserl remarks that even God would not be able to see spatial things except as adumbrations given in perspectives, he is not challenging the religious sense of God by imposing restrictions on his omniscience or omnipotence.[60] Instead, he is challenging the metaphysical God's-eye view, arguing that apart from the limited perspective of perceptions of things, there are no spatial objects to be experienced.[61] The metaphysical idea does not reach things as they "really are," but is essentially devoid of meaning.

Something similar is expressed when Merleau-Ponty renounces Leibniz's dream of a perspective from which all possible perspectives are joined in the totality of an object. As Merleau-Ponty argues, to see an object from everywhere is tantamount to seeing it from nowhere. The only way to actually see an existing thing is to see it from somewhere.[62] Theology, Merleau-Ponty claims, has a tendency to cling to similar ideas, fixating being in a static manner, invoking eternity as a frozen state, or imagining human perfection beyond the bounds of our finitude.[63] Indeed, true philosophy would "die upon contact with the absolute," because such absolute entails a fixed view of the world from nowhere and thus overcomes ambiguities and paradoxes.[64] But this will not do, because to Merleau-Ponty, it is the very ambiguities and paradoxes that signify the perceptual world in the first place, the only world available to us.

The incarnated and finite perspective implies that we are situated in a world that surpasses us and outruns our grasp on all sides. Perspectival perception means that we cannot see all sides of a thing at once, but that they are given in profiles. Nevertheless, we do not only see one side of a house, as if it were a two-dimensional stage prop, but we apprehend the house as a whole. How? Since Merleau-Ponty refuses to portray the whole as a product of intellectual syntheses, the hidden sides must somehow be co-given with the thing perceived by means of horizons. More precisely, the profile given entails the inner horizon of the thing, sketching out a specific style that invites new explorations along the direction invoked by that style. The horizon suggests something more than what is strictly speaking given, as if the whole thing is both part of my perception and yet transcends it. This is why we cannot remove the ambiguities and paradoxes belonging to the finitude of perceptions: "Thus there is a paradox of immanence and transcendence in perception. Immanence, because the perceived object would not be able to be foreign to the one who perceives; transcendence, because it always involves a beyond of what is actually given."[65]

Indeed, the paradox of immanence and transcendence can be generalized to our very perceptual relation to the world, which, on the one hand, remains inalienably mine, and at the same time indicates a world that is beyond any of my perceptual acts. Merleau-Ponty does not want to resolve the contradictions encountered in perception but rather to preserve them. "I wish only to point out that the accusation of contradiction is not decisive, *if the acknowledged contradiction appears as the very condition of consciousness.*"[66] It is the paradoxes and ambiguities that simultaneously make the world mine and more than mine—in short, make it real. We must say that the world is only available to incarnate subjects, and yet that the world perceived is not my creation or construction—it transcends, is always open to further explorations, it contains mysteries, opacities, and depths that cannot be exhausted. Any philosophy of transparency— particularly onto-theological ideas of God—will only deprive us of the kind of depth that belongs to our being-in-the-world.[67]

Merleau-Ponty on the Specific Incarnation

If subjectivity and the world only make sense for an incarnated being, the question still remains: What should one make of the incarnation in the specific sense of the Word made flesh? Unlike Husserl, Merleau-Ponty occasionally comments on the incarnation of Christ. Although religion is not among Merleau-Ponty's primary concerns, many of his central notions have religious connotations; incarnation, Logos, flesh, the visible and the invisible are all, in fact, found in the Nicene Creed.[68] In "The Primacy of Perception," Merleau-Ponty addresses the incarnation while problematizing God as the metaphysical absolute. Following his general criticism of detached speculation, Merleau-Ponty rejects any sense of the absolute insofar as it has no experiential basis. Still, he argues that there might be a sense of the absolute, and it is indeed in this sense that Christianity radically altered the idea:

> To tell the truth, Christianity consists in replacing the separated absolute by the absolute in men. Nietzsche's idea that God is dead is already contained in the Christian idea of the death of God. God ceases to be an external object in order to mingle in human life, and this life is not simply a return to a nontemporal solution.[69]

In this interpretation, inspired by Hegel, Merleau-Ponty claims that the incarnation of Christ is a reversal of the metaphysical idea of God, which again anticipates Nietzsche's announcement of the death of God. However, Nietzsche's madman's declaration of the death of God is not news, as it had already taken place at the cross. This death is the culmination of the story of "a God who takes on the human condition," as Merleau-Ponty puts it elsewhere, by becoming part of the finite, vulnerable embodied life of this world. In doing so, Christ becomes in effect "the most resolute negation of the conceived infinite."[70] By negating any detached absolute or intellectual idea of the infinite, Christianity radically transforms the understanding of transcendence in immanence—in the figure of a human body.

Another way Merleau-Ponty contrasts abstract metaphysics with the Christian idea of incarnation is by interrogating the vertical transcendence found in metaphysical thought. Vertical transcendence, from above to below, indicates both hierarchy and power, along with inaccessibility and distance. "Christianity is, among other things, the recognition of a mystery in the relations of man and God," Merleau-Ponty claims, "which stems precisely from the fact that the Christian God wants nothing to do with a vertical relation of subordination."[71] Nevertheless, such a vertical transcendence has become central to the Christian tradition and led it to blend transcendence with power. Yet, according to Merleau-Ponty, the incarnation resists verticality; incarnation means a reorientation of all fundamental vectors, of above and below, verticality and horizontality, omnipotence and impotence:

> There is a sort of impotence of God without us, and Christ attests that
> God would not be fully God without becoming fully man. Claudel goes
> so far as to say that God is not above but beneath us—meaning that we
> do not find Him as a suprasensible idea, but as another ourself which
> dwells in and authenticates our darkness. Transcendence no longer
> hangs over man: he becomes, strangely, its privileged bearer.[72]

If such a radical reversal of the metaphysical power structure is the implication of the incarnation, Merleau-Ponty believes that its consequences
have not yet been fully realized. He can at times distinguish between the
"religion of the Father" which clings to the vocabulary of verticality and
which tends to be conservative on the political plane. Such a religion
eclipses the revolutionary—philosophical, theological, and political—
impact of the incarnation, according to the "religion of the Son," where
God fully participates in human life and society.[73] No God above us, therefore, only God with or beneath us. It remains unclear whether Merleau-
Ponty thinks of God as becoming completely transformed to humanity—
at the risk of idolizing or, at best, divinizing humanity (*theosis*)—or more
traditionally, as God taking part in the human condition in solidarity with
the world. What is clear, however, is that the incarnation entails a radical
change in how we think of both God and humanity. The God beneath
us outlines a God not of power but of weakness, not of metaphysics but
as embodied, along the lines that have later been elaborated by Jürgen
Moltmann, Paul Ricoeur, Hans Jonas, and more recently, John Caputo
and Gianni Vattimo.

God becoming human means that God assumed the entire human
condition and underwent its extremes from the inside, in darkness and
depths. In a manner parallel to Merleau-Ponty, Hans Urs von Balthasar
writes:

> If God himself has lived out this ultimate experience of this world . . .
> he will no longer be a God who judges his creature from above and
> from outside. Thanks to his intimate experience of the world, as
> the Incarnate One who knows experientially every dimension of the
> world's being down to the abyss of Hell, God now becomes the measure
> of man.[74]

God's embodied experience of the world means that the world is no longer alone; height and depth, transcendence and immanence intersect
in the incarnate God. God has entered our flesh and historicity, and no
longer hangs above us, but has poured himself out through God's self-

emptying kenosis (Phil. 2:7–8).[75] Everything remains as it was, and yet, "the incarnation changes everything."[76] The notion of God has changed, and along with it, what it means to be human. It reopens the distinction between spirit and body, inner and outer, subjectivity and world.[77]

By negating any detached metaphysical idea of the infinite, the incarnation does not exclude any sense of absolutes or transcendence. Rather, Merleau-Ponty thinks it must be sought along other paths. Figuratively, he reminds us that there is always an "other side of things," some sort of irreducible surplus to what we perceive. Such thought not only makes incarnation a special revelation tied to the God-man in Christ, but prepares a general revelation in which God is revealed in the world just as he withdraws from it. However, Merleau-Ponty is not talking about grand ecstatic visions or exposure to the wholly other, but rather an attentiveness to the wonders that are part of the familiar world we inhabit. Revelation, incarnation, and reversal are the invisible of the visible: "In my view this 'reversal' takes place before our eyes. And perhaps some Christians would agree that the other side of things must already be visible in the environment in which we live."[78]

The invisible other sides that are inscribed in the visible have far-reaching consequences; for Merleau-Ponty, it suggests that Husserl's transcendental reduction must necessarily remain incomplete. The transcendental reduction can only lead us back into pure immanent givenness and absolute consciousness, where all that is given to me is what I have constituted. Such reduction thereby ignores the depths and hidden sides of the world never constituted by me—an insight Merleau-Ponty thinks Husserl gradually came to acknowledge: "Originally a project to gain intellectual possession of the world, constitution becomes increasingly, as Husserl's thought matures, the means of unveiling the backside of things that we have never constituted."[79] Elaborating on the figure of the backside of things in his latest writings, Merleau-Ponty emphasizes the outer horizon, the thickness of the fields, and the opaqueness of the inner horizon of things. They no longer only indicate possible perspectives not yet entertained, but suggest the inexhaustible depth of being. This depth is spelled out less in terms of immanence and transcendence, as in his earlier accounts, but more in terms of the visible and invisible. The invisible is not a void or something non-visible, but as given along with the texture of the flesh—as "the invisible of the visible."[80] The backside of things is not simply a reference to the perspectival ways in which things are given, but has become a figure of the depth and inexhaustibility belonging to being, to the flesh.

Both the specific revelation of Christ and the general revelation imply a sense of surplus, "the backside of the things," in keeping with

Merleau-Ponty's general criticism of transparency. "It is no longer a matter of rediscovering the transparency of God outside the world but a matter of entering body and soul into an enigmatic life," which does not lift the obscurities contained in God but enhances them.[81] According to Merleau-Ponty, this general revelation is nonetheless condensed in particular sites, such as the reflection on incarnation, original sin, the parables of Jesus, and the sacraments.[82] In his unfinished sketches for an ontology of the flesh written toward the end of his life, one might glimpse another, more ontological way of conceiving incarnation as the movement in the depth of the flesh.[83] If the flesh is the anonymous medium from which both visible and invisible emerge, then it seems to allow for God's invisible presence, and in this wide sense, God as incarnated in this flesh. Perhaps this direction must be explored in light of one of the earlier remarks Merleau-Ponty made: "A God who will not be simply for us but for Himself, could, on the contrary, be sought by metaphysics only behind consciousness, beyond our ideas, as the anonymous force which sustains each of our thoughts and experiences."[84] In short, a God that does not hang over our heads but has become one of us will have to be phenomenologically sought along with the incarnate experience and, according to the late sketches of Merleau-Ponty, also along with the flesh, which the human body is a part.

Henry on the General Incarnation

Within the phenomenological tradition, it seems safe to say that no one has penetrated as deeply into both the general and the specific sense of incarnation as Michel Henry. For him, the incarnation of Christ is not only analogous or relevant to but also crucially interwoven with our understanding of ourselves. In becoming human, Christ takes a flesh like ours, Henry holds, which raises the question of how our flesh should be conceived in the first place.

Initially, Henry defines the human sense of incarnation broadly, referring to "a being who possesses a body or, more precisely, a flesh."[85] In this respect, he follows in the footsteps of Merleau-Ponty, but only initially so, because the possession of flesh, in Henry's sense, is a different matter than possessing a body. While Husserl draws a line between the lived and objective body, Henry's distinction goes significantly further. According to Henry, there are two fundamental modes in which phenomenality appears in general: visibly, according to the world, and invisibly, according to life in the flesh. Corresponding to this fundamental binary, the objective body pertains to the visible world and the flesh to invisible life. Importantly, Henry's notion of the flesh must not be confused with Husserl's lived body or Merleau-Ponty's intentional body, because the flesh is prior to and independent of both the objective, visible body and the lived body with its intentional involvement with the world. All intentionality, according to Henry, implies that its object or noema is put at a distance, whereas the phenomenality given to the flesh is given without distance, immediately to itself. In this way, the flesh seems to be the privileged place in which the phenomenological requirement of immediacy and adequacy can be fulfilled—notably by dropping the central notion of intentionality.

In its simplest form, Henry argues, the flesh is impressional, both in the sense that flesh is the milieu where impressions come to pass as they reveal themselves, and in the sense of defining flesh as a totality of impressions.[86] For Henry, pure impressions do not refer to any externality, because empirical sensation needs to be rooted in impressionality. Unlike empirical sensation, impressions are immediately given to the immanent flesh without distinctions and distance.[87] Impressions do not only come to pass in the flesh but are always affectively charged. Impressions affect themselves according to their auto-affection. While auto-affection takes care of its own givenness, it does not exclude subjectivity or ipseity, but implies it. Incarnation entails subjectivity, for the simple reason that the affections are always lived by someone: "the human is thus a carnal living Self."[88] Such a self is inextricably given along with the flesh; otherwise, the impressions and affections would be lost in an anonymous stream known to no one. Ipseity must not, however, be confused with Husserl's subject who holds sway over its body, and certainly not as a transcendental pole beyond bodily givenness. Ipseity is given passively along with the life of the flesh.

While it is hardly anything new to argue that incarnation takes a self internal to the flesh, Henry's understanding of the flesh stands in contrast to the tradition of Husserl and Merleau-Ponty. If the great achievement of Merleau-Ponty is that he installed the subjective body in the world, one may wonder why Henry should insist on the radical immanence of the impressional flesh. Is not the point of invoking impressions—along with kinesthesis, spatial location, and perspectives—to shed light on the way the world appears to our incarnate being and how we participate in that world? How can Henry make phenomenology of something that is essentially invisible to the world, that is, an invisibility that does not live up to the definition of a phenomenon (*phainesthai*), that shows itself as visible?[89] No doubt, Henry asks us to reorient the entire understanding of incarnation. He explains:

> To be incarnate is not to have a body, to put oneself forward as a "corporeal" and thus material being—an integral part of the universe, which one awards with the same qualifier. To be incarnate is to have flesh, and, perhaps more precisely, to be flesh.[90]

Henry alludes to Merleau-Ponty's—and before him, Marcel's—distinction between having and being a body, along with Husserl's objective and lived body. Henry follows Husserl in granting the lived body constitutive priority; it is only the latter that can found the founded, objective body, not the other way around.[91] However, according to Henry, reducing the objective to the lived body is not sufficient for a transcendental founding of the body. In order to gain phenomenological access to the self-givenness— the flesh in Henry's sense—a radical reduction must be enacted.

To understand Henry's motivation for such a radical reduction, we need to follow him back to the basic question of what phenomenology essentially is. Henry detects a certain indeterminacy within phenomenology, particularly in Husserl and Heidegger, an indeterminacy that has allowed un-phenomenological and metaphysical prejudices to slip into phenomenology despite its own aspirations. Phenomenology's fundamental task, Henry contends, is the investigation not of the "what" or the content of particular phenomena, but of the "how" of the appearing itself; that is, of the essence of pure phenomenality. Among what Henry regards as the four principles of phenomenology, Husserl's "principle of all principles" is central. In *Ideas I*, Husserl states that the intuition of originary givenness in its bodily presence (*leibhaften Wirklichkeit*) is the source and limit of phenomenological inquiry.[92] Intuition plays a key role here, but this intuition, Henry argues, is in its essence already shaped by intentionality. Intentionality, in turn, is consciousness of something which is given at a distance. According to Henry, intentionality creates this distance by a movement that "*throws itself outside itself when it goes beyond itself toward what is now placed in front of its gaze*, and which Husserl calls its 'intentional correlate' or 'transcendent object.'"[93] For Henry, his description holds true, whether intentionality is conceived as consciousness (Husserl), ek-stasis (Heidegger), or as bodily self-transcendence (Merleau-Ponty).

In addition to intuition as intentionality, the "principle of all principles" demands that any object of phenomenological investigation must itself be given in person or bodily presence. If intentionality itself outlines the basic "how" of phenomenality, it must be the privileged object of phenomenological description of how it is given in person. Here, Henry claims, traditional phenomenology runs up against severe difficulties, for how can intentionality itself be given as an object present in person? Perhaps there must be another, more primordial intentionality

CHAPTER 1

to which the first is given, and yet another to which the second is given—but that only leads to an infinite regress.[94] The conclusion Henry draws is that phenomenality must have another, more original way of appearing than that according to intentionality in order to fulfill its own goal. The distance implied in intentionality never reaches the immediate presence of the givenness. Hence, phenomenality as such must appear, from itself and to itself, without distance or distinctions, which is to say, it must be self-revealing.

Returning to the question of the general incarnation, we must ask what consequences Henry's general view of phenomenology has for the conception of the human body. Clearly, the objective body will be just another intentional correlate put at a distance. More surprisingly, perhaps, Henry argues that something similar holds for the lived body. Although it is not regarded as an object of the world, the lived body is still modeled on intentionality, or more precisely, as the subjective correlate of intentionality. Furthermore, the lived body implies the intentionality of the world, which means that far from being immediately given to itself, it needs to gain access to itself through the detour of a world, a world that it has previously thrown out in front of itself. This means, however, that the lived body is not immediately given to itself.

To reach a notion of the body that appears in its phenomenality, Henry undertakes the radical reduction of the body, all the way back to the ultra-transcendental flesh. All traces of the visible world are undone; only the flesh is given to itself in pure immanence. According to Henry, the flesh offers the only milieu where pure phenomenality can be found, simply because it does not depend upon intentionality. It consists solely of self-revealing impressions and affections. Unlike the body that lends itself to the world, the flesh "is nothing other than what *feels itself, suffers itself, undergoes itself and bears itself, and thus enjoys itself according to impressions that are always reborn* . . . [The flesh] is thus an impressional substance *beginning and ending with what it feels.*"[95] Henry develops his notion of impressions by drawing on Husserl's pre-intentional impressions or *hyle*, with the important modification that for Henry such impressions do not await any intentional form to become manifest. In the pure suffering of impressions, one is not directed toward anything in the world but is solely filled with one's own affections. Starting and ending with themselves, the impressions reveal themselves in the flesh, and can without remainder manifest themselves immanently, from themselves to themselves.

Henry proposes both a new sense of the body as flesh and a new sense of phenomenology, not as intentional phenomenology, but as what he calls a "phenomenology of life." Henry claims that only a phenomenology of life is able to fulfill phenomenology's aspirations of pure phenomenality. His account of phenomenology does not end in the infinite regress of intentionality unable to feel itself, nor does it direct itself toward the "unreality" of Husserl's noema or life-world. The essence of phenomenology can be found in the awareness of the flesh transparent to itself.[96] However, Henry suggests that there is yet another level beneath this auto-affective flesh, namely life. The constant producing and receiving of auto-affection are not engendered by the ipseity itself. It is rather life that makes the flesh possible; life "whose property is precisely revealing itself to itself in its pathos-filled self-affection."[97] Moreover, the life animating the flesh refers to the absolute Life, from which the very movement of life finally springs forth. Such absolute Life—God—is what makes the incarnation in general meaningful: Life coming in flesh.

Henry on the Specific Incarnation

The general view of life coming in flesh obviously corresponds closely with Henry's more specific approach to the incarnation of Christ. For Merleau-Ponty, the incarnation of Christ signifies a reversal of the onto-theological God, since God, by taking a human body, is no longer above us, but has become one of us, sharing our earth and our world, and dwelling even beneath us. What sense of the specific incarnation does Henry's phenomenology of the flesh lead to?

Henry's approach to the specific incarnation is strongly influenced by the Gospel of John, where the coming of Christ signifies both incarnation and revelation. In *I Am the Truth*, Henry's starting point is revelation. The coming of the Word is revelation because the Word (logos) made flesh is the embodiment of Truth. Such fundamental truth has nothing to do with a correspondence between propositions and facts, or, as in Heidegger's view, about Being unconcealing itself. All such manifestations of worldly truths remain situated in the visible exteriority, according to Henry. In contrast, the Christian truth reveals itself without remainder or distinctions. More specifically, God is the self-revelation that arrives in Christ, and thus there is no distance between the Life and the flesh that lives, and there is no distinction in the way Christ is God, either.[98] The question then arises: How can we account for the incarnation, as the Son's coming into the world? Does it not necessitate that Christ comes into the visible, and hence, must the revelation not be regarded by intentionality? Is not the point, as Merleau-Ponty asserts, that incarnation means that "God has been externalized" and hence is "diametrically opposed to 'spiritualism'"?[99] To believe so, Henry argues, means that we

CHAPTER 1

have not yet grasped the distinction between worldly appearances and revelation. While the former are conditioned by someone perceiving the appearance, truth is unconditional because God reveals himself without the distance imposed by a perceiver. Not only is revelation without distance, but it does not interfere with the visible world. There are no appearances to perceive, for according to John: "my kingdom is not of the world" (John 18:36).

Henry's position challenges the most common understanding of truth and revelation, in a manner that raises numerous questions, one of which Henry addresses to himself:

> If the Revelation of God owes nothing to the world's truth—if its pure phenomenological matter is not identified with the horizon of light that is the world, in such a way that this Revelation cannot show itself within the world and will never show itself there—how then can we have access to Revelation?[100]

Revelation has no manifestation in the world and yet we must somehow access the revelation. Henry contends that the truth revealed is God as absolute Life (John 14:6), and since the revelation is a self-revelation, it does not need to go outside itself. Not only is Life revealed, but it is revealed in and through life. Life is both the "what" and the "how" of the givenness. Insofar as we, as fleshly beings in general, are living creatures, we participate in that life. This means that there is access to the revelation for any living being, namely through life itself.[101]

According to Henry's aspiration to develop a Christian philosophy with its inherent Trinitarian structure, he cannot attribute revelation to God the Father alone, but must differentiate between the Father and the Son. This fundamental distinction aligns with the ancient creeds: God creates, or as Henry prefers, engenders life ("the maker of heaven and earth"); but the Son makes Life manifest ("His only Son, who was conceived by the Holy Spirit"). In terms of God engendering Life in himself, Henry refers to God as absolute Life. It is this absolute Life that in turn engenders the life of human beings, with Christ as the firstborn and only Son.[102] Because Life is revealed to itself, it can therefore be experienced in and by itself. Importantly, such experience entails a self. This self sheds light on the role of the Son vis-à-vis God: The Son is precisely a self or ipseity in which the Life of God is gathered, individuated, and experienced in the flesh. The inextricable relation between the Father and the Son can thus be further specified, for while the Father engenders the Son, the Son is the ipseity through which the Father experiences himself. The self-experience of God must come about through the incarnation of the Son, so that God can affect and enjoy Himself through the Son. As Henry puts it: "The Father . . . by which Life is cast out into itself in order to experience itself, this Father eternally engenders the Son within himself, if by the latter we understand the First Living in whose original and essential Ipseity the Father experiences himself."[103]

Revelation appears as a circle, the appearance of Life from within Life, accessible only through the participation of Life. And yet, there is no revelation without the incarnation. Incarnation is often thought of as uniting heaven and earth, God and humanity, but Henry approaches it differently: Christ is not born in the sense of coming into the visible world. John does not speak of birth at all, and in Henry's rendering, the stories of the virgin birth, as accounted for by Luke and Matthew, serve only to elucidate that Christ derives Life from God.[104] Strangely enough, the empirical person of Jesus of Nazareth is not central to the revelation; for Henry, the man Jesus is just one among other men. "If the Word of God comes to dwell with humanity under the guise of the objective body, the Word's journey would take place in such a way that Christ would remain insurmountably incognito."[105] There is in principle nothing to be seen in the revelation according to the light of the world, since invisible Life is fundamentally heterogeneous with the world.

Such a radical denunciation of any worldly aspect of Christ is highly problematic because it paradoxically denies any visible, material, and hence bodily implications of the incarnation. However, Henry does not deny the significance of the flesh of Christ; on the contrary, while the objective body proves to be irreal, the flesh is the very center of Life and Truth. Incarnation is nothing other than the Word's *"arrival in a flesh."*[106] The Word (logos), according to the Prologue of John, is crucial for the understanding of the incarnation of Christ. Although the Greek word *logos* is used in John, Henry argues that its content is entirely un-Greek. The content of the Greek logos is conceived as the rational human power that illuminates the world, a power that distinctly separates rational humans from animal flesh in general. In contrast, the Christian understanding of logos situates flesh as the site of the logos. According to Christianity, Henry writes, "its Logos is no longer the Logos of the world but the Logos of Life, and its conception of the body is no longer the Greek conception of a mundane body but precisely the conception of a flesh that only exists in life."[107]

Henry's notion of the specific incarnation does not pertain to the mundane body, but to the manner in which life becomes flesh: "Incarnation no longer refers to this actual flesh which is considered to be the paradigm of all factuality. *It refers to the arrival in a flesh,* to the process from which it came and in which it remains."[108] By eternally arriving in flesh, Christ reveals Life and thereby opens a phenomenological realm beyond the visible. Alluding to a central trope of the Church Fathers, Henry sums up the meaning of salvation in this simple schema: "God's becoming-man is the basis for man's becoming God."[109] By identifying oneself with the Word, one simultaneously participates in God. But if such participation is not made possible through knowledge or speculative reason, and not through sacraments or sacrifice—how then is it to be achieved? The crux is the common flesh of Christ and all humans. This means, on the one hand, that incarnation is the divine affirmation of the human condition, acknowledging that humanity essentially is flesh. On the other hand, since incarnation implies salvation, this salvation depends on Christ's true communion with both God and humans at once. The notion of Christ as the mediator is classic. As Irenaeus famously puts it: "For unless man had overcome the enemy of man, the enemy would not have been legitimately vanquished. And again: unless it had been God who had freely given salvation, we could never have possessed it securely."[110] According to Henry, it is less a matter of vanquishing the enemy, and more a matter of revealing the true life in our flesh. While there is neither flesh nor life without a self, nor is there any incarnated self without the life that lies at the foundation of any of its powers. Our sin, Henry argues, is that we tend to refuse to accept life as given to us, wanting instead to hold on to it as our own possession. Thus, we deny life and invoke death. It is against the backdrop of sin and death that God's arrival in flesh brings salvation by reuniting our life with absolute Life.[111]

Assessing the General Incarnation

Having looked at some of the motives that make both the general and specific incarnation significant for Merleau-Ponty and Henry, it becomes evident that their respective projects head in different directions. While Merleau-Ponty expands on some of Husserl's groundbreaking insights regarding the lived body, he portrays the lived body as far more actively engaged in the world. There is no closed immanence of our conscious life, quite the contrary: "Consciousness is transcendence through and through."[112] For Henry, in contrast, the transcendence that Merleau-Ponty has in mind is but a derived mode; the body is still a form of intentionality, beyond which there must be another, more fundamental mode of manifestation that conditions the former. This is the immanence of the auto-affective flesh. Reconciling these accounts is no easy task, but assessing their respective contributions can lay the groundwork for further elaboration of the phenomenology of incarnation.

Neither Merleau-Ponty nor Henry significantly illuminates one central ambition of Husserl's second volume of *Ideas*: to provide a phenomenological account of the various strata of our embodied being. Husserl seeks to account for the personal sense of being embodied, as well as having an extended, objective body, while attempting to do phenomenological justice to both in their own right. In his treatment of the middle term—the animal body—Husserl aims to elucidate the relationship between the lived and the objective body. His exploration of the relationship between materiality and sensation, and between causality and motivation by such notions as "somatological causality" may not appear immediately persuasive unless it becomes evident that such causality can unify essentially different modes of givenness. Unfortunately, it is doubtful that his explanation goes beyond psychophysical parallelism.[113] However, the problem Husserl raises persists as a challenge even after considering the contributions of Merleau-Ponty and Henry: exactly how can we account for the fact that we live our bodies and yet that they are part of the world? If we wish to maintain that the lived and objective bodies are aspects of one and the same body, I believe that we require a phenomenological approach that recognizes the objective body as more than an external correlate and the lived body as open to more than its own immanence. Can we experience the material dimension of the body from a first-person perspective, rather than a third-person perspective? If so, might this suggest a way in which the objective and lived body is traversed and reveals a primordial experience of incarnation?

Starting with the general notion of human incarnation, Merleau-Ponty's strength lies in his ability to demonstrate the mutual implication of body and the world. The incarnate subject becomes a mere abstraction without taking into account the primary unity of being-in-the-world. Although Merleau-Ponty's elaborations of the lived body in *Phenomenology of Perception* are fruitful, they remain anchored in its transcendental ambitions, and revolve around the constitutive contributions of our sensations, movements, positions, and habits as we situate ourselves within our surroundings. As Merleau-Ponty in retrospect saw it, his problem was the transcendental approach, which led to "that in part I retained the philosophy of 'consciousness.'"[114] This may explain why he offers little insight into the more material and carnal dimensions of the body or the objective body as such. To encompass not only the perceptual but also the material aspects of our corporeality in the concept of incarnation, it seems necessary to move beyond *Phenomenology of Perception*.

CHAPTER 1

Drew Leder compellingly argues that Merleau-Ponty's notion of the lived body is limited to the intentional or ecstatic body. More specifically, Leder posits that what remains unaddressed is an organic basis that, although not perceptible, enables perception. He refers to this presupposed basis as "the visceral body." "My inner organs," Leder writes, "are for the most part neither the agents nor the objects of sensibility. They constitute their own circuitry of vibrant, pulsing life, which precedes the perceptual in fetal life, outruns it in sleep, sustains it from beneath at all movements."[115] The visceral body, though not strictly part of subjectivity, supports the body that is under my sway. Other elements of our material constitution, such as bones, muscles, veins, and blood, also sustain us from beneath. The implication is that it is insufficient to invoke the lived body in order to account for fully incarnated subjectivity—we must also include the material and visceral strata that enable it. Incarnation must encompass, in Leder's apt expression, flesh and blood.[116]

Leder's invocation of flesh and blood is not intended primarily as a critique of Merleau-Ponty's position, but rather as a means of supplementing a certain one-sidedness of Merleau-Ponty's account of the body. The implications of flesh and blood are, I believe, not exhausted by addressing the organic stratum beneath intentionality; they also suggest the common substance that unites body and world. The materials composing flesh and bones, which we exchange in metabolism, are part of the world opened by the lived body but also elude it. In his later writings, Merleau-Ponty identifies the common ontological element of the flesh as the basis for interlacing and chiasms.[117] This idea allows for a complex structure of unity and difference, both between the two aspects of the body and their shared rootedness in the flesh. Merleau-Ponty describes the two aspects of our body as "a being of two leaves, from one side a thing among things and otherwise what sees them and touches them; we say, because it is evident, that it unites these two properties within itself, and its double-belongingness to the order of the 'object' and the order of the 'subject.'"[118] The two leaves belong to one another, the perceiving body on the one hand, and the body that belongs to things on the other; a body, that is, which is made of the same "stuff." This "stuff" is not alien to the perceiving body, since it is what is sensible to us.[119] Merleau-Ponty occasionally also speaks of nature as that which both founds our bodies and resists phenomenological reflection, preserving an opaque dimension of the body.[120] All of this, I believe, points in the direction of a comprehensive understanding of incarnation in terms of flesh and blood, although Merleau-Ponty never elaborates on it in these terms.

In one respect, the appeal to the visceral body seems to converge with Henry's position on the immanent body, as Henry also directs attention away from the world and toward the body's interiority. Nevertheless, there are reasons to believe that Henry would resist any such identification. Flesh and blood simply seem to fall outside the scope of his concept of the flesh. Organs, bones, veins, and blood are naturally not denied by Henry, but they remain parts of the visible, objective body that, by definition, does not feel and affect itself. Only flesh is self-affective and self-revealing, thus opening itself to phenomenological givenness in the first place.[121] While it is phenomenologically challenging to account for the visceral dimension, as it is not immediately apparent to us, Henry simply dismisses the entire material side of the body along with our perceptual bonds to the world.[122]

Anthony Steinbock argues that an adequate treatment of the body must take into account both its immanent and transcendent aspects. Referring to Henry, he writes that just because "the body is not essentially *res extensa*, does not mean that the only phenomenological aspect of the body is the Invisible body."[123] For this seems to be the choice Henry leaves us with: either an objective body projected into the world, or a flesh in which visibility and materiality have no part. This does not mean, however, that Henry denies the world or somehow annihilates it. Indeed, he maintains that there are not one but essentially two modes of givenness: manifestation according to the visible world, and revelation according to the invisible flesh. Hence, Henry states that our body "must be able to appear to us in two different ways. Our body offers us the crucial experience in which the duality of appearing is decisively confirmed."[124] What has become of the reduction to the flesh and to immanence as the milieu of auto-revelation? It turns out that Henry soon sharply distinguishes between the ways the bodies appear; while the flesh is emptied of all exteriority, the objective body is "the derealization of a flesh in and by the appearing in the world."[125] This argument is consistent with his overall view. Having entered immanence through the radical reduction, Henry is no longer able to shed light on what difference the life in the world means for us. While his reductions bring him back from the worldly body into the flesh, Henry finds a self-constituting immanent life that is heterogeneous to all transcendence, and therefore cuts its ties to the world. This leads to a position where no path leads from the self-subsistent auto-affective life back to exteriority, from the flesh back to the body in the world.[126] The radical reduction appears to be a one-way traffic, or worse, a dead end.

Take sensations, for example. Henry rightly holds that any seeing or hearing must imply that the sensation is sensed by itself, as pointed out by Descartes.[127] But seeing or hearing entails that one sees something other than itself, which is the essential teaching of intentionality. If impressions are fundamentally the movement of the inner life affecting itself, we can no longer account for how impressions relate to the sensation of our surrounding world. We are left with a strange notion of sensation that is not sensing anything beyond itself; it just makes up a closed circuit of auto-affection. The same holds for kinesthesis. Henry is well aware of the importance of the feeling of effort and movement.[128] He writes: "Because it is not constituted, because it is a transcendental experience, the movement of the hand has nothing to do with a displacement in objective space or in any transcendent milieu whatever; the original and real movement is a subjective movement."[129] The problem that occurs, following Renaud Barbaras, is that this feeling of efforts that knows no alteration in objective space, is tantamount to immobility. It undercuts the most fundamental sense of movement from which the analyses set out.[130] Admittedly, there are impressions and affections given without intentionality and distance, such as pain, but these can hardly serve as representative of sensations in general and even less for kinesthesis. It seems to me that Henry has made a strong case for the non-intentional affections we do have, but his phenomenology becomes problematic as they are absolutized and purified. Is it possible to see Henry's flesh as only one dimension of the body, while other dimensions transcend Henry's immanence, both toward the world and toward the material density of flesh and blood?

Materiality and Incarnation

Turning to the Christian idea of incarnation, it is fair to say that Merleau-Ponty does not elaborate on this in any detail. Still, the perspectives he does sketch out are telling: incarnation prohibits any form of onto-theology, eliminates metaphysical hierarchies, and advances the meaning of incarnation for humanity as such—all of this because God becomes one among us. The direction of this inquiry begins with the phenomeno-logical disclosure of the human embodiment in general and approaches the specific incarnation of Christ sketched out on the horizon of the former. Henry, in his far more elaborate and theologically qualified account, reverses this direction. Since truth is first revealed in Christ, it is only by starting from the specific incarnation that Henry can reach the truth of the general human incarnation. For Merleau-Ponty, the body of Christ must be modeled on the intentional, lived body; Henry's account of incarnation has nothing to do with the intentional body, but centers around the flesh of the invisible Life.

The difference between Merleau-Ponty's and Henry's accounts of incarnation resonates like a distant echo of the Christological battles waged in the first centuries of the Christian church, which revolved around the implications of the incarnation. What certainly makes Christ's incarnation exceptional is, as Henry emphasizes, that Christ is simultaneously generated by God and participates in God—indeed, that Christ is God. However, in becoming flesh, Christ is human. Since Henry regards human birth as insignificant to the incarnation, one must ask if he thereby leaves out a decisive mark of the finite human body, as natal and mortal. To Tertullian and Irenaeus, the point of the birth narratives of the Gospels is to highlight the complete humanity of Christ. For them, any adequate Christology must both appeal to the generation from above and the birth from below. As Irenaeus argues: "He therefore, the Son of God, our Lord, being the Word of the Father, and the Son of man, since He had a generation as to His human nature from Mary—who was descended from mankind, and who was herself a human being—was made the Son of man."[131]

The flesh of Christ that Henry invokes does not take our ordinary natal and material body as its paradigm; its paradigm is rather some extraordinary flesh of Christ in which Life reveals itself. As Emmanuel Falque convincingly argues, the point of the incarnation cannot be its bodily extraordinariness, since incarnation is not in the service of enhancing ordinary bodies into its exceptionality. Rather, the paradigmatic expression of incarnation follows the kenotic or descending movement of the divine into the ordinary. Referring to the patristic era, Falque directs his reproach toward Henry: "They [the Church Fathers] did not wish to proclaim a God of the extra-ordinary but, rather, the unlikelihood of the Word's incarnation in the daily ordinariness of our simple material corporeity."[132] In the early church, it was crucial to hold fast to the ordinariness of Christ's body in order to ward off conceptions of Christ's body as un- or super-human; conceived, for instance, as angelic in nature as the Gnostic Valentinus held.[133] Given Henry's rejection of Christ's ordinary corporeity, Falque accuses him of "angelism," alluding to Valentinus's position. Such strange neglect of the ordinary body is not, Falque contends, unique to Henry; Henry just gives a very overt expression of a tendency that Falque believes is lurking under the surface of the entire phenomenological movement. Indeed, I believe Falque points to the heart of the discussion as he writes: "Phenomenology does not know how the body is material, unless it is made objective (*Körper*). To appear 'in flesh and bone' (*leibhaft gegeben*) in phenomenology, is paradoxically to have neither flesh nor bone."[134]

I want to draw out two important points from this quote. First, although phenomenology can appeal to the objective body as a correlate to the lived body or flesh, the objective body is so conceived that it can never be experienced from the inside, and the lived body does not include organs and materiality. Second, Falque alludes to Husserl's "principle of all principles" in which intuitive presence, literally something bodily given (*leibhaft gegeben*), serves as the source of phenomenology. For Falque, it is paradoxical that phenomenology has nevertheless deprived bodies of their "flesh and bone." Is this necessarily so? Falque's sweeping critique may go too far here, but he puts his finger on an important tendency. Mainstream phenomenology, we have seen, basically tends to provide us with two approaches to the body that are mutually exclusive: either lived or objective body. The important thing is that neither of them includes the material or organic body as given to the subject. Obviously, the most promising notion with respect to incarnation is the lived body or flesh. According to Falque, however, this phenomenological approach doubly misses the mark, both with regard to the general and the specific incarnation: it neglects that incarnation is not only about becoming lived body (*Verleiblichung*), but about becoming objective body (*Verkörperung*) as well.[135] If the specific incarnation follows the kenotic movement, it should at least inspire a notion of the body that embraces what we take to be below us. It suggests the inclusion of our corporeal dimensions, all the way down to the "dust" and "earth" from which our bodies are drawn.

If this is so, then one of the basic obstacles to an adequate phenomenology of incarnation seems to be the very dichotomy between *Körper* and *Leib*. Husserl, we know, draws a sharp division between them as he holds that the "physical body and living body are essentially different; living body, that is, understood as the only one which is actually given to me as such in perception: my own living body."[136] Otherwise put, whereas the lived body is given exclusively in the first-person perspective, the objective body is only available in the third-person perspective. With reference to the constitutive role, Merleau-Ponty writes that "the objective body is not the true version of the phenomenal body, that is, the true version of the body that we live; it is no more than the latter's impoverished image."[137]

Invoking the lived body in its difference from the objective body may well overcome the body-mind dualism. But it also raises another problem, the so-called body-body problem, concerning the relationship between the different notions of the body, where the different notions of the body and their corresponding perspectives eclipse one another as two perspectives on the same body.[138] When it comes to Henry, he insists that there are two irreducible ways of appearing of the body. But since this comes with a distinction of reality (flesh) and irreality (objective body), it seems that he, unlike Husserl, embraces an ontological split of the two bodies.[139] In any case, it is far from obvious that these perspectives on the body exhaust the full sense of our incarnation: flesh and blood are still left out. The first-person perspective and the lived body have priority in phenomenological research, but this tends to exclude the visceral and material dimension. Correspondingly, the visceral and material dimensions are relegated to a third-person perspective on the objective body, which is thereby detached from the first-person perspective.[140] The situation is not made better when Henry deepens the cleft between the invisible flesh and the visible world as two completely heterogeneous modes of manifestations.

Incorporating flesh and blood into the sense of incarnation is challenging. Can phenomenology make sense of the different intuitions we have, namely that the body is given to itself as part of our immediate self-awareness (Henry), and is intentionally directed toward the world (Husserl, Merleau-Ponty), but also involves material and organic density (Leder, Falque)—all within the first-person perspective? If so, I believe we need to move beyond the dichotomous understanding of the objective and the lived body. My bones, veins, and organs are not given to me as an object in front of me, because they imply some sense of mineness, even though they tend to be absent as I engage in the world.[141] Nevertheless, such flesh and blood is part of me prior to their objectification. For similar reasons, Falque has coined the notion of the "spread body." Interestingly, Falque claims that the spread body is indeed phenomenologically given to subjectivity. It appears, for instance, when we slumber or lay on the operating table. In those cases, we encounter an experience of our very own body, both familiar as mine, and yet strange in its density and weight. Such experiences, Falque argues, open us toward a bodily region beyond the objective and lived body:

> The in-between of the spread-out body—neither flesh nor body, neither purely subjective nor exclusively objective—is then, as I see it, what philosophy needs to recover and what theology needs to deal with.[142]

Such a notion of the spread-out body, or what I have called flesh and blood, seems to me indispensable to an understanding of incarnation, general and specific, since they refer to a third bodily dimension that must be taken into account. Falque's perspective entails that it is possible to experience the material and visceral dimensions of my lived body. Interestingly, Henry can at times speak of the resistance of the body, as a thingly body that resists my will. But Henry attaches no constitutive significance to such experience, since the resisting body turns out to belong to the outside world. What this resistance demonstrates to him is rather the will's ability to bend whatever resists us.[143] This is not where Falque is

CHAPTER 1

heading; he instead points to an inner experience of resistance precisely without switching to a body projected into a visible world. Phenomenology must rather seek those occasions, such as slumbering or feeling a dull pain, because on such occasions one's own body is given to oneself in its thickness, resistance, and weight.[144] While bones, muscles, and organs are part of my own body, they retain a strange sense of opacity once they make themselves felt. In fever or when about to fall asleep, we feel that our grasp of the body is slipping away, which enables another experience of the body, the body as "thinglike" in its heavy and dense materiality.[145]

I believe it is possible to draw a further consequence from Falque's suggestion. The spread body does not only denote one region of the body among others, however fundamental, but an experience of the body *prior* to the splitting into lived and objective body. Such a primordial bodily sphere is, similar to the lived body, given as originally mine, but at the same time it is given with the kind of resistance and density that we otherwise assign to objective bodies. Consequently, the spread body, or as I prefer, flesh and blood, blurs the distinctions that later will evolve into the lived and the objective body. Put another way, flesh and blood is given in an ambiguous manner, both as mine and in its material density. If this is the case, we must follow Merleau-Ponty in preserving the ambiguity in the most primordial experience, for as he says: "What is ambiguous is the human condition."[146] Because of the way it is given prior to the split between lived and objective body, and due to its inherent ambiguity, flesh and blood might turn out to be the soil from which those other senses of the body can evolve.

Since our primordial sense of the body as flesh and blood is mostly not apparent, phenomenology must pay attention to the special occasions when it does appear, and ascribe relevant significance to them. Falque mentions situations such as drowsing or lying on the operating table, but pain too seems to be an exemplary occasion, which I will discuss later in more detail. But why not just stick to the established notions and say that on such occasions it is my objective body that is given to me in an immediate phenomenological experience?[147] The reason why this does not work is that the objective body presupposes a higher, intersubjective constitution and thus entails mediation and distanciation. However, I can experience my spread body prior to any distanciation, and my flesh and blood as belonging to my primordial ambiguous body, for example when I suffer from pain in my leg. Moreover, such a notion of the body as flesh and blood has repercussions for how to think of the incarnation of Christ. If Christ were solely incarnated as flesh, as Henry has it, he cannot be truly given as an objective body, and vice versa. To Falque, in becoming flesh, Christ did not become either flesh or objective body, but assumed a body like ours, including its organic and material conditions.[148] Merlau-Ponty's understanding of the incarnation—God becoming one among us and thus authenticating our darkness—can now be given a further twist: in the incarnation, God embraces all of our humanity because the incarnation participates in all of our being, including its flesh and blood.[149]

2

The Body between Matter and Form

I have taken the Christian idea of the incarnation as a guide to understanding the depth of human embodiment. This approach includes the objective and lived body, as well as the organic and material dimensions of the body as it is subjectively given. However, little light has been shed on the experience of one's flesh and blood, and how it can be given a more accurate phenomenological description. If the problem in post-Cartesian philosophy has been how to put the mind back into a lived body, I want to take a step further and ask how that incarnated body can preserve its materiality. This chapter, therefore, picks up what I see as a challenge to phenomenology; namely, how it can account for the material dimension—the raw experience of the givenness of flesh and blood—without giving up the role of the lived body. To this end, I will pay heed to the notion of matter (*hyle*) and form (*morphe*) in its various applications inside and outside phenomenology. Admittedly, Husserl's notion of *hyle* at first seems to be restricted to sense data or impressions that fulfills the intentional form or *morphe*. Departing from this view, Henry has made *hyle* central to his notion of the flesh, but his take drifts toward a certain de-materialization. Can phenomenology preserve the materiality of matter at all? Phenomenology cannot simply state the reality of matter but must study how it is given in experience, which means that a phenomenological approach to materiality is bound to the first-person perspective. According to such perspective, I suggest that Husserl's notions of *hyle* and *morphe* can serve as conceptual tools for analyzing the density and resistance of the body, which arguably is the way its materiality appears.

To approach the materiality of the body, I will shortly visit two non-phenomenological approaches to the body's materiality: first, Judith Butler's performative feminism, which seeks to move beyond the constructivism/essentialism distinction; and secondly, some suggestions made within the recent current of speculative realism. Performative feminism and speculative realism are picked out because they represent almost opposed approaches to the material reality of the body. The former emphasizes the ways in which our perceptions of our body are shaped by discourses, while the latter insists on reality, including bodily reality,

THE BODY BETWEEN MATTER AND FORM

beyond any correlation with subjectivity. Both of these positions serve as a contrast which puts the phenomenological approach I want to propose into relief.

Matter without Materiality:
Butler's Constructivism

With the telling title *Bodies That Matter*, Judith Butler discusses the problematic notion of body and matter through a Foucault-inspired discourse analysis coupled with notions of performativity derived from ordinary language philosophy and Derrida's theory of iterability. In speaking of matter that matters, Butler attempts to show how signification cannot be divorced from materiality. Her account takes issue with feminist thinkers who have tended to revolve around, not *Leib* and *Körper* exactly, but the distinction between gender (culturally conceived) and sex (naturalistically conceived). Butler is critical of how such a distinction between gender and sex was treated in much literature in the postmodern wave of the 1980s. Often, gender has been taken as a construction that tends to make the body into a sign, or worse, a fiction that can in principle be changed at will, or even disposed of. Other feminists, Butler points out, have argued that real bodies are not reducible to signs but really exist here and now; they feel pain and pleasure, live and die. These feminists tend not to deny any further meaning of the gendered body, but assume that the cultural construction of the gendered body is superimposed on a stable nature or sex.[1] However, if there is no unmediated access to anything like a stable nature, then the problem recurs: if "everything is discourse, what about the body?"[2]

Butler thus portrays the dilemmas posed by the postmodern wavering between essentialism and constructivism within feminism. The relevance of these discussions is, however, not restricted to feminist philosophy, for they also have repercussions for the phenomenological discussion of the distinction between the lived and objective body. Moreover, here one needs to come to terms with how the lived and the objective body both mutually support and exclude each other, along with the constitutive significance of intersubjective and cultural mediation.[3] The challenge for phenomenology seems to be this: if such mediation is constitutive of the body, it seems to lose its resistance and materiality, and conversely, if the body is pure materiality, the mediation is only superimposed on an essential structure.

Butler holds that what matters is the materiality of the body, but what does materiality mean in her lingo? She obviously does not want to align herself with constructivism, nor is essentialism a viable option. Her point is that even the notion of unmediated, pure sex (or for that matter, a purely objective body) is itself mediated. According to Butler, this is not to deny the reality of materiality, nor does it refer to something given, say, some kind of naked reality beyond the concept. Culture and nature, gender and sex, are distinctions made possible by a matrix that underlies all these distinctions. Drawing on Foucault, Butler argues that the body is neither constructed by the sign nor does it exist before the sign: body and sign come simultaneously into being. Indeed, Aristotle adopted his form/matter distinction in order to stress the impossibility of severing the intelligibility of form from matter. The body is always already invested with structures of significance, and such significance implies structures of power. The significance of the material body implies power because it will sustain some structures and exclude others. To Butler, such a view demands that we come to regard matter as historical sedimentations, shot through with earlier investments of power. As she explains:

> "Materiality" designates a certain effect of power or, rather, *is* power in its formative or constituting effects. Insofar as power operates success-fully by constituting an object domain, a field of intelligibility, as taken-for-granted ontology, its material effects are taken as material data or primary givens.[4]

In other words, the materiality is taken as an empirical given, with power imposing itself completely and thereby masking the genealogy that made such conviction possible in the first place. Butler draws on Foucault's vision of the disciplinary forces of normalizing discourses throughout history, where the normal tends to appear as the given, as a matter of fact. This obscures the fact that matter is a "process of materialization that stabilizes over time to produce the effect of boundary, fixity, and surface we call matter."[5] What we take as our body is therefore mediated by historical power structures that mold our conception of the normal body.

Now, Butler has more to say that directly bears on the matter/form distinction. The way in which this process of materialization has shaped our body discourse is through heterosexual or heteronormative logic. One significant way in which this has come to expression is by the form/matter distinction, essential to Plato and Aristotle. Following Butler's reading, Aristotle regards matter as potentiality and form as actuality. The soul is the actualizing or forming principle of the material body. They belong together in an intimate way that prohibits any sharp division of body and soul. Aristotle does not appeal to pure matter by which we can superimpose linguistic signs. Form and matter make up a unity apart from which matter hardly makes sense at all. Indeed, matter is always invested with sense, since matter "means at once 'to materialize' and 'to mean.'"[6]

Butler points out that in Plato, the opposition between form and matter is less pronounced than in Aristotle but certainly operative. Interestingly, Plato argues that there is yet another, more excessive sense of matter that is located below the form/matter distinction. In this excessive sense, matter is understood as the receiving principle that originates all that is. This matter has no form, nor does it await any, and therefore it cannot be further defined or thematized. "This excessive matter that cannot be contained within the form/matter distinction operates like the surplus in Derrida's analysis of philosophical oppositions."[7] As a surplus, matter is produced as the outside of discourse and yet it secretly works on the inside. This sense of matter remains on the outside of the form/matter distinction, while simultaneously originating both. Historically, after Plato, the form/matter dichotomy became hegemonic, and the notion of the original raw matter was gradually excluded. Through the course of history, form gained the upper hand, and it did so through acts of exclusion. Indeed, it is through this exclusion that philosophical intelligibility is constituted.[8] One way to challenge the borders of philosophy is to attend to how the excluded femininity is cut off from the normative discourse on form and matter—and yet it is impossible to get rid of. The excessive matter haunts our discourses as what Freud would call the return of the repressed. Thus, it seems that the excessive matter is not easily subsumed by power discourse but strongly resists it. Butler grants us the possibility to consider this matter as both the excluded outside (secretly enabling the inside), and simultaneously a surplus that evades the domestication into conceptual schemes of form and matter.

Butler's central move beyond the essentialism-constructivism divide in feminism rests on the claim that matter and discourse cannot be separated. Matter is not simply a given fact, but an internal part of the process of materialization which comes through the heteronormative discourse that makes matter significant to us. It is, however, due to this claim that Butler is criticized for neglecting the materiality of the body, especially because the resistance of materiality seems to evaporate along with the agency that belongs to matter.[9] Butler denies that one can regard matter as simply given facts, and there is no way that its meaning or essence can be directly extracted from it. However, she does not deny materiality. The body is indeed shaped and structured by the way performatives iterate older discourses, but one may still wonder if the body seems to be all too malleable and without any resistance of its own. Can the matter of the body be fully transformed into an enacted text? Isn't there still at least a remainder, some silent matter, that resists meaning? The question is whether it is still possible to insist on an unconstructed dimension to which meaning-making responds but cannot itself construe or constitute. Form presupposes matter. To suggest, as I will, that there is a sense of matter that both enables and withdraws from discourse, is not to fall back on an essentialist biologism, but to propose that our bodies at times reveal themselves in their brute and resistant materiality, as flesh and blood.

I find Butler's invocation of Plato's original matter more fruitful, as it indicates a dimension of matter that always evades form and hence meaning. It seems phenomenologically adequate to say that bodily materiality evades any easy integration into signification and form. But since matter is what usually goes up in the form, can we experience bodily matter as such? I believe there are occasions when we can. Take an instance of acute pain: I am not solely the "I can" that holds sway, because, in the passivity of experiencing pain, I sense the opacity of the body addressing me: it announces itself from the dark matter of my body prior to any meaning-giving form. As Butler notes, Aristotle argues that matter cannot be defined, and Plato speaks of it as formless.[10] In accordance with the example of pain, this lack of definition suggests that any possible comprehension of pain arrives, as it were, too late. When we try to grasp the pain or give form to its matter, pain is already there. Alternatively put, the matter of pain is like a call that precedes a response that bestows form on it, where the point remains the same: the response cannot fully appropriate the call to which it responds.[11] Pain speaks first, as an insistent matter with its own density and affectivity. While Butler preserves the sense of a surplus of matter, it too becomes a function of the discourse, namely as its outside. In absorbing our materiality into the unfolding performativity of the body, Butler leaves little room for the phenomenology of materiality in its own terms.

Reality without Correlation: Speculative Realism

Moving from Butler's materialization as the outcome of signification and power to the other extreme, there has been a growing interest in realism in general and particularly in one of its avatars, called speculative realism, over the last decade or so. Admittedly, the relationship between form and matter is less of an issue for speculative realism, but it nevertheless prepares the ground for a view of the body that contrasts starkly with Butler's account. If there is a convincing realist approach to the body,

THE BODY BETWEEN MATTER AND FORM

it follows that the body cannot be taken up into discourses, at least not without remainder. The movement of speculative realism was founded at a conference in 2007 and is made up of an association of members with different projects, most prominent among them Graham Harman, Quentin Meillassoux, and more recently, Tom Sparrow.[12] They all share the conviction that post-Kantian philosophy suffers from an idealist or antirealist bias that closes philosophy off from reality. What is called for, they hold, is a philosophy that can come to terms with reality beyond the strictures of consciousness and language and thus guide philosophy to the "great outdoors."[13] While both Harman and Sparrow draw heavily on phenomenology, they nevertheless have come to see it as the major obstacle to realism within contemporary philosophy.

To Meillassoux, the fateful step taken with Kant's Copernican revolution is encapsulated in what he calls "correlationism." From Kant onward, he claims, the major trends in Continental philosophy cling to the essential correlation between thought and world, consciousness and things, subjectivity and objects. According to this correlationism, "we only ever have access to the correlation between thinking and being, and never to either term considered apart from the other."[14] It is not hard to see that this captures a central phenomenological commitment. Husserl writes that he discovered the essential correlation in his first major work, *Logical Investigations*, which "affected me so deeply that my whole subsequent life-work has been dominated by the task of systematically elaborating on this a priori correlation."[15] If one strives for a reality beyond this a priori correlation, one must have good reasons for giving up such a compelling idea. Indeed, Meillassoux believes he has such reasons: he will drop correlationism because it debars us from reality as such, which he takes to be the reality that science addresses and describes. However, it is one thing to appeal to reality as such, and another thing to account for how it can be approached. One may wonder: If reality cannot be approached from subjectivity, and not from a God's-eye view—then from where? From the view from nowhere?

For Harman, the problem with what he dubs the "philosophy of access" is that it does not respect the autonomy of things. Harman's own readings and extensions of Heidegger's philosophy primarily concern Heidegger's famous notion of tools. According to the context-dependent know-how of tools, which Heidegger calls "ready-to-hand," things become transparent and invisible as they are absorbed into successful handling. But tools can break, Heidegger notes, and in breaking, the tools disclose themselves in their objecthood. So far Harman's interpretation does not deviate from the standard reading. But then Harman argues that such breakdowns are not only a matter of switching from ready-to-hand to present-at-hand, from practice to theory, as it is often rendered; more profoundly, the breakdowns let the objecthood appear in a way that indicates our limited access to things in the first place. What is made manifest is how things ultimately evade our access to them and withdraw into their own independent being.[16]

While Harman trusts Heidegger's phenomenology of the tools, he nevertheless finds that Heidegger fails to transcend the dynamics between ready-to-hand and present-at-hand. Thus, Heidegger never fully gives up the commitment to the closed circle of human access. The problem is the self-imposed limitation of such a philosophy: "While philosophy is charged with knowing the whole of reality, the Philosophy of Access reduces the reality to the tiny portion of it directly available to humans."[17] This criticism of philosophy of access is meant to pave the way for Harman's alternative, namely his object-oriented ontology, which is furnished with hidden causality and panpsychism. Limestones, gorillas, and hurling winds are all treated on the same footing as consciousness, and knit together in a web of relations. But if object-oriented philosophy implies such a network of relations, one might wonder if Harman has not in fact overcome correlationism, but rather broadened it drastically to include any objects correlated with others, conscious or not.[18]

What unites Meillassoux's and Harman's concerns is their criticism of deep-seated assumptions, found in phenomenology, that debar it from thinking of reality beyond and independently of human access. But what led phenomenology astray, when it initially wanted to give a pure description of things themselves? A possible defense of phenomenology must, it seems, convincingly account for its basic principles, the principles that phenomenology must adhere to in order to establish itself as a methodologically coherent enterprise. Tom Sparrow argues that this is precisely what phenomenology fails to do. It not only fails to live up to its principles, but ever since Husserl's first initiation of phenomenology, there has never been established commonly recognized principles of phenomenology at all. Sparrow's lack of confidence in the phenomenological movement is motivated by a double conviction: "It first implies that speculative realism, as noted, brings phenomenology to a close . . . Second, it suggests that phenomenology has perhaps already come to an end."[19] In the first case, Sparrow thinks speculative realism is the only viable way to redeem phenomenology's implicit realistic aspiration, encapsulated in its slogan "back to the things themselves." However, such a slogan cannot be redeemed by phenomenology, because it only recognizes what falls within the strictures of the consciousness-world correlation, where the things themselves are strangely absent.[20]

Sparrow's second conviction, that phenomenology has already

come to an end, follows from the phenomenological movement having to a great extent turned its back on Husserl's principles—such as the eidetic and transcendental reductions—but even Husserl himself never managed to conceive a clear and stable methodological bedrock for his phenomenological enterprise. The only coherence left is what Merleau-Ponty calls a certain "style" of thinking, uncommitted and unconvincing as this sounds. Sparrow concludes that phenomenology was stillborn, and for the remaining time has been a zombie: "it is extremely active, but at the same time lacking philosophical vitality and methodologically hollow."[21] The high standards Sparrow invokes must not only be applicable to phenomenology, but apply to all movements worthy of the name. But how many philosophical movements do in fact obey such a strict, static, and systematic set of principles as Sparrow demands of phenomenology? The diverse movement of speculative realism, for one, seems not to do so. And perhaps it is impossible, especially since a philosophical movement develops over time. Sparrow's demands seem to require a place for philosophy outside history and finitude, which is, perhaps, the secret aspiration of realism.

Importantly, speculative realism has some repercussions for how the body is conceived, especially its material or objective dimensions. In *Plastic Bodies*, Sparrow does not so much pursue speculative realism as what he dubs "speculative aesthetics."[22] Some of the same ambitions adhere to this study: "aesthetics" in that phrase refers to the "comprehensive sensory life of the body, whereas the speculative aspect is meant to counter phenomenology's insistence on evidence, givenness, and perception, and thus point beyond the correlationist enclosure."[23] His position is at this stage not anti-phenomenological, but one that seeks to overcome phenomenology from within through a novel understanding of sensation. Since Sparrow clearly has realist ambitions, according to which objects and their qualities exist independently of human subjects, his notion of sensation is meant to hold another metaphysical position than that typically found in phenomenology. Sensation, Sparrows holds, must be regarded as material and must be granted autonomy in its own unfolding. According to him, such a notion of sensation is out of reach of phenomenology's main means of access, that is, intentional perception; sensation is pre-perceptual, pre-conceptual, pre-personal, and non-intentional.[24]

Given Sparrow's aspiration to overcome correlationism, one might have expected a defense of the objective body, as real and material. But materiality in *Plastic Bodies* seems to denote nothing but sensations as they are exposed to external forces. We are offered a description of a body open to the sensations and forces that it encounters prior to intentionality. Conceived on this basic level, Sparrow argues that the body is essentially plastic. This plasticity does not mean that the body is infinitely malleable, but that it comes into being in the dynamic exchange with its environment. In this exchange, the body displays its ability to receive form as well as the capacity to give form, both receiving sensations from its environment and molding its own responses to it.[25] As this position builds on Levinas's non-intentional sensation and Merleau-Ponty's habitual body, one might wonder if Sparrow's own position can survive the criticism of correlationism. It is true that it does stress the immediacy of sensation, but it also emphasizes the way we make sense of the world by responding to it. Moreover, given his realist aspirations, it is surprising to find that Sparrow's account of the body seems almost deprived of resisting materiality of its own. There is no thingly dimension of the plastic body, but a field of the dialectic of surroundings and responses.

In a critical note, Meillassoux pushes toward a more realistic notion of the body. He points out that phenomenology thinks of transcendental subjectivity as a finite perspective on the horizon of the world, and also that such subjectivity is always already in the world. To occupy a place in the world means to be incarnate in a body, and to phenomenology, such an incarnation is supposed to be something more than merely a relation to a contingent body. Meillassoux argues that this view leads phenomenology into an aporia: transcendental subjectivity necessarily takes a body, but the body is, he claims, inescapably a matter of the empirical, contingent order of the world. The embodied subject must be placed in real space and time that precede the horizon spread out by the transcendental subject. Accordingly, Meillassoux thinks the transcendental notion of the body must presuppose a world and its "ancestral space-time" that has existed prior to and independently of humans. Since the transcendental and the empirical body are mutually exclusive, we must choose— and the only reasonable option is that of the empirical body. Only such a body can do justice to the reality in space and time that is available for scientific accounts.[26]

The upshot of these sketches seems to be that the speculative realists leave open two options: they can either, as Meillassoux does, surrender a strong sense of the lived, transcendental body and aim for a realistic perspective based on science, or they can struggle with phenomenology from the inside, as Sparrow does, at the risk of falling prey to some form of correlationism. Constructively, these perspectives remind phenomenology of some important insights: it should preserve the sense of the body as more than the lived body, over which I hold sway and through which I confer meaning on the world. My body is also a body in the world and of the world. While it seems impossible for phenomenology to abolish correlationism as such, the correlation does not need to be conceived as a bridge between a separate subject and object. Arguably, the point of the a priori correlation is that subjectivity is never closed in on itself but is essentially self-transcending, transcending toward a world. Or as Renaud Barbaras has argued, the correlation even signifies the relation from which both poles of experience grow; for as the world first becomes fully manifest to an incarnate subjectivity, this subjectivity in turn is constituted by its intentional relation to the world.[27]

Nevertheless, one may object that there are experiences that point beyond what we normally take as the subjectivity-world correlation. Harman's broken tool is meant to point this out. However, the fact that tools slip from our grasp and show themselves in their inaccessibility does not make them independent of subjectivity. It is still an experience for someone confronted with what cannot be managed. Something similar is at stake when one experiences the body as becoming "other." In becoming ill, for instance, the experience of our body alters, but the body's strangeness is still someone's experience. What remains to be explored is whether phenomenology has the resources for spelling out such experiences beyond the lived body and its entanglement with the world. Even if our ordinary life can be described in terms of lived body and objective body, there are indeed instances revealing that there is something more and other to the body—not as a mind-independent reality, but as something that cuts across the lived and objective body.

Phenomenology on *Hyle* and *Morphe*

Neither performative feminism nor speculative realism aims at contributing to the phenomenology of the body, but there are important findings from both that are fruitful for further discussion. Despite the fact that she ends in a rather immaterial understanding of matter, Butler's discussion of form and matter is helpful because it shows how form remains necessary for intelligibility and—more importantly for my purpose—that there is a sense in which matter evades the dichotomy of form and matter. As for speculative realism, it is clear that phenomenology cannot accept the speculative realists' "great outdoors." But if read charitably, their criticism of correlationism can be seen as attempting to address a sense of bodily reality which has not been sufficiently taken into account within phenomenological frameworks—even if they have not presented a satisfying account of it themselves. I will later attempt to show how phenomenology can respond to these findings. In order to do so, I will first give attention to the role that Husserl has ascribed to matter. I will

CHAPTER 2

therefore first examine matter as it is presented according to Husserl's understanding of *morphe* and *hyle*.

Even if Husserl defines consciousness as intentional, he underlines from the start that our intentionality contains elements that are not intentional, namely sensual content. In *Logical Investigations*, Husserl makes it clear that real (*reell*) sensational content is crucial for the upbuilding of intentionality, since it is the carrier of intentional acts. Otherwise put, such a sensation is the content of apprehension. A simple example illustrates Husserl's point: when I regard a yellow ball in front of me, the color-sensation of its different shades is no doubt part of the experience of the thing, yet my intentionality does not aim at the color but rather at the ball itself.[28] Thus, it is possible to distinguish between the identical thing that appears and the varying sensations that belong to it. We must draw this distinction, for while the shades of the color can vary as the ball rolls over the floor, the thing remains identical.[29]

The same position is retained in Husserl's *Ideas*, but is now analyzed functionally, in terms of *hyle* (matter) and *morphe* (form). While applying the Aristotelian distinction, Husserl does not want to commit himself to any sense of realism, and certainly not to substance metaphysics in an Aristotelian sense. *Hyle* and *morphe* rather serve to elucidate the model of intentionality, where matter is regarded as what fulfills an empty intention, so that they together constitute perceived phenomena. At this point of his analysis, Husserl leaves that which is intended, the noema, to one side, and focuses on the experience that constitutes intentionality itself, that is, on noesis and sensual data. While the intentional and non-intentional elements make up a functional unity, this unity is constituted by two essentially heterogeneous components, respectively "dead matter and animating meaning." Animating function bestows meaning on what is otherwise dead matter to us and makes apprehension possible. Alternatively, Husserl can speak of these heterogeneous components in functional terms, as "*formless materials* and *materialless forms*," where they are mutually locked together by means of a logic of lack and fulfillment.[30]

By affording matter with sense, the form takes up matter, gives unity to the manifold, and thus constitutes meaningful phenomena.[31] This entails an activity of giving form and meaning to sensual matter. But what does Husserl more accurately mean by matter or *hyle*? He repeatedly outlines three different classes that fall under that notion, each one having its own generic unity.[32] The first class, already outlined in *Logical Investigations*, concerns sensual content, which is the raw material that is given to our senses, such as sense data of color, data of touch, data of sound.[33]

THE BODY BETWEEN MATTER AND FORM

At times, Husserl speaks of sensual content as inherent to the object perceived, as its particular adumbration, roughness, or color. He emphasizes that *hyle* in this sense is not meant as an adumbration of the noema and hence as belonging to the thing, but as the material from which noema is eventually built up by means of noetic animation. The second class of matter concerns sensations such as pain and pleasure.[34] Such matter is not intentional in itself because it does not by itself aim at anything. The third and final class is that of drives. Husserl does not think of drives as inherently intentional either, because they operate prior to or even independently of consciousness and therefore still await sense.

Husserl's point is not to tear matter apart from form, but to analyze their functional unity. Where empiricism and psychologism regard consciousness as a bundle of senseless matter in various relations, Husserl regards intentional consciousness as inherently meaningful, that is, as formed matter. That said, Husserl believes it is possible to undertake separate analyses, both for the affording of sense, which falls under his analysis of noesis, and similarly for a pure hyletics in its own terms, apart from its functional unity with noesis. Admittedly, Husserl never provides any elaboration of this pure hyletics, perhaps because his later turn to genetic analysis made it hard to retain an idea of pure hyletics.[35] Already in *Ideas*, he makes it clear that such hyletics would under no circumstances demand the kind of attention that the noetic analyses would, since hyletics ranks "well below the noetic and functional phenomenology."[36] It seems to me that Husserl's account of *hyle* entails a tension between *hyle* as integrated into *morphe*, and *hyle* as at least in principle able to appear apart from *morphe*.

The distinction between form and matter has met significant resistance in the phenomenological tradition.[37] Merleau-Ponty, for instance, expresses his dissatisfaction with Husserl's position in *Ideas*, particularly the dualism between apprehension and sensation, *morphe* and *hyle*. According to Merleau-Ponty, such a distinction implies that cognitive operations are an intellectualist abstraction cut off from the unhesitating manner in which our habitual body responds to situations where everything is already given as meaningful gestalts. *Hyle* is conceived as isolated sense data, Merleau-Ponty argues, but such atomistic data are in fact never given, just as no self-sufficient *morphe* exists either.[38]

> There is no hyle, no sensation which is not in communications with other sensations or the sensations of other people, and *for this very reason* there is no morphe, no apprehension or apperception, the office of which is to give significance to a matter that has none.[39]

CHAPTER 2

Indeed, the entire hylomorphism drops out of Merleau-Ponty's thinking. In his view, no data will do, since everything is always related in fields and presents itself to us according to pre-reflective gestalts that give things and surroundings their familiar physiognomy. Merleau-Ponty makes a strong point when it comes to the strict way in which Husserl draws the distinction between form and matter. However, it is hardly fair to say that Husserl believes *hyle* to be atomistic data. As Husserl makes clear in his analyses of passive syntheses, *hyle* appears to us as pre-given, that is, as an already passively constituted rudimentary field.[40] However, if this is the case, Husserl's distinction between *hyle* and *morphe* should be less strict, since the *hyle* must come with an outlined content that already informs and restricts the way it can be apprehended.

What Sartre rejects is the very idea that *hyle* can bridge the gap between consciousness and the world. For Sartre, being-in-itself (non-conscious being) and being-for-itself (consciousness) are distinct onto-logical categories that mutually exclude one another. Matter, as Sartre points out, does not belong to any of these categories. It seems as though Husserl attempts to square the circle of a thing and consciousness, but only succeeds "in creating a hybrid being which consciousness rejects and which can not be a part of the world."[41] Indeed, sensations never appear as such—they are always part of the world. "One will have to admit," Sartre writes, "that I apprehend only *the green* of this book, of this foliage and never the sensation of green nor even the 'quasi-green' which Husserl posits as the hyletic material of which the intention animates into green-as-object."[42] Given our intentional orientation, it seems reasonable to say that we normally first see the green book, and only afterward can we, by means of abstraction, single out the sensual components—not the other way around. However, upon closer inspection, we need to draw a distinction, for the greenness of the book may vary according to different light sources, while the noema, the book, remains the same.

More crucial to my concern is that neither Merleau-Ponty nor Sartre allows for *hyle* to be able to stand forth in its own right, for instance in pain. To them, *hyle* does not make sense, because all sensual content is nothing but the qualities of perceived objects; apart from them, "pure sensation would amount to no sensation and thus no feeling at all."[43] But is that so? It seems reasonable to me that I can, for instance, have a hyletic experience of pain before I identify it as a headache, and even after I have identified it, the hyletic experience does not disappear but continues to affect me.[44] Thus, the price to pay for Merleau-Ponty and Sartre's position is, as indicated by Sparrow, that they lose the conceptual devices for articulating the confrontation with a sensual, hyletic experience prior to its intentional meaning.

Henry's main concern draws in a different direction than Merleau-Ponty's criticism: the problem is not so much that matter, or impressions, as Henry prefers to say, relies on an atomistic conception, but almost the opposite; namely, that matter from the start is deprived of its autonomy and self-sufficiency. Lacking such self-sufficiency, matter becomes for Husserl "not the matter of the impression, the impressional or impressionality as such; instead, it is the matter of the act that informs it, a matter for this form."[45] In other words, as soon as Husserl opens the opportunity for grasping the essence of impressions, he subordinates impressions to intentionality, making them into the blind *hyle* under the reign of *morphe*. Moreover, Henry believes that the intentionality of outer perception is the operative model for Husserl's construal. For outer perception, *hyle* either becomes the raw material for constituting outer objects, or else it is reduced to adumbrations of a fully constituted noema that can be analyzed via the reduction. In both cases, *hyle* only fills in what is determined by intentionality's bestowing of sense. However, to Henry, the most promising understanding of *hyle* is Husserl's primal impression or *Urimpression* that occurs in his time analyses. Husserl suggests that primal impressions are at the core of the present; these impressions are not derived by anything else, but make up the absolute source without which time consciousness is unintelligible.[46] Nevertheless, Henry thinks that even Husserl's self-sufficient and self-revealing primal impressions finally are subjected to the form of the internal time consciousness. Concerning the tension in Husserl's notion of *hyle*, Henry concludes that Husserl deprives *hyle* of its initial promise.[47] What Henry misses in Husserl, and what his own phenomenology is meant to provide, is the full acknowledgment of an immanent impressionality with its own self-affecting power, prior to and independent of any form and any intentionality.

Merleau-Ponty's and Sartre's position vis-à-vis Husserl is almost diametrically opposed to that of Henry. Whereas Merleau-Ponty and Sartre profess a situated understanding of perception to the point where the distinction between *hyle* and *morphe* drops out, Henry seeks to preserve the autonomy of *hyle* at the expense of *morphe*. It seems to me that neither of them is entirely wrong nor entirely right, and it should therefore be possible to prolong Husserl's model in a way that points beyond the impasse. If, contrary to Merleau-Ponty and Sartre, *hyle* is more than the senseless fulfillment of intentions, but is pre-given as rudimentary formations and organizations, then it must be granted the power to inform and even resist the bestowing of sense from *morphe*.[48] In his later writings, Husserl explicitly criticizes any atomistic account of matter and underlines the manner in which matter always belongs to a field that is constituted prior to the active ego.[49]

As mentioned, Husserl distinguishes between different classes of *hyle*, where the first concerns *hyle* connected to outer perception, the second concerns inner sensations, such as pain, and the third concerns drives.[50] Merleau-Ponty's and Sartre's criticism concerns the first but hardly captures the latter two. Inner sensation and drives can hardly be internally interwoven with backgrounds or fields, at least not in any straightforward sense. In contrast, Henry seeks to preserve and revise the second sense of *hyle*, which he interprets as auto-affecting impressions that are resolutely non-intentional and do not await any *morphe*. But is it clear that Husserl rules out such non-intentional *hyle*? Henry is correct that Husserl tends to treat *hyle* and *morphe* as a functional unity, but Husserl is also open to the possibility that *hyle* can be given, without animating *morphe*. He writes: "Here is not to decide whether such sensual experiences in the stream of experience in every case necessarily bear in themselves some sort of 'animating construal' . . . or as we may also put it, whether they always stand in *intentional functions*."[51] Admittedly, Husserl does little more than raise the question of the possibility for *hyle* unchained from *morphe*, but if we consider this alongside the notion of primal impressions found in his lectures on time, it should at least be possible to argue that there are resources in his phenomenology for a more robust concept of *hyle*. As I see it, such a conception does not necessarily lead to Henry's autonomously self-revealing impressions with the fundamental constitutive power he assigns to them, but it does suggest that *hyle* can appear as distinct from the functional unity with *morphe*.

Hyle and the Body

The notions of *hyle* and *morphe* seems to be designed to analyze the functional components of intentionality, but they may also have bearing on the constitutive levels of the body. Shaun Gallagher argues that it is because the critics take *hyle* to be part only of our outer perception that they cannot find it. They search in the wrong place and thus fail to see that "hyletic experience is an experience that belongs to the body."[52] Indeed, both the lived and the objective body entail form and matter; the first as the living organ of our intentional life and the latter as an intentional correlate. Thus, even if *hyle* belongs to the body, as Gallagher points out, the question of the relationship between *hyle* and *morphe* recurs. Now, Butler points out that there is a sense in which original matter cannot be contained completely in the form, which for her is the reason why the negotiation of the line between what is excluded and what is included should not be settled. It will be important to ask if such a lack of complete overlap between form and matter can also be detected in a phenomenological approach. But can matter be given without form, apart from the animating sense? This is exactly what Henry claims and what Merleau-Ponty and Sartre deny.

It is, to my mind, worth exploring a middle position, where *hyle* is not given complete autonomy from the form but where hyletic sensations can still be felt as they resist or withdraw from the form. There are bodily experiences, such as pain, where we live through the experience without being fully able to identify or objectify that experience. The experience of *hyle* then comes about as the unity of form and matter cracks open from within. That *hyle* can make up such resistance does not make form superfluous, but rather discloses a limit internal to its function. In this way, the experience of pain can have a certain intentional form—if burned by fire the pain is taken to refer to the fire—but in addition, there is something opaque in pain, a remainder or intruder of the raw *hyle* that cannot be fully comprehended by form. Thus, the body in pain seems to put us in touch with its hyletic stratum; indeed, our entire consciousness refers back to it. Husserl writes: "Hence in this way *a human total consciousness is in a certain sense, by means of its hyletic substrate, bound to the Body [Leib]*."[53] The hyletic substrate is neither external nor internal effects on the body, nor is it tied to the representation of the body, but it is what makes any experience present and lived through.[54]

How does such embodied experience relate to the division between the lived and the objective body? According to Ricoeur, what Husserl in *Cartesian Meditations* calls my "sphere of ownness" makes my lived body the closest of all things, but it also represents my original otherness. Ricoeur detects the lived body as the otherness of passivity, or again, as *hyle*: "the flesh is the matter (hyle) in resonance with all that can be said to be hyle in every object perceived or apprehended. In short, it is the origin of all 'alteration of ownness.' "[55] From a related angle, Didier Franck argues that if the lived body is what is given in the sphere of ownness, it is challenging to see how it can achieve the status of an objective body, since the objective body must be mediated by the other's body. The problem is that if we start from the lived body in the sphere of ownness, we cannot apperceive the other as an alter ego, since the sphere of ownness is by definition restricted to my pure ownness. The otherness of the other must therefore be presupposed, Franck argues, which means that my sphere of ownness must be shot through with references to some otherness from the start.[56] The upshot of both Ricoeur's and Franck's perspectives is that for the lived body to become an objective body, there must be some form of original alterity inherent in the lived body.

CHAPTER 2

In the last chapter, I attempted to anchor the experience of flesh and blood in the lived body, and it seemed to convey some sense of inner alterity. According to such a perspective, Derrida seems to call for the right thing, namely a sense of the "objective" body "that is no longer essentially alien or external with regard to 'flesh' (*Leib*)—or rather that pertains or 'belongs' to it . . . but as something foreign."[57] The question I want to raise is whether *hyle* is what we need to consider in order to understand how flesh and blood can contain something "foreign" that still "belongs" to our lived experience. Ricoeur fruitfully asserts that the hyletic stratum of the lived body may serve as this foreignness belonging to the lived body. However, *hyle* seems to occupy a double position vis-à-vis the ego and the sphere of ownness. Typically, neither *morphe* nor *hyle* will be taken note of, since we are directed toward their correlate, the noema. In such cases, both seem to be integral parts of our experience in our sphere of ownness. However, Husserl can at times stress that *hyle* or sensual impressions are not always immanent to the sphere of ownness but can occur as foreign to it, in the sense that they stem from elsewhere and thus affect us as something foreign:

> The word "impression" is appropriate only to original sensations; the word expresses well what is "there" of itself, and indeed originally: namely, what is pregiven to the Ego, presenting itself to the Ego in the manner of something affecting it as foreign.[58]

As pre-given and foreign, impressions can be taken up and animated, but they also have the power to resist form. Arguably, this is what happens when our anticipations are disappointed and the noema "explodes" or is "crossed out."[59] Let's say I thought I saw a person, but as I draw nearer, it turns out to be a mannequin. In this case, *hyle* steps up as foreign to our intentions and with the power to cancel the intentional object. Moreover, it is interesting to note how *hyle* is given in these cases, namely *to* the ego. As Husserl excavates the deep layers of experience, the passivity to which our active comprehension corresponds begins to stand out. What is pregiven to us is not simply raw material that fulfills our empty intentions, but rather something arriving as if from elsewhere, something that affects us as passively shaped.

Hyle is in this sense deeply intertwined with affectivity.[60] Before we turn our active attention toward something, our attention is already addressed, invited by some form of an affective allure that demands our response. Even at this passive level, something stands out, either by contrast, intensity, or some form of rupture.[61] Husserl seems, paradoxically, to treat *hyle* as both a real part of experience, since sensations and impressions are the source of our experience, and yet as foreign and non-ego—as the structural antipode to noema, which is not a real part of consciousness and yet never external to it. This is perhaps not paradoxical once we acknowledge that our own conscious life has sources outside its own achievements. As non-ego, *hyle* does not stem from ego's spontaneity, but is affecting us as impressions for which no further grounds can be given: "Primal sensibility, sensation, etc., *does not arise out of immanent grounds*, out of psychic tendencies; it is simply there, it emerges."[62] Where such insights are the ultimate source for Henry's phenomenology, they seem to be the limits of Husserl's phenomenology, for there is not much more to say than the fact that *hyle* is clearly there, affecting us as pre-given, yet resistant to further static inquiry.[63]

In his analysis of passive synthesis, Husserl notes that when hyletic sensations make up a homogeneous field, they call for no particular attention when they are taken up into the active formation. Yet, in cases where the field is not homogeneous, where some kind of heterogeneity interrupts its uniformity, the hyletic sensation stands out in the field and calls for attention. The affectivity of the sensation will demand attention and call on the active I to turn its intentional ray toward it.[64] The same holds for the body. When it functions normally, the body recedes into the background. In the case of pain, however, our attention is drawn toward the part of our body that hurts. The otherwise smoothly functioning lived body is suddenly ruptured, as the painful body stands out, but now as foreign to the intentional, lived body.

While the experience of pain puts us in touch with hyletic experience, it does not follow that such experiences are completely divorced from form. If form is what makes any experience meaningful, it would be strange to insist that my own pain has no sense at all, even if minimal. There are, after all, ways I can direct myself toward it and things to be said about it. Yet, the meaning is quite limited, words soon become insufficient, and the experience of pain retains a sense of foreignness and non-I. The point is that none of our meaning-giving activities seem to exhaust the experience of pain, or otherwise put, the hyletic experience is not taken up into form without remainder. I cannot even say that I initially direct myself toward the pain, since it is the hyletic givenness that takes the initiative in affecting me. The bestowing of sense can only work as a response to pain, a response that cannot fully appropriate the affective call. There remains something that is no doubt there, but which at the same time withdraws from *morphe*, as if both within and outside it. Unlike the sensations of the color of a ball, pain is always a bodily experience: it is located in the body and is felt as part of the body which I inescapably am. While this experience is lived in my body, it is not the intentional body that reaches out for pain, since pain contains something that resists full integration. It is pain's resistance and density, along with the intruding character of the foreign *hyle*, that awakens the presence of the body as flesh and blood. While pain's matter has the character of non-ego welling up from strata of the body beyond our intentional command, it still remains partly connected to the lived body. Levinas rightly says that what surfaces here is impressionality as "an 'other' penetrating the 'same.'"[65]

In instances of pain, or for that part, being ill or being completely exhausted, we experience how flesh and blood so to speak penetrate the lived body. In these cases, my body does show some kind of inner resistance; it is neither the transparent lived body, nor the objective body that I relate to as a noematic correlate. Both of these concepts lack the lived density and resistance of materiality stemming from hyletic sensation. This material density alludes to a dimension of the body which, on the one hand, relates to the lived body, insofar as it is doubtless lived through. On the other hand, it points beyond the lived body insofar as it possesses the density of materiality, and yet it is not an objective body viewed from a third-person perspective. It is both foreign and yet mine.[66] This elucidates the notion of flesh and blood as initially outlined in the previous chapter.

Theodor Adorno has discussed the limits of the unity of Aristotelian form and matter. He argues that it cannot be a complete unity, as *hyle* will always entail a reference to something beyond the form or, as Adorno prefers, something beyond the concept. Not only is matter nonconceptual, but there is also a resistance to form internal to matter. This resistance keeps the interval between form and matter open.[67] As the form has run its course, something still evades its grasp, and it is this "something" which Adorno calls the "addendum" (*das Hinzutretende*). In agreement with Adorno, I will say that Husserl's notion of the form without matter and matter without form hits the target, insofar as they entail the difference between matter and form; but it nevertheless fails, since it suggests that they make up a seamless unity. However, as I have pointed out, Husserl leaves the door open for a hyletics in its own terms, which suggests a relative autonomy of matter. Moreover, Adorno claims that this addendum can be experienced, if not appropriated conceptually. The addendum can be experienced in disappointments and failures where the addendum wrests free of the form. Yet it is physical pain that serves as Adorno's principal example. Against rational systems of morality, such as Kant's, one must always keep the experience open to what falls outside its form:

> I say to you that the true basis of morality is to be found in bodily feeling, in identification with unbearable pain . . . The metaphysical principle of the injunction that "Thou shall not inflict pain"—and this injunction is a metaphysical principle pointing beyond mere facticity— can find its justification only in the recourse to material reality, to corporeal, physical reality, and not to its opposite pole, the pure idea.[68]

The point I want to retain is that acute pain in itself puts one in touch with a material dimension that resists any complete assimilation to form. This is not an appeal to the real beyond the correlation between form and matter, in the way speculative realism proposes, since that neglects the manner in which the addendum disrupts the lived, intentional body and thus presupposes it. Nor can we assert that the production of meaning through power structures and discourses is all there is to the body and its matter, since that suppresses the non-intentional hyletic level and its agency. According to Adorno's negative dialectic, pain does not manifest pure matter as such, devoid of any form, for thus it would be absolutely private, unintelligible, and impossible to elevate into the realm of concepts and speech. Pain is an experience where a surplus of matter resists form as it shows up in the internal tension to form. This relatively open structure of *hyle* and *morphe* in the case of pain has thus supported the more general outlines in the previous chapter. The otherness or non-I of *hyle* is not something external, but designates the relative autonomy of the flesh and blood evading my intentional grasp, or better, on the fringes of my intentional grasp. As I identify my pain as a toothache, there is always more to the hyletic experience than such identification entails.

It is true that our relationship to our body is ambiguous, since the body appears irreducibly as both part of oneself and strangely foreign, both as a lived and a material body. "From the day of his birth on," Helmuth Plessner notes, "everyone has to come to terms with this double role." This double role is the frame within which our embodied lives unfold, to which Plessner adds: "The frame itself is never broken."[69] Is that true? It rather seems to me that the frame can be, if not entirely broken, at least fissured when pain, fatigue, and various illnesses confront our lived, intentional body with the body as flesh and blood. This does not negate the ambiguity of which Plessner speaks, but adds a more profound ambiguity beneath it, one that cannot be resolved neatly. Confronted with the affective call of *hyle*, the functional intentionality of the lived body cannot without remainder subsume the matter in its form. Something remains. A remainder, or addendum, persists. It signals flesh and blood as it penetrates the lived body but without becoming an objective body. As non-intentional, the hyletic bodily experience creates a gap between *hyle* and *morphe,* reminding us of the profound ambiguity inherent in being incarnate.

3

"I Cannot"—The Passivity of the Body

In my account of flesh and blood and how it can be phenomenologically elucidated by matter, I have repeatedly drawn on the example of pain. In this chapter I will not address pain in any detail—that must wait until chapter 5—but rather outline the broader region of bodily breakdowns where the normal, active body is brought to a halt. While some forms of illness and impairment involve pain, many do not. Instead of pain, I will in the present chapter focus on bodily breakdowns, where the "I can" transforms into "I cannot." The incapacities of the body I have in mind typically manifest differently from pain. Acute pain, I have claimed, puts us in touch with the body as intensely lived, and yet it also reveals the body's dense otherness as flesh and blood. In "I cannot," it is not so much the flesh and blood that appears, but a deep passivity that comes to the fore when the body is unable to act in its usual ways. The standing possibility of such breakdowns belongs to our vulnerable bodies, as it occurs in illness, injuries, and various dysfunctions. I suggested in the previous chapter that inner experiences of *hyle* stem from a passive level genetically prior to the intentionality of the ego. I will in this chapter investigate what the occasions of "I cannot" disclose about the passivity of our incarnation.

"I cannot" is logically dependent on "I can," and it is one of my aims to critically investigate how "I can" and "I cannot" relate in phenomenology. I will argue that much previous phenomenology has taken the "I can" for granted as the paradigmatic case for the analysis of human incarnation. In so doing, the "I cannot" only enters the analysis as a deviation from normality, and as such it has not been subjected to a study of its inherent meaning and structure to the same degree.

From "I Think" to "I Can"

The classical expression of the modern ego is Descartes's cogito. One of the obvious problems with Descartes's conception is that it is intellectually conceived, with no internal relation to the sensing and moving body. As Henry points out, even if Descartes does ponder the intimate connection with bodily movement, he fails to give any account of how that connection between the two opposing substances of *res cogitans* and *res extensa* is made. Movement for Descartes remains imprisoned in the thinking substance, and as such, it does not transgress the pure *idea* of movement toward real, bodily movement.[1] When the cogito recurs as a central topic of Kant, the "I think" is purged further of psychological and empirical traces and recast as a purely transcendental ego. "It must be possible for the 'I think' to accompany all my representations,"[2] is Kant's way of putting the fundamental critique of every empiricist or otherwise construed representationalism that does not trace the representations back to a transcendental ego: without the I, whatever appears comes to nothing. "I think" not only stresses the necessity of an ego to whom representations are given, but is simultaneously the principle that secures unity for the manifold of all representations. Despite his insight into the transcendental ego and the unity of experience, which became important to Husserl, Kant's account of the ego still appears static, intellectualized, and strangely discarnate.

Phenomenology, particularly Merleau-Ponty's phenomenology, strives to reintegrate the transcendental I into the body. Alluding to Kant, Merleau-Ponty states unequivocally: "Consciousness is in the first place not a matter of 'I think that' but of 'I can.'"[3] Moving away from intellectualism, this perspective starts from perception and movement as they work together in the embodied experience of the world. The complex ways and different strata of the experience that feeds into passive and active constitution still point back to a principle that secures their unity. This unity must belong to someone, that is, to an ego. One sometimes gets the impression that Husserl has prolonged the static model, a form of philosophy of consciousness where the intentionality aims at its objects. However, as many of his manuscripts make clear, both the body and bodily activity are important to him—and moreover, even a significant sense of the ego is identified with such activity. Since they are given different constitutive roles, Husserl can both speak of the pure transcendental ego, but also of the practical and functional ego. The functional ego is shorthanded as "I move," "I do," or more generally, "I can." "I can" suggests the powers or capabilities of an incarnated ego, and such an ego already suggests a transposition from Kant's intellectual ego to a practical and embodied ego that Merleau-Ponty later voices.

When we reach out to the life-world, we do so through sensations and movements. Yet it is not as if our various sensations and our feelings of movement (kinesthesis) run alongside each other. Rather, they make up a kinesthetic-sensual totality (synesthesis) that mutually inform each other so that when I move around an object, the movements will flawlessly correspond to my changing sensations of that same object. Insofar as "I can" makes up the center of practical life, it also constitutes the unity of embodied experience and movement. In one passage, Husserl gives the following description of how sensibility, kinesthesis, and the lived body are intertwined:

> Thus sensibility, the ego's active functioning of the living body or bodily organs, belongs in a fundamental, essential way to all experiences of bodies. It proceeds in consciousness not as a mere series of body-appearances, as if these in themselves, through themselves alone and in their coalescences, were appearances of bodies; rather, they are such in consciousness only in combination with the kinesthetically functioning living body, the ego functioning here in a peculiar sort of activity and habituality.[4]

In short, our functional I, with sensibility and kinesthesis, activity and habituality, is implied in every perception of things.

"The Ego has the 'faculty' (the 'I can') to freely move this Body—i.e., the organ in which it is articulated—and to perceive an external world by means of it."[5] "I can" is not just a pole, but a power that implies a system of potentialities that can be actualized by me. To actualize such potentialities is the outcome of my will, which takes all my capabilities under its sway. In the last resort, the various capabilities spring from the original, spontaneous capability (*Urvermögen*) of the ego:

> With regard to my own centralized Ego-acts, I have consciousness of the *I can*. They are indeed activities, and in their entire course we have precisely not a mere lapse of events but, instead, the course they take continuously proceeds out from the Ego as center, and as long as that is the case, there reigns the consciousness, "I do," "I act."[6]

Any conscious acts, therefore, refer back to the active ego of "I can," or better, continuously proceed from it.

When we ask how the lived body appears in accordance with the actualization of the "I can," the answer is that it tends not to appear. Rather, it disappears in favor of the perceptions and tasks that the I is involved with. Along with the body, the functional centrum of the I tends to fade into the background of our intentional focus.[7] This strange eclipse of fundamental constitutive layers is familiar to phenomenology, with Heidegger's analysis of the "ready-to-hand" as the most obvious example of how Dasein forgets itself as it "goes up" into its handling of tools. It is this pre-thematic absorption that makes the world familiar. Heidegger points out, however, that in this "familiarity Dasein can lose itself in what it encounters."[8] Similarly, Merleau-Ponty notes that although the body opens us to the world, it remains in the background, like the darkness that makes the screen light up in the cinema.[9] The preoccupation with the things of the world we usually entertain invites a forgetfulness of the bodily conditions upon which it depends. In turn, Merleau-Ponty argues that such forgetfulness paves the way for the objectification of our own body, as if it were a thing among other things.[10]

But if this is the case, one may wonder how phenomenology gets access to the "I can" in the first place, since it seems precisely not to be given in person, but already withdrawn from us. At least, an access seems to call for some kind of reduction or reflective turn, but such a turn must itself be motivated. This motivation seems rooted in the natural attitude by which we live in the world. But again, the smooth course of the embodied subject does not call for our attention, and even less for reflection. Perhaps it is rather when the body becomes the obstacle to our will that it first calls for attention and thus motivates a thematic reflection in the first place? Perhaps the breakdowns of the body's smooth functionality must serve as phenomenology's point of entrance even for the functional ego? As we will soon see, Husserl, Merleau-Ponty, and Heidegger do take abnormalities and breakdowns into account for reasons like these.

It is safe to say that the active, well-functioning body serves as the paradigm for most phenomenological accounts of the lived body. After all, this is how the body is given most of the time for most people; it is the underlying way we operate in the everyday.[11] However, I suspect that such a paradigm leads phenomenology to provide a somewhat one-sided account of that body. From the ability to sense and move, to the capabilities to perform complex actions, the body is often portrayed as active rather than receptive and passive. Due to the paradigmatic role that the active functional body tends to be granted, I will refer to this as an underlying philosophical activism. While the constitutive role of activity is undoubtedly crucial, there may be other aspects of our incarnate being that are eclipsed by the focus on "I can." Perhaps there are central dimensions of our incarnation that are overlooked, not because they do not appear, but because their appearance falls outside the established paradigm of activity. It is hardly news that humans are vulnerable to bodily breakdowns, incapabilities, and dysfunctions of various sorts—we can transition from "I can" to "I cannot" at any moment. What, then, does "I cannot" signify phenomenologically?

"I Cannot"

Philosophical activism can be traced in Heidegger's *Being and Time*, even if Heidegger significantly altered his views in his later period.[12] In that seminal book he analyzes the constitutive role of active engagement in opening the world. But he also stresses Dasein's activity in taking over its own possibilities, its resoluteness, which entails a transition from the inauthentic to the authentic mode of existence.[13] Still, one of the most fruitful aspects of Heidegger's analysis, as I see it, is the way he detects how breakdowns and disturbances have the function of disclosing phenomena from their often veiled and unthematic state. In *Being and Time*, Heidegger has surprisingly little to say about how this affects the perception of the body, even if his earlier and later publications and lectures indicate that the bodily dimensions are indeed implied in his analyses of Dasein's careful concerns.[14] Much later, Heidegger suggests how the body fits into our ordinary practical concerns, noting that when we engage with things, our bodies are away. And yet, this "being-away" is not exactly nothing, he points out, but the strange way in which the body withdraws.[15] This is also the case with the tools that we take for granted: they become transparent to us. However, when our tools appear unusable, whether they are lacking, occluding the operation, or breaking down, they call for attention. When our broken tools draw attention to themselves, their implications and tie-ups will also "light up."[16]

In other words, Heidegger finds in these breakdown situations a way to let the phenomenon come to the fore beyond its average concealment—precisely because it becomes obtrusive. This analysis seems to shed light on the body as well. Nonetheless, Heidegger will later state that however fruitful the analyses of the tools are, the lived body is not a tool: in contrast to tools, the body is mine in a sense that cannot be dispensed with.[17] Whatever modifications such a statement implies, Heidegger's detection of phenomenological breakdowns seems to apply to the body; indeed, it gives us the motivation for turning our thematic reflection toward it. The breakdowns are occasions where otherwise non-apparent dimensions of our incarnation become manifest. For the latter, Heidegger has unfortunately little to say.

I previously underlined Husserl's functional ego, "I can," but it might be worth considering other aspects before brushing him aside as a one-sided phenomenological activist. Husserl was after all the first among the phenomenologists to pay attention to "I cannot." Indeed, what makes the notion of "I cannot" promising is that it registers the failures and impediments of the functional ego. There are, Husserl initially points out, different grades of "I cannot." One can meet different degrees of external resistance that can be overcome with lesser or greater efforts. But there are also occasions when the resistance is insurmountable, such as when encountering things that are too heavy to lift or mountains too steep to climb. In both cases, the resistance opposes my will, but it is first with the insurmountable resistance that the will is originally elicited to me, precisely in its failure.[18] There is, moreover, a third case where the "I cannot" is not externally impeded but is blocked by the lived body itself. Husserl points out that there are different grades of inabilities between "I can" and "I cannot." One example is: I used to play the piano, but I have not practiced for a long time, and the piece is no longer playable by me. With some practice, however, I will recover my skills. But there are cases where I simply cannot do even habituated practices, such as when I am impaired or fall seriously ill. Husserl provides the following examples: "But if I have been laid up sick for a long while, then I have to learn how to walk again, though it comes back quickly. Nevertheless, I can also have a nervous disorder and lose the mastery of my limbs; 'I can't do it' [*Ich kann nicht*]."[19]

From these sets of examples, it is clear that Husserl wants to bring out the fact that disabilities come in grades: a disability can be a matter of special expertise that does not affect the functional "I can" in general, or it can be a passing illness where I soon regain my abilities, but it can also be a serious illness that deprives me of mastery over my limbs, temporarily or permanently. As for the first cases, Husserl pays no particular attention to how the impediments affect the body or the person in question, either because the inabilities are regional and peripheral or because the lived body will soon return to its normal functional order. The most interesting case is the severe "I cannot," one without any immediate prospects of recovery and which strikes at the heart of the functional ego. The central question for me is how the embodied ego can be phenomenologically accounted for when activity is deprived, when "I can" turns into "I cannot." Unfortunately, Husserl does not pursue the phenomenological analysis as one might expect. Faced with the loss of control of one's limbs, all Husserl has to say is: "In that respect I have become an other."[20] Certainly, the pure ego has not changed. It might mean that the normal activity of "I can" has changed because my normal range of acts is blocked. Then my relation to my body will change into something that is no longer mine, perhaps along the lines that Jan Patočka will have it: "A body that does not respond, which does not yield, which is not skillful, ceases to be my body in one sense and becomes an object for me."[21] Patocka seems to leave the subject intact, only adopting a new, objectified relation to the no longer functional body.

But there are other possible interpretations of Husserl's "I have become an other." He might mean that, insofar as the "I can" is no longer operative, the person changes from a functional I to a dysfunctional, passive I and thus falls outside the scope of Husserl's central notion of selfhood: the normal, functional ego at the center of all acts. I have become an other in the sense of no longer being fully myself. Husserl continues the quote above: "'I am normal as to the Bodily and practical'—that is, I have the ability, as a permanent normal substratum, to move my organs in a 'natural and free' way as perceptual organs and as practical organs of sensory life."[22] As far as the incarnated subject is concerned, Husserl's notion of bodily selfhood seems to be intimately tied to an activism which is fixed to the normality of "natural and free" abilities. It seems to me that such activism prevents Husserl from pursuing the "I cannot" further. He instead takes it as a dead end, a state of otherness, about which there is nothing more to say.

Merleau-Ponty explores various forms of abnormality and illness as well. For instance, he provides the famous analysis of phantom limbs. The question Merleau-Ponty pursues is how it can be that someone can still feel a limb when it is no longer there. There is, according to Merleau-Ponty, no satisfactory physiological or psychological explanation for it, yet there is a phenomenological one. The habitual body, structured by the body memory of past acquirements, continues to direct itself toward the world and its tasks, even if such directions no longer correspond to the actual body. The phantom limb depends on a kind of repression of the actual, impaired body and its actual situation. The habitual body has become fixed to a past state at the cost of the way the body and the world actually present themselves. For Merleau-Ponty, the upshot is not so much the account of the lacking limb as the way the analysis sheds light back on aspects of our body that normally are lost from sight. Under normal circumstances, we make the world ours, not by psychic or physiological means, but by our actual body acquiring habitualities that can be adjusted to differing situations.[23]

Another of Merleau-Ponty's cases is that of Schneider, who has suffered physical damage in the back of his head, with strange results for his being in the world. Schneider can perform simple operations and understand concrete messages, but he fails to see their wider implications. Merleau-Ponty believes that Schneider's movements have lost their inherent "motor intentionality" which makes them meaningful; he can only perceive them in a mechanical way. He has lost the organic way in which movements take on meaning as springing off from a background and constantly projecting themselves into new situations.[24] To Schneider, the world appears frozen and ready-made. The point Merleau-Ponty is making is that Schneider's privations shed light on the temporal, horizonal, and synesthetic role that motor intentionality normally has. For Schneider, the body is no longer an organ for "I can"; rather, he illustrates the philosophical position of the discarnate "I think," for which sensations and movements must be synthesized intellectually.[25]

While the case of Schneider is meant to highlight the normal functioning body, Merleau-Ponty warns against drawing a hasty conclusion from the abnormal to the normal, since the former makes up a world of its own. The insights we can gain from such cases are more indirect, through the way those who are impaired develop substitutes for lacking functions: "We must take substitutions as substitutions, as allusions to some fundamental function that they are striving to make good, and the direct image of which they fail to furnish."[26] In other words, substitutions point to what they lack, which is what Merleau-Ponty expects the normal body to possess.

Critical Perspectives

Phenomenologically, something first comes to light when the usual course breaks down, as Heidegger points out. Undoubtedly, both Husserl's and particularly Merleau-Ponty's accounts can be seen to employ this insight, since they treat breakdowns as occasions that shed light on aspects of our normal body that tend to become invisible to us. However, it is striking that according to their conception, the normal and able body serves both as the point of departure, from which "I cannot" deviates, and the point of arrival, since the detour through "I cannot" reflects back on the normal body. Because this strategy is operative in Husserl and Merleau-Ponty, they fail to draw attention to the phenomenology of the experience of illness itself, such as its altered experience of the body, its transformed abilities, and the role of passivity. In his analysis of the phenomenology of pain, Christian Grüny even speaks of the "extreme activism" in Merleau-Ponty's phenomenology. He argues that there is no autonomous weight given to illness or to being in pain. What Grüny more specifically misses is attention to materiality and passivity as part of the body in the way these manifest themselves in the experience of pain.[27] The underlying reason for such neglect, I suspect, is that Merleau-Ponty and Husserl grant the "I can" a privileged, constitutive role, and according to this role, "I cannot" will only play the role of a deviation from and contrast to the normal. "I cannot" only confirms "I can." An illustrative example is Husserl's discussion of the changes that occur when a hand is burnt. The thing touched will occur differently, but the central point for Husserl is not the new tactile sensations, but the way he regards them as a deviation from sensations of a normal, non-injured hand. His principal claim is that: "this modified givenness refers back to the normal."[28]

There is within phenomenology a widespread tendency to regard various bodily limitations, illnesses, and breakdowns in this way. Shaun Gallagher and Dan Zahavi, for example, follow up this line of thought, writing that "core features of subjectivity can be sharply illuminated through a study of their pathological distortions. Pathological cases can function heuristically to make manifest what is normally simply taken for granted."[29] I am not contesting that this strategy has proved to be fruitful; I only want to point out that it does not capture the full story and that something tends to get lost. Gallagher and Zahavi's interest is not invested in the meaning and phenomenology of pathologies themselves, but as means to explicate normality in more accurate ways. However, it seems to me that there is room within phenomenology to explore, as it were, the opposite path, taking the broken body not as pointing beyond itself, to normality, but as manifesting its own modes of givenness.

A first step towards this is to address the relationship between the abnormal and the normal. Richard Schusterman argues that something is misleading with the distinction itself in the way it is employed in *Phenomenology of Perception*: "This simple polarity [between normal and abnormal] obscures the fact that most of us so-called normal, fully functional people suffer from various incapacities and malfunctions that are mild in nature but that still impair performance."[30] The perspective Schusterman suggests does not start from the abnormal to reflect back on the normal. It reverses the perspective so that the normal is already taken to integrate the abnormal, thereby undermining the strict polarity between them. In a more radical manner, Joel Michael Reynolds regards such a distinction to be upheld by what he terms "enablism." To Reynolds, it is not a matter of deconstructing the distinction between normality and abnormality, but disclosing the normative powers that are invested in it. To regard the disabled body in terms of lack and privation mirrors the ideal functioning body as "the normate."[31] From Socrates onward, Reynolds claims that the metaphysics of presence has produced oppositions that still guide our view of the body: "it presumes a binary between perfect and defective, between what things really are and what they should be and what they really are not and shouldn't be."[32] In sum, the normal body is simply better than the non-normate body.

Some of phenomenology's presuppositions are targeted by this critical perspective. One should observe, however, that the phenomenological use of normality is a flexible one. In Husserl's case, the abnormal tends to moderate or change our notion of normality, making it wide enough to integrate what otherwise shows up as abnormal.[33] Merleau-Ponty also has more to say about the constitutive role of the abnormal as it encounters us in ill people and children. In a series of broadcasted lectures, he questioned the priority of the normal, well-functioning adult when we try to understand children and the sick. The investigation of children and sick persons has tended to be posed from the perspective of a healthy, adult person, Merleau-Ponty claims, and this is precisely the reason why no progress has been made in understanding their lives and the world they occupy.[34] Their world might not be coherent—but does anyone live in a completely coherent world? Should we not question the conceptions of adulthood and health? Merleau-Ponty writes: "It follows that the 'normal' person must remain open to these abnormalities of which he is never entirely exempt himself; he must take the trouble to understand them. . . . These leave his knowledge of the natural world riddled with gaps, which is how poetry creeps in."[35] Such an outlook makes the distinction between normality and abnormality more complex because there is no absolute line dividing them, with the gain of opening richer perspectives on both sides. This makes phenomenology less vulnerable to Schusterman's and Reynold's critique, but apart from some general traits, it still does not provide a phenomenological analysis of the "I cannot."

If the upshot of the phenomenology of the body is that the body is not something we have, but something we are, in other words, if we take the incarnated subject for granted, then any changes that affect the body will have to affect the sense of subjectivity. This seems to be implied when Husserl says that in severe illness, I have become another. While Husserl and Merleau-Ponty do not explore the phenomenological meaning of such an altered subjectivity, and while, as I have suggested, their over-arching interest in the functionality of the capable subject leads them away from such explorations, there are noteworthy exceptions in the phenomenological tradition, particularly in approaches to the philosophy of health.

S. Kay Toombs has written extensively about the lived body from her perspective of having multiple sclerosis and on illness more generally. She emphasizes that a threat to one's body is at the same time a threat to one's very self.[36] The most pressing and fundamental changes are those that affect one's ability to engage in the world, that is, the manifold ways in which one handles and perceives the world. When some of my limbs or sensory organs are impaired, the body intentionality that made the bodily activities taken for granted, is now frustrated. Toombs underlines that the automaticity on which one relied has now been broken, and one's surroundings demand a new measure of effort in order to move and act. But this also changes our perception of the situation—even one's home can change from an inviting field to a challenge. The tools that could be relied upon are not only things "in order to," but are as much obstacles to the free employment of my embodied self. "Thus, the sphere of bodily action and practical possibility becomes circumscribed. The 'I can' is rendered circumspect. The character of lived spatiality and lived temporality changes in significant ways."[37] Spatiality changes. Steps are no longer utilizable to get me upstairs but present themselves as barriers. Temporality changes, too. The future is not an open horizon of my projects, but might be severely curtailed.[38] Indeed, the body tends to present itself as out of control, even as alien, not complying with the ego. While Toombs provides a valuable descriptive account of the phenomenology of "I cannot," the question of what becomes of the capable subject is not really answered. Does that subject change to another, become narrowed, or is it perhaps granted new access to itself as embodied?

For an incarnated subject, where the body is who I am, "I cannot" must lead to change. But in what way is the conception of the self changed? Heidegger is relevant here. As mentioned earlier, he emphasizes Dasein's activity and potentiality. His equivalent to "I can" is Dasein's Being-able-to-be (*Seinkönnen*). Being-able-to-be belongs to Dasein as one of its existential structures (*Existenziale*). In this way, Heidegger makes Dasein's Being inextricably related to its active abilities. These abilities come to the fore not only as acts but also in our ability to understand, since we always understand in light of a future goal that we actively pursue. We are indeed thrown into the world—the sheer facticity of our existence—but we have a horizon of future possibilities that opens up projects based on our abilities.[39] The active Being-able-to-be thus is forward-looking in the sense that it points to who we can potentially become, which in turn reflects back on who we presently are and already have become. However, according to Dasein's inclination to fall away from itself, its fallenness, the range of these possibilities and the way they are intertwined with who we are, tend to be covered up. But in anxiety, the call of the conscience, and most clearly, in our confrontation with our mortality, the possibilities are reopened, and Dasein's innermost Being-able-to is uncovered as a possibility for authentic existence.[40] When confronted with the impossibility entailed in death and finitude, the possibilities of Dasein are not closed, but rather empowered: "In anxiety, Dasein finds itself *faced* with the nothingness of the potentiality-of-being [*Seinkönnen*] of the being thus determined, and thus discloses the most extreme possibility."[41]

Regarding Heidegger's emphasis on potentialities and abilities for the self-understanding of Dasein, Havi Carel poses a timely question:

"But what about the other part of life, the one in which we become gradually *un*able to do things, unable to be? . . . Does Heidegger's definition exclude this important aspect of life, that of decline, inability, failure to be?"[42] Despite the clear activist tendency in Heidegger that she addresses, Carel does not wish to dismiss Heidegger, but instead aims to complement his thinking with what remains unexplored in his account. On the one hand, she proposes a broadened understanding of "being able to" to include decline, inabilities, and failures within it. In doing so, Carel shifts the focus away from Heidegger's more heroic overtaking of abilities and towards the transformation of one's horizons by adapting to the limitations and possibilities of the actual body. More importantly, she claims that we need to recognize that an "inability to be" is also a way of being. "Acknowledging an inability and learning to see it as part of life's terrain are important lessons that illness can teach at any age. This knowledge enables the ill person to embrace the unable self as part and parcel of human existence."[43]

No doubt, both Toombs and Carel reveal dimensions that are hardly captured by Husserl, Merleau-Ponty, and Heidegger, even though they all focus on cases of breakdowns, impossibilities, or "I cannot." What Carel suggests is not so much that illness makes us other, as if excluded from the normal ego, but that illness brings "important lessons" about the human condition. But what exactly does this lesson tell us about the human condition? One lesson is that inabilities can always lead us to adapt to new abilities so that our conditions are transformed. This is important and often stressed. However, I want to suggest that the lesson about our condition can go even deeper, concerning a passivity beneath both "I can" and "I cannot."

Paul on Weakness

While there has been growing philosophical attention paid to Saint Paul, he is seldom taken as helpful when it comes to his understanding of the body, particularly because his notion of the body or flesh (*sarx*) is often associated with desires and sin (e.g., Romans 8:2–9). Yet Paul operates with a far richer concept of the body, spreading out in different directions; it figures as the bearer of the self, as the whole human person, and as a metaphor for the congregation. It can be argued that the body makes up a nodal point from which all the major topics of Paul's anthropology can be oriented: law and desire, members and unity, sin and redemption, sin and holiness, mortality and immortality.[44] Moreover, I will argue that Paul's letters lend themselves to a phenomenological reading that corresponds neatly to the topic under discussion, such as the capable, active, and strong body versus the incapable, passive, and weak body.[45]

In the Second Letter to the Corinthians, Paul's authority seems to be challenged by someone in Corinth who boasts of some form of spiritual superiority and strength. At first, it appears as if Paul is engaging in a battle of spiritual superiority. He claims that he has had ecstatic visions, which only a few in the Hebrew Bible have been granted. As he recounts it, he was

> caught up to the third heaven—whether in the body or out of the body I do not know; God knows. And I know that such a person—whether in the body or out of the body I do not know; God knows—was caught up into Paradise and heard things that are not to be told, that no mortal is permitted to repeat." (2 Cor. 12:2–4)

It soon turns out, however, that Paul's aim is not to hammer home his spiritual superiority. Even if such boasting would make Paul the equal, if not the superior of his opponent, the point is that, as a criterion of apostleship, the boasting of visions misses the mark. He brings it forth only to undermine it. It turns out that the emphasis is not put on the ascension to the third heaven, but on the descent from it. Indeed, to prevent the ascension from making his ego inflated, Paul is violently brought down to earth. "Therefore, to keep me from being too elated, a thorn was given to me in the flesh, a messenger of Satan to torment me, to keep me from being too elated" (2 Cor. 12:7). It is as if the thorn pricks the inflated self, like a puffed-up balloon, and returns him, deflated, firmly into his own body.[46]

The thorn in the flesh is one of the famous tropes in Paul's epistles, and much ink has been spilled on pinning down what exactly the thorn refers to. From the early church onwards, there have been different theories put forward, such as some form of physical illness—epilepsy, eye problems, stammering, or malaria—to some sort of spiritual trial, or even persecution during his missionary work.[47] The exact reference is not decisive here; it is enough to assume that Paul refers to some form of bodily suffering that has violently interrupted his activity and strength (Gal. 4:13; 1 Cor. 2:3). It is for this reason that his repeated appeal to weakness now takes on a very specific carnal meaning, as if his very incarnation is laid bare through the thorn's aversive presence. The thorn has nailed the flesh to the self without changing the self to another, but by putting it firmly back into the body. The fact that it hurts makes Paul impotent and incapable; it overthrows the sway of the "I can," and puts Paul in the position of "I cannot."

I pointed out earlier that Heidegger takes various breakdowns to disclose otherwise hidden dimensions of phenomena, and that the analysis of being-toward-death follows the same structure. In Paul, the thorn occasions a similar breakdown of his normal functional body and thereby discloses experiences of his incarnation that were previously concealed. Nevertheless, Paul's breakdown does not lead his attention back to the normal body of "I can," as Husserl and Merleau-Ponty tend to take it, and it certainly does not empower capabilities and possibilities, as in Heidegger's interpretation of death. Rather, for Paul, the thorn becomes a privileged occasion for understanding the meaning of weakness and passivity. Even as they arrive uninvited, weakness and suffering become, for Paul, ways to identify himself with the crucified and risen one, which implies a reevaluation of weakness and power.

The power Paul speaks of does not mean lifting his suffering. "Three times I appealed to the Lord about this, that it would leave me," Paul reports, "but he said to me, 'My grace is sufficient for you, for power is made perfect in weakness'" (2 Cor. 12:8–9). The power here is obviously not the reversal of bodily weakness, as the thorn does not leave him. God's reply: "my grace is sufficient for you" is a tough message in this context. But still, the final time Paul appeals to boasting, it is neither of human strength nor of his own weakness, but of a power at another level, one coming towards him, as a gift received from a source outside himself. Since it does not stem from himself, this power can only be received passively. It is when the normal powers and capabilities no longer appear as the source from which he lives, that is, precisely when the usual capabilities are blocked, that Paul is made attentive to a power of life that he can but passively receive. Hence, the thorn in his flesh discloses a new asymmetry of weakness and power that motivates Paul's inverted boasting—not of himself, but of what he receives. "So, I will boast all the more gladly of my weaknesses, so that the power of Christ may dwell in me" (2 Cor. 12:9).

Apart from Paul's religious conviction and conception, what, if anything, can this power phenomenologically denote? It cannot be investigated with the means of the usual understanding of the lived body, since that body is essentially body-intentionality that correlates with the world. But for Paul, the power does not show up in our engagement with the world, quite the contrary. Nor does it stem from the hidden powers of the body itself, since it precisely arrives in the "I cannot," that is, when the body is deprived of powers. It is not even a supernatural power that works miracles, since it does not heal the brokenness of Paul's biological condition. The power that is made perfect in weakness means that the power first reveals itself as power when human passivity is laid bare.

Paul poses a double challenge to philosophy. On the one hand, he suggests that our embodiment is not to be sought along the line of philosophical activism, but in passivity and receptivity; on the other hand, he suggests that the power of life both enables any ability and yet is disclosed in moments of inabilities. I want to argue that these challenges are taken up and replied to in the phenomenology of Henry.

Henry and Passivity

While he does not address bodily breakdowns as such, Henry sheds considerable light on the body in its passivity that Paul invokes. Henry agrees with Husserl and Merleau-Ponty that the transition from "I think" to "I can" is paramount for phenomenology, both in the sense of putting the transcendental ego into the body, and in the sense of assigning the powers of human activity their constitutive role.[48] In an early study, Henry offers an account of the moving and sensing body by way of a phenomenological reading of Maine de Biran's philosophy. Henry notes that our first and most original reality is not of the intentional correlate or the world, but the original reality of the flesh's innermost powers of sensation and movement, in short, the original "I can." In line with the analyses of Husserl and Merleau-Ponty, the unifying principle is indeed the practical or functional I. For Husserl and Merleau-Ponty, "I can" unfolds in the world, but Henry strictly treats it as an a priori power that belongs to the immanent flesh. This power is, more specifically, identified as what Maine de Biran calls feelings of effort, an effort that must be given prior to space and things, that is, independent of intentionality.

The ego does not bring movements about through the instrument of our body, nor do we need reflection in order to uncover our movements. Original efforts of movement, Henry claims, are non-reflectively given with subjectivity itself; they are transparently given in immanent experience, not just as any feeling but as an original pathos welling up from life itself.[49] It is in this feeling of effort that the ego both reveals itself to itself and also discovers the most basic sense of reality. The original reality shows up in the feeling of resistance that confronts our fleshly efforts. Clearly, this reality is not the outcome of any perceptual synthesis or representation, nor even of motor intentionality.[50] Following Maine de Biran again, Henry sees reality originally as the "resisting continuum" that makes up the transcendental terminus of immanent efforts.[51]

Thus, Henry will not give up the importance of "I can," and up to a certain point, he will not object to what he calls Maine de Biran's "activist philosophy."[52] But only up to a certain point. I have previously pointed out the weight Henry gives to impressions as self-revelations, which are like Husserl's *hyle* insofar as they are an immanent part of the experience, but they are unlike Husserl's *hyle* insofar as Henry's impressions are not non-I that arrives from beyond the active ego. For this reason, Henry's impressions do not restrict the unfolding of "I can." Rather, impressions together with affectivity are never foreign, but are internal parts of the flesh bestowed with powers and freedom, revealed to itself by itself. If this is so, it seems unlikely that Henry provides the phenomenological resources for articulating the human fractured state that I have called "I cannot."

Even in his otherwise sympathetic reading of Maine de Biran, Henry finds that Maine de Biran lacks any positive account of passivity and has little to offer when it comes to affective life.[53] For Henry, the problem is that Maine de Biran's philosophy remains within the confines of the Kantian heterology between the active ego and passive impressions. This heterology can to some extent be softened, Henry admits, by a better understanding of passive synthesis, as Husserl has provided, and by leading it back to a common root of habituality in which activity and passivity interact. But Henry does not think this is sufficient. There must be an even more profound passivity, beyond the analyses of sensation, living experience, or the will; there must be an "original ontological passivity" that pertains to life itself.[54] Lacking such a theory of passivity, Maine de Biran is confronted with an absurdity inscribed in his philosophical activism, with relevance for the shortcomings of Husserl and Merleau-Ponty, as well. Their common activism comes with a price:

> If subjectivity is actually present only when it decides to act according to a specific motor intentionality, then each time such an intentionality becomes blurred or is interrupted, this same subjectivity must also cease to be the very real experience which is but one with our very existence, actually it must cease to be the experience of any existence, it is no longer anything more than nothingness.[55]

The embarrassment of philosophical activism confronted with interruptions of its intentional achievements, or more generally "I cannot," comes from the fact that it has no conception of the non-active ego and thus

"I CANNOT"—THE PASSIVITY OF THE BODY

no way of integrating it. As if the alternative to activity is nothingness. Perhaps this is the reason why Husserl, faced with "I cannot," loses all of the ego's identity and concludes: "I have become an other."[56] And yet, as Henry points out, Maine de Biran is certainly on to something when he, in some late letters, welcomes a dimension of the passivity of grace. It is precisely in this direction that Paul's thoughts lead and which comes fully into focus in Henry's later accounts of the flesh.

Despite the fact that Henry insists on the flesh as self-revealing immanence internally tied to "I can," this flesh is nonetheless the site of radical passivity. This is the paradox at the heart of his contribution: the more self-affection and auto-revelation are closed into immanence, the more Henry emphasizes the depth of flesh's passivity. Even if flesh is always given to itself by itself, revealing itself in its affectivity and its powers, it nonetheless is indebted to Life that generates it. This life is not an anonymous, general power of nature or a cosmic will. Life is irreducibly mine, signifying how I am incarnated, the form of my ipseity. Still, it is paramount that life is not of my own making. Thus, from within the very mineness of flesh, my auto-impressions and auto-affections are always stamped by Henry's sense of radical passivity:

> The life that arrives by itself in experiencing itself in its flesh is precisely not what brings about this arrival. If it streams through us . . . independently of our power and will, then it is indeed a question of this life, which precedes us at the very heart of our being, and which is not solely our own—because always and already, before a single moment allowed us to turn toward it to welcome or reject it, or say yes or no to it, life is in us and we are in it, in the radical passivity that strikes the impression, but our entire life as well.[57]

The life of the flesh does not emerge from anything beyond itself, from a cause or a creation ex nihilo, but from a passively received power, as Paul would agree. It is from the hither side of immanence that we are generated in the constant arrival of life, independently of all our efforts.[58] Henry's rendering of life as generated has a Johannian twist to it, but it is also derived from Paul. The weakness and powerlessness that the thorn in the flesh leaves Paul in reveal to him a power of life that arrives in him. Henry cites Paul as summing up the generosity of life: "What do you have that you did not receive? And if you received it, why do you boast as though you did not?" (1 Cor. 4:7).[59]

While the occasion for Paul is some form of "I cannot," I said that Henry emphasizes "I can." Yet, it would be more precise to say that Henry claims that both inabilities and abilities are stamped by a radical passiv-

CHAPTER 3

ity. In fact, "I can" invites two perspectives. On the one hand, it appears as an absolute power, enabling movements, sensation, and indeed any free undertaking that is within my compass. On the other hand, those very powers refer to a "before," a coming of life into flesh, and they are made particularly manifest when my own powers fail: "*Every power collides in itself with that about which and against which it can do nothing, with an absolute non-power.*"[60] The radical passivity in question concerns a lack of sufficient self-grounding, an inability to bring itself into existence, which means that while the self and its powers appear autonomous, they do ultimately depend on the arrival of life. Life can only be received passively regardless of my abilities or inabilities. At the bottom of any activity on our part lies another power: "Every power bears the stigmata of a radical powerlessness."[61]

The stigma of powerlessness inscribed in the "I can" echoes Paul's stigma, the thorn in the flesh. Henry's account of the ultra-transcendental notion of life, as I take it, is a phenomenological explication of Paul's grace and power: life arrives in me and becomes the essential part of me, remains unaltered by mundane strength or weakness, and yet makes all of my abilities possible in the first place. While Henry believes that powerlessness and passivity are inscribed in all of our powers, Paul seems to regard the suffering, breakdown, or "I cannot" to be a privileged occasion for the radical passivity to surface. Not only is Paul's thorn an intrusive experience that turns him toward his bodily constitution and finitude, but more than that, it entails a kind of radical reduction to the strata of powerlessness and weakness. Paul's metaphor of the clay jar brings this point home: "But we have this treasure in clay jars, so that it may be made clear that this extraordinary power belongs to God and does not come from us" (2 Cor. 4:7). The metaphor of the clay jar is meant to suggest a certain hollowness that makes it possible to receive and contain the treasure in the first place. While "I can" no doubt plays a vital role in our lives, it would, according to the metaphor, be an illusion to believe that it can fill the hollowness. Rather, the hollowness designates the receiving subjectivity. The fragility of the clay jar parallels the way Paul in other places boasts of his weakness; it is not that the weakness has a value in itself, any more than the fragile jar does, except for the treasures stored therein. Hollowness and weakness are a privileged human condition insofar as they make the reception of power possible. Unlike strength, hollowness and weakness produce no illusion of where the treasure comes from: it stems not from me but is granted to me from elsewhere. This view does not exclude activity and achievements, but it entails that any such activity is enabled by powers received according to what Henry calls our radical passivity.

Flesh as Withdrawal from the World

Returning to the critique of Husserl's and Merleau-Ponty's activism, I earlier conceded that it needed some qualification, since they do pay attention to various forms of disability and illness. Nevertheless, they fail to take the manifestation of the dysfunctional body as having a phenomenological meaning in its own right, that is, in what Henry calls its radical passivity. However, Henry's valuable contribution also has problems of its own. I have already suggested some problematic aspects of Henry's notion of the flesh, which seems strangely purified from any materiality. To Henry, there are two fundamental modes in which the body appears: as visible in the world and as invisible according to the immanence of life. The constitutive functions move, according to Henry, only in one direction. In an almost idealist fashion, Henry argues that only from the self-revealing immanence can a transcendence be cast outside.[62] The world is placed in front of intentionality, as a visible unreality, or more accurately, "a pure imaginary dimension."[63] While I agree that "I cannot" returns us to the passivity of the flesh, it seems strange to leave out the world and the worldly body. The typical way in which "I cannot" shows up is precisely tied to worldly situations, where I fail to cope with my tasks or am overpowered by the resistance of things. Or take the visceral body, where my legs cannot move, my arm is broken, or an internal organ fails—for Henry, these are only worldly matters, inessential to the flesh. They still need to be revealed, that is, given to the self-affecting flesh, Henry argues. If I have a fever, I can feel my pulsating flesh affecting itself. But is this pure auto-affection? Is there not also a feeling of hetero-affection at work here? In lying stretched out in my bed with fever, I feel an impenetrable heaviness and density to my body too, a sense of what I have called flesh and blood. If this is so, it seems to me that the auto-affection is less pure than Henry will have it, since we are being affected by the otherness of the body. I will leave such inner tensions of the body for now and return to this in chapter 5.

How can Henry neglect the lived and objective body along with the world it is entangled with? Is it something about the way in which such a body is given that invites the neglect? Perhaps it is, due to a form of forgetfulness. At one juncture, Henry points out how strange it is that we often come to forget the very conditions that make life possible, particularly when we are free of obstacles. He notes: "Health is forgetful, as forgetful as life."[64] Our healthy, well-functioning body tends to forget itself, but illness, one must assume, deprives us of such happy forgetfulness. Inspired by Heidegger's analyses, Leder has spelled out a similar transition with precision: "Insofar as the body tends to disappear when functioning unproblematically, it often seizes our attention most strongly at times of dysfunction; we then experience the body as the very *absence* of a desired or ordinary state, and as a force that stands opposed to the self."[65] The reason why the body becomes absent is due to its intentional or ecstatic nature: it recedes in order to let something other appear. In its normal functioning, the body has a tendency toward self-concealment, receding into the background of our thematic awareness.[66] When the smooth functioning of the body breaks down, this tendency is reversed: the background now becomes the figure, and the absent body becomes present. "In disease, one is actively *dis-abled*. Abilities that were previously in one's command and rightfully belong to the habitual body have now been lost. This could be termed the phenomenon of 'I can no longer.'"[67]

Such occurrences of dysfunction of the body are precisely those occasions in which one is thrown back on one's body. The decisive question I keep coming back to is what is revealed therein. Leder's analysis does not shed further light on this. Arguably, in typical experiences of "I cannot," something like Henry's radical reduction is taking place: one is turned away from the world and back into the fundamental experience of being alive despite one's nonfunctional body. However, unlike Henry's reduction, I hold that the reduction is initiated from a lived body that is intertwined with the world. This is not only a decentering of the initiative of the reduction, but it alters what Henry takes to be our primary mode of the body. The immanent flesh is not the beginning or the foundation from which we project a world in front of us; it rather marks the *withdrawal* from the primary state in which the body is already installed in the world. "I cannot" is not the lighting up of immanence as the body's original site, but signifies a retreat from the world in which we live, thereby making a particular dimension of our body, our flesh, become salient. It is this intimacy with the world that changes in "I cannot," now occurring as overpowering resistance or something beyond reach for the broken body. Only in the passivity of our life which then comes to the fore can we speak of something like the flesh. While discovered in withdrawing from the world, its significance is no less decisive, for as this chapter has argued, it marks the decisive passivity of our body of which the active body is forgetful.

I will therefore contend that there are not two unbridgeable ways of bodily appearance—the visibility of the worldly body and the invisibility of flesh—but rather different levels of the same body that appear from the perspective of "I can" and "I cannot." Jean-Louis Chrétien is right when he notes that we do not start in a state of auto-affection from which we never reach out to the world: "Each and every sensation starts by consenting to the world, and from this ground only can it ever return back to itself."[68] But if we start from worldly engagements, how do we return to ourselves? One way, Chrétien suggests, is in illness: "Illness is the paradigm of auto-affection."[69] While Chrétien alludes to Henry, he thinks the role Henry ascribes to the auto-affective flesh is displaced: it is not the ultimate source, but a derived mode from our original consent to the world. To me, this approach rightly aligns "I can" and "I cannot," world and interiority, the lived body and the flesh. The way my movements, sensations, intentionalities, and projects mold the world has a constitutive privileged role. In a different sense, however, undergoing "I cannot" is phenomenologically privileged, not in opening our world but in disclosing dimensions of our incarnate being that are otherwise covered up. Put differently: the active, lived body installs us in the world at the same time as it makes us forgetful of our flesh; our inabilities withdraw us from engagement with the world at the same time as they disclose the flesh. To make full sense of the notion of incarnation, I hold, we must include the functional, lived body, but also take into account the passivity that silently makes any activity possible.

Although the received life is always there, at the root of our capabilities and powers, our activities tend to cover over the fact of our passivity, as if we tend "to forget the most original gift of life."[70] But left to itself, to the "I cannot," the radical passivity of which Henry speaks has its proper occasion to appear as the received power of life: "power is made perfect in weakness" (2 Cor. 2:9). Henry concludes his *Incarnation* with the following statement: "The more each of our sufferings happens in us in a way that is pure, simple, stripped of everything, and reduced to itself and its phenomenological body of flesh, the more strongly the unlimited power that gives it to itself is felt in us."[71]

4

Touch and Skin

Having shown how analyses of the structure of the "I cannot" reveal the passivity of the body, I now want to elaborate on another dimension that bears directly on our incarnation, namely touch and its medium, the skin. For all their associations with surface, touch and skin are by no means superficial matters to a phenomenology of incarnation. Aristotle, at the inception of the metaphysical tradition, in fact grants a privileged status to touch, pointing out that all the other senses imply touch, whereas the sensation of touch can be present without the others.[1] Historically, Aristotle's insight was soon overturned by the metaphysical tradition, where vision replaced touch as the paradigmatic sensation. This replacement is probably due to the way vision fits into the ideal of detached knowledge, since it is able to discriminate and identify objects at a distance.[2] Arguably, such a privilege granted to vision in turn paved the way for the discarnate view of subjectivity.[3] With Husserl and the ensuing phenomenological tradition, touch returned to philosophical attention—paradoxically, perhaps, because one of phenomenology's key notions, intentionality, seems to be modeled on the visual ray. Such a return was by no means completely unprepared by undercurrents of philosophical and religious traditions. It is perhaps no surprise that religious traditions have preserved the centrality of touch given the role it plays, particularly in the Gospels.

Since touch cannot take place at a distance from our own body, it works as a corrective to any form of discarnation. In touching, the subject is there, bodily present to itself and simultaneously to the tangible world. But such presence also makes the body exposed and vulnerable to pain. I will take this double structure, at once referring back to the embodied subject and to the world, as my guiding thread as I work through the relation between touch, pain, and the skin.

Touch and Incarnation

Husserl sketches out analyses of touch in several places, but his most penetrating and influential treatment is found in *Ideas II*. In investigating our basic sensibility, independently of the intentional form, Husserl lays out the distinctions and overlaps between vision, hearing, and touching. Among the different senses, Husserl follows Aristotle in giving priority to touch. Why? The primacy of touch cannot be deduced from its role in knowledge, where vision, Husserl admits, seems to play a more principal role; its primacy rather stems from the role touch has in the constitution of our bodily self-awareness. Husserl notes that if we abstract the hand's tactile sensation, the hand becomes a mere physical thing among others. However, if we include tactile sensation, we do not simply make a richer and more adequate account of our body, but we allow for a complete change in its status: "*it becomes Body [Leib], it senses.*"[4] Husserl's point is that touch belongs to our lived body in a special way. Husserl even claims that it is only thanks to tactility that we have a lived body at all: "The Body as such can be constituted originarily only in tactuality."[5] Touch constitutes the lived body because it implies the immediate presence of the body—there is no mediation, analogical apprehension, or distance between the touching body and what is touched. Touch entails an embodied subjectivity because no one can touch through a distant medium, but only with the body that is inalienably mine. Even though the object one touches is exterior to oneself, one is simultaneously made aware of oneself touching.

In a much-quoted passage, Husserl gives the following example:

> My hand is lying on the table. I experience the table as something solid, cold, and smooth. Moving my hand over the table, I get an experience of it and its thingly qualities. At the same time, I can at any moment pay attention to my hand and find on it touch sensations, sensations of smoothness and coldness, etc.[6]

What Husserl illustrates with this example is how the touch of the hand can be attended according to two directions: I can feel the object's qualities, such as a smooth and cold table, but I can additionally feel the smoothness and coldness as given in my hand. Touch has this remarkable character of double sensation, as Husserl dubs it, as at once reaching toward the world and reflecting back on the body. Due to these two directions, Husserl distinguishes between two meanings of sensation. He reserves the term *Empfindung* for those sensations that adhere to objective qualities, while coining a neologism, *Empfindnisse*, for those sensations—or "sensings" as it is rendered—that occur on the sensory organ.[7] Yet, these are not two classes of sensations that exist separately—in which case it would not be a double sensation—rather, they are distinguished by different directions of our attention belonging to one concrete experience of touching.

The reason why tactility is bound up with bodily self-awareness

CHAPTER 4

relies on one of its essential traits: touch will always appear as localized in my lived body. I do not only feel the smoothness and coldness of the table, but I feel smoothness and coldness at a particular place, in this case, in the palm of my hand. "All the [tactile] sensations thus produced have their localization, i.e., they are distinguished by their place on the appearing Corporeality, and they belong phenomenally to it."[8] Since these sensations are not yet intentional and as such do not belong to intentional perceptions of things, the localization is not a coordinate in objective space. Of course, I can point to a spot on my objective body in space, say a splinter pricking my left hand, but my only confirmation of this being the right spot is that it overlaps with a localization already given. Such an objective localization presupposes a pre-objective localization that is immediately felt in the lived body.[9] Any reference to localizations on the objective body must await a higher order of the constitutive process.

To understand why touch has this central role, Husserl provides a comparison with other senses. He makes it clear that touch, vision, and hearing do not display the same phenomenological structure. For all its importance, vision lacks the features essential to touch, namely its double sensation and localization. Husserl says this about vision:

> An eye does not appear to one's own vision, and it is not the case that the colors which would appear visually on the eye as localized sensations (and indeed visually localized corresponding to the various parts of its visual appearance) would be the same as those attributed to the object in the apprehension of the seen external thing and Objectified in it as features. And similarly, we do not have a kind of extended occularity such that, by moving, one eye could rub past the other and produce the phenomenon of double sensation.[10]

In this passage, Husserl points out at least two things. First, vision does not have the kind of localization in the organ the way tactile sensing has. He distinguishes between the color that falls on the eyeballs and the color we see on the external thing, as the latter is not a sensation but the result of a constitutive process where the sensational qualities reappear as ascribed to the thing. In contrast, touching has a double structure inscribed in the very sensation where the same sensations refer to both the touching and the touched. Secondly, vision lacks double sensation, not only because our eyes do not "rub past" one another, as hands can, but also because such a rubbing would no longer be a matter of seeing at all, but of touching. We simply do not see our seeing, not even when we see our own eyes in the mirror. In the mirror, we only see the objectified organs, not the seeing itself. Thus, touching essentially relates to our own body in another manner: "What I call the seen Body is not something seeing which is seen, the way my Body as touched Body is something touching which is touched."[11] What appears to sight is only the external body, which is categorically distinct from touching one's own lived body with its sensing surface. The same structures found in vision, Husserl adds, can be transferred to hearing, since the sound is not localized in the ear, and to be sure, you cannot hear yourself hearing. The lack of immediate localization on the body, along with the lack of self-reference of double sensation in vision and hearing, undergirds touch's priority with regard to the constitution of my incarnation. Put negatively: "*A subject whose only sense was the sense of vision could not at all have an appearing Body.*"[12]

Touch and Pain

One often thinks of roughness, hardness, smoothness, warmth, and coldness when one thinks of touch. What about pain? Once taken note of, it is striking that Husserl repeatedly makes pain an example of tactile sensations. For instance, he notes the implications of tactile sensations if one is pricked by a splinter or cuts one's own finger; in both cases, the tactile pain sensation immediately changes the apperception of our physical body into a lived body.[13] "Obviously," Husserl notes, "the Body is also to be seen just like any other thing, but it becomes a *Body* only by incorporating tactile sensations, pain sensation, etc." According to another similar formulation, Husserl enumerates sensations of touch, "for example, warmth, coldness, pain, etc."[14] One looks in vain for any extended treatment of pain as tactile sensation; pain simply figures among Husserl's examples. It is nevertheless clear that Husserl thinks that there is an internal connection here, or more precisely, that pain belongs to a group of tactile sensations. Among the few who have given some attention to pain and touch, Augustin Serrano de Haro points out that pain belongs to the hyletic layer and comes with localization. He argues that pain "is particularly linked with tactual sensibility, which is spatialized from within."[15] This same point is confirmed by Saulius Geniusas, who says that because "pain is an *Empfindnis*, it belongs to the group of those tactual sensations through which the lived-body is constituted."[16]

I suggested earlier that pain plays a unique constitutive role in our incarnation, one that even goes beyond what is usually implied in the lived body and awakens our sense of flesh and blood. For this to hold true, pain must significantly differ from other tactile sensations, perhaps due to its aversive quality that breaks into our flow of occupations and demands our full attention. While such characteristics distinguish pain, it may still belong to the wider group of tactile sensations, not as a typical example but as tending toward one pole of the spectrum of tactile sensations. As Husserl contends, a defining feature of tactility is the immediate and reflective manner in which it makes us aware of our incarnation, and that is even more pronounced in pain. Moreover, tactility and pain both appear as localized. Indeed, pain never manifests itself except as—more or less distinctly—localized.

This pre-objective localization is given without any distance, immediately and inextricably alongside my body, but it becomes particularly salient in pain. Pain's aversiveness causes us to try to distance ourselves from it, but to no avail. Husserl's remark here takes on gravity: "In popular terms, everything in the whole world can escape from me, except for my own Body."[17] The body in pain is exactly what I want to run away from, and yet I am bound to it. To suffer pain consists precisely of the inability to escape it. Inescapably, I am my body, I am incarnated. For Husserl, the hyletic sensations that are immediately given to me in pain are part of my body and my consciousness: "*a human being's total consciousness is in a certain sense, by means of its hyletic substrate, bound to the Body.*"[18]

Sartre does not regard pain as a localized, embodied experience, as his analysis of having pain in the eyes while reading illustrates. Having established his fundamental division between being-for-itself (of consciousness) and being-in-itself (of what is not consciousness), pain must belong to the former. Sartre argues that pain does not originally manifest itself as a sensation in my body as it is lived through, but is indicated by the objects in the world in which I am bodily engaged. Sartre observes that we can be so absorbed in reading that we even ignore the pain. I can, however, stop my reading and reflect on my pain and thus posit it as an intentional object, but in that case, the pain is no longer lived through but turned into an object of reflective thought. In the latter case, the pain becomes something different, a psychological object or a state that Sartre more broadly calls illness.[19] However, in the case where the pain is lived through, pain is simply implied in consciousness as I am reading. Because consciousness is always consciousness of the world, the non-intentional pain can only participate in consciousness if it "slips" into intentional acts and becomes part of the appearance of the world to which the intentional acts are directed. As Sartre puts it, "we apprehend [pain] only through the world. For example, it is given in the way in which the book appears as 'having to be read in a hurried, jerky rhythm.'"[20] It is as if the pain is neither here nor there, but fades into the background that colors the reading itself.

According to Sartre, pain only appears as localized as we break away from the reading and objectify it. Otherwise, it is only indicated by the world. But is this how pain typically arrives? It is certainly not how Husserl has it; he regards localization as essential to the primordial way we live pain. Merleau-Ponty also emphasizes the localization of pain. When a nail pierces my foot, Merleau-Ponty asserts, pain does not appear to me as an effect of a cause, and certainly not as part of my walking: "I mean that the pain is localized . . . 'the pain comes from my foot,' or again 'my foot has pain.'"[21] Following such accounts, pain cannot primarily be given as a background that informs the objects we deal with. There are instances that fit Sartre's description, but they are not instances of pain, at least not acute pain, but perhaps irritation or dull aching. Once pain becomes intense, it does not manifest itself in one's reading, but precisely in one's eyes. For now, it seems appropriate to say that pain primarily occurs in the body, and only in specific circumstances is it indicated by objects we engage with.

I have addressed the location of pain, but does pain share the other characteristics of tactile sensation, namely double sensation? In Sartre's case, double sensation is impossible, as pain is either being-for-itself or being-in-itself—that is, either part of the lived experience or an object of reflection, but not both simultaneously. However, when cutting one's finger with a knife, one seems to sense both the lived experience and the external object at once. For do we not both feel the sharp edge of the knife and the growing pain in our finger? So it may appear in mild pain. However, once the knife cuts deeply, the situation changes significantly; the intensity of the pain now demands all our attention, focusing on the cut itself rather than the knife. Elaine Scarry has emphatically claimed that such pain is unique in the sense that it totally blocks out the intentional object and solely becomes a "state without an intentional object."[22] In the case of such intense pain, there is, no doubt, a localized pain in the body being hurt, but this pain lacks the double sensation that is characteristic of touch.

Where does this leave us regarding double sensation and pain? There seem to be cases where it applies and where it does not. If it remains valid to consider pain as a special tactile sensation, the picture has undoubtedly become more complex. This complexity might well be due to the different ways in which pain is given. I think one needs to consider how the givenness of pain varies with its intensity, because the intensity of pain is not simply a quantitative matter, but in fact modifies its qualitative appearance. This point can be clarified by inspecting the different phenomenological appearances of irritation, moderate, and acute pain. First, in Sartre's case of the pain in the eye, it bypasses the tactile sensation and slips into worldly engagement. This, I believe, holds only for the mildest forms of pain—better understood as irritations as opposed to suffering—where the attention to the localization is so light that the intentional pole of our engagement will still be at the fore of our attention.[23] In the second case, when the intensity rises to a moderate level, for example when I am suddenly pricked by a splinter, my awareness is turned around. I am made aware of the splinter that painfully touches me at a certain localization in my lived body. In this case, the double sensation becomes manifest, such as in Husserl's example where the slightly burnt hand refers us to the hot oven.[24] Thirdly, in the case where the pain gets severe, where the edge of the knife not only touches me, but cuts deep into my flesh and blood, Scarry is right in holding that the awareness of the knife drops out, and I am only left with the pure sensation of pain localized in my hand.[25]

In the latter case, where the pain is given in its most pure state, it seems difficult to speak of a double sensation at all. As the last chapter argued, any breaking down of the body, for instance in pain, reverses the dominance of the active engagement and throws us back on ourselves. Pain gives itself, comes over us, and we undergo it passively. Intense pain seems to tip the balance completely over to the passive reception, where all intentional references at some point vanish, and we are filled with only the affectivity of pain. It is as if the world of engagements is annihilated, as all our attention is reinvested in the hyletic givenness of pain as such. This consideration does not mean that pain is not related to touch. I will uphold that pain remains a special form of tactile sensation, but it obviously has its own unique essential traits that vary according to the intensity and various quality that comes with it. There is, as I have argued in chapter 2, a sense of something non-I and foreign in the painful exposure to one's own body. Such inner tension between foreign *hyle* and one's own body is essential to the phenomenality of pain, as I will purport to show in the next chapter, but the tension can also shed light on double sensation at another level, not between one's lived body and an exterior tactile quality this time, but as oneself being simultaneously touched and touching.

Touch and Otherness

Touch makes contact, it makes present. When touching oneself, one seems to fulfill the dream of a metaphysics of presence, as absolute proximity here and now, without distance. Husserl's much-commented upon example of the right hand touching the left reads as follows:

> Touching my left hand, I have touch appearances, that is to say, I do not just sense, but I perceive and have appearances of a soft, smooth hand, with such a form. The indicational sensations of movement and the representational sensation of touch, which are Objectified as features of the thing, "left hand," belong in fact to my right hand. But when I touch the left hand I also find in it, too, series of touch-sensations, which are "*localized*" in it, though these are not constitutive of properties (such as roughness or smoothness of the hand, of this physical thing).[26]

Without going into exegetical issues or the rich reception history of this passage, let me simply note that Husserl believes this touching of one's own hands both illustrates double sensation and marks out a defining structure of the lived body that we are, as at once a subject and an object of touch.[27] But is such touching pure self-affection, or does it imply something else, something foreign? And what about my incarnation, the body that unites the two hands—is it really a closed circuit the way the self-touching seems to presuppose?

In one of his last working notes, Merleau-Ponty writes: "To touch is to touch oneself,"[28] and thus he apparently confirms Husserl's analysis of touch and the incarnate subject. Nonetheless, already in his rendering of Husserl's example in *Phenomenology of Perception*, his emphasis is different from Husserl's. As Merleau-Ponty concurs that the double touch manifests the lived body as different from any other objects, the main lesson from the example of the touching hands is for him the impossibility of full coincidence or unification of the two hands: "We have just seen that the two hands are never simultaneously in the relationship of touched and touching each other."[29] Husserl already distinguishes between the ways the left hand appears to the right hand and vice versa, using the distinction between representational sensation and merely localized sensation. Although this implies the presence of both the objective and the lived body, Husserl does not elaborate on its phenomenological implications. For Merleau-Ponty, the active touching hand and the passively touched hand can change roles, but touch cannot be lived in the same way at the same time. Even though the touching of the two hands can be reversed, they will never render the body fully transparent to itself. Merleau-Ponty does not suggest that there is any ontological cleavage between the two hands of the same body; rather, their difference illuminates a certain ambiguity inherent to our body. On a more general level, this indicates that the lived body is not transparent to itself, and the world it casts out will remain only partially given. The point of ambiguity and reversibility of the two hands is later inscribed in the ontology of the flesh,

CHAPTER 4

but the point remains that the immediate coincidence of touching and touched is always eclipsed.[30]

In *Cartesian Meditations,* Husserl introduces "the sphere of ownness," but to what degree and in what sense does our body belong there? To analyze that sphere, Husserl conducts what he alternately calls an "abstractive epoché" or "primordial reduction," which puts in brackets everything foreign to the ego. Every intentional achievement that stems from others will be put in brackets, such as our cultural world, the natural sciences, and indeed, objectivity as such. We are finally left with what is purely my own as absolutely non-alien and familiar.[31] According to Husserl, my lived body will remain within the sphere of ownness. The body is my own as far as it is the only animate organism that falls under my sway and expresses my "I can." As expected, the central example of my immediate presence to myself is also mentioned: within my sphere of ownness, I can experience me touching one hand by the other.[32] No reference to non-I is presupposed here, no distance, difference, or alterity, only my own sphere filled with myself—or so it seems. The picture becomes more complex if we hark back to the account of the two hands in *Ideas II,* where Husserl points out the congruence of lived and objective body in the touching hands. However, in *Cartesian Meditations,* the objective body is bracketed in the primordial reduction toward the sphere of ownness. Husserl can still claim that I feel my two hands touch, but this time without any implication of the objective body. This must be so because the access to the objective body is mediated by the other, and more broadly, by intersubjectivity—which the primordial reduction has precisely left out. However, the question is whether it is possible to reduce such a sphere of ownness, with my lived body at its center, to a pure state of mine-ness, purged of otherness.

Merleau-Ponty's emphasis on the ambiguity of the body should already cast some doubt on the purity of such ownness, but Didier Franck has explored this doubt further. Drawing on Husserl's own resources, Franck emphasizes the necessity of accepting some form of alterity to be an integral part of the sphere of ownness from the very outset. For, as Franck puts it, "there is not a single concept employed to describe the sphere of ownness which does not already refer to the other."[33] However, if there is an implied alterity within the sphere of ownness, this seems to undermine Husserl's aim of establishing a pure sphere of the ego in the first place. Franck develops his argument in various directions throughout *Flesh and Body,* always moving toward the same conclusion. If the other is by definition other than me insofar as the other exists and yet must be constituted by me, then the other must already be presupposed in my innermost sphere of ownness. Similarly, if the distinction between the lived and objective body is to remain a distinction within the unity of the body, intersubjectivity must be presupposed from the start, since no objectification of the body is possible without it. Moreover, if I imagine the other's position in space "over there" from my sphere of ownness, the intersubjective is already presumed. And finally, if the sphere of ownness must be given as temporal, the otherness of retention of the past is already assumed as the prerequisite of the present. Hence, contrary to what Husserl holds, Franck concludes that "flesh [lived body] as original ownness is originally not mine and originates from what is not my own."[34]

What about touch? To repeat, touch seems to be the most promising candidate for pure auto-affection, completely locked into the circuit of my sphere of ownness, where my lived body is affecting myself. It is by such auto-affection that I am constituted as embodied. However, in making contact, the lived body is pushed to its outer borders, its sensible skin, and toward something transcending it. According to Franck's overall argument, the self-touching is not paradigmatic for touch, it is rather a derived mode of touching the other. According to Franck, to touch is to be at the border, already turned to the outside, where my lived body encounters the other. If this is true, Franck argues, the other cannot be added to my lived bodily sphere closed in itself. Instead, the other enables my sphere of ownness: "The first non-me is the other me, and, from the other me, the flesh is the first given."[35]

This notion of alterity within the same naturally appeals to Derrida, who posits that for me to experience the other, the other must be presupposed as part of me. Derrida elaborates on the implications of this view for the two touching hands, predictably denying the possibility of achieving absolute presence, auto-affection, or immediacy through self-touching. Derrida's argument stems from Husserl's phenomenology of the alter ego and expands on Husserl's notion of analogical appresentation, which is often rejected since it appears to derive the alter ego from the ego. However, Derrida interprets it differently. Analogical appresentation of the other is decisively not an appropriation of the other, he argues, but the best way to preserve the otherness of the other. As the other is given analogically to me, I am debarred from claiming direct access. Derrida takes a step beyond Husserl, claiming that we need to apply analogical appresentation not only to others but also to ourselves. Thus, in touching oneself, there is a difference operative between touching and touched which makes touch possible. We should, Derrida holds, start to "extend rather than reduce the field of appresentation and to recognize its irreducible gap even in the said touching-touched of my 'own proper' hand, my own body proper as a human ego, and so forth. And this would strictly be neither Husserlian or Merleau-Pontyian."[36] In contrast to Husserl and Merleau-Ponty, Derrida holds that my self-touching is given to me not in intuitive fulfillment, but indirectly, since the gap between the hands is never overcome.

To better understand the gap between the hands, Derrida refers to Husserl's conviction that touch is given as localized in the lived body, a localization essentially differentiated from extension in objective space. Yet, according to the structure of double sensation, there is at the same time a touching of an object, that is, the other hand that is given in objective space. Apparently, Derrida argues, touch collapses spatial distance, but in fact, for contact to be made, it must presuppose an interface between two different "spaces," namely the objective and the bodily localization.[37] In the act of touching, this interface is the surface of the body, or more precisely, the skin. The skin is at once the outer limit of the lived body and the borders of the objective body. Thus, according to Derrida, there remains an interval between my lived body touching and the objective body touched that cannot be filled. Without such an interval, there would not be a double touch and hence no touching at all. This lack of complete presence and immediacy holds regardless of whether the object is a thing, an other, or my own hand.

There are obviously crossing paths in Derrida's and Franck's rendering of Husserl's phenomenology. Both strive to challenge the conception of the ownness of the body purely conceived by detecting alterity and difference at the heart of it. Neither Derrida nor Franck believe that alterity is overcome by the primordial reduction, since alterity is inevitably implied in the sphere of ownness. As for touch, they hold that alterity or difference is part of what makes up its condition of possibility. The alterity of the human other, between the two hands, between inflections of space and time, or between past and present, all work in a similar way to burst Husserl's pure sphere of ownness open from the inside.

What to my mind remains problematic in Franck's and especially Derrida's account, is how the alterity loses its phenomenological concretion and becomes a formal and generalized emblem comprising many things, such as difference, heterogeneity, alterity, or spacing, which again can be applied to temporality, spatiality, the human other, intersubjectivity, or two hands touching.[38] While Derrida is especially concerned with irreducible differences, one might question whether he underestimates the distinctions between those differences. In any case, this abstract and formal detection of alterity contrasts with how Husserl elaborates on the essential traits belonging to various regions of our experience. Conversely, one could argue that even if a kind of difference exists in touch, touch would not occur if the touching and touched were not present to each other in the first place. Although differences cannot be denied and absolute immediacy cannot be maintained, the lesson, as I understand it, is not that we must draw the analysis in a new direction. It should be possible to acknowledge the difference, separation, and otherness inherent in touch without forgetting that the phenomenal weight lies elsewhere, namely on presence in contact, however impure. For the phenomenon of touch gives itself in a manner that tends to let the presence appear while the differences and alterities recede into the background. This is not to deny forms of separation, but to assign them to their appropriate phenomenological mode of (dis)appearance. Moreover, it may seem too obvious to mention, but it is tempting to remind Franck and Derrida that, yes, it takes two to touch—hence difference and alterity—but touch is the event where the two meet.

The same holds for the sphere of ownness. My lived body is irreducibly mine because it is given to me differently than any other body, even though my lived body includes traces of alterity and difference. This proves important for the analysis of pain. There is no need for the subject to initiate a primordial reduction to prepare the analysis of pain at will. Irritation and moderate pain do not necessarily throw us back on ourselves, but show up as moods or slightly disturbed practices in the world. Yet in severe pain, there is something like a spontaneous primordial reduction taking place, initiated by the affective appeal of pain itself. In this case, we could say that the irruption of pain puts the world in *epoché* and leads us back into our sphere of ownness. The experience of the sphere of ownness is inalienably and even inescapably my own. Yet, we must address alterity, not in a generalized sense, but as it manifests in pain itself. Being in pain, the sphere is invaded by a concrete, non-egological phenomenon. In pain, there is something foreign there that already occupies my territory, namely the aversive, non-welcome appearance of a *hyle* that resists complete subjection to *morphe*. In this sense, it is still a form of touch or self-touch. If we should speak of alterity in being touched by pain, it is neither a question of the other, due to spacing, nor of non-coincidence, but an encounter with the strange denseness of the material dimension of my own flesh and blood, as if both mine and yet foreign.

The Double Character of the Skin

As touch exhibits a double structure, at once in touch with the outside and reflecting back on itself, it does so by its surface—the human skin. The skin opens the body and the world to one another, enabled by the line it draws between them.[39] At the core of the phenomenology of the skin lies a certain ambiguity, which follows the double logic of the limit: it simultaneously encloses us within ourselves and opens us to the world, delineating our outer borders and facilitating our encounters, protecting us and exposing us.[40] The ambiguity is perhaps unsurprising given touch's double sensation, since the skin is the very organ of touch.

Jean-Louis Chrétien, in his analysis, agrees with the tradition from Aristotle to Husserl that touch is the primary sense. For Chrétien, this primacy is not due to the central role touch plays in the constitution of our embodied self-awareness, but because it entangles us with the world.[41] Nevertheless, he does not deny the skin's ambiguity. The skin is both exposing us to the adventures of the world, and protecting us from its dangers. The skin is protecting us in the sense of offering a retreat behind. But the skin preserves the interiority to the same degree that it opens us to the exteriority. Such ambiguity follows from the skin as a limit and a line that divides. Yet, this line of the skin is not for the most part manifest to the lived body because touch itself tends to veil it. Chrétien writes:

> The experience of touch seems to be an experience of contact, in which our skin and our flesh apply themselves to the surface of things, abolishing distance and interval. The flesh is supposed to form a continuum with things by touching them. Yet as Aristotle shows, the interval is never abolished, only forgotten.[42]

This insistence on skin as distance and interval sounds similar to Derrida's analysis. Nevertheless, Chrétien decidedly does not aim at deconstructing the closures of phenomenological theories or bringing out their dreams of pure presence; rather, he attempts to provide a renewed phenomenology of touch. For Chrétien, it is not the clandestine movements of metaphysics of presence that lead us astray, but the skin that enables the phenomenon of touch that withdraws in the touch's own manifestation.[43] Aristotle claims that air and water do not give themselves as objects, but as the media through which objects appear, and the same holds for the skin. The skin becomes the untouchable medium, the membrane through which contact is made, precisely because in touching, the skin withdraws from our awareness. Nevertheless, the skin unites by separating. In this sense, Chrétien will hold that touch is not exhausted phenomenologically by its proximity pure and simple, for there is a certain distance that comes with the medium of the skin.[44]

As the analyses of the skin are related to touch, Chrétien goes on to note how the Husserlian analysis of touch emphasizes its self-referential dimension, which explains its unique role in constituting the body as mine. In contrast, Chrétien proposes that the primary direction of touch should be reversed. He is not denying that in the case of my right hand touching the left, the touching does reflect back to me, but both Husserl and Merleau-Ponty seem to take the self-touching as the paradigmatic case of touch in general—which is exactly what Chrétien contests. Instead, Chrétien suggests that we must seek the paradigm elsewhere, namely in touching external things. In this perspective, the self-touch must be seen as a derived and special case. He holds that touch is primarily transitive, not reflexive; in touch, we reach out for the otherness of things, or better, we respond to them. According to Chrétien, this is true of all sensations in general: "Each and every sensation starts by consenting to the world, and from this ground only can it ever return back to itself."[45] Touch does eventually refer back to the subject, but it does so via the world because touch can only receive itself as a response, through the detour of otherness. What, then, about the indisputable instances when we feel ourselves, listen to ourselves, or touch ourselves? These instances are indeed possible and do happen, but, according to Chrétien, they refer to abnormal situations, such as illness. In normal circumstances, I feel the heat of the surroundings, not my own body. Only in abnormal cases, such as fever, do I feel my own heat. The paradigmatic cases are not auto-affective, but abnormal cases are, such as fever or nausea.[46] The same holds for the hetero- and auto-affection of touch.

Not surprisingly, Henry's account of touch and the skin moves in the opposite direction from Chrétien's. For Henry, touch is fundamentally about self-revelation rather than the transitive meaning of touching worldly things. Since an objective body does not feel touch and the organic body does not feel its own feeling, the proper sense of touch can only unfold where affections affect itself without distance, surface, or otherness, that is, in the flesh. Henry will therefore hold the opposite position of Chrétien: self-affection is primary, and the transitivity of touch is a derived mode of it.[47] But what does Henry's approach tell us about the phenomenology of the skin? Since there are two fundamental modes of givenness—one visible and one invisible—Henry can account for the doubleness that pertains to the skin. As belonging to the visible, the skin can be seen and touched like any other surface in the world. As belonging to the flesh, the skin registers resistance to movement and touch from within.

Henry seems to allow for a more mutual relation inscribed in the skin than Chrétien. For as he writes: "We call this frontier between the invisible universe of our flesh (to which our own thingly body belongs) and this same body perceived from the outside, our skin—this visible and invisible line on which our kinesthetic sensations and those that come from our senses are built up."[48] Many of Henry's phenomenological concerns are interlaced with the skin: the flesh and the thingly body, the visible region of the world and the invisible dimension of our immanence. As a consequence, the skin itself must be understood as an ambiguous line given both as visible to the world and as the invisible frontier of our interior powers. Despite the observance of both the visible and invisible aspects of the skin, Henry's account does not maintain any symmetry between the two dimensions. Since the objective body can only be felt by an organic or lived body, and the organic body, in turn, must be referred back to the flesh that senses itself sensing, the analysis of the skin first finds its transcendental foundation in the latter. Henry therefore primarily invests interest in the skin as the limit of the invisible flesh.

Both Chrétien and Henry speak of the ambiguity of the skin: Henry emphasizes the skin as the limit of the flesh, while Chrétien gives priority to the way it exposes us to the world. The problem with Henry's account is that it forecloses any distance or difference that makes us touch something other than ourselves, which Derrida has rightly pointed out. The issue with Chrétien's account is that he fails to recognize that abnormal and non-paradigmatic cases, such as illness, can be revelatory and thus disclose the passivity at the root of all activity. For Chrétien, as for philosophical activism in general, such cases are considered nothing more than deviations from the normal, paradigmatic case. As a way out of this deadlock, it seems to me that it is worthwhile to recall Husserl's double sensation, which suggests a fine balance of the double character of the skin. As the skin exposes me to the world, it does not have to await the detour via the thing in order to return to itself, as Chrétien argues. Nor does it solely refer us to the invisible flesh that senses resistance to its powers while remaining ignorant of its worldly correlates. According to Husserl's example, as my hand slides over the table, the skin opens me at once to the table and the tactile sensation in my hand, both to the world and to my lived body simultaneously.[49] In this sense, the metaphor of the membrane is pertinent. As a membrane, the skin draws a limit and yet lets the diffusion go both ways, inwards and outwards. This does not contradict the point made by Derrida and Chrétien, namely that contact implies separation or difference, for the skin disallows for a fused unity: it draws a line. The skin is neither a wall nor an unbridgeable gap, but rather the condition that makes the presence of contact possible in the first place.

The skin implies further ambiguities. As Chrétien notes, the more refined the sense of touch is, the more alert to dangers it becomes. However, having delicate skin also implies increased vulnerability. Chrétien explains: "Yet for touch to be more discriminating, greater exposure is required. The being who best guards against peril must be the one who is most vividly exposed to it."[50] Chrétien draws this lesson from Aristotle, who observed that in comparison to other species, the human body is the softest and is wrapped in the most vulnerable skin. The skin and its tactility make us open to and also unprotected from the presence of the outside. Whereas all the other senses can be closed—I can plug my ears or shut my eyes—the naked skin cannot withdraw from its exposure to the world.[51] With regard to the affective tonality, this means that the skin opens us to the enjoyment of touch as well as to pain and suffering. According to Aristotle, pleasure and pain, along with joy and suffering, inevitably follow from our having tactile skin.[52] It exposes us to both the best and the worst of our incarnate experiences.

In order to delve deeper into the enjoyment and suffering associated with the skin, Levinas's analyses prove valuable. Levinas is well aware of how the skin makes joy as well as suffering possible. In *Totality and Infinity*, Levinas does not restrict his notion of sensibility to the sensations of touch or vision, but more broadly takes sensibility to denote our fundamental belongingness to our environment. Still, such belongingness has clear relevance for the phenomenology of the skin. Unlike Sartre and Merleau-Ponty, Levinas refuses to make sensation merely an integral part of intentional perception, and instead insists on its phenomenality and significance on its own terms.[53] He claims that sensation is not intentional, and therefore unfolds prior to any objectification. For this reason, he argues that vision should not serve as the paradigmatic model for sensibility. Vision has held a prevalent role in the history of philosophy due to the way it opens the horizon and fixes salient objects in front of our gaze. From the priority of vision, touch is consequently subjected to a role of grasping the objects that vision already has picked out.[54] In Levinas's own analysis, by contrast, the tactility of the skin is representative of sensation's role in the enjoyment of our environment. Unlike knowledge, enjoyment does not know of any distance: "The world that I constitute nourishes me and bathes me. It is element and 'medium.'"[55] To bathe in the elements, to become part of and belong to the world, centers on the sensibility of the skin, for it is through the skin that such belongingness is given as enjoyment.

Levinas observes that the skin is imbued with affectivity. The caress evokes an erotic sense of enjoyment, but now in interpersonal relations that he calls "the feminine"—a notion that does not necessarily suggest gender but rather a particular mode of givenness.[56] There is a crucial distinction between enjoyment and caress, for while enjoyment is tied to interiority, prior to any separation, caress presupposes the separation that arises with the other. While enjoyment denotes a pre-ethical immersion in the sensible elements, the caress knows of no such immersion, according to Levinas. The caress does not establish pure contact through

CHAPTER 4

the skin and does not attain immediate unity with the other. Even when caressing the other's naked skin, it still preserves the other's alterity. The exposure in the caress enables both mutuality and division, as the contact is made possible by the skin's ambiguous line. According to Levinas, this line suggests both the nudity of the other's skin and the mystery of the other, who is never appropriated but withdraws from the caress into the future.[57] In *Otherwise Than Being*, Levinas writes: "The caress is the not coinciding proper to contact, a denuding never naked enough. The tenderness of the skin is the very gap between approach and approached, a disparity, a non-intentionality, a non-teleology."[58] Clearly, for Levinas, the skin entails separation, but a separation that makes possible the non-intentional relations to the feminine, more intimate than the ethical relation to the face.

Caress and enjoyment make up one side of the affective ambiguity of the skin; the other side consists of vulnerability and pain. As Chrétien noted, the skin's delicate surface is not a solid shield against danger; it can easily be injured or violated at the hands of others. Whereas sensibility in *Totality and Infinity* is deployed in terms of enjoyment, *Otherwise Than Being* adds another dimension: because sensibility conveys vulnerability, Levinas considers sensibility in terms of both enjoyment and suffering.[59] Vulnerability can therefore be made manifest in pain:

> It is the living human corporeality, as a possibility of pain, a sensibility which of itself is the susceptibility of being hurt, a self uncovered, exposed and suffering in its skin. In its skin it is stuck in its skin, not having its skin to itself, a vulnerability.[60]

In this dense passage, Levinas explicitly links the skin to the possibility of pain. Being incarnated in our skin means that we are constantly exposed to exteriority. We are, however, not only exposed to the exteriority, for the same skin also makes us stuck within it. While we do not feel imprisoned in our skin during ordinary engagement with the world, the infliction of pain turns the skin into our imprisonment because it awakens the urge to escape our painful body. What makes pain into suffering, Levinas repeatedly insists, is the frustration of this urge: it is impossible to escape our embodied condition, and we remain trapped within our skin.[61]

Starting from the polarity of Chrétien's and Henry's account of the skin in order to hold on to a middle path that preserves the irreducible ambiguity of the skin, this reading of Levinas has added a further dimension to its ambiguity: pleasure and pain, as well as enjoyment and suffering, must all be seen as tied up with the ambiguity of the skin. Pleasure primarily concerns the interiority of the subject on the hither side of the skin, for even as enjoyment reaches out into its environment, it always leads back to the ego. Pain follows the opposite trajectory, starting from some form of externality that thrusts itself into the vulnerable skin and leaves us caged. In the following chapter, I will return to a more detailed analysis of pain, but the crucial point for now is simply to emphasize how the ambiguity of the skin both opens and restricts, exposes and protects, and is accompanied by both pleasure and pain.

Divine Touch

One important aspect of what Heidegger calls onto-theology is the metaphysical influence on the Western conceptions of God. It is therefore only to be expected that those conceptions have been shaped by the primacy of vision. Luce Irigaray argues that this privileging of vision functions as some form of repression of the tangible. Such repression makes us forget our fundamental belongingness to the flesh, which is foreshadowed in the prenatal relation of mother and infant. This repression can, Irigaray argues, already be traced back to the biblical story of the Fall, where touching the untouchable fruit leads to the exile from the carnal happiness of the Garden of Eden. This story suggests that while touching is our primary opening to the world, there has come to pass some form of constriction of its primacy, replacing it with vision. This replacement, in turn, "opens up the question of 'God,'" she claims, "but in a certain forgetfulness of the primary maternal-feminine. Which entails the fact that God is always entrusted to the look and never sufficiently imagined as tactile bliss. Who imagines the beyond as an infinitely blissful touching? Being touched by God, for example."[62]

While I concede that there is more than a grain of truth in Irigaray's account, it seems a little too hasty. One reason is that the Old Testament God primarily speaks and thus announces himself to hearing rather than vision; another is that Christian currents—not least mystics—do indeed speak of divine touch. In keeping with the latter, Chrétien holds that the relation between touch and God is essential. His lengthy analysis of human touch is intended to pave the way for his theological analysis of the divine touch, both in the sense of being touched by God and touching God. Whereas ordinary touch ceaselessly covers the gaps and distance entailed in touching and leads onward, spiritual touch implies no distance. It is transparent and completely immediate, because, as Chrétien holds, in God there is no skin, no medium, and hence no distance. This difference follows from the fact that human touch consists of contact between bodies, while spiritual touch is purely intellectual.[63]

For Chrétien, there is no contradiction in speaking of an intellectual touch. Rather, it brings touch to its perfection: "touch is also what allows us to name the highest act of pure mind, at its supreme summit."[64] Chrétien here follows Thomas Aquinas, for whom the spiritual touch is a pure coincidence establishing pure identity. And yet, this coincidence is unlike the self-touching of two human hands, for the divine touch is fundamentally God's intellect that is touching itself without distance. The human, finite mind can still come into touch with the divine intellect in a way that intimates the human caress of the other. But to Chrétien, this intimation is imperfect, because the divine touch does not allow for any gradual ascension from the sensible to the intelligible but demands a leap of discontinuity. The divine is not anything given to bodily sensations—it is inherently iconoclastic, without image or representation. This means that we cannot reach proximity to God through any active initiative on our part. Although the initiative rests with God, Chrétien argues that there is nevertheless some form of reciprocity, albeit asymmetrical, for as God touches us with grace, we can touch back in loving God.[65]

Even as Chrétien takes the corporeal dimension fully into account in his treatment of human touch, he displays a purely intellectual orientation as far as divine touch is concerned. Drawing on Thomist intellectualism and mystic metaphors of divine touch, Chrétien arguably ends up betraying the most significant theological trope with regard to touch: the Word becoming flesh. However, a more careful reading of Chrétien will reveal that the incarnation is not completely absent. He can, for instance, claim that immediate mystic contact does not remove us from the incarnation of the Word, but brings us to it. Chrétien does not fail to note that the touch comes to us by the Mediator. As the Word mediates between divine intellect and bodily creatures, Chrétien preserves the bodily dimension of the revelation. With reference to Saint John of the Cross, he speaks of God's touching hand as a form of mediation, and the metaphor of the hand refers us to the Mediator: "The 'merciful hand of the father' with which he touches us is the Son."[66]

It is telling that Chrétien prefers to speak of the Son not as the incarnated but as the Mediator, which is to say the bridge between eternity and temporality, divine and human. The logic of mediation presupposes an existing rift between humans and God, a rift corresponding to the discontinuity between the human and the spiritual touch. While the Mediator is invoked, the bodily dimension of the incarnation plays no significant role. One might wonder why Chrétien, after having developed

TOUCH AND SKIN

his phenomenology of human touch in such detail, finds it necessary to turn so abruptly away from the carnal touch when he moves on to the divine touch. He seems to take no interest in the "hand of God" as the assumption of flesh and how it takes on meaning in the concrete events that follow from Christ's worldly life. But if God becomes flesh, it is not necessary to remove the divine touch from its bodily implications to hold on to its theological centrality—on the contrary. For God to become flesh must also imply coming into human skin and thus being able to both touch and be touched.

A swift look at the Gospel accounts makes it clear that touch is remarkably present, especially in Jesus's healing of the sick. Seen from one perspective, the narratives are about a touch of grace, as intimated by Chrétien, but first and foremost the stories are about the concrete contact made between specific bodies, as if the divine touch comes to pass through human touch. Derrida has no doubts about the centrality of touch in the Gospels, noting that if one starts from "the Greek word that translates touching, which is also a divine power, and the manifestation of God incarnate, one can take the Gospel's for *general haptics*."[67] Derrida claims that the narratives make up two groups, one portraying Jesus as touching, and the other portraying Jesus as touched. Among the first group we find the accounts of Jesus purifying the leper by stretching out his hand and touching him (Matt. 8:3), and his healing of Peter's mother-in-law by touching her hand (Matt. 8:15). There are also stories of restoring the sight of the blind by touching the eyes (Matt. 9:29–30), ears that are opened, and tongues that are loosened (Mark 7:32–36). They all portray how the divine power came out from him to restore their bodies (Luke 6:19).

As for the other group, the Gospels bear witness to Jesus being touched. Exemplary among these stories is the one about the woman who had suffered from hemorrhages for twelve years. She is the one touching his garment this time, and Jesus at once reacts to being touched: "Immediately aware that power had gone forth from him," he turns to the crowd, looking for the one touching him (Mark 5:30). The divine touch is not portrayed as intellectual in nature, but takes place between bodily beings. The power going forth reminds the reader of the divine touch that proceeds from God, but at the same time, there is a purely human sense of the power in touch. Taken together, the two groups of healing narratives attest to the fact that touch is inherently reciprocal, a reciprocity that plays out in the double sense of touch prior to thematization and intentional apprehension.[68] In and through such barely human touch, the incarnate God is revealed.

These stories of healing are central to Elisabeth Moltmann-Wendel's

CHAPTER 4

attempt to erect the place of the body in recent theology. Commenting on the woman with the hemorrhages, she says: "Though the story may smack of magic to some enlightened people, it is a physical story, the story of bodies, which in Christianity have been forgotten: crucified and never raised."[69] The physical story does not point beyond, toward a transcendent God, but downward, to the bodily presence of God among humans. Already Tertullian points out that touch is precisely what Marcion and other Gnostics cannot acknowledge, for "touch or being touched . . . cannot be believed to be truly done in the absence of all reality in His body itself."[70] In the same vein, Moltmann-Wendel holds that Jesus's touch is not meant to let our soul ascend to divine touch or to make human beings divine (*theosis*). Rather, it is meant to transfigure our understanding of both humanity and divinity by letting us appreciate that Jesus's "deepest humanity makes up his divinity."[71]

Apart from the stories of healing, I want to propose that there is a deeper current in the stories of Jesus, a current that concerns skin and touch. God comes under our human skin, first as a naked child, helplessly handed over to the hands and touch of his parents, then in touching and being touched to restore broken bodies, and finally stripped naked to the skin, exposed to violence and torture. It is not difficult to detect how skin and touch play a double role in these accounts, both actively in acts of love and passively in suffering pain. Skin and touch, in this context, open up to the other and make the body's integrity vulnerable to the other. The skin that makes Christ's healing touch possible is the very same skin that makes him exposed to violence—they are two sides of the same coin. It is the fineness of the human skin that makes up both the possibility of the caress and our susceptibility to pain. From the narrative trajectory of the Gospels, these two dimensions of the skin weave the events from cradle to cross together, as if to underline the depths to which God is incarnated in a human body.

5

The Inner Contradictions of Pain

Pain makes otherwise hidden aspects of our lived body present, not least what I have called flesh and blood. For this reason, I have repeatedly come back to the example of pain, but without providing any in-depth analyses of the phenomenon. In this chapter, I will attempt to work out the phenomenology of pain in more detail, drawing on previous findings and explicating their implications more systematically. In approaching the phenomenology of pain, one soon faces a set of theoretical dilemmas much discussed in the literature: Is pain intentional or not? Is it an auto-affective or hetero-affective impression? Does the painful body fully belong to my lived body, or does it signify another dimension of the body? Does pain bring out the incarnate self as fully at home in its body, or does it reveal the body as foreign to the self? These are sets of exclusive either-or options, and we seem forced to make an assessment and choose the most adequate option.

It is, however, very hard to choose sides in these cases, since there seems to be good phenomenological evidence for each of the options in the questions above. Hence, another approach should be considered: Is it possible to approach pain without resolving the dilemmas? And more, can there be good phenomenological reasons for doing so? If so, these reasons must link the contradictions and ambiguities back to the phenomenon of pain itself, as if they were already inherent components. Drew Leder has explored such an approach to pain. "Such ambiguities *are* the topic," he argues. "Pain, I will suggest, and especially persistent pain, involves negotiating a series of dialectical tensions and experiential paradoxes."[1] Although refusing to take sides with regard to different positions may seem unsatisfactory as long as pain is regarded as an intellectual problem, things change if we hold fast to the experience of pain as the lodestar of the phenomenological explication. From the assumption that a phenomenological description must preserve the inner contradictions, I will approach the contradictions at three different levels. After an account of pain's most elemental givenness as sensorial impressions, I will consider the ways the body is given in pain, and finally, account for how pain relates to the ego.

CHAPTER 5

Pain: Intentional or Not?

I previously discussed pain with respect to Husserl's notion of *hyle* and *morphe* (chapter 2), and later as a subcategory of tactile sensations (chapter 4). However, I have not yet extensively addressed pain and intentionality. Does Husserl himself believe that pain is intentional or nonintentional? After all, intentionality is the very essence of consciousness, which should lead us to assume that pain must be intentional, but Husserl also speaks of non-intentional matter, such as sensation. As Husserl raises this question in his first major work, *Logical Investigations*, his answer turns out not to be straightforward. On the one hand, pain seems to be emphatically sensual and given prior to any intentional comprehension. Unlike outer perception, fantasy, willing, and memory, pain does not seem to have any directedness or reference. It is not about anything; pain just hurts. On the other hand, Husserl also refers to instances where pain does relate to something, such as when one burns oneself *on* a hot oven or cuts oneself *with* a sharp knife. In these situations, pain seems to be intentional. In considering the intentionality of feelings in general, Husserl discusses the prevalent positions of his time, namely those of Brentano and Stumpf. Whereas Brentano argues that all feelings, including pain, must be intentional, Stumpf regards feelings as essentially nonintentional sensations.[2] Both make generic claims about the intentionality or non-intentionality of feelings, but that is exactly what Husserl refuses to do. Rather, Husserl suggests drawing a line between intentional feelings and non-intentional feelings which he calls feeling-sensations (*Gefühlsempfindungen*).

Sensorial content is given in outer perception, such as coldness, smoothness, color, and the like. While such sensations in themselves are not intentional, they are normally taken up by intentionality and accordingly interpreted as properties belonging to the object we are directed toward. These sensations will fade into the background of our attention as we focus on the intentional object. Husserl agrees with Brentano that there are feelings that have intentional structure. Sorrow is inconceivable apart from something sad, just as the "essence of pleasure demands a relation to something pleasing."[3] But at the same time, following Stumpf, Husserl recognizes that we have feeling-sensations, such as in intense pain, that are different from intentional feelings. These feeling-sensations are not directed to objects but are sensations given in and for themselves. Consequently, we have two classes of feelings, intentional and non-intentional ones.[4]

Husserl is quick to point out that most feelings are complex, which

THE INNER CONTRADICTIONS OF PAIN

means that they are built up in several levels and thus can integrate components of both non-intentional sensations and intentional feelings. The relation between them can overlap and vary in different ways, so that the same feeling can be given differently: we can still enjoy a meal even after the sensual taste has vanished, or we can have a sensation of pain even as the intentional feeling is lacking. As Husserl puts it: "such unities may at one time seem to depend on sensational features (e.g., pleasure or urge-sensation), at another on act intentions which rest on these."[5] The reason why we easily run into confusion when we speak of feelings, Husserl claims, is because we do not distinguish clearly between the two ways in which we speak of them. As for pain, Husserl is not conclusive, but leaves us with a double determination of the sensation of pain: it can be both non-intentional and intentional.

Except for mediating between two opposing views of feelings and distinguishing between different forms, I want to stress the possible consequences of embracing both non-intentional and intentional pain. Aligned with Husserl, I suggested in chapter 4 that pain as mere irritation remains intentional, which I took Sartre's example of reading to illustrate. However, once the pain gets sufficiently intense, the worldly objects drop off and one is immersed in one's own non-intentional affective flesh. However, there is a way one can regard the distinction Husserl draws as reappearing even in intense pain. In chapter 2, I pointed out that Husserl cites pain as an example of hyletic sensations during his discussion of *hyle*. Although these hyletic sensations are evidently non-intentional in themselves, Husserl tends to treat them as the raw material for *morphe*. When *morphe* shapes and animates *hyle*, they together make up the concrete intentional consciousness of something. Nevertheless, Husserl can indicate the possibility that *morphe* and *hyle* can be studied independently.[6] Husserl asserts that no phenomenological reason compels us to regard hyletic sensations as part of intentional presentations.[7] As I argued in chapter 2, we can go beyond what Husserl writes and argue that this possibility opens up an ambiguous space between *hyle* and *morphe* which seems to capture the inherent tensions of pain. According to my proposed understanding, pain arises from the hyletic sensation to which *morphe* responds and lends its sense, but without fully encompassing the surplus inherent in *hyle*. From this perspective, it should be possible to argue that the distinction between intentional and non-intentional feelings in *Logical Investigations* suggests that pain sensation involves an unresolved inner tension. At least, this is a possible way to extend Husserl's analyses, and it is, at any rate, the avenue I wish to explore further.

Sensation as Non-Intentional Impressions

Michel Henry's analysis of pain shares Husserl's focus on sensation, impressions, and intentionality. Unlike sensations, Herny's notion of impressions is not imprints of the world. According to Henry, impressions never appear in the world. Consequently, they must be described strictly according to their immanent givenness. For Henry, the most striking characteristic of pain is its lack of intentional reference to anything beyond itself. There is therefore no way in which Henry can agree with Husserl's view that pain sensation can be taken up into complex acts and become part of intentionality. Henry rather sides with only one aspect of Husserl's analysis, namely where he treats pain as non-intentional. As with any impression, pain is not sensual matter through which we perceive the world or objects in it; pain is simply auto-affections: *"The original reality of pain is not in the world and does not manifest itself therein . . . The reality of pain is its manifestation, its first arising, its revelation, yet in such a way that this revelation is constituted by pain itself and finds in it, in pain as such, the effectiveness of its phenomenality."*[8] There is no intentionality in pain, it does not refer beyond itself, pain does not even allow for any escape. If pain were intentional, there would be a possible escape, because the function of intentionality is to project impressions outside themselves and thus put them at a distance, as an irreal noema. But pain is essentially without distance and thus without relief. Henry also denies that pain follows the succession of time, for in that case, it would soon fade into the past and unburden the present. But pain lingers in its auto-affection beyond time. Pain, like in principle any impression, is immediately "given over to itself, immersed in itself, submerged by itself, and crushed under its own weight," which is to say, affecting itself without any distance or escape.[9]

One important consequence of Henry's view is that pain, or at least pure pain, has nothing to do with hetero-affection. Pain does not contain the impression of something external that puts pressure on or penetrates the body, such as a hammer or a knife. This is so because impressions are distinct from the empirical sensibility that mediates the external world.[10] If the impression of pain were hetero-affective, Henry contends, then we should be able to alleviate the pain by manipulating its causes. However, pain remains unaltered by such manipulation. Pure pain is not a result of external circumstances; rather, suffering "is not affected by something else, but by itself; it is *a self-affection* in the radical sense that suffering is what is affected, but it is by suffering that it is so."[11] Henry has no patience for Stoicism or other strategies that seek to render pain manageable; he simply thinks they have lost touch with the impressionality of pain, splitting it off and turning it into an intentional correlate.[12]

Henry's understanding of auto-affection gives it a sense of agency and activity as it affects the flesh in pain. But being auto-affected by pain also means the passivity of undergoing pain, and it is this passivity that is central to Henry. Husserl has analyzed passivity, both as the passive synthesis of association, but also in the sense of *Ursinnlichkeit*, that is, arch-impressions given prior to the ego and situated at the heart of temporality. Henry is well aware of Husserl's treatment of passivity, but he is not satisfied with the way Husserl accounts for the passive synthesis, which in Henry's reading subsumes the passively given to an anonymous intentionality. The radical passivity of which Henry is speaking is more aligned with Husserl's sense of *Ursinnlichkeit*, for the passivity is inscribed in the impressions themselves, prior to and independent of syntheses and intentionality. The impressions do not bring themselves about spontaneously but flow from life itself.

For pain, such a fundamental passivity means that it is powerless to bring itself about and escape itself, as it attests to the "powerlessness of every originary impression to rid itself of itself, to escape itself in any way whatsoever."[13] Since pain excludes external references, as well as the self's powers over it, pure pain suffers itself. It is, according to Henry, in "absolute identity with itself."[14] The same identity also holds for the opposite tonality of pain, namely pleasure, which also enjoys itself, as it is both given and received from itself. Although we must differentiate between the tonality of pain and pleasure, suffering and joy, they are identical in essence. "Suffering is joy because in it, in its content and in what it is, the Being-given-to itself, the enjoyment of Being is realized . . . Joy is suffering because the Being-given-to-itself of Being, its enjoyment, resides and is realized in the self-experience of the self of its suffering."[15] Both joy and suffering imply undergoing life in passivity.

While Henry's analysis can be interpreted as an extension of one aspect of Husserl's two-sided account of pain, his examination of pain occupies a different position within his phenomenology than in Husserl's case. For Husserl, the class of feeling-sensations of pain is treated as a special case due to its complex relation to intentionality. This lays the groundwork for a regional analysis of pain's specific phenomenological characteristics—its structure, character, and implications for embodiment and intentionality. In contrast, Henry's central notion is impressionality, and pain serves as its most significant example. But it could just as well have been joy, since in essence, suffering and joy converge:

> In the accomplishment of "self-suffering," however, life experience itself, comes into *it*self, augments itself with its own content, delights in

CHAPTER 5

> itself—it is enjoyment; it is joy. It is clear that these two original and fundamental phenomenological tonalities, a pure "suffering" and a pure "enjoying," root themselves a priori in the "self-experiencing" which constitutes the essence of every conceivable life.[16]

Granted the way impressions are given in their unique affective tonality, Henry's question becomes: "How can we sustain the idea that amid precisely this suffering, confusing me with its impressionable and suffering flesh and identifying me with that suffering, I am yet happy?" And the answer is that all impressions are self-impressions, and as such, they stem from life. Life is received and suffered. In stripping us bare of any illusion of self-sufficiency, suffering points back to the life from which any impressions generate. And yet all suffering is also joy in the sense that suffering *"leads to the 'rejoicing' implied in any 'to suffer.'"*[17]

Henry's contribution to the phenomenology of pain lies in his analysis of how pain causes the world to recede and intensifies the immanence of the flesh. However, one might question whether Henry is correct in identifying joy and suffering. After all, isn't the opposition between them foundational to the polarity that orients significant aspects of our lives? Furthermore, asserting that pain and pleasure, suffering and joy are essentially one is difficult to reconcile with their givenness in experience. Their structure, inner movement, scope, and temporality do not appear homogeneous. It is far from clear that reducing pain and pleasure, suffering and joy to a single essence aligns with "the things themselves." Even if such identification is located at the depth of life itself, Henry must maintain the strange conviction that suffering and joy are entirely impervious to changes in the world and their effects on our lived body. So why does Henry arrive at such a conclusion? It seems to me that the critical step is taken already in his initial approach to pain, where pain is treated as exemplary of impressions in general. In this way, Henry focuses solely on the characteristics that apply to all impressions despite their differences and varying tonalities, that is, their pure essence. But what if pain is not paradigmatic but rather an exception to typical impressions?

Indeed, why choose pain as exemplary in the first place? In fact, enjoyment seems to better fit Henry's account. One can conceive of a deep satisfaction and joy, where joy originates from itself, relishes in itself, and thus remains within the circle of immanence. However, the idea that suffering pain is similarly closed in on itself is far from self-evident. Even if both pain and pleasure are affective impressions, they may very well differ in their essential structure. In fact, most phenomenologists argue for their essential opposition. Let me just mention a few examples. Ricoeur has argued that pleasure comes from fulfillment of some form of lack, whereas pain is not at all about fulfillment, but is a sign of a threat to our bodies.[18] F. J. J. Buytendijk argues that enjoyment implies self-movement and self-realization, whereas pain turns them into a restricted state of helplessness.[19] Grüny speaks of pain as a disruptive way that puts an end to normality and enjoyment.[20] If nothing else, these different examples indicate how contested Henry's position is, and suggest that the difference between enjoyment and pain does not lead back to one essence, but is an original duality rooted in the phenomenological structure of our incarnation.

Pain, I will suggest, does not display the same structure as enjoyment; that is, it is not enclosed in the circuit of auto-affection. It also takes some form of hetero-affection. Pain implies the most basic form of negativity, the experience of "something that should not be," and as such, it breaks the closed sphere of Henry's absolute self-identity. While pain affects the body within its own sphere, we must also take into consideration how pain emerges as an unwelcome stranger. Husserl seems more convincing on one important point, because he emphasizes that the feeling-sensation of pain is not representative of intentional consciousness as such, but rather its exception. I would even say that not only is there tension in the way the impressions of pain relate to intentionality, as *hyle* to its *morphe*, but that the reason for this tension resides in the phenomenological quality of pain itself: it is given with a certain resistance to the intentional form and the homogenous milieu of Henry's immanence.

Jean-Francois Lavigne has made the important point that Henry is incorrect in asserting that it is suffering that suffers itself. Rather, it is I who suffer something, something that is precisely opposed to me, "not only as that which is affected by an 'impression,' but more properly as *aggressed* by a hostile enemy, or an adverse and unbearable quality."[21] Henry's analysis of pain lacks the negative structure of pain, but also its inherent affective power as aversive. There is nothing in Henry's analyses that encapsulates how pain turns against us; rather, his description treats it as the most natural manifestation of the passivity of life. Henry stresses that there is no escape from any impressions, as they are given without distinction and distance, but his immanentism prevents him from shedding any light on why we have the urge to escape pain in the first place. But this urge to escape must be inscribed in its sensual content upon its arrival: pain violently breaks into our sphere of ownness and constantly turns, as it were, against us. Jay Bernstein notes: "The primary feature of pain is its sheer averseness."[22] Scarry rightly argues that pain stands out "by its aversiveness, [which] makes most pressing the urge to move out and away from the body."[23] Without its unwelcome, aversive presence, we would lack the urge to flee, and without aversiveness and negativity, we are no longer talking about pain.

Sensation "in-Spite-of-Consciousness"

Although Henry captures some of the central characteristics of pain as impressions and the way pain tends to imprison us, the phenomenological description cannot be exhausted by pure immanent auto-affection. There is also a sense in which pain appears to be hetero-affective, and Levinas emphasizes precisely the latter. However, Levinas shares several key insights with Henry. Levinas, too, focuses on pain's sensorial impressions and notes that, just like our lived experience of color, sound, and touch, they are given independently of intentionality.[24] Moreover, Levinas also stresses the passivity of pain and the impossibility of escape from it. As for the latter, it was in fact Levinas who first made the often-repeated observation that in "suffering there is an absence of all refuge. . . . It is made up of its impossibility of fleeing or retreating."[25] However, an important contrast soon appears, for where Henry insists on the immanent self-identity of pain, Levinas thinks that physical pain comes with a kind of transcendence or excess.

There are various dimensions of Levinas's central notion of "excess." Starting with the sensorial impression of pain, the impression is excessive in the sense that it is given to consciousness as "in-spite-of-consciousness," which means that it arrives somehow against the structures of consciousness. Pain impressions resist integration into the consciousness to which they are given, or in Levinas's words, they remain "unassumeable."

> "Unassumability" does not result from the excessive intensity of a sensation, from some sort of quantitative "too much," surpassing the measure of our sensibility and our means of grasping and holding. It results from an excess, a "too much" which is inscribed in a sensorial content, penetrating as suffering the dimensions of meaning which seem to be opened and grafted on to it.[26]

The excessive "too much" does not simply surpass sensibility, since pain is certainly made up by its specific, hurtful sensorial content. It is not exterior to consciousness either, but conveys a qualitatively "too much" that cannot be contained. The content of pain is, according to its own

THE INNER CONTRADICTIONS OF PAIN

essential quality, over against the receiver and denies any integration or syntheses: the content resists being taken up into intentionality. Where Husserl remains ambiguous on this point, Levinas resolutely sides with Henry by regarding pain as essentially non-intentional—not, however, due to impressions' general auto-revealing power, but due to pain's specific hyletic content.

Moreover, there is another sense of pain's excess that relates to meaning. Pain has often been taken as the very breakdown of meaning, as the non-sense that appears in contrast to the reasonableness of life in general.[27] Meaning might, however, signify different things; it might refer to the power to unite, to bring into association with other experiences, and subsume content to conceptual grasp; or it might, in a more Husserlian way, entail bestowing sense by means of noesis. According to Levinas, pain resists meaning in both these senses. Pain is essentially the very manifestation of disturbance; what makes it evil is "this very *non-integrability*."[28] In its very "how" of appearing, pain arrives violently over against the consciousness to which it both belongs and which it opposes. Serrano de Haro has similarly argued that even if we stick to Husserl's model of acts and fulfillment, pain remains nonsense: "The adequate fulfillment that pain enjoys as lived experience is as well a counter-fulfillment, an accomplished negativity, not merely an intentional deception."[29]

Meaning can, moreover, also refer to a telos, a purpose that bestows sense on projects or on life itself. It is in this inflection of meaning that pain enters the problem of evil and theodicy. To Nietzsche, clinging to a transcendent telos is typical of Christianity, and it stems from our inability to stand the utter meaninglessness of pain.[30] Levinas, however, never denies the meaninglessness of pain. In fact, he invariably denies that suffering has any purpose—indeed, he argues that imposing purposes on any suffering is fundamentally a denial of ethics. Any serious discussion of pain must acknowledge that its excess utterly lacks purpose or sense: "The evil of pain, the harm itself," as Levinas puts it, "is the explosion and most profound articulation of absurdity. Thus, the least one can say about suffering is that, according to its own phenomenality, it is useless, and 'for nothing.' "[31] Levinas is clearly not speaking of a simple cut on one's hand, but is alluding to the Holocaust. While the grand questions of evil may seem distant from Levinas's initial analysis of the sensual content of pain, he intimates that both are, in fact, rooted in pain's most elemental givenness as senseless.

The way pain sensation refuses meaning leads to Levinas's final understanding of excess, namely excess as exteriority, and consequently—in opposition to Henry—a rupture into immanence. In this context, exteriority does not denote the physical world but refers to an excess that

CHAPTER 5

cannot be derived from interiority, and that takes the face of the Other as its paradigm. Levinas explicitly denies that pain is merely an affective "coloring" of consciousness, which assumes that it is just a modality of the general structures of consciousness. Rather, pain's sensual content arrives without anticipation, it arrives as impossible to welcome, and it is impossible to integrate—it must appear alien and, in *"this sense, transcendence!"*[32] As such, the exteriority of pain also affects the ego in its power to turn its active mastery into submissive passivity. The passivity which Levinas, here as elsewhere, invokes has nothing to do with being an effect of a cause. Levinas also denies Husserl's passivity understood as receptivity: "In suffering, sensibility is a vulnerability, more passive than receptivity; it is an ordeal more passive than experience. It is precisely an evil."[33] The suffering of pain is beyond the scope of passive synthesis and active intentionality—it interrupts prior to preparation or anticipation. The passivity in question is a matter of undergoing sensations that outstrip all defenses.

Given the excessive nature of pain, in all its inflections, does Levinas fall into the opposite pitfall from Henry? Does he, instead of enclosing the suffering of pain within immanence, make it into an alterity that leaves little room for the way pain is emphatically mine to suffer?

Inner Contradictions in Pain

Despite some of their common phenomenological starting points, Henry and Levinas draw almost opposite conclusions. Where Henry emphasizes the immanent self-affection of pain to the point where its invasive and aversive nature is neglected, Levinas underlines the intrusive and excessive nature of pain but has little to say about pain's auto-affective power. According to the principle of the excluded middle, it seems that both cannot be right. But such mutual exclusion is not self-evident in the case of pain, for, as I have suggested, pain is not simple but implies inner tensions and contradictions in itself. If this is so, a descriptive account must precisely not resolve the tensions but articulate them. Occasionally, Levinas comes very close to this point, commenting that pain entails a "quasi-contradictory structure, but a contradiction which is not formal like that of the dialectic tension between the affirmative and the negative which arises for the intellect; it is a contradiction by way of sensation: the plaintiveness of pain, hurt."[34] Levinas encircles the tensions of externality and interiority, of the urge to escape pain along with the impossibility of doing so, but he leaves us without sufficient means to deal with Henry's important point, namely that in pain I am not suffering something else, but myself. I am in pain.

Pain is mine, as felt solely by me, and simultaneously resist my grasp and appropriation. Pain is certainly not under the sway of "I can." Rather, pain has an agency ensuing from itself, an "it can" that is turned against me and my will.[35] There is at once an experience of the invasion of an excessive sensation, and at the same time, the pain sensation is mine to the point of no escape or distanciation. The double movement and inner contradiction of pain are well captured in Bernstein's account of its aversiveness:

> Aversion refers to the action of turning away from oneself, and so against oneself. Pain is the occurrence of such a turning: pain is an attack on the body, the sensational experience of negation, a feeling of something being against one, which is always with pain one's body itself. With pain one's own body turn against one; in pain one is turned against oneself.[36]

The assault on the body is against the body yet also part of the body itself. Similarly, Jean Améry speaks of the body in pain. Experiencing a toothache, one desires to be rid of it, have the dentist remove it as an alien *res extensa*; yet the toothache is mine, or more precisely, it is "a realization of my flesh in the self-denial of my flesh: it is both an addition to my ego and a loss of ego."[37] What can phenomenology tell us about such strange tensions inherent in pain?

Even though Husserl never pursued the phenomenology of sensation of pain in detail, I have in previous chapters noted that there are resources found in his thinking that can shed light on its contradictions and dynamics, especially his notion of *hyle*, understood in its fundamental sense as an impression. In a Kantian way, Husserl distinguishes between two fundamental sources of knowledge: on the one hand, the original spontaneity that pertains to the activity of reason, and on the other, the original *Ursinnlichkeit*, or primal impressions, that belong to passivity and sensation. These original sensations are pre-given in the sense that they are already provided for as I turn toward them. They are by no means derived from the spontaneity of reason—they are simply there.[38] Primal impressions are the most basic givens toward which subjectivity can turn its intentionality. These impressions also seem to direct themselves to the I in its affectivity—not as internal to auto-affection, but precisely as foreign: "the word ['impression'] express well what is 'there' of itself, and indeed originally: namely, what is pregiven to the Ego, presenting itself to the Ego in the manner of something affecting it as foreign."[39] Pain, too, consists of impressions, charged with affectivity, which as foreign occur, in Levinas's words, "in-spite-of-consciousness." While pain appears foreign, occurring over against us, Henry's emphasis on the immanence of pain must somehow also be accounted for. For Husserl, the foreignness of the impressions is described ambiguously, for *hyle* is not external to the ego, either as something wholly other or as a hidden physical cause. Hyletic impressions are certainly also a real (*reel*) part, that is, immanent to experience, since it is only as a real part that they can serve as matter for intentional form. And yet, in pain, these impressions are given as foreign.

As Henry has made perfectly clear, even if Husserl at times can prepare the ground for the autonomy of impressions, the overarching tendency pulls the other way: *hyle* is swallowed up in *morphe*. Thus, in normal perception, sensations—of colors, contours, tactile impressions, and so on—will be taken up into the constitution of intentional objects without further notice. Pain is an exception to this rule, because here those aversive impressions will resist integration—and yet they belong to experience. To repeat, the fruitfulness of this Husserlian account consists in its preservation of the inner contradiction or double movement that pertains to pain itself, as at once belonging to the sentient beings we are and at the same time turning against us, as foreign.

Body and Flesh

Having examined the inner contradictions of pain sensation, I will now broaden the scope and take the body into account. There are good reasons for doing so; it can even appear strangely reductive to treat pain only as sensation, for as Buytendijk has pointed out: "a painful impression is an extreme abstraction."[40] Pain always tends to spill over into the experience of our entire body. Max Scheler has highlighted different constitutive levels of suffering in order to bring out how sensation feelings spread from vital, bodily feelings to personal dimensions, and even into metaphysical-religious worldviews.[41] In my view, such descriptions do not make the previous analyses fruitless, but put them in relief: impressions and sensations can only be treated separately as long as one keeps in mind that such treatment is a reflexive abstraction, discerning only one part of a concrete whole. As experienced, pain takes place within a multileveled unity of our embodied subjectivities. Even if pain is typically localized, our entire bodily awareness is certainly affected by it, following the logic that if "one member suffers, all suffer together with it" (1 Cor. 12:26).

Husserl's *hyle* is not detached from our lived body.[42] As Shaun Gallagher has pointed out, it is telling that the majority of Husserl's examples of *hyle*—including pain—belong to the immediate bodily sphere. Informed by Merleau-Ponty's and Gurwitch's critique of *hyle* as atomic data given independently of pre-theoretical fields, Gallagher attempts to develop an embodied notion of *hyle* in which it is always already given as a rudimentary gestalt. *Hyle* is not blind and abstract but rather a meaningful unity, and it appears primarily in embodied experience.[43] It is, however, far from clear that pain is meaningful, but it does come with a certain recognizable profile that marks the way we embody it. In this way, pain seems to be the paradigmatic example of how subjectivity and body make up a concrete unity, because pain makes the embodied conditions manifest, or even inescapable to the incarnate subject. However, if Levinas is right in claiming that pain is given in-spite-of-consciousness, then the *hyle* cannot easily be assimilated into the lived body. While doubtless affecting the whole body, the hurting limb or organ also gives itself as an unwelcome intruder with an affective agency of its own. It has been noted that pain patients tend to speak of the painful part of the body as "it"—signalizing a strangely detached perspective over against the body.[44] Such utterances reflect the strange bodily experience of pain as both embodied and yet against the body. As Scarry aptly writes: "Even though it occurs within oneself, it is at once identified as 'not oneself,' 'not me,' as something alien that must be gotten rid of."[45]

Again, we face the aporia where two opposing views of the body in pain both seem appropriate: the body as inescapably mine versus the body as not myself. One radical solution to such a Gordian knot is, of course, just to cut it. That is what Henry in effect suggests in turning away from all other perspectives of the body, such as the lived and objective body, and turning toward the impressional flesh. Since the flesh is affective and immediately mine, it seems to be a good candidate for the body in pain.

> The original reality of our body is not our mundane body that is situated in the world and opens onto it, instead it is our flesh in the auto-impressionality through which all powers are placed in themselves and thereby able to be exercised. . . . Yet *our flesh can only provide access to this body and through this body to the world, because it first provides us with access to itself—because it is impressionally given to oneself where all self-givenness occurs, namely, in and through life.*[46]

Life arrives in flesh and calls flesh into being, whereas impressions, such as impressions of pain, mold how the flesh is given in concrete affective tonalities.[47] Any attempt to detect pain and suffering in the world, in lived and objective bodies, is in vain; pain never appears in the light of the world, it doesn't even have anything to do with empirical sensation. As a mode of life itself, pain reveals the absolute immanence of our flesh.[48]

Does Henry's notion of flesh capture the body in pain? Although pain makes the inescapable immanence of my body present, as flesh, pain also makes that very same body occur as foreign to me—as an "it," turned against me. Paradoxically, the state of pain is at the same time the paradigm of auto-impressional flesh and of the estranged body; it is both an immediate affective flesh and the body experienced as solid, opaque, and dense.[49] What Henry's flesh neglects is one side of the tension, namely the body as flesh and blood. "The massive *stampede toward the flesh*, characteristic of contemporary thought," according to Falque's diagnostics, "neglects Husserl's attachment to the *body*, to the point sometimes of *dis-corporating* the flesh."[50] While shifting the gravity from flesh to a solid body, Falque does not end up with a body without flesh, but argues that we must add a neglected layer of incarnation, namely the "spread body." Applied to the tensions of the various perspectives on the body in pain, it is interesting to note how the spread body is located in an ambiguous zone, as it "demarcates a kind of border zone, or an intermediary body, between the *extended body* (simple materiality) and the *lived body* (pure subjectivity)."[51] Granted the way the phenomenology of pain gives rise to conflicting accounts of the body, Falque's suggestion is attractive. Even if he does not elaborate on the phenomenology of pain, the spread body seems to allow for a perspective on the body where the inner conflicts of pain can be embraced. The spread body does not replace or repress the objective or lived body, but provides a deepened account of the body where the otherwise neglected material and organic dimensions are retained in between the lived experience and the objectified body.

The spread body also allows for an account of how the foreignness of pain can be acknowledged while not denying that it is indeed my own body that undergoes that foreignness. Although this level of the body is for the most part invisibly implied in engaged bodily activities, it can also come to the fore. Falque argues that my painful body is not phenomenologically captured by Henry's auto-affection "of self by itself in its pathos (or in its flesh)," but must take into account the sense we have of something foreign to our own circuit, that is, "hetero-affection of self by the other in his or her body (or *bios*)."[52] The hetero-affection in Falque's rendering encircles the central tension, in which I remain affected by some alterity in my own body. I find it even more precise to say that in pain, we are exposed to the crossings of hetero-affections, thus referring to the sense of foreignness of the "non-I," and auto-affection, preserving the sense that it nevertheless remains my own body that feels and affects itself.

The body in pain entails the same inner contradiction and double movement that was accounted for with regard to sensation. Pain enters the flesh, for unless there is an incarnate self-awareness, there is no pain; and yet pain is not the occurrence of an immaterial flesh closed in its own self-affections, but one that is affected by an otherness internal to the carnal condition. In pain, our spread body appears in-spite-of-flesh, to draw on Levinas's lingo. Pain is carnal in an almost literal sense: the knife penetrates the skin, cuts into tissue, runs into flesh and blood—to which it is an unwelcome guest. This does not dispense with the impressional body or lived body, since without the mineness of the carnal experience, nothing will be felt. Yet it is not completely identified with the flesh, but poses itself in contradiction to it, as our material and animal levels wrest free from the ego's dominion and set themselves up against it. Saulius Geniusas captures the central tensions of the body, as he states that

> the experience of pain is the experience of an inner cleavage, in which my lived-body unwillingly becomes the one and only *object* of experience, while still retaining the sense of being the subject of experience. *The body-in-pain splits into two, while still remaining one.*[53]

Pain and the Self

No doubt, pain makes the body salient in its different levels, but since it takes place in my body, the question of subjectivity is also brought up. Milan Kundera once wrote: "*I think, therefore I am* is the statement of an intellectual who underrates toothaches . . . However, when someone steps on my foot, only I feel the pain. The basis of the self is not thought but suffering, which is the most fundamental of all feelings."[54] Suffering pain is so fundamental, Kundera suggests, that it amounts to an experience of subjective existence. But exactly how does the body in pain relate to the self? On the one hand, pain seems to be the most prominent way in which incarnation manifests itself, as my own embodied being in the modality not of "I think" but as "I am in pain." This "I am in pain" captures the self in its inescapable singularity with a concretion and acuity absent in thinking, communication, and actions. It thus seems like pain belongs to what Henry calls immanence or "the transparency of subjectivity."[55]

CHAPTER 5

Yet on the other hand, it also seems equally clear that what comes to the fore in severe pain is not so much the lived body that I am, and perhaps not even the body that I have, but the body that is turned against me, sentencing me to inner exile. In that case, how transparent is this incarnate subjectivity?

In his sketch of a phenomenology of the flesh, Jean-Luc Marion makes the relation between flesh and ego his central theme. In our everyday engagements, he notes, there is a strange absence of the self to itself. If not in the everyday life which I lead most of the time, then where is the self given to itself? The self must somehow be made concrete and manifest if we are to have a phenomenological account of it, and it can only be so, Marion argues, when the self finds itself incarnated: "I come back to myself in experience myself, and I experience myself in taking flesh."[56] It is not by chance that Marion uses the word "flesh" rather than "body" or "living body," since his reflection unfolds in the territory already mapped by Henry. Moreover, his expression "taking flesh" alludes to the coined idiom in the ancient Christian church where theologians spoke of logos "assuming" or "taking" flesh. However, Marion's first approach to the givenness of the ego taking flesh is worked out through a reading of Descartes. Even if Descartes is regarded as the father of modern body-soul dualism, Marion points out that parts of his writings invite another reception. Here, *res cogitans* does not, Marion argues, originally come to itself through a reflective thought that is thinking. Before such proof of the ego, the ego must already be given to itself, not intellectually but by the capacity of being a body gifted with senses. Most originally the ego feels itself feeling.[57] This is another way of saying that the ego's original givenness is provided by affections that reveal themselves in the flesh.

Marion goes on to explore how the self is given through analyses of pleasure, aging, and most interestingly here, pain. As for suffering physical pain, Marion repeats Henry's findings about its auto-affection and lack of distance.[58] Marion's own contribution consists in the way he thinks that pain singles out the self. Against Heidegger, he holds that individuation of the self does not come about through resolute decisions in the face of facticity and finitude; rather, the self initially finds itself individuated by pain. While the ego takes flesh, there is also a sense in which the flesh takes the ego, indeed fixing the self as riveted to the flesh by pain. This self riveted to the flesh is not taken hostage in some inner realm, but is held fast by the ground that supports it. Accordingly, Marion finds Husserl's notion of "earth" to be a fitting metaphor: just like the earth is the unmovable ground that makes any other movement possible, so is my flesh the indispensable ground that conditions the self:

> As soon as the *ego* takes flesh, it finds itself stuck to itself as to its
> ground, to its phenomenological earth (the one that does not move):
> as earthed, the taking of flesh assigns the *ego* definitively to itself and
> itself alone. Or rather, in assigning it to a place that it can neither deny
> nor shake nor flee, flesh and its earthing identifies it finally as it*self*, as
> an *ipse*.[59]

Not only does the ego only fully become itself as it relates to its flesh,
but its origin does not arise from the ego's spontaneity or choice; rather,
the flesh precedes the ego and preempts any choices that can be made.
Such a reversal of initiative is central to Marion's phenomenology in
general, and it also has further implications for pain. It is not sufficient
to stress the mineness of pain, because the ego does not take pain into
its possession—the reverse is rather true. I never choose pain, but pain
chooses me.[60] Marion will even say that the self receives itself in pain, as if
the self emerges in being passively received as a gift: "I do not give myself
my flesh, it is it that gives me to myself. In receiving my flesh, I receive me
myself—I am in this way gifted to it."[61]

While there is no doubt that pain can lay bare a fundamental passivity of the self, it is not pain itself that produces the flesh, but pain is a privileged way in which flesh is disclosed to the self and also posits the self as
a given by the flesh. Moreover, it seems that Marion's one-sided emphasis
on passivity leaves out an inner tension, this time between activity and passivity. Whereas pain arrives without invitation or initiative on our part, it
does arouse reactions; pain simultaneously leaves us helpless and yet provokes active protests. However, while protests and what Buytendijk calls
"flight reactions" are inscribed in pain itself, we will never succeed in escaping pain. Since pain is inseparable from the incarnate self, Buytendijk
helpfully suggests that the suffering of pain consists of a double movement of the urge for flight and the impossibility of escaping, that is, of a
responding activity held fast by passivity.[62] This much must still be granted
to Marion: there is a fundamental sense in which passivity has both the
first and last word, for pain originally places the self in the mode of the
receiver, and deprives the receiver of the power to end it at will.

Far from conceiving the self in terms of spontaneity, thinking, or
choosing, Marion finds its origin in an initiative arriving from elsewhere,
according to the logic of the gift.[63] Such an understanding relies on another of Marion's signature concepts, that of "saturated phenomena,"
which signifies phenomena with an excess of givenness of intuition that
overwhelms the intentions. In the arrival of saturated phenomena, the
direction of the intentional act is reversed; it is no longer our intentions
that seek fulfillment in different degrees, but the givenness of the phe-

CHAPTER 5

nomenon that addresses and overflows our intentionality and its capacity to respond. Such reversal is a paradox in the etymological sense of *para* (against) *doxa* (expectation), signifying how intentions and anticipations always come too late to an initiative that has already been taken. The relevance for the present is that Marion takes flesh to be a saturated phenomenon that precedes the ego and exceeds its possessive grasp. This is especially salient in the case of pain, which occurs without my expectations and "invades me without ceasing even before I know its meaning."[64]

Whereas the other types of saturated phenomena Marion accounts for refer to a surplus that comes towards us, flesh simply manifests itself to itself. In a manner similar to Henry, Marion says that "flesh only ever refers back to itself, in the indissoluble unity of the felt and the feeling."[65] But as I have repeatedly argued, this only captures half of the story. What Marion does not give sufficient attention to is how pain turns the experience of the body into a stranger to the self. In pain, the self is not only gifted with itself and its affectivity, but feels itself invaded by non-I that resists the identity of auto-affection. Still, in one passage, it is as if Marion realizes exactly this. Writing about the possibility of subjectivity after metaphysics, he says: "it can only come from flesh, where *hetero*- and auto-affection are mixed."[66] This is exactly what must be said of the self in pain, but Marion does not develop this argument, and it is hard to see how he can consistently do so, given his reliance on Henry's flesh.

In any case, I will hold on to the fruitful perspective of the self as at once hetero- and auto-affective, both foreign and familiar. Since Marion takes his cue from Descartes, it is interesting to note that the phenomenology of pain can lead to a reappropriation of one aspect of Descartes's dualism. In general, a phenomenology of incarnation cannot dogmatically assume the two distinct substances of the thinking ego and the extended body. However, in pain, the self is riveted to the flesh, but is also put at a certain distance from our body as the hurting limb turns strange. When the hand or the foot is hurting in pain, the sufferer tends to perceive the body part as "thing-like," as if my own hand or foot is put over against me. But why this sudden return to *res extensa*? David Bakan has pointed out that in normal circumstances, the self coincides with the boundaries of the body, so that however immersed I am in my tasks, I can nonetheless draw a line between myself and my surroundings. In pain, however, this distinction is reversed, transferring the feeling of my own body to the outside world and letting it return to my consciousness as if external to myself. According to Bakan, the motive behind this reversal arises from our inability to distinguish ourselves from invasive pain. As a defensive response, Bakan argues that the ego attempts to distance itself from the body. To phenomenology, such alienation of the painful body might smack too much of psychological projections, but it captures well the inner contradictions of the body in pain as at once inseparable from the ego and yet strange to it: "Phenomenally, however," Bakan explains, "pain appears to the conscious ego as not a part of itself but as alien to it, as something happening *to* the ego, with the ego as it were, the victim of external forces."[67]

The ego taken by flesh is, according to Marion, more original than Descartes's *ego cogito*. The lack of distance between the ego and the afflicted body marks their identity: "I do not have it [i.e., the body], I am it."[68] However, the conclusion Drew Leder draws from the Cartesian perspective on pain is very different: "I no longer simply 'am' my body, the set of unthematized powers from which I exist. Now I 'have' a body, a perceived body in the world."[69] Marion's and Leder's perspectives may seem mutually exclusive at first: is the body in pain something I am or something I have? I have argued that we do not have to choose between these two options in this case.

One reason why being a body and having a body are not mutually exclusive is that the body is given differently to us according to its strata. Whereas phenomenology has tended to privilege the constitutive role of the lived body, there might be good reasons to retain the multileveled analysis of the body right down to its material and animal levels. A multileveled analysis of the body is already operative in Husserl's analyses in the second volume of *Ideas*. For my purposes, the relevance of such an approach is not due to its explication of various constitutive levels of the concrete body, but rather due to how it allows us to reflect on the internal tensions and contradictions within one and the same body. There are different ways in which the various levels of the body are given to the ego. My habitual lived body is under the sway of my "I can." But there are also animal and vegetative levels pertaining to the visceral body that normally function beyond my conscious awareness, such as heartbeats and digestion. This is no longer "I can," but "it can." Yet, as cases of illness and breakdown attest to, this level can also revolt against the self and rob me of my powers over my body. A heart attack will certainly leave me in a state of "I cannot." The organic body is certainly part of the body, but it is something I "have" rather than "am." Finally, there is also a material level, one that can be experienced in the body's resistance toward us, as heavy, dense, or opaque. But this level, too, can turn against us, as the skin is cut open or bones break. This suggests that pain can occur both in the flesh that we are and in the body that we have, that is, in the animal and material body. In short, physical pain can encompass both flesh and blood. Insofar as we are incarnated in all the levels of the body, the suffering self can simultaneously be riveted to the lived body that it has and feel alienated from the way its organic or material levels appear.

Incarnation entails that there is no subjectivity without a lived body. Yet the self cannot be completely identified with its own body: its organs work independent of its will, and its materiality usually supports the ego, but both can turn "in-spite-of-ego." In acute instances, Buytendijk argues that "in pain alone, we actually experience a cleavage in the most natural of all organic unions—that of our personal and physical being." Buytendijk goes on to argue that this cleavage has a direct impact on the self as it results "in a cleavage of the self and the body."[70] In normal cases, the ego is at home in its body to the point that it can take it for granted; the body becomes the transparent medium through which I engage in the world. But as Freud's analysis of the uncanny has highlighted, the home also harbors the unhomely.[71] In pain—or for that matter, in illness, paralysis, and other forms of bodily breakdowns—the self is no longer fully at home. The self undergoes, to employ the Freudian model, the return of repressed deeper levels of the body—ones not external to the self, nor completely familiar to it either. Being in pain, the self is pushed against itself by means of its very embodiment, as if it is at home in an unhomely way. Against the tendency to close the embodied self in an autistic circle of auto-affection, Waldenfels has reminded us of the implication of the Freudian legacy: "Freud's dictum: 'The ego is not master of its own house' means that this foreignness already begins in my own life and in my own body."[72] The fact that we are not fully masters of our own body not only dethrones the ego from its absolute mastery of itself, but also acknowledges the passivity and vulnerability that belong to our incarnation. Pain reminds us that we are at once familiar and strange to ourselves as embodied.

6

Communicating Pain

One reason why philosophy is drawn to the problem of pain is that it seems so clear and concrete, and nonetheless, it gives rise to deep philosophical complexities. We have strong pre-philosophical intuitions of the nature of pain, but closer examination reveals that these intuitions lead in different directions. On the one hand, pain seems to epitomize the private inner realm; for example, when an axe hits my leg, I am filled with intense pain, cut off from all exchange, and imprisoned within myself. On the other hand, pain can manifest itself as immediately intersubjective, as when we instinctively comfort a crying child with a bleeding wound without questioning her internal experience. In the latter case, the pain is unquestionably there, right in our midst. These contrasting intuitions have implications for how we understand the communication of pain.

Let me provide some examples from the literature. It is widely held that pain can isolate us from our shared world. Hannah Arendt observes that among our experiences, bodily pain is "the most private and least communicable of all. . . . There seems to be no bridge from the most radical subjectivity, in which I am no longer 'recognizable,' to the outer world of life."[1] The costs of such separation are that the shared world becomes irrelevant to the sufferer, and the sufferer's subjective states become unrecognizable to others. In a similar vein, Scarry's study of pain begins by noting that whatever "pain achieves, it achieves in part through its unsharability, and it ensures this unsharability through its resistance to language."[2] Both Arendt and Scarry suggest that pain unfolds within a private subjectivity, and that our expressivity and language are not immediately able to lift that experience into intersubjective life. Nonetheless, at times pain can indeed be shared, in gestures, cries, and language; there are even times when it is impossible to ignore others' pain. Following Merleau-Ponty, this may be so because we do not start out as separate beings, but from a primordial intercorporeality from which individuals gradually emerge. Granted such an approach, it is no wonder that we can express and immediately respond to pain—in fact, it is hard to see how the problem of unsharability occurs.[3]

However strong an inclination we feel toward these positions, they cannot both claim to be an exhaustive description. They can, nonetheless, be parts of the more overarching tensions that unfold between our

CHAPTER 6

sense of separateness and relatedness in pain. To my mind, the most adequate philosophical elaboration of the problem of communicating pain is found in Wittgenstein's as well as Scarry's contributions. But since I read these contributions in a phenomenological spirit, I will prepare the ground with a brief look at intersubjective communication in phenomenology, particularly in Merleau-Ponty.

Phenomenology of Communication

One of the challenges that pain brings to philosophy is related to the problem of the other. If we cannot prove the other's inner state, such as pain, skepticism toward the other's mind arises, correlated with solipsism on the side of the ego. But before such doubt arises, there must be something that gives us a preliminary conviction that the other is in pain. What is it that makes us thus convinced? How can pain be signalized at all to others? In analyzing humans as persons immersed in cultural worlds, Husserl points out that our community with one another is established through our expressions. Although I can adopt an attitude to a book as a compilation of papers with written lines, this is hardly how I regard the book. Rather, I pick up a book for the purpose of reading it. Of course, the material support of the book does not vanish, but it will be taken up as part of the book meant for reading.[4] In a related manner, Husserl argues, the other person will not primarily appear as a physical body with a soul somehow connected to it and located on the inside. Instead, the body manifests the spirit by expressing it, in dancing, walking, chatting, discussing, or laughing. To understand another person, one must start from the expressive unity of the other's body: "The apprehension of the man is such that, as 'sense,' it completely penetrates the apprehension of the body."[5] There is nothing hidden or enigmatically connected to the body. The expressive unity of the other belongs to a wider unity of meaning, and to the unity of a communal world.

For Merleau-Ponty too, communication with others is made possible by the inherent expressivity of the body, which always already transcends the biological body. Humans cannot avoid meaning, for even the most primitive behavior "creates meanings which are transcendent in relation to the anatomic apparatus."[6] As verbal language becomes incredibly complex and fine-grained, it remains grafted on the lived body, or more precisely, on the primordial layers of the body with its silent gestures beneath the words. According to Merleau-Ponty, language originates in bodily gestures and develops gradually into verbal signs.[7] The transition from bodily gestures to verbal signs is safeguarded by the fact that meaning is not superimposed but inherent from the start. Just as an angry face does not invoke some hidden idea of anger but manifests the anger itself, gestural words do not invoke translation into inner thought, or what Wittgenstein calls private language, since they realize their own meaning.[8] Language, as an existential mimic, expresses the body's relation to the world and others. This relation to others means that all communication implies mutual exchange: "The communication or comprehension of gestures comes about through the reciprocity of my intentions and the gestures of others, of my gestures and intentions discernible in the conduct of other people. It is as if the other person's intention inhabited my body and mine his."[9]

In order to argue convincingly that such an exchange takes place between separate people, Merleau-Ponty takes the interlocutor, the other, more fully into account. At this point, the old ghost of skepticism reappears. For as long as the meaning we find in the other's gestures and speech is perceived by me and me alone, the question arises whether the other's inner experience is not a mere analogical transference from my own solipsistic experience. Merleau-Ponty's general response to skepticism is a transcendental argument: skeptical doubt already presupposes a pre-reflective relation to what is doubted, or as Merleau-Ponty puts it: "Rationalism and skepticism draw their substance from an actual life of consciousness which they both hypocritically take for granted."[10] In the case of solipsism, the skeptic presupposes a private ego already complete in itself, having others and the world in front of its gaze. If the ego reconstrues or even creates the world, there is no room for another constituting consciousness.[11] However, Merleau-Ponty argues that this neglects the primordial way in which we are initiated into the world in the first place. There is initially neither a pure subject on the one side, nor a pure object on the other, but originally a "third genus of being," a pre-reflective life in which consciousness, body, world, and others are already interlaced. When we come to discover our subjectivity, that subjectivity has already evolved from that prior state. Merleau-Ponty admits that there is some truth in solipsism, for in the end, it is solely the ego that can experience the other. Nevertheless, this ego is not closed in on itself, since the other is already inscribed in the ego from a primordial level. The reflection that the skeptic employs must be reconnected with the pre-reflective experience without which it is empty:

> Solitude and communication cannot be the two horns of a dilemma, but two "moments" of one phenomenon, since in fact other people do exist for me . . . Reflection must in some way present the unreflected,

> otherwise we should have nothing to set over against it, and it would not become a problem for us. Similarly, my experience must in some way present me with other people, since otherwise I should have no occasion to speak of solitude, and could not begin to pronounce other people inaccessible.[12]

By such a move, Merleau-Ponty reverses the thrust of the skeptic argument. The problem is not whether the other exists, but how one can arrive at a skeptical position in the first place. Simply to speak of my solitude dialectically presupposes that there are others from which I come to conceive myself detached. What is true, though, is that others and the world can turn strange and that I can become opaque to myself. For Merleau-Ponty, this is not so much a limitation that confirms solipsism as it is a testimony to our being as incomplete and unfinished. My own opaqueness reminds me of my incompleteness, which again indicates that there is always more to explore in the inexhaustible world of things and other persons. Moreover, my incompleteness also makes me dependent on others and their perspectives on the world in order to become who I am.

From such a point of view, Merleau-Ponty writes that "the perception of other people and the plurality of consciousnesses no longer present any difficulty."[13] A happy solution, to be sure. But is it too happy? Are there no instances where all communication with the other breaks down, in which the other becomes alien, or in which I feel locked into myself? And what about the case of pain? Arendt argues that bodily pain is the most private and least communicable of our experiences; it makes the subject "removed from the world of things and men."[14] Pain seems to put Merleau-Ponty's primordial bond with others and the world to the test. In passing, Merleau-Ponty does in fact mention a similar problem: "If I am forever incapable of effectively living the experience of the scorching the other suffers, the bite of the world as I feel it upon my body is an injury for anyone exposed to it as I am—and especially for the body which begins to defend itself against it."[15] There is no question of my having the other's experience of scorching pain, but I understand the other's gestures nonetheless, both because I am vulnerable to the same pain, a universal feeling ("for anyone exposed to it as I am"), and because I recognize the reactions it causes ("the body which begins to defend itself against it"). But the problem remains, for the feeling I cannot live can well up from the interiority of the other's body in ways that do not affect me. In such cases, the other remains inaccessible and his or her pain unshareable. It is as if skepticism cannot be correct in its account of our general relation to the other, but it nevertheless has captured something essential in the case of pain.

Merleau-Ponty is well aware of instances where things strike us as lacking sense. I can try to read a book and fail to make sense of it. But in such a case, we do not come across something utterly alien to our understanding, for what strikes us as incomprehensible stands out against the background of something we understand. What we often do, Merleau-Ponty points out, is to start reading over again until a certain phrase unlocks the book and leads us to a new understanding. Similarly, in the social world, I can encounter others that I simply cannot make sense of. They will, however, never become completely unintelligible because the conversation can always lead us to new perspectives and new knowledge. We must let the other's speech be "capable of remaking us in his image and to open us to another meaning."[16] The recurring argument Merleau-Ponty makes is similar to what in chapter 3 I argued Husserl is making: in stumbling upon anomalies, strangeness, or brokenness, there is always a way to integrate the foreign into an overarching familiarity, or in Merleau-Ponty's case, to broaden the horizon of the understanding. In short, for Merleau-Ponty, communication seems never to be radically broken, since it invariably leads back to a common soil of intercorporeality. According to such view, language "*is no longer a means; it is a manifestation, a revelation of intimate being and the psychic link which unites us to the world and our fellow men.*"[17] However, does this fully capture the communication of pain? Can the intimacy and unity with others be portrayed in a way that doesn't allow for the breakdown of communication? Might not pain also involve a profound sense of isolation? I find Merleau-Ponty's account lacking in its representation of the tension between our commonality and separateness, particularly in the context of communicating pain.

Privacy of Pain

There must be a shared foundation that makes understanding and communication possible. I believe Merleau-Ponty and Wittgenstein shed light on this in overlapping yet distinct ways. However, Merleau-Ponty's account leaves little room for the skeptical experience of *solus ipse*, either in the sense of being sealed within one's own experience or others being shut out from it. While we typically communicate without issues, there are experiences that are difficult to convey, and it is these difficulties that motivate skepticism. Although the skeptical conclusion may be extreme, it seems to stem from rather common experiences: experiences like pain, Arendt claims, fuel the distrust of the world in all modern skepticism.[18] That does not rule out the shareable communication of pain, but it suggests that such communication implies both our connectedness as well as our separateness. Both must be given due philosophical attention to achieve a satisfactory account of the complexity of communicating pain. Bernstein argues that undergoing extreme pain parallels the typical skeptic argument. Descartes's initial skepticism entails doubt of the outer world, coupled with the certainty of the thinking ego, which mirrors the way pain renders the world a more or less irrelevant background, while it makes the self unavoidably present to itself. Hence, pain seems to be absolutely present to myself but absent for others, just as the skeptic assumes.[19] Yet, there is something exaggerated in such a skeptical interpretation of pain, for instance in the way it draws a general conclusion of other minds from the particular case of pain. Besides, there are certainly also ways in which pain can be expressed and responded to by others. Can we grant skepticism at least some truths without denying the other? And if so, can we strike a balance between privacy and the claim to community?[20]

Scarry draws attention to the peculiar split between the sufferer's sense of pain's reality and its unreality for other persons. In her view, experienced pain seems to be the paradigmatic case of what certainty amounts to. Scarry writes:

> So, for the person in pain, so incontestably and unnegotiably present is it that "having pain" may come to be thought of as the most vibrant example of what it is to "have certainty," while for the other person it is so elusive that "hearing about pain" may exist as the primary model of what it is "to have doubt." This pain comes unsharably into our midst as at once that which cannot be denied and that which cannot be confirmed.[21]

The skeptic argument returns, now as mapping out the asymmetry of my certainty in contrast to the doubt of others. As pain enters our common life, it is destined to oscillate between presence and absence, between what cannot be denied and what cannot be confirmed. Following Scarry, pain manifests itself to the sufferer as essentially unsharable and private. Unsurprisingly, such unsharability bears on the relationship between pain and language—or rather the lack thereof. Language's failure to capture pain is for Scarry not due to the scarcity of our vocabulary for expressing pain, but due to how pain resists assimilation into words. "Its resistance to language," Scarry writes, "is not simply one of its incidental or accidental attributes but is essential to what it is."[22] Even so, Scarry will eventually argue that pain can get lifted into shareable language, but only by employing metaphors. But why claim that pain essentially resists language in the first place?

Scarry's argument relies on an assumption that is similar to the phenomenological notion of intentionality. Going over the field of different modes of intentionality, physical pain stands out as a remarkable exception. Like Levinas and Henry before her, Scarry points out the strange lack of intentionality in pain, as it has no referential content. Pain is not about anything. Precisely because it takes no objects, pain resists language more than any other phenomenon.[23] The lack of intentional object does not make pain empty, however, for pain comes with a strong sense of affective presence—an undeniable, aversive presence even.

Apparently, Scarry's account flies in the face of many of Wittgenstein's most famous insights into the grammar of pain and the impossibility of private language, at least according to mainstream analytic readings. And of course, critical responses to Scarry based on such Wittgensteinian readings have not been lacking.[24] Scarry's split between pain's presence to the sufferer and its absence to others seems to fit well as the target of Wittgenstein's remark: "Only I can know whether I am really in pain; another person can only surmise it," to which Wittgenstein's correcting voice immediately replies: "In one way this is false, and in another nonsense."[25] The reason why this is nonsense seems to be that knowledge concerns empirical propositions or any statement that can be believed, denied, or doubted, according to publicly available procedures, whereas my own sense of being in pain cannot qualify as knowledge in this sense at all. The grammar of pain does not concern knowledge, doubt, or surmise. To hold that the first person knows his pain, must consequently rely on some form of a grammatical illusion.[26]

What about the resistance of language—does not Scarry, here too, come close to the illusion of a private language, locking the experience along with its private meaning into a realm inaccessible to the outside? She seems to say that ordinary public language does not reach into the opacity of pain. And yet, Scarry has been able to write a whole book on pain, not just about its shareable metaphors, but about the nature of pain made accessible to her audience. Regardless of whether she draws on her own pain experience or those of others, pain cannot be entirely severed from shareable language. Perhaps Scarry is imagining that, despite pain's resistance to public language, an inner procedure makes it possible to connect the private experience of pain to a private language. But in that case, Wittgenstein points out, it will become impossible to identify and distinguish pain from other experiences, since such identification lacks the publicly available criteria for the application of the words. In this case, a right application of a word is nothing but what seems to be right. However, since we do have ways of expressing and speaking about pain, there must be a public application of pain language, some form of manifestations that make it meaningful and shareable.[27]

CHAPTER 6

Scarry takes one step further as she writes: "Physical pain does not simply resist language but actively destroys it, bringing about an immediate reversion to a state anterior to language, to the sounds and cries a human being makes before language is learned."[28] Again, we find something at once resembling and yet at odds with Wittgenstein's remarks on the language of pain. Wittgenstein also highlights the sounds, cries, and other reactions that children exhibit before acquiring language, but he does so not to illustrate a regression from linguistic meaning, but rather its progression—or, more accurately, how the language of pain initially develops:

> How does a human being learn the meaning of names of sensations?
> For example, of the word "pain"? Here is one possibility: words are connected with the primitive, natural, expressions of sensation and used in their place. A child has hurt himself and he cries; then adults talk to him and teach him exclamations and later, sentences. They teach the child new pain-behaviour.[29]

For Wittgenstein, primitive pain behavior serves as the foundation from which a child can enter the language of pain, while for Scarry, such preverbal behavior attests to the breakdown of language. The issue at stake here is the different perspectives on the role primitive reactions play in our lives with words. For Wittgenstein, meaning appears to be rooted in pre-linguistic reactions and expressions, from which it evolves into far more complex practices that are tied up with language. This supports Merleau-Ponty's notion that language arrives late, having already been prepared by bodily habits and gestures.[30] In contrast, Scarry contends that primitive pain behavior demonstrates that we are stripped of our language, having reached a state of muteness of bodily movements and inarticulate sounds.

Pain behavior is, of course, not always accompanied by words, for there are occasions of sudden, intense pain that do not allow for anything but inarticulate cries. But such outcries are also expressive of pain. The grammar we learn as we enter language involves different expressions, from sounds and gestures to words, embedded in particular situations. However, Wittgenstein points out that the others' response to pain is as much a part of the grammar of pain as the first person's utterances. "It is a help here to remember that it is a primitive reaction to tend, to treat, the part that hurts when *someone else* is in pain; and not merely when oneself is."[31] Thus, Wittgenstein emphasizes that the grammar of pain encompasses primitive reactions of both the sufferer and bystanders. The other's response to pain might take different forms, such as giving attention, patting on the shoulder, or comforting.[32] These different responses are various ways in which pain is acknowledged. Acknowledgment, as Stanley Cavell has argued, is not about knowledge understood as certainty (sufficient evidence and reasons). Acknowledgment goes beyond such knowledge, both in the sense that it relates to expressions that reveal something about a person, and in the sense that it entails a personal response to that expression. I must, Cavell says, be aware that "your suffering makes a *claim* on me. It is not enough that I *know* (am certain) that you suffer—I must do or reveal something (whatever can be done). In a word, I must *acknowledge* it, otherwise, I do not know what '(you or his) being in pain' means."[33] Far from directing ourself to an objective body, we respond to a person; and far from being a matter of epistemic conviction, the conviction is revealed in our response. One might, for instance, show pity: "Pity, one may say, is one form of being convinced that someone else is in pain."[34] Such an account shifts the ground significantly away from Scarry's narrow focus on the privacy of pain, toward many aspects of our natural and cultural shared form of life, from primitive expressions to different responses.

Publicness of Pain

If Scarry's account of pain depicts it as too private, one can suspect that Wittgenstein ends up making it too public, as if primitive reactions take care of the entire communication and the pain itself drops out. "Aren't you nevertheless a behaviourist in disguise? Aren't you nevertheless basically saying that everything except human behaviour is a fiction?" Wittgenstein quickly discards this charge as a misconception, since he is not denying the experience of pain but mapping how its grammar works and how philosophy often fail to attend to it: "If I speak of a fiction, then it is a *grammatical* fiction."[35] But even if there is no question of denying pain experience, it remains the case that our primitive pain reactions, such as outcries, sobbing, or groaning, can express us beyond our will and intentions. Despite all her distrust of the linguistic transmission of pain, Scarry is correct in holding that loss of control and integrity belong to the grammar of pain. Our primitive reactions bypass our demands for integrity and dignity and give ourselves away in a potentially shameful and obscene manner. Scarry argues that this is part of the workings of torture. In undergoing torture, the victim is at the same time invaded and exposed, indeed, turned inside out: "This dissolution of the boundary between inside and outside gives rise to . . . an almost obscene conflation of private and public. It brings with it all the solitude of absolute privacy with none of its safety, all the self-exposure of the utterly public with none of its possibility for camaraderie and shared experience."[36] According to Scarry's analysis, torture is designed to exploit the grammar of pain in order to deprive the victim first of their community with others, and second, of their integrity and privacy. All that remains is pain behavior exposing the victim beyond control.

If one focuses on the overarching structure of Wittgenstein's so-called private language argument, which is usually taken to span over more than seventy paragraphs in *Philosophical Investigations,* one sees how it moves the reader from one extreme to the other, from regarding pain as a private sensation to regarding pain as utterly public, punctured with transitory moments of clarity and relief.[37] It starts with the conviction that only I know that I am in pain and that a private language is the only language that can pick out pain with certainty. Once such convictions of the inner break down, we are led outward, to public criteria, to visible bodies, and manifestations of behavior. But from this position, the inner seems only to evaporate. How should we come to terms with our separateness as well as relatedness? Sensitive to the complexity of the situation, Cavell offers this perspective:

> It is felt that Wittgenstein's view makes language too public, that it cannot do justice to the control I have over what I say, to the innerness of my meaning. But my wonder . . . is rather how he can arrive at the completed and unshakable edifice of shared language from within such apparently fragile and intimate moments—private moments—as our separate counts and out-calls of phenomena.[38]

In this passage, Cavell questions the common view that Wittgenstein denies any sense of privacy, and instead affirms the complete publicness of language. Cavell interprets Wittgenstein as taking private moments for granted in order to investigate how we nevertheless arrive at a shared language. This perspective reopens the question of the relationship between separateness and relatedness that lies at the heart of Wittgenstein's philosophy. For does Wittgenstein really deny all senses of privacy?

There is, no doubt, a sense of defining sensations privately, along with a cluster of pictures that go with them, which for Wittgenstein pass for grammatical illusions. But since such illusions are so hard to get rid of, couldn't that be because they spring forth from a strong intuition of something valuable to us, something that we want to preserve within philosophy? Is there not, as Scarry says, a sense that I, in contradistinction to others, know that I am in pain? At this point, it is crucial to recognize that Wittgenstein does not so much deny all senses of privacy as ask in what sense sensations are private. He writes: "It cannot be said of me at all (except perhaps as a joke) that I *know* I'm in pain. What is it supposed to mean—except perhaps that I *am* in pain?"[39] My relation to my pain is clearly not one of knowledge construed as the subject's privileged access to a quasi-objective fact of an inner realm. But there is still another way of knowing my pain, Wittgenstein suggests, one that simply means "I'm in pain." Such a statement does have an important use—say, in some form of confession or acknowledgment when asked.

When Wittgenstein asks "in what sense" sensations are private, there is indeed a sense, for the saying "sensations are private" is comparable to the saying "one plays patience by oneself."[40] One may read Wittgenstein as saying that "sensations are private" is pointless and empty, for the parallel definition of patience (i.e., solitaire) seems at best trivial. A more charitable reading takes Wittgenstein to be reminding us of what we usually imply when we say that sensations are private. Accordingly, the point is that for both sensations and patience, the first-person perspective is inextricably interwoven with its use. Just as the player of patience has a different role if playing cards with others, so do sensations play another role in the first-person perspective than in the second- or third-person perspective.[41] That another cannot have my pain is not so much a limitation imposed on us as a constitutive feature of the communicative situation between me and the other. Moreover, the remark about playing patience alone sheds light on a different sense of privacy than the picture that dominates the image of the private linguist. To point out that playing patience is done alone is not to deny its dependence on the common institution of playing cards with others. Similarly, to claim that sensations are private is not to deny that the words we employ in expressing pain presuppose the common practice of the shared language.

From such a perspective, it makes sense to say that pain is not only undergone privately, by me, affecting my flesh and blood. But it can also leave us in a position where the shared language and all our expressive resources fail to provide the desired understanding—a possibility that I find marginalized in Merleau-Ponty's account. Feeling impotent, unable to share how it is with me, is a terrifying experience of isolation, for in such cases, we are not acknowledged by others. As Scarry pointedly writes: "the lack of acknowledgement and recognition becomes a second form of negation and rejection, the social equivalent of the physical aversiveness."[42] What I am getting at is this: apparently contrary to Scarry, there must be an obvious public dimension to pain, but then she does not, at least not consistently, deny this, given that she believes that pain can expose us to others in unwelcomed ways. And conversely, apparently contrary to what Wittgenstein holds, there seems to be some sort of privacy to pain, but then neither does Wittgenstein deny this; what he denies is a particular philosophical conclusion drawn from it. What is public and shareable is not just verbal articulations, but must also embrace the meaningfulness of our most primitive gestures, reactions, and outcries. What is misleading in Scarry's account is that she starts from a real experience of isolation in pain and goes on to propose a picture where pain is surrounded by epistemological barriers, which implies that while the first person has perfect access to pain, others' access is inexorably infused with skepticism. However, pain is private in the sense of always being subjectively given, which is not necessarily a barrier, but rather the condition for what we can intelligibly understand as a human relatedness in pain, a relatedness across separation. Relatedness and community run incredibly deep, but they do not prevent us from falling out of the community or experiencing the breakdown of communication and acknowledgment. There are cases where words and our expressivity fail to reach the other, and it is in these instances, and only in these, that we must grant skepticism a limited truth.

Job's Broken Dialogue with His Friends

The problem of communicating pain is not a discovery of twentieth-century philosophy, but has occupied literary texts for a long time. I want to illustrate and elaborate on this problem by paying attention to some aspects of the biblical book of Job. The choice of the book of Job might seem strange, since much of its reception history has revolved around its dramatization of the problem of evil, or more precisely, of innocent suffering in the face of God.[43] While I will not deny the legitimacy of such reading, I will focus here on some less obvious features of the text. I will contend that the evil Job is confronted with primarily strikes him as physical pain, and that the focus on pain will shed new light on the nature of the strange dialogue between Job and his friends, and more particularly on why that dialogue rarely seems to reach mutual understanding.

Why claim that Job's most pressing suffering has the character of physical pain? In the prologue of the book of Job, it is worth noting that Satan strikes twice. In order to prove that Job is far from the righteous servant God takes him to be, Satan is granted the opportunity to test Job. First, he deprives Job of all his possessions, his livestock, and his children, but this time God forbids Satan to stretch out his arm and touch Job himself. Satan's first ordeal is of no avail; Job tears his robe, shaves his head, and falls on the ground to worship God, saying: "Naked I came from my mother's womb, and naked shall I return there; the LORD gave, and the LORD has taken away; blessed be the name of the LORD" (Job 1:21). For all the deprivation and all the sorrow it brought, it did not alter Job's relation to God. It is with the second stroke that Satan is allowed to stretch out his arm against Job himself, and the story takes a dramatic turn: "But stretch out your hand now," Satan says to the Lord, "and touch his bone and his flesh, and he will curse you to your face" (2:5). Satan is allowed to touch Job in his bodily existence, inflicting him with aching sores from head to foot (2:7, compare 13:21, 30:21). Of course, the infliction of pain may be taken as just another blow, a blow that makes the total amount of suffering too much for Job, to which he consequently reacts with a mixture of resignation, despair, and protest.

There is, nevertheless, something about the very physicality of his pain that calls out Job's response.[44] It is evidently first when Satan strikes Job with painful sores that the drama takes off. Despite the fact that classical Jewish and early Christian commentaries read the book as a story of the patient hero, much speaks for the opposite. True, Job remains patient and pious after the first attack, but that alters significantly after the second: Job cannot stand the pain that afflicts him for no reason; he starts to cry to God. There seems to be something particularly unbearable about physical pain, which perhaps Satan has suspected all along. As David B. Morris comments: "People can accept the loss of external goods, Satan reasons, but intense pain suffered within our own bodies is finally unacceptable and unendurable."[45]

Job's remaining family and friends initially react in fear to his disease, because they probably see it, as Job himself would otherwise see it, as a stigma of impurity, one form of punishment that attests to former sins (6:21). Or perhaps they fear the intolerable truth that all flesh is susceptible to pain and mortality. It is, therefore, better to cling to the cover story of punishment for transgressions instead.[46] But in Job's case, as the reader knows, it does not add up, for Job is righteous and innocent (1:1, 9:15, 9:20). Or perhaps Job does, at this phase of the drama, share their presuppositions, only to find himself the exception. His growing feeling of utter isolation is enhanced by the fact that his case does not fit into the unbreakable logic of the Law: he has been righteous but still he suffers. Because the exception can no longer appeal to the shared scheme of the worldly and divine order, Job's situation would lead us to assume that he should remain silent, shut into his privacy. But this is not how the story goes. It is his friends who are initially silent. For seven days and seven nights they keep quiet, "for they saw that his suffering was very great" (2:13). It is in fact Job who breaks the silence: "After this Job opened his mouth and cursed the day of his birth" (3:1). It is as though he *must* speak, even though the intelligibility of what he says cannot rely on shared frames and orders. His initial speech is like a primitive reaction transformed into articulated cries that push forth, pressing out, literally, as ex-pressions. Despite the difficulty of conveying his agony, Job goes on expressing himself—as if the nature of his suffering itself demands expressions, such as complaints, curses, and protestations. But what is it about the pain that Job finds so unendurable? What is its nature?

In the poetic discourse of the dialogues in the book of Job, the expressions of pain will first and foremost surface as metaphorical speech, in line with Scarry's understanding of expressions of pain. A minimal requirement of a metaphor is that it unites at least two otherwise separable semantic fields and creates new meaning in the tension between their dissimilarity and similarity.[47] In the present text, the metaphors draw on the tensions and similarities between Job's pain and various objects of the shared world. The particular fragility of metaphors in the region of pain lies in the fact that one of the two semantic fields draws on the first-person experience. This means that an understanding of the metaphors calls for special empathy on the side of the listeners. But pain has a public aspect too, which is shown through behavior or is related to visible marks on the body. The text suggests that Job's pain is caused by some kind of skin disease: loathsome sores from head to toe, blisters that harden and break out again, and skin turning black (2:7, 7:5, 30:30). It is, however, beside the point to insist on the disease's physiological nature, for the text does not display any interest in its etiology. What matters is the pain that is lived through and how Job constantly strives for its possible articulations. The point of holding on to the putative fact of his skin disease is to keep the reader aware of the nature of both poles of the metaphors: although the book will evoke storms, weapons, strokes, stabbing, and so on, these are to be taken as expressive of qualities of Job's pain.

Arguably, the most central metaphor for pain in the book of Job is the arrow. It is, for instance, evoked by his friend Zophar: "a bronze arrow will strike [you] through" (20:24), and by Job: "he set me up as his target; his archers surround me" (16:12, see also 6:4, 7:20). The metaphor of the arrow is not only significant because it is often invoked or alluded to, but more importantly, because it implies a phenomenology of pain. Being hit by an arrow captures the passivity in which the suffering Job finds himself: Job never invokes or welcomes pain. Pain as such is aversive, and therefore not something that anyone would naturally want. Consequently, pain is not actively achieved but is coming over Job, or according to the metaphor of the arrow, is something hitting him. Being hit, moreover, corresponds to the feeling of being hit from outside, which does not necessarily designate a spatial externality or external cause, for as has been repeatedly pointed out, severe pain does not refer to its cause—it has no reference at all. The externality of the arrow is the flip side of Job's passivity; it signifies an excess that arrives beyond the sufferer's own will and control. This arrival from the outside is a sign of the strange power that pain executes over and against Job, before he can resist, give in to, deny, or affirm it. The way the text portrays pain as a weapon that acts on Job is not exceptional in the grammar of pain. As Scarry has pointed out, it is rather the rule: pain is often metaphorically spoken of in ways that invoke weapons as well as their inner agency.[48] Despite the arrow's arrival from outside of Job's control, the suffering of pain essentially belongs to the interiority of his lived body. The arrow hits him from outside, leaves him passive against its workings, pierces through Job's borders, and thrusts itself into his living self: "For the arrows of the Almighty are in me" (6:4).

Admittedly, the expressions of pain witnessed in the book of Job do not merely take the form of metaphorical speech, but additionally through what Wittgenstein calls primitive reactions, such as bodily contractions, sweat, lack of breath, and cries. But for the speaking animal that Job is, pain is primarily articulated verbally. Acute pain is hard to convey by words; it gives rise to the feeling that our words do not reach all the way into the concrete phenomenon in question. With reference to the book of Job, Donn Welton points out pain's isolating effect: "There is a splitting, special to disease and suffering, which isolates the person and effects a reduction of their existence to their afflicted flesh, even beyond their 'bone' (2:5). This is the state in which the soul becomes lost in a body that threatens to devour it."[49] This sense of isolation consists in feeling trapped in the body, but the most marked way it cuts the sufferer off from the community is by the impotence of expressive speech. No doubt, pain can isolate the sufferer from the speaking community, but it is also a state in which the desire for community is at its most urgent and is made most intimate where it succeeds. It is the threat of isolation and longing for community that lies behind David Biro's observation that there is "no other setting where the absence of language is so terrifying and the need for it so urgent."[50] Job's pain is certainly expressed and meant to be acknowledged, but the tormenting fact for him is that he is not understood, or at least not properly acknowledged.

If communicating pain is so hard, why does Job speak in the first place? The pain leaves Job with questions, such as: "Why have you made me your target?" (7:20), that is to say: "why me?" Such questions seem to stem from the phenomenon of pain itself, not because it leaves us with an epistemic puzzle to be solved, but because pain arrives as a call that awaits an answer. Yet pain does not provide any answers; it provokes the

CHAPTER 6

question to which all responses are doomed to come too late. And yet, the call demands an answer in the way it singles Job out for no reason. It is true that his friends provide him with all kinds of theological explanations. But the grammar of Job's "why?" does not seek explanations, for Job knows that ordinary explanations cannot really satisfy him, especially not the kind of explanations provided by his friends: "If you would only keep silent," Job replies to his friends, "that would be your wisdom!" (13:5). The "why?" is like an empty intention that no longer awaits its fulfillment, but still must continue to resound as long as the suffering lasts. Although he rejects insufficient replies and suspects that no replies will do, Job keeps raising his questions throughout the dialogue.

Job's lack of satisfaction with answers is just one aspect of the dialogue between him and his friends. On the face of it, it is not the case that pain is the central theme of the dialogue. It seems to revolve around various aspects of the appropriateness or inappropriateness of Job's suffering with regard to God and the Law, particularly the possibility of an exception to the unbreakable logic of transgression and punishment inscribed in divine justice. It is, however, beneath the thematic level, in its underlying structure, that we can discern how pain animates the dialogue. In Socratic dialogues, there are misunderstandings, confrontations, and corrections, but always on the horizon of mutual understanding and in pursuit of a deeper understanding. No such development can be traced in these dialogues. Job and his friends seem unable to get across to each other, not, however, because they are initially reluctant to engage or because they are strangers to one another—they are, after all, friends. Instead, it is as if everything the friends utter fails to bring anything significantly new, or at least it is not sufficiently in touch with what Job holds to be the problem. As Job puts it: "What you know, I also know; I am not inferior to you," or, "Who does not know such things as these?" (13:2, 12:3). It is as if Job and his friends do not discuss in an ordinary sense, since normally, opposing views presuppose a common framework for the discussion. But here, they are not really addressing each other's views at all, and it is not even clear that they reply to one another. Thus, there is a striking lack of reciprocity between questions and responses, and no clear progress in terms of mutual learning. Why this lack of recognition and progress? Why such strangely broken dialogue?

The first clue is given at the beginning of the friends' reproach, as they argue that Job himself has patiently guided others in their suffering: "But now," Eliphas says, "it has come to you, and you are impatient; it touches you, and you are dismayed" (4:5). The friends accuse him of inconsistency that, as Kant has made clear, is typical of an individual's immoral responses to the Law: Job affirms the Law, but makes an exception of himself. Strange as it seems, Job will later turn the same argument against his friends, this time making it the reason for their failure to understand him: "I also could talk as you do, if you were in my place; I could join words against you, and shake my head at you" (16:4). In other words, the accusations of transgressing the Law are intelligible from a second- and third-person's perspective, and if the discussion solely concerned these perspectives, no disagreement would occur. For Job, however, it is not at all a matter of such perspectives, for his problem appears in his own first-person's perspective, and the latter is exactly what Job takes the friends not to recognize. This is where the separateness in pain becomes relevant: the experience of pain can be expressed, but the first person is the only one undergoing it. It is not so much that the friends' words or considerations are unintelligible to Job, but that those words do not acknowledge his suffering; they even avoid it. At times Job feels the powerlessness of language as such: "If I speak, my pain is not assuaged, and if I forbear, how much of it leaves me?" (16:6). Through the course of the dialogue, Job's sense of isolation and powerlessness constantly grows.

The friends do not sideline suffering and God's part in it, but they will invariably be speaking *about* God, in juridical, philosophical, or theological terms. They put forward various explanations of Job's suffering in terms of the unbreakable wheel of justice, at times underpinned by reference to truth and wisdom professed by the ancient fathers (8:8, 15:18), or more theologically, the fallible human condition in contrast to the inscrutable nature of God (3:17, 15:15–16, chap. 25). While these are certainly meant to shed light on the suffering that Job undergoes, they are all matters of theoretical considerations. But Job, being hit by the arrow, has no patience for theoretical considerations about God. Being in a state of pain, he will primarily respond by expressing how things are with him, or by referring to the place from which the arrow at least seems to originate—from God. Hence, at crucial points, Job changes the discourse; turning away from his friends' discourse about God, he starts addressing himself directly *to* God:[51] "Only grant two things to me, then I will not hide myself from your face: withdraw your hand far from me, and do not let dread of you terrify me. Then call, and I will answer or let me speak, and you reply to me" (13:20–22). The externality implied in pain is conceived as a divine "You" from beyond the world. Whereas the inner development of the story significantly bears on the way Job comes to alter his understanding of God, the point, for now, is that such a You at the core of Job's concerns is not what the friends speak about. Pain leaves no room for disengaged reason.

The profound mismatch between the interlocutors, I will hold, has its roots in the nature of the phenomenon of pain. While expressions of pain—their primitive as well as their linguistic expressions—are publicly available, they of course will not convey the sensations and affections of pain undergone in the sufferer's body. As Wittgenstein points out, the subjective character of the phenomenon of pain is not so much a limitation as part of its grammar: we play patience alone.[52] If there is no subject having pain, then it is not a matter of pain. And conversely, if all shared the same experience of pain, the language game of pain would simply not play the role it does in our intersubjective lives. Since the friends do not have Job's pain as subjectively given to them, it is obviously possible to ignore it, as Scarry has pointed out.

While the friends are not modern skeptics who doubt Job's inner state, they still flee the way it addresses them, deflecting it and turning the question in other directions. Whether their theodicies are meant as consolation or not is less important, for in effect, none of their talks respond to Job's suffering. In not acknowledging the state he is in, they fail to offer relatedness in his separation; that is, a sense of sharing his privacy, such as careful listening and responding in kind. But there are also reasons to believe that Job is unable to respond properly to the gestures of his friends. He is filled with affliction (10:15), which means that the world will fade into a more or less undifferentiated background without relevance to him. Philippe Nemo claims that the impact of physical pain has the power to deprive words of their usual sense. From Job's perspective, the friends become distant figures: "Job's friends look like characters trapped in a silent film: Job cannot understand what they say, and uselessly addresses them with words they do not understand, although they hold fast to the mistaken belief that they can read his lips."[53]

Nemo, much like Scarry, goes too far in insisting on the total breakdown of communication of pain, which is strange in the context of the book of Job, since one of the text's finest achievements is its poetic articulations of pain. It is true that pain puts signification and communication under extreme pressure, not, I will say, because the words are devoid of semantic meaning, but because the point of addressing such words, their real relevance and aptness, has become distorted. But again, why? On the one hand, there are primitive reactions as well as linguistic expressions that should make Job's pain conveyable to his friends, and conversely, his friends' utterances are in principle accessible to Job. This leads to a further assumption, namely that their blindness to one another is not so much due to linguistic or perceptual limitations as it is to an active imposition of ignorance.[54] To follow Cavell's lead, for a sufferer to insist that a private language is incomprehensible to others is a strategy to deepen one's separation from the other by avoiding letting oneself be exposed to them. This is hardly descriptive of Job's position because he relentlessly tries to express his suffering and asks for recognition. On the other side, applied to his friends, the Cavellian perspective seems to fit. Their speeches appear like a clever way to mask the fact that they are avoiding acknowledging Job's pain. Job's case is not threatening because it drives a wedge into the moral universe and the just God—the friends are not lacking explanations—but because it exposes them to the fragility of the human and the human community.

To engage in the dialogue—a real dialogue where the parties acknowledge one another—would mean to be exposed to one another, confessing, and responding to feelings of pain. It would mean engaging in a dialogue where communication is particularly fragile: Job's way of expressing himself can fail to reach out to his friends, and the friends' response might fail to reach into him as significant, consoling, understanding. Normally, we take for granted our intersubjective world and our shared sense of language, but in communication of pain, these become problematic. The shareability of pain has no guarantee as it is torn between separateness and relatedness. But that fact makes its demands all the more urgent and the outcome possibly more valuable. What the book of Job demonstrates is how the breakdown in communicating pain might rely on the incapacity to stand the tension between acknowledged separation and a willingness to extend our relatedness.[55]

Pain Expression and Secondary Sense

The broken dialogue running through significant parts of the book of Job highlights how pain at once pushes forward to expression and solicits acknowledgment in return, along with the costs of its failure to do so. It also lays bare the fragility of communicating in these regions of human experience, since the relevant words can always fail to reach out to others and others can fail to acknowledge the person in pain. While the continuity between bodily reactions and verbal expressions is particularly visible in the case of pain, verbal language certainly provides the richest and most nuanced expressions. I want to return to Wittgenstein's perspective in order to explore the conditions for such a subtle language.

When *Philosophical Investigations* introduces the role of primitive reactions and pain behavior in learning the word "pain," it is worth noting that Wittgenstein is not putting forth theses.[56] Starting his account with "Here is one possibility: words are connected with the primitive, natural, expressions of sensation and used in their place,"[57] Wittgenstein notes that he will not present a theory about learning the use of the word "pain."

CHAPTER 6

The suggested example is meant to counter the way we otherwise tend to be pulled too quickly toward certain philosophical theories. However, one interesting aspect of the possibility Wittgenstein suggests is that primitive reactions are replaced, implying, I assume, that pain behavior will be differentiated, nuanced, and enriched as it becomes grafted onto linguistic expressions. For Merleau-Ponty, habits and expressive gestures are the pre-linguistic ground from which language evolves, but it is also crucial to maintain the inherent link between speech and gestures. Speech does not translate ready-made thoughts into external signs, but gives expression by means of "*gestural meaning* which is immanent in speech."[58] In the appropriate context, this gestural meaning manifests immediately. Wittgenstein adds that the language game of pain expression is remarkably flexible, rather than being controlled by a fixed set of rules.[59] There is no doubt that primitive reactions are decisive for bridging pain to shared language, but these reactions soon run out. Humans need to advance to a more subtle language, because our feeling of sharing privacy depends on whether we find the right words expressive of our exact state and whether others recognize those expressions in turn. This rests on the ability to find oneself and others finely attuned in language.

Arguably, Wittgenstein is sensitive to the fragility of communicating pain and how it transcends more conventional speech. Expressing pain does not stop with the replacement of reactions by words, but extends along different routes into the flexible expressive means of human language, with its manifold registers and various pitches. Communicating pain is more than just signalizing pain. It is often conveyed in a fine-tuned language that captures, or seeks to capture, the particular shade of the state in question. The trope of "fine shades of behaviour" keeps recurring in the second part of Wittgenstein's *Investigations*, where he tries to make sense of the immediacy as well as the nuanced sensitivity of how we respond to what we experience. From one philosophical angle, these fine shades in our responses seem hardly worthy of attention, since they do not deal directly with classical epistemological questions. Yet from Wittgenstein's perspective, they are held to have very important consequences.[60] One way in which such fine shades of behavior are important is the manner in which they are inherent in how we respond to other persons' facial expressions. Wittgenstein notes:

> Consciousness in another's face. Look into someone else's face, and see the consciousness in it, and a particular *shade* of consciousness. You see on it, in it, joy, indifference, interest, excitement, torpor and so on. The light in other people's faces.[61]

COMMUNICATING PAIN

In looking at the joy or indifference in another's face, there is no question of Husserl's analogical apperception, if that is a transfer from my case to others, nor do I arrive at the other's state of mind as a conclusion based on patterns of behavior. There are no inferences. "Think of the recognition of *facial expressions*," Wittgenstein suggests, and points out: "[it] does not consist in giving the measurement of the face."[62] Yet we immediately perceive them. In the same way, Merleau-Ponty insists that facial expressions do not demand inferences, as if there were a psychic fact behind the gesture; "The gesture *does not make me think* of anger, it is anger itself."[63] If we need to speak of evidence, it must be evidence of another order, namely what Wittgenstein calls the "imponderable evidence" betrayed in "subtleties of glance, of gesture, and of tone."[64] Judgment and discernment in this region can be learned, but not by taking classes. A person who masters such a form of judgment might be able to give hints to others, but not much more. But what about the rules of the language game? "There are also rules, but they do not form a system, and only experienced people can apply them rightly."[65] Rules seem to be of derivative importance for the game of expressing and understanding the pain of the other. Discerning the other's pain seems to take some other form of learning through life experience. Almost in a Wittgensteinian style, Merleau-Ponty sums this up nicely: "But conventions are a late form of relationship between men; they presuppose an earlier means of communication, and language must be put back into this current of intercourse."[66]

Since linguistic expressions of different states, such as pain, do not follow rules, we cannot expect words to work the same way as they otherwise do. Scarry notes that there are attempts to capture utterances of pain in systems, such as the McGuill Pain Questionnaire elaborated by Ronald Melzack as a diagnostic tool. This account of typical words used for pain—such as throbbing, burning, pulsing, pinching, pressing—is systematized according to different parameters. The philosophical gain of such an account is limited, since the parameters do not establish a foundation but are rather based on the already existing language used by patients.[67] Despite its rigidity and lack of inventive plasticity, the McGuill Pain Questionnaire does suggest one important thing about pain language: whereas there is a great variety in our expressions of pain that can be stretched in various directions, it implies that somehow there exists an agreement about their meaning.[68]

Admittedly, expressions of pain can be stereotypical and conventional, but the possibility of new linguistic inventions and the plasticity of their use suggest that conventions are not constitutive, but the end products of a spontaneous ability to bring our inner life into subtle language.

CHAPTER 6

Novel metaphors of pain do occur, and it takes a remarkable capacity to bring one semantic field into relation to another in an immediate and striking way. When it succeeds, it has the ability to capture the exactness of an experience, for the subject as well as for the other. The richness of Job's expressions is an illustrative case in point. In these cases, we are far removed from the private linguist who attempts to secure an unbreakable bond between sensations and words for him- or herself. We are instead in a region of our language where we can arrive at a shared understanding in the absence of fixed conventions and rules. In such absence, the shareability of new and subtle expressions of pain must presuppose something at once more fragile and yet deeper. We are not depending on agreements of words and reference, of rules and application, but on something beneath all that: a deep attunement to one another.[69] To be able to use words in new ways and still make sense, we must master all the intricate paths and patterns with which those words are usually tied up. To recognize pain as a piercing arrow takes such things as knowing what experiences these words normally convey, the interest and value they have for us, the different contexts of application and related practices; in short, what Wittgenstein calls our forms of life. From within such a shared form of life, we can start to see how we can improvise in languages beyond rules.

For the language of pain to signify what it does, Wittgenstein suggests that we must recognize its distinctive place in that life: "The concept of pain is characterized by its particular function in our life. Pain has *this* position in our life; *these* connections."[70] The functions and connections in a particular region of our life will over time be assimilated into the words with which they are involved. As we continue using words, they tend to store the implications of their use that go with them. This sedimentation shapes words' feel and quality, and due to their particular feel and quality we can project them into new contexts—in contexts where no fixed application is prescribed. Poets celebrate this possibility, and people in pain employ it, and so did the authors of the book of Job.

What we draw upon when we feel the impact of words in this way is what Wittgenstein refers to as a "secondary sense" where we can "experience the meaning of words."[71] To use Wittgenstein's example, if I feel inclined to say that the vowel "e" is yellow, I do not use words according to their primary or ordinary sense. In the latter case, to say that "'e' is yellow" is pure nonsense. But the secondary sense is not meant in this way; it is intended to draw out the sedimented experience of the word "yellow" that Wittgenstein perceives as capturing the feeling of the vowel. It is this secondary sense that also makes metaphors possible. If a metaphor for a particular sensation of pain is to make sense, we must already be willing to see a connection between two distinct realms that are not ordinarily connected and that require a form of familiarity with words that goes beyond their semantics. Such familiarity can bring along implications that allow for metaphorical transference, blending two fields in a way that produces the most fitting account of a distinct experience. Words can suggest connections and overlaps where their primary use does not. We can navigate among words because it is as if the secondary sense can bring new experiences and connections to the fore. Words acquire their own gestural meaning or feel as they absorb the patterns of language into what both Merleau-Ponty and Wittgenstein speak of as their physiognomy.

If our initiation into our primary language takes us into the community of speakers, the ability to speak in the secondary sense can bring out one's individual voice.[72] Its strength as well as its weakness resides here. The expression of pain certainly belongs to our individuality, and is inherently tied to our subjectivity. Since the communication of my individual experience of pain depends on a deep attunement beneath conventions and rules, there is no solid ground that supports it. This makes communication vulnerable, for its misunderstandings cannot be ruled out a priori. Discussing expressions of pain, Wittgenstein aptly points out that just as someone can be transparent to us, so can a person be "a complete enigma to another," not necessarily because we do not recognize the meaning of particular words, but because we "can't find our feet with them."[73]

When Scarry speaks of the unsharability of pain, it must be such cases she has in mind. Nevertheless, as Talal Assad has rightly observed, Scarry's point holds true only with significant modification: "It's not that one's own pain can never be convincingly conveyed to others, but that *when* one feels the urgent need to communicate one's pain, and the communication fails, *then* it may come to be thought of—with added anguish—as unshareable."[74] The shareability within such forms of life takes us astonishingly far, but it cannot exclude the threat of our remaining strangers to one another. We are deeply connected, but there is a sense of separateness that can end in isolation, to which pain in general and Job's pain in particular bear witness.

Primitive Reactions and Forms of Life

What about primitive reactions? If pain becomes manifest prior to words, as a hard-wired response in our biological nature, do we not have a stable ground that supports our communication of pain? It is worth recalling that in Wittgenstein as well as in Merleau-Ponty, there is no ontological gap but rather a continuity between reactions, gestures, and language. Linguistic utterances for pain are developed from the bodily ways in which we react. One may still wonder whether reactions and words belong to two separate and heterogeneous realms: our natural makeup on the one hand, and our cultural and conceptual capacities on the other. Arguably, Wittgenstein's notion of "forms of life" is designed to comprise both. It refers to the forms of *life*, which means "the general facts of nature,"[75] and to our *forms* of life, our "agreement in judgments."[76] Similarly, in his notion of natural history, Wittgenstein sees these two dimensions as essentially intertwined: "Giving orders, asking questions, telling stories, having a chat, are as much a part of our natural history as walking, eating, drinking, playing."[77] Wittgenstein proposes a perspective from which the natural (walking, drinking, etc.) and the cultural (giving orders, asking questions) are not split, but appear as two dimensions that are inextricably interwoven. For humans, nothing is purely natural or purely cultural.[78] Wittgenstein's point in invoking forms of life is to remind us of the background which we tend to take for granted. We have not agreed upon those deep structures that enable our meaningfulness. Rather, those structures enable and inform every meaningful utterance we make.

As previously pointed out, primitive reactions play an important role in our initiation into the language of pain. Scarry sees such reactions as falling below the threshold of language, supposedly because they are too primitive to pass for linguistic utterances. Wittgenstein questions such a view of primitive reactions, since, as he takes it, they do not inhibit language but condition it: "But what is the word 'primitive' meant to say here? Presumably that this sort of behavior is *pre-linguistic*: that a language-game is based *on it.*"[79] Although initiation into verbal language marks the decisive step in human maturation, it does not miraculously emerge from a dumb and brute state, but develops gradually from reactions that are expressive in their own right.[80]

Pain pushes the interconnection of primitive reactions and linguistic articulation to the limit—and this might itself be taken to be part of the grammar of intense pain. While words abandon us in intense pain, there are still reactions and cries, but we are not thereby returned to a dumb, unintelligible state. Indeed, such primitive reactions cannot but manifest meaning, for as Wittgenstein reminds us, inarticulate sounds, too, have a place in a language game.[81] What makes pre-linguistic reactions able to convey meaning is that they are part of a game, embedded in an intricate web of practices and implications, and eventually in our form of life. At the basis of our common attunement is the shared interest we take in certain events and utterances: some reactions prove crucial, while others are trivial. It is because pain reaction occupies a distinct role in our lives that we respond to it with comfort, pity, or various other forms of acknowledgment. In this perspective, primitive reactions are not beneath the level of language, as Scarry seems to hold, nor do they provide direct evidence for inner states beneath our linguistic community.

Primitive reactions can be acknowledged as well as neglected, embraced as well as ignored. There is no way in which the communication of pain can be guaranteed. It is open to rejection, deflection, and various skeptical strategies. But expressions of pain can also convey a deep sense of relatedness where they reach out and are responded to. It is the precariousness of pain language that institutes the intimacy of those who share in it. If such sharing or attunement is what upholds our communication, one might easily feel that it is based on a shaky foundation, as if all we rely on is a net over an abyss.[82] But then we forget how incredibly far the commonality reaches: we immediately understand bodily reactions, and we can recognize subtle utterances with astonishing precision. In sum, both the sense of separateness and relatedness irreducibly belong to the communication of pain.

7

Incarnation and the Cross

In revisiting the theme of chapter 1, where the broad outlines of a phenomenology of incarnation were introduced, I aim in this chapter to focus more narrowly on the body of Christ and the cross as the phenomenologically privileged site for the special incarnation. This implies a shift. While the first chapter approached the theological topic of incarnation broadly through phenomenological philosophy, in this chapter I will reverse the order, starting with a theological outline of incarnation and subsequently addressing its philosophical implications. This reversal is intended as a way to expand the phenomenological exploration of incarnation and pain through a deepened conversation between theology and philosophy.

According to the Christian understanding, the special incarnation of Christ entails a double revelation: both of God and of the true humanity of man. If this humanity essentially entails embodiment, the question arises: How do we conceive such embodiment in phenomenological terms? To recall, Merleau-Ponty focuses on the event of the incarnation as a subversion of metaphysical depictions of God and transcendence: "Transcendence no longer hangs over man: he becomes, strangely, its privileged bearer."[1] While this opens a perspective from which to regard transcendence from below, anchored in the earth and world that we all share through our embodied being—which is precisely what Merleau-Ponty's phenomenology attempts to articulate.

Henry, however, does not begin with what we take as our ordinary conditions, because revelation cannot be about what is already revealed in our worldly being. Incarnation has nothing to do with entering the world, it concerns divine Life and its "*arrival in a flesh*."[2] With the incarnation, we are granted a new paradigm of the reality of the body, the true body as flesh. But has the movement of incarnation thereby shifted away from its descending movement? It seems that Henry no longer implies the movement from on high to the lowliness of the ordinary human condition, but rather reconceives the human condition according to the extraordinary paradigm of the Word arriving in the immanence of flesh. What happens to our relation to the world, and what about our organic and material bodies? Does Christ even assume such a body? And if phenomenology offers different notions of the body—the lived, the objective, the flesh,

flesh and blood—the question of which applies still remains. Questions like these are far from new in the theological and philosophical tradition of Christianity. In fact, they were remarkably alive in its earliest centuries, particularly in the debate surrounding the Gnostic appropriations of Christ. It seems that their intense preoccupation with human embodiment has recurred in phenomenology, to which recent discussions of major figures, such as Irenaeus and Tertullian, bear witness and to which I will soon turn.

To understand incarnation, I have argued that pain plays a particular role in phenomenology because it lays bare otherwise concealed structures of our embodiment. Accordingly, I will argue that pain has a similar function in the case of the special incarnation of Christ. For if God has become fully human, it is reasonable to think that pain can serve as a guiding thread to the understanding of what it implies for God to become a body. Thus, if pain has disclosing power, then the revelation of Christ's incarnation is not only to be found in the Prologue of John and in the birth narratives of the Gospels, but, as I will argue, even more so on the cross.

Incarnation and the Created Body

The acute attention paid to the human body of Christ, especially in the second and third centuries, was probably initiated as a response to the spread of Gnosticism, both outside and inside Christian circles. Due to its sharp dualism between the realm of light, goodness, and spirit on the one hand, and darkness, evil, and materiality on the other, Gnosticism regarded the human body as the material confinement of the soul. Accordingly, Christ figures as the savior who conveys the secret knowledge (gnosis) that can free the soul from its bodily imprisonment.[3] As such, Christ cannot be truly part of the material world and consequently, Gnosticism holds a Docetic view of the body of Christ, that is, denying the bodily reality of Christ's suffering and resurrection. Already Ignatius, at the beginning of the second century, warns against Docetism, underlining that the Lord truly suffered bodily, "not merely in appearance as some of the unbelievers say."[4] Clearly, different interpretations of incarnation have been at stake from early on, ranging from flesh without body to some material notions of the objective body.

It was Irenaeus and Tertullian who first developed a comprehensive theological response to Gnosticism at the turn of the third century. Irenaeus's view of the general and specific incarnation is contingent on

CHAPTER 7

his conception of creation. In strong opposition against Gnostics in general and Marcion in particular, who separates the Creator from the Redeemer, the God of the Old Testament from Christ of the New Testament, Irenaeus insists on the identity of one and the same God. According to one line of argument, Irenaeus points out that only insofar as it is the same God that creates and establishes the Law, can this God also re-create and redeem.[5] According to another line of argument, Christ the redeemer is at once one with the Creator but is also becoming part of the creation, which for Irenaeus means that in being incarnated, Christ is formed by the dust of the world in the same manner as Adam. Christ is therefore fully human: "His only-begotten Word, who is always present with the human race, united to and mingled with his own creation, according to the Father's pleasure, and became flesh . . . in every respect, He is man, the formation of God."[6] There is no paradox, dialectics, or synthesis of two natures in Irenaeus's rendering, but an organic unity between the creation of the first Adam and Christ. Humanity, in the figure of Adam and Christ, are of the same matter.

> But if the Lord became incarnate for any other order of things, and took flesh of any other substance, He has not then summed up human nature in His own person, nor in that case can He be termed flesh. For flesh has been truly made to consist in a transmission of that thing molded originally from the dust.[7]

In a manner that comes close to Merleau-Ponty's view of incarnation, Irenaeus emphasizes the earthliness of Christ's body. The point of the incarnation is lost if one weakens or denies the material commonality of Christ and humanity, for the redemption works in and through the creation. In taking on a created body, Christ affirmed and transformed creation, which Irenaeus often speaks of in terms of a recapitulation that sums up human nature. Recapitulation means a forward movement, towards a renewal of the creation consummated in God, which simultaneously points back to the original goodness of the creation as it was in the beginning.[8]

In this perspective, Christ cannot be some disguised heavenly being or a messenger from a transcendent eon, as some Gnostics had it; nor can he be properly conceived as starting from a distinction between eternity and temporality or two separate natures, divine and human, as the dogma of Chalcedon presumes. Irenaeus's conception of incarnation follows from a more straightforward observation, namely that since God is the creator of all humans, he can become one with the creation. Irenaeus notes that the humanity of Christ shines forth most clearly where it contradicts our expectations of divinity: Christ makes no exception from

INCARNATION AND THE CROSS

human weakness, needs, and affections. There is no question of Docetism or that Christ could be impassible, for then the salvation would not concern humanity. What the incarnation entails is rather "the invisible becoming visible, the incomprehensible being made comprehensible, the impassible becoming capable of suffering."[9]

For Irenaeus, then, the incarnation is not primarily seen through the prism of resurrection or through the Trinitarian relationship, but by holding together Christ with the creation of man. The affirmation of the good creation makes up Irenaeus's bulwark against any form of Docetism because it affirms the positive value of Christ's human body in its very materiality. This stress on materiality, Thomas Weinandy argues, reflects Irenaeus's overall attitude to the world: "Irenaeus possessed a childlike enthusiasm and delight in the materiality of the material, the physicality of the physical, and the bodilyness of the bodily. He insisted that God did indeed create man from the dust and slime of the earth."[10] According to Irenaeus's notion of matter, it is precisely the materiality of the body that exposes us to affections, so that Christ feels hunger, thirst, anxiety, and physical suffering. This is obviously not a mere objective body incapable of feeling. Even as the image of the anthropomorphic God that forms a human out of dust with his hands may appear mythical or obsolete, its point still deserves attention: the affective body that Irenaeus affirms is still part of the world, which is not of our own making.

The fact that Tertullian shares many of Irenaeus's concerns for the body as an integral part of God's creation follows from their common stance against Gnosticism. However, while Irenaeus underlines the typological and thus historical link between the creation of Adam and Christ, Tertullian elaborates the created matter in a more systematic manner. Falque argues that we can discern the two with respect to the role that visibility and material solidity play for them respectively: "If Irenaeus strives to disclose in Adam the *visibility* of the flesh of humanity, Tertullian attempts to feel the weight of the flesh of the incarnate Word in all its *solidity* and makes of his weight the defense against all our attempts to angelize the Incarnation."[11] There is no doubt that Tertullian comes to emphasize the flesh's carnal solidity, precisely when he is connecting the incarnation to what is essentially human. Like Irenaeus, Tertullian argues that the fundamental flaw of his Gnostic opponents is their view of creation according to which the materiality of this world is the work of an inferior god. Only the spirit is left with some divine spark. For Tertullian, such a position leads to the complete devaluation of all God's creation, not least embodied human beings.

Tertullian suggests that the Gnostic disgust for the body makes them unable to embrace the incarnation in its true sense: that Christ has come

CHAPTER 7

in human flesh. As a rhetorical strategy, Tertullian directly invokes what his opponents hold as unfit and repellent about the idea of humanity: "unclean from its first formation of the dregs of the ground, uncleaner afterwards from the mire of its own seminal transmission; worthless, weak, covered with guilt, laden with misery, full of troubles."[12] To Gnostics, Christ cannot possibly be divine and yet be part of such obnoxious conditions, since they are held to be products of the lower creator god. Consequently, Christ's body must either be but a phantom or else made of another celestial substance. But if there is one God, both creator and redeemer, as both Irenaeus and Tertullian hold, nothing of the creation can be foreign to Christ, except non-created, dehumanizing sin. Tertullian emphasizes that it is in the very same flesh and body which all humans have that the divine is incarnated. This in turn means that the incarnation entails the reevaluation of our lowly materiality into dignity. It is precisely the filthy human body, originally made from the dust of the earth, that should be cherished because Christ has fully affirmed it.[13] We know that Jesus commands us to love our neighbor, Tertullian notes, and he believes this to have repercussions for our relation to our bodies, too: "He will love the flesh which is, so very closely and in so many ways, His neighbor." From which the encouragement follows: "Let, then, the flesh begin to give you pleasure, since the Creator thereof is so great."[14]

Christ's body is far from any spiritual or celestial substance, but made up of earthly materiality: "I mean this flesh suffused with blood, built up with bones, interwoven with nerves, entwined with veins, a flesh which knew how to be born, and how to die, human without doubt, as born of a human being."[15] Whatever effect the rhetoric has had, the theological point is to underline how incarnation includes even the most basic, animal, and material dimension of human existence. Tertullian's point is not to deny the extraordinariness of Christ, but to argue that the extraordinariness must be correctly located. It is not about extraordinary substances, but his sinlessness and mighty deeds. To Tertullian, the latter in fact presupposes Christ's ordinary human nature: "As the case stood, it was actually the ordinary condition of His terrene flesh which made all things else about Him wonderful."[16]

Having underlined the biological makeup of the body, Tertullian does not fail to note Christ's human affections: "He hungered under the devil's temptation, He thirsted with the woman of Samaria; He wept over Lazarus; He trembles at death (for 'the flesh,' as he says, 'is weak'); at last, He pours out his blood."[17] Affections are central to Michel Henry's concept of the flesh as well, but only insofar as they are uncoupled from the objective body. According to Greek thought, affections belongs to human beings as physical beings, and are especially significant since they differentiate humans from gods. In feeling and suffering, the incarnated God, however, has also taken on human affections. Unlike Henry, Tertullian does not think affections are at odds with his materialist convictions, but holds that affections belong to the body and to the soul mediated by that body, as if welling up from our flesh and blood. Even as he conceptually distinguishes between soul and body, Tertullian goes remarkably far in tying them together. He can claim that the soul is created together with the body; indeed, Tertullian defends the Stoic notion of the corporeal soul. For an incorporeal substance cannot suffer, he claims; only a corporeal soul can suffer with the body.[18] "For he suffered nothing who did not truly suffer; and a phantom could not truly suffer."[19] Christ attests by his Spirit that he is God, and he attests by his suffering that he is truly human. It can be claimed that Christ's suffering becomes the touchstone of the incarnation, for if the pain and suffering are true, no other options—phantoms or celestial bodies—than the human body of Christ are viable. It is on the cross that Christ is nailed to his physical body, indeed, inescapably so, not as an outer appearance detached from the subject, but as hurting in its material and affective presence.[20] Before I attempt to show how such a reappraisal of the concrete body of Christ leads to a phenomenological account of the cross, I will discuss to what extent Irenaeus's and Tertullian's accounts can be retrieved phenomenologically.

Henry's Responses to Irenaeus and Tertullian

Since Henry has made incarnation central to his phenomenology, it comes as no surprise that he picks out Irenaeus and Tertullian as his theological interlocutors, since they encircle the focal points of his project: flesh and incarnation. They all share the basic assumption that Christ takes a flesh similar to ours and in that sense affirms it. However, as soon as one moves closer to the notion of incarnation, disagreements start to emerge. For Henry, incarnation is modeled on the Gospel of John, which to him means that the Word is generated by God and became flesh. Tertullian is unable to make sense of this, Henry holds, because he is led astray by his metaphysical schema—he "still thinks Greek."[21] Both Irenaeus and Tertullian claim that Christ has a double origin: as the Son of God, Christ comes from God, but as a human being, Christ is grafted onto the human race by being born of a woman.[22] Moreover, as fully human, Christ has both soul and body. Even as soul and body are closely interwoven in Tertullian's account, the Greek distinction nevertheless prevails. Henry argues that, following the Gospel of John, there is neither a question of the substance of the soul nor of a material body born from the womb. But there is reference to the flesh, the flesh understood as the complete and undivided definition of the human.[23] As for the origin of human flesh, both Irenaeus and Tertullian insist that it is fully earthly, made of dust on the ground, and bestowed with the divine breath of life. While Henry accentuates the inbreathing of Life, he contends that their readings of the creation story are misleading, because they do not see that the full meaning of the story must be conceived retrospectively, in light of the incarnation as accounted for in the Prologue of John. John says nothing of dust and materiality: "In the silt of the earth, there are only bodies, but no flesh. Something like flesh can happen and come to us only from the Word."[24] Inert matter implies no self, Henry contends, and cannot have affections such as pleasures, sufferings, hunger, and thirst, and thus the Word can only arrive in flesh.

To Henry, the problem with Tertullian's Greek dualism is not so much his notion of the soul as his notion of the body as the material counterpart of the soul. The body, in Tertullian's rendering, is, to repeat, "suffused with blood, built up with bones, interwoven with nerves, entwined with veins."[25] Henry sees this as an account of the objective body inscribed in the ontological horizon of the visible world. On such a horizon, the content of the world is given as dust or material bodies, and the body therefore cannot be accounted for as affective flesh. Henry argues that in such a universe of material things,

> there is never the feeling they inspire for Tertullian or Marcion, and no feeling in general, for that matter; no impression either: neither hunger, nor fatigue, nor pity, nor anguish, nor joy, nor suffering. No suffering, actually, none of the suffering by which Irenaeus and Tertullian alike will define the reality of Christ's flesh, and the reality of our own flesh too.[26]

Clearly, Irenaeus and Tertullian do not neglect affections like the hunger, anguish, or suffering of Christ, and Henry recognizes that these are central to their definition of Christ's humanity. Moreover, Tertullian makes the relation between the soul and the body intimate, writing that "so intimate is the union, that it may be deemed to be uncertain whether the flesh bear about the soul, or the soul the flesh."[27] What Henry is arguing is that even so, Tertullian's conception of the body leaves out the affective flesh. Incarnation, Henry writes, "is a matter of flesh and not of the body; and if the difference between flesh and body appeared essential to

INCARNATION AND THE CROSS

us from the outset, it is because flesh and not the body must serve as the central theme for understanding incarnation in the Christian sense."[28]

Nonetheless, Henry appreciates Tertullian's emphasis on birth, precisely because there is no mortal flesh without birth. Tertullian writes: "Come now, beginning from the nativity itself, declaim against the uncleanness of the generative elements within the womb, the filthy concretion of fluid and blood, of the growth of the flesh for nine months long out of that very mire."[29] There is no attempt to downplay the organic dimension of the birth of Christ; on the contrary, Tertullian underscores it. Moreover, he contends that birth is also a sign of finitude: only those born can die, for what has a beginning in time must also end in time. While Henry agrees with this correlation, he does not concur with Tertullian's understanding of birth. Tertullian's account of Christ's birth misses the mark insofar as he exclusively addresses the birth of the external, organic body on the horizon of the world. Henry disregards the nativity stories in Matthew and Luke, relying solely on John for these matters. For Henry, "birth" is central to coming in flesh, but he does not refer to the arrival of an objective body in the world. Rather, "birth" means generation, which is to say, a self that is arriving in flesh.[30] The distinction between being generated and created goes back to the patristic era where God's generation referred to the Son, and creation to the world and the humans in it. According to Henry, however, both the Son and the sons (all human selves) are equally generated. Life can only be generated in the phenomenological substance available to it: the affections and impressions of a self. These affections and impressions are not of their own making but are generated by Life itself. Hence, birth is not childbirth, not even the biblical forming of dust. *"Life reveals flesh by generating it, as what takes birth in it, being formed and edified in it, and drawing its substance (its pure phenomenological substance) from the very substance of life."*[31]

It was no doubt central to Tertullian's anti-Gnostic argument to hold that Christ could suffer and hence be fully human. But his operative split between objective body and flesh is never mended, as Henry reads him, and never could be, once he had started out "thinking Greek." "Body and flesh are thus distinguished through the radicality of an originary phenomenological dualism."[32] Henry maintains that suffering is important, particularly because suffering is what makes incarnation manifest. In suffering "life touches its own Depth. It is not an accident that in the affirmation of the reality of flesh, its suffering is ranked first."[33] Henry is aligned here with my central claim, namely that suffering, or more narrowly, pain is privileged in making the flesh (and the body) manifest. But suffering entails the self as well, because the suffering of the flesh is always given

CHAPTER 7

along with its ipseity. And finally, suffering reveals to me that life is not of my doing, but is given to me passively, in Henry's terminology, from Life.[34]

While Henry discards Tertullian's account of the body, he surprisingly finds that Irenaeus has it right. Henry claims that Irenaeus does not confront Gnostic images of Christ's otherworldly body by defending his objective body. Rather, Irenaeus is concerned with flesh in Henry's sense: "The explicit theme of the fundamental problematic Irenaeus addresses is the definition of the reality of the flesh, not through the material of the world but through suffering and thus through life's phenomenological material."[35] The obvious problem with Henry's rendering is that Irenaeus sounds more like a mirror of Henry's own phenomenology than the one that emerges from a careful reading of his texts. As I pointed out above, Irenaeus repeatedly traces Christ's body back to the dust from which God created Adam. What has Henry found that makes him think otherwise?

Henry turns to Irenaeus's way of addressing life as his central insight. Irenaeus underlines that humans must be capable of receiving the power of life. If that is denied, the way Gnostics do, one is in effect already dead, which is an absurd self-contradiction. Henry quotes Irenaeus: "And if they are now alive, and if their whole body partakes of life, how can they venture the assertion that the flesh is not qualified to be a partaker of life, when they do confess that they have life at the present moment?"[36] Henry takes Irenaeus to suggest that the Christian self has not derived a body from the world but has its flesh from Life. However interesting this reading might be, a closer look into the relevant section suggests another reading. In the current section, Irenaeus is discussing life as the power coming into the weakness of the human flesh in order to argue that this power grants the mortal flesh immortality. Notably, Irenaeus claims, right before the passage quoted above, that such resurrection of flesh requires that we see the resurrection anchored in the wonder of the whole creation, so that all of us, our life as well as our material parts, is both created and will be re-created along with the world. Here he deals with dimensions Henry leaves out:

> And surely it is much more difficult and incredible, from non-existent bones, and nerves and veins, and the rest of man's organization, to bring about that all this should be, and to make man an animated and rational creature, than to reintegrate again that which had been created and then afterwards decomposed into earth.[37]

If we set aside antiquity's problematic yet widely held image of the reintegration of matter, it at least seems clear that Henry is correct in asserting that, to Irenaeus, life is essentially received from God. However, Henry ignores Irenaeus's conception of life as an integral part of material bodies, both in the present world and in the world to come.

Moreover, Tertullian and Irenaeus see the body as an integral part of the created world. Henry will by no means deny creation, but again the question is what it means. Henry draws a distinction between creation, as accounted for in Genesis, and his notion of generation. Read through phenomenological lenses, the creation story is a transcendental theory about human beings, in which humans are placed within the totality of being, with a world spread out as the horizon for everything that appears on it.[38] But, as already suggested in Genesis, humans are at the same time created in the image and likeness of God, which Henry takes to mean that humans are essentially not of the visible world. The full implication of this will first be drawn in the Gospel of John, where creation is replaced by generation. "Man has never been created, he has never come in the world, He has come in Life . . . Man can be understood starting from the idea of generation alone."[39] With this reinterpretation of birth and creation in terms of generation, Henry moves away from Tertullian as well as from Irenaeus. But can Henry nevertheless preserve some of their key insights into the human body of Christ?

Assessing Henry

Body and flesh, according to Henry, hold nothing in common but make up the two distinct ways of appearance: either given invisibly in affection according to its immanence, or visually in the world as an externality. In line with the common trend of phenomenology to regard the lived body as primary, Henry grants the flesh constitutive priority over the body. But due to the uncommonly strong divide between them, Henry goes remarkably far in splitting externality from the flesh. One might even wonder if Henry overcomes Tertullian's dualism of body and soul, or whether he replaces it with another dualism, this time between flesh and body. Does Henry in fact suggest a flesh without a body, as Falque has argued?[40] Where the objective body, its physicality and biological nature, is never in doubt for Husserl, it has, strangely enough, become inessential to Henry, even evacuated from the flesh. Of course, the objective body appears, Henry will say, but solely as an object of the world, put in front of my intentional gaze. For this reason, it is never given to itself, felt by itself, and revealed to itself. Henry masterfully detects problems within phenomenology, such as its one-sided focus on intentionality and its lack of attention to impressions, as well as the neglected

CHAPTER 7

passivity at the heart of activity. Nevertheless, his proposed solutions are too extreme, as if they represent a defensive overreaction to the problems he identifies, resulting in a flesh that knows no matter, visibility, or worldliness.

Although Henry draws on Tertullian and Irenaeus to shape his own position, their battle against Gnosticism reemerges in an unexpected way. Several commentators have noted that Henry's approach itself seems to drift toward a form of Gnosticism.[41] Hans Jonas points out that one of the defining features of Gnosticism is the sense of exile and alienation from the material, created world. Hence, the deep antithetical dualism at work is not primarily between soul and body, but between man and world and correspondingly, between the world and God.[42] To be sure, Henry does not speak of the world as a manifestation of dark, evil matter produced by a demiurge, but rather one of light and horizons. Yet he repeats a similar dualism found in Gnosticism, this time between human flesh and world, since the visible world is always at a distance from the flesh as a mere appearance never given in itself. Perhaps Henry's position is covertly motivated by a sense of exile in the messy world from which he retreats into the pure immanence of self-revelation. In a similar vein, Rudolf Bernet holds that Henry's "hyper-transcendentalism" entails a "purist conception of a transcendental life that is foreign to all compromises with worldly affairs."[43]

Since truth and human life reside in auto-affection, man as a creature in the world is cast out as the correlate to intentionality, or even more strongly: *"The man of the world is merely an optical illusion."*[44] Although Henry does not propose a dualistic Gnostic view with a lower creator God and a saving God of Christ, by separating the world from immanent life, he risks making creation insignificant, which is precisely what Irenaeus accused the Gnostics of doing. Far from merely concerning immanent Life, Irenaeus's main concern is to confront Gnostic dualism by holding creation and redemption together. Christ arrives in the creaturely condition of earth and life to redeem it from within.[45] When Merleau-Ponty writes that "incarnation changes everything," this implies a new evaluation of the human body through the "externalization" of God in becoming human, which simultaneously disrupts metaphysical hierarchies since "God is not above but beneath us."[46] According to such a view, incarnation signifies a transition from the metaphysical God above to the God who embraces the conditions that Genesis portrays as dust, and which Tertullian elaborates on in terms of bones, nerves, and veins. In my interpretation, this means that Christ does not only come in flesh, but also in flesh and blood. When Henry excludes Christ's created, appearing body, he presents a flesh that, like the Gnostic Valentinus suggested, is more angelic than human: no creation, no matter, just pure impressionality and affection. As Falque has argued, Henry's phenomenology results in a peculiar angelic flesh without a body, that is, Valentinus's Gnostic conception of Christ.[47]

While Henry acknowledges that some form of arch-gnosis must be embraced, he does not want to embrace Gnosticism; he even confronts its dangers directly. In fact, he argues that his own view of incarnation represents "the true reversal of the Gnostic position."[48] Henry challenges us to reconsider what a true body is, in contrast to the merely apparent body that Gnosticism desires. The merely apparent body must be one that is discarnate in the sense of not being given to anyone, and thus not fully real. "Where is the flesh only apparent? In the world. The world's appearing strips every flesh of its reality. And this concerns our flesh as well as that of Christ, as well as that of the Word."[49] Henry ingeniously turns the tables, identifying any appeals to materiality and worldliness of the body not as an anti-Gnostic position, but as the Gnostic position itself. However, does this reversal really undercut Falque's criticism? The auto-affecting flesh that knows nothing of the world still evokes a Gnostic distaste for material bodies, even if it is deemed more real. Seen from Irenaeus's perspective, Joseph Rivera argues, the accusation against Henry's doctrine of the incarnation would be "that it is a Gnostic rendition of divine subjectivism, which in turn must abandon any doctrine of participation of the world in God."[50] What happened to the world and the worldly body in Henry's account? Is it not precisely such ordinary bodily conditions that the Word assumed to become one of us?

According to Henry, we cannot begin with the assumption of some ordinary bodily conditions. Christ's flesh is extraordinary since it is nothing less than the Son arriving in flesh. But is not such exceptionality what the Gnostics called for, referring to Christ's otherworldly origin and constitution? However, such a charge would be misplaced, for the point Henry is making is that no human flesh is ordinary flesh in the first place; not only the Son but also us, the sons, live from Life.[51] What we ordinarily consider the human body belongs to the man of the world, but to Henry, this is precisely not the human flesh. In contrast, Tertullian insists on the ordinariness of both our and Christ's embodiment: "His was an earthly flesh like ours is; but anything new or anything strange I do not discover."[52] The ordinariness involves the body's finitude (natal and mortal) and the way it is interwoven with matter and organic life (dust)—all of which becomes dubious in Henry's rendering. While I agree that Christ must be granted extraordinary and exceptional status as far as he is the Son of God, it remains crucial for the notion of incarnation that it makes the extraordinary appear amidst the ordinary.[53] In

CHAPTER 7

fact, the Prologue of John states that the Word came to dwell among us, meaning that he came to his own, that is, the world of his own making, even as he was not welcomed (John 1:10–11). What this seems to suggest is that the extraordinary coming of the Word is first recognized if we hold onto the ordinariness of the world and bodies in which the Word proceeds. The moment everything is regarded as extraordinary, nothing is any longer extraordinary; for something to be extraordinary, it must stand out against the ordinary, just as a figure only stands out against a background.

Nevertheless, the full significance of assuming a body like ours can first be realized in its trials. Irenaeus, Tertullian, and Henry all emphasize the fact that Christ underwent human affections: he was hungry, thirsty, cried, felt anxiety, and experienced pain. When Henry suspects that the Greek thinkers employed notions of the objective body that prevented them from thinking about affectivity, he does not consider it possible to have an internal experience of one's flesh and blood that is not yet distanced. But if we are to apply phenomenological concepts to the way Tertullian speaks of materiality along with affectivity, the most appropriate notion is not that of the objective body, but that of flesh and blood. Flesh and blood situates the body beyond the impasse (in Falque's reading) of Henry's flesh without a body and (in Henry's reading) of Tertullian's body without flesh. In order to interrogate this possibility, I will again turn to pain, more specifically to Christ's pain on the cross. For if it is true that pain is privileged in making flesh and blood manifest, then the cross should be the test case of a god said to have become truly human.

The Cross: Incarnation Revealed

Christ's suffering is exceptional because it is the Son of God that undergoes it, but it is not exceptional with regard to his pain and suffering. The pain on the cross is rather exemplary than exceptional, as he suffers the same way all humans can suffer. Only because Christ is fully human can he suffer, take part in our darkness, and live through the depth of our common bodily condition.

The cross has long since become a symbol, invested with layers of symbolic meaning—of atonement, salvation, death, and life—to the degree that it has become hard to see the literal event underneath it. To approach the pain of Christ, it is necessary to bracket off those symbolic layers for the purpose of letting the brute appearance of the tortured body reappear. Despite the simple construction of the cross, it does bring

INCARNATION AND THE CROSS

with it a certain sense—not one that invites imagination, abstraction, and the play of semantic meanings, but rather through the concrete way in which it makes pain explicit and phenomenologically apparent. To be sure, this torture device is meant to produce pain, humiliation, and death, but the way in which it does so is by rendering the victim's privacy public, by stripping away clothes, stretching out the limbs, and thus putting all bodily pain behavior on outward display.[54] Central to the deterrence of the cross is the uncompromising manner in which it renders pain visible and palpable. I propose that the torture scene itself mimics the experience of pain by literalizing it. In nailing the body to the cross, the crucifixion literalizes the body nailed to itself in inescapable pain. In drawing on previous chapters, I will pursue seven different ways in which the cross literalizes the suffering of Christ.

First, I want to draw attention to the fact that Christ was hung on the cross. The passivity of being hung implies that Christ has no agency or activity; he is effectively stripped of any resistance and compelled to accept the actions of others in the mode of "I cannot." His fate is quite literally "betrayed into the hands of sinners" (Mark 14:41; Matt. 26:41). The Latin word *passio*, as in the passion of Christ, conveys a sense of passivity. Interestingly, the word contains a certain ambiguity between passivity and activity. While Christ's passive suffering is the primary focus of the so-called passion narrative, the active sense of "passion" is more commonly understood today: as an desire, even erotic desire, by which one is drawn to and pursues an object.[55] Although erotic desire is largely absent from the Gospels, outward-reaching love is certainly present. Jesus is depicted as actively engaged with others through teaching, healing, and touching, embodying a being-in-the-world. According to the Gospels, the passion narrative marks the turning point between activity and passivity. When this active sense of passion turns into the passive sense, activity and passivity must be seen as two sides of the same coin. Jürgen Moltmann has hinted at this inner unity, writing that "the story of Christ is the story of great passion, of a passionate love; for that very reason, it is also a story about deadly anguish."[56] What unites the passion of love with the passion of deadly anguish is a love with nothing held in reserve. For the crucified Christ, this means that the lived body that opens up into engagement in the world is the same body that becomes vulnerable to suffer the rejection of the world in passivity.

As far as the cross marks the transition from active passion to passive passion, the "I can" turns into "I cannot." In being hung on the cross, the absence of bodily powers and capabilities are revealed along with the passive exposure to the pain inflicted. Pain suggests passivity in the sense that it comes over us and invades us to the point where there is no distanciation or escape from it. Our helplessness against pain is literalized in the body riveted to wood with no way out. This helplessness underlines the lack of control and heroism on Jesus's part; no Heideggerian resoluteness in the face of death awaits the one hung on the cross. Nothing awaits except more pain, and then death. In a reversal of Heidegger's being-toward-death which enhances our abilities, Levinas writes: "What is important about the approach of death is that at a certain moment we are no longer *able to be able*. It is exactly thus that the subject loses its very mastery as a subject."[57] Being spread out on the cross and faced with "I cannot," nothing is left of bodily activity and ability.

As a second point, the Gospel narrates that Jesus was stripped naked before they divided his clothes among them (Mark 15:24; Matt. 27:35; Luke 23:34). The fact of nudity underlines the humiliation of stripping away the clothes that shelter the body from the surrounding world, along with all signs of a social role and identity. Moreover, nakedness comes with shame because there is no hiding from the exposure to the look of others.[58] Additionally, the stretched-out body is made fully visible in a way that makes the experience of pain turned inside out for the inspection of others, with no chance of withdrawal. This forced loss of control over one's integrity is, according to Scarry, one important purpose of torture as it seeks to accomplish an "almost obscene conflation of private and public." A naked man nailed to a cross seems to be the most fitting picture thereof. It is an enforced exposure to others, but without any community or "shared experience."[59] This utterly public display is matched by one's utter isolation, underlined in the fleeing of the disciples in the passion narratives.

The nakedness exploits the phenomenology of the skin: the naked skin signifies exposure, vulnerability, and defenselessness. As I discussed in chapter 4, the skin is marked by an inherent ambiguity, both drawing a border around the interiority of myself and simultaneously making me perceivable to the world, both shielding me from its dangers and exposing me to the tactile world. As with the ambiguity of passion, the ambiguity of the skin necessarily comes with vulnerability. In being stripped naked, the activity of Christ's touch is reversed into a surface that can be invaded and exploited. In Jean Améry's reflection on his own experience of torture, the ambiguity of the skin is neatly captured:

> The boundaries of the body are also the boundaries of my self. My skin surface shields me against the external world. If I am to have trust, I must feel on it only what I *want* to feel. . . . At the first blow, however, the trust in the world breaks down. The other person, *opposite* whom I exist physically in the world and *with* whom I can exist only as long as he

does not touch my skin surface as border, forces his own corporeality on me with the first blow.[60]

The nudity and skin undergo a radical change in the act of violence: the skin that gives access to but simultaneously protects me from the world becomes the medium of harm caused by powers outside my own powers. The naked crucified is stripped of clothing, of social dignity, and not least, stripped down to a flesh and blood in its pure vulnerability: "the tortured person," Améry claims, "is only a body, and nothing else besides this."[61]

Thirdly, the crucifixion means that nails were driven into hands and feet. While Jesus is reported as both flogged and mocked, the nailing to the cross initiates the final death process, literalized as inescapable. The border of the skin is not only exposed but transgressed, invading the flesh and blood. As a subcategory of tactility, pain is always located, as Husserl has emphasized. In intense pain, the sensation is not only located but drags all our attention toward the painful location of the body. The otherwise outward-going movement of the intentional ray is reversed, now coming toward me from the concrete location of pain. From the focal point, the centripetal force of pain spreads through the body and can have a totalizing effect in a way hardly shared by other sensations.[62] In a remarkable fragment, Simone Weil expounds on the implications of the penetrating nails:

> It is impossible to handle this piece of iron without suddenly reducing the infinite which is in man to a point on the pointed part, a point on the handle, at the cost of harrowing pain. The whole being is stricken on the instant; there is no place left for God, even in the case of Christ, where the thought of God is no more at least than that of privation. This stage has to be reached if there is to be incarnation.[63]

The localized pain makes everything else recede into the background or eclipses it completely. There is no room left for anything but pain at the tip of the piece of iron. Weil suggests that there is a double consequence of this. On the one hand, she suggests that in pain there is not only no place for the world, but even the radical thought that there is not even room for God, whose sonship constitutes Christ's very identity and mission. On the other hand, Weil claims that such a painful state is inherent to the notion of incarnation—which may seem paradoxical because the pain represses the divine relation. The nails that affix Christ to the cross undoubtedly cause pain, but they also literalize another aspect: this man is riveted to his humanity with no reprieve. It reveals the material, affective, natal, and mortal body that Tertullian describes. This man endures human pain, and is fastened to the cross just as he is anchored to his own human flesh and blood, with no escape or sanctuary.

As a fourth point, I will more closely draw attention to the meaning of the nail's piercing. Gabriel Marcel has argued that physical suffering can be regarded as the prototype of all suffering, and one could add, the prototype of physical pain is when some device—a knife or nail—pierces the body.[64] This is prototypical because it makes plain a phenomenological feature of pain, namely how something non-I is forced into the embodied I, as a piece of iron cuts into one's flesh. The nail thus graphically mimes the phenomenology of pain, positioned at the irresolvable tension between being a part of my interiority and yet remaining something foreign to it.[65] The body in pain is set over against me, it addresses me as the one affected by it. The pain is interior to me, without distance, and yet the painful body is given as not being fully mine. Scarry argues that the pain I feel does not appear as identical to myself, and yet, the experience of pain is doubtless mine.[66] In this sense, pain remains an excess in Levinas's sense: impossible to integrate, directed against me contrary to myself, even as it is grafted onto me.[67] While the crucifixion renders this visible as the iron nail driven into the body, it is not the foreign materiality that hurts; for at a certain intensity, the pain experience will leave out all references to its cause. The alienating sense is internal to the tensions it provokes within the familiar milieu of the body. Thus, the crucifixion, or indeed any torture, is an assault on the body, but more profoundly, it turns one's own body into a weapon turned against itself. Pain has, as it were, its own agency even as it is my own body that is hurting itself in a strange mix of hetero- and auto-affectively.[68]

In chapter 2, I argued that such affectivity could be analyzed in terms of *hyle* and *morphe*, where *hyle* resists full integration into the *morphe* that otherwise grants *hyle* its meaning. Here *hyle* refers not to the immaterial arch-impression of the temporal flow, but to the non-I that affects the body from within as the opacity, heaviness, and resistance of our flesh and blood. Pain wells up from these regions of our body. It is therefore particularly in pain that Tertullian's account of the body of Christ proves adequate: a flesh that feels itself, but also as turned over against itself, as blood, veins, nerves, and bones. The body stretched out on the cross can neither be adequately captured by Henry's flesh that affects itself without inner antagonism, nor as an objective body put at a distance. As mentioned in chapter 1, Falque has fruitfully suggested a third notion of the spread or stretched-out body as a way to capture experiences that otherwise evade phenomenological conceptions. He writes:

INCARNATION AND THE CROSS

> There is a biological aspect to myself that is not quantifiable (not extended in the geometrical fashion in the body) but that nonetheless cannot simply be reduced to subjective qualities. The body spread out—on the operating table, certainly, but also dozing on a bed or even crucified on a cross—is more than the simple extension of matter (the objectivity of the body) and more than pure selfhood of the flesh (subjectivity of the flesh).[69]

To stick with the primacy of the flesh over the body, or even to imply a flesh without the body, means to cut oneself off from the phenomenology of crucifixion.[70] Falque does not abandon the phenomenological notions of the flesh and the lived body, but points out how certain situations reveal to us levels of our own body that cross the lived and the objective body. With the stretched-out arms pierced by nails, Christ must have experienced his own body in its density and weight—literally being suffocated by the weight of his own materiality, his flesh and blood. This is the radical implication of being made of dust, or better, returned to dust.

Related to the latter, the fifth point concerns the fact that Christ being nailed to the cross also implies being nailed to his own flesh and blood. Once pain has arrived, it gives itself in unmediated presence. "This can be recognized," Henry rightly notes, "by the fact that there is no gap that separates suffering from itself." And with an allusion to the cross, he continues: "Riveted to itself and crushed under its own weight, suffering does not allow one to establish any distance from it."[71] The more we long to put pain at a distance, the more it becomes clear that we cannot. We can shut our eyes, and block our ears, but there is no way to shut pain out from the body it invades. Levinas's most significant contribution to the phenomenology of pain, to my mind, is his elaboration of the dynamism of pain: between the exigency to get out and the impossibility to escape. Among the various shades of suffering that Levinas's earlier writings attend to, his description of nausea is the one that captures this dynamic with the most precision: "There is in nausea a refusal to remain there, an effort to get out. Yet this effort is always already characterized as desperate. . . . In nausea—which amounts to an impossibility of being what one is—we are at the same time riveted to ourselves, enclosed in a tight circle that smothers."[72]

The figure of the crucified Christ in Matthias Grünewald's Isenheim altarpiece is a precise depiction of the unresolved tension between the need to escape and its impossibility. His bruised skin along with its pale color signalize agony in the proximity to death, and the horizontal beam of the cross literally bends, as if to underscore how Christ is tortured under his own weight. Yet, it is especially the expressive gestures of his hands and fingers that are most telling. While being nailed to the wood, they simultaneously twist vigorously. The hands express the urge to escape, along with the absolute hopelessness of such an urge as robust nails fix the hands to the wood.

Sixth, I want to attend to Jesus's last words: "My God, my God, why have you forsaken me," at the moment of death (Mark 15:34; Matt. 27:46). These are strong words, raising questions of blasphemy as well as the trustworthiness of Christ's self-proclaimed mission—so strong that there have been attempts to avoid them from early on. Both the Gospel of Luke and John compose different versions. Whether it is historically correct that Jesus cites Psalm 22 on the cross is of course beyond the scope of verification. Yet, for Jürgen Moltmann, Christ's last words sum up the real significance of the cross. As Moltmann points out, the depth of this crisis can first be recognized when one takes into consideration the fact that Jesus had devoted his entire life to this God; Jesus lived and taught the kingdom of God and even dared to call God his Father. Yet, in the crucial moment, God is absent. Jesus's isolation is absolute. Moltmann sees this as introducing a rift within God, specifically between the Father and the Son—a rift that will only be reconciled in the resurrection. However, prior to the resurrection, "Jesus ends with an open question concerning God."[73]

Because Moltmann conceives the final words in terms of the Father-Son relationship, he offers little reflection on the concrete body on the cross and, consequently, the connection between incarnation and the cross. Yet it is possible to approach godforsakenness from the phenomenology of the body. Pain puts all relations on trial. One important reason for this is that pain is always undergone alone, and is therefore often difficult to communicate to others. Under normal circumstances, expressions of pain are pleas for consolation, and, correspondingly, to understand and acknowledge the other's pain means to meet those pleas. Under torture, however, such pleas are in vain, since the situation is designed to prevent any form of help or consolation. When Jesus is hung on a high beam, others can only watch him from afar, but not respond to him. In this way, the torture scene dramatizes what is true of acute pain: pain often comes with isolation.

Unacknowledged pain comes with a loss of community. Moreover, when sufficiently intense, pain will suppress everything else—the world and others in it. The presence it holds fills all of our attention. As Weil said, there is no longer room for others, not even for God. As for Christ, the universe is compressed to a lived body, condensed in the iron nail. It is not by chance that Christ utters his godforsakenness in the most painful state. His utter solitude, feeling abandoned by the community and by God, does not need further explanation since it is inscribed in the phenomena of intense pain itself.

Seventh, the cross is often regarded as the symbol of salvation, but taken more straightforwardly, it is also a manifestation of evil. The sensation of pain, Levinas has claimed, already contains the basic structure of evil, in the form of an excess that refuses to be assimilated to meaning or purpose. Accordingly, the experience of suffering pain gives itself in a way that undercuts any theodicy. Theodicy, understood as a justification of evil in the face of a loving and almighty God, makes evil a rational problem that calls for conceptual solutions, such as Leibniz's invention of the best of all possible worlds.[74] In acute pain, however, a detached view of the world, or of all possible worlds, is no longer available, and certainly not the free exercise of rational thought. As Henry argues, if we follow Leibniz's search for a rational explanation of the present state, evil will only appear insofar as it is made visible in the world. But for that reason, the important part is left out: to speak meaningfully about evil, there must be someone affected by it, someone able to feel and suffer it. Whatever sense evil has according to worldly representations, Henry argues that it is not suffered by anyone and still lacks a phenomenological foundation.[75] Insofar as we live life in enjoyment Henry claims that the why-question simply does not appear. But what about pain and Christ in pain? Does it not raise the question of evil?

In the preaching of Jesus, there is a tendency to abort all explanations of suffering. When the question is raised whether someone who was born blind is a punishment of the parents' sin, Jesus unequivocally replies no (John 9:1–3); and similarly, when eighteen men are killed as a tower fell down on them, he likewise refuses to see it as divine punishment (Luke 13:4–5). What about his own innocent suffering? In the face of all theories of atonement and sacrifice, Falque argues that suffering leads not only to an absence of response, but, in Jesus's case, to "a negation of any affirmative response."[76] On the cross, there are no answers given, no supernatural intervention, no voice heard from above. For Falque, the pain on the cross leaves us with the imperative: "let all discourse cease and let pain speak."[77] To finite human beings, imposed pain appears utterly meaningless, devoid of conceivable purpose—and not even Christ is given any answer to why this is happening to him.[78] Christianity therefore, in Falque's view, does not provide any escape or catharsis from pain, and he contends that its meaninglessness must be maintained in its bodily manifestation.

Falque's contention closes off the horizon on which any possible theodicy could be spelled out, and it also prohibits any why-questions

CHAPTER 7

from arising in the first place. However, this flies in the face of the Gospels' "My God, my God, why have you forsaken me?" In other words, if no answer is proposed, at least there remains a question. This leaves us with a problem. For while Henry and Falque have pointed out how totalizing pain annuls the distance that makes the question possible, the accounts of the Gospels capture the sense in which evil comes with a troubling "why?" In Henry's case, the interiority of pure suffering does not refer to reasoning beyond its own auto-affection. Yet, Henry does not fail to register the crucial role the why-question plays, and he even confirms that the "why" springs up from suffering itself:

> It is from the ground of the interiority of suffering that the cry of this question emerges to the subject. By casting the horizon of the question beyond itself, suffering instinctually invokes the world of exteriority which, putting everything outside of itself, would unburden suffering itself.[79]

The why-question both wells up from the interiority in pain and creates a distance from itself by projecting the question onto the world. This reflects the first step of the dynamics of suffering as suggested by Levinas: being in pain, one cannot help but want to flee it. At the same time, again in proximity to Levinas, Henry underlines that any distanciation or escape cannot succeed: "But this distancing of suffering from its internal and living reality, this way of alienating itself from itself and casting off the weight of its own being, does not and cannot ever occur."[80] The why-question is caught in a strange loop, where the question inevitably occurs at the same time as it is undone.

The need to escape the inescapable means despair. When Christ cries out his abandonment, posed as the question "why?," this is precisely the expression of despair. His exclamation on the cross is a perfectly human cry directed to God. It is a question of meaning, relation, and comfort, in a situation that does not allow for any of these. According to its structure of despair, the evils of pain must always raise the question anew and yet it can never reach a final answer. Hence, Henry is right in claiming that theodicy seeks an answer outside the suffering itself that cannot match the pain. Yet we must add that it is nevertheless pain itself that makes us seek explanations. The cross does not provide any such explanations either. It is rather a powerful manifestation of the evils of human pain, and beyond that, the unrestricted divine solidarity with human pain.

These seven interconnected aspects of the crucifixion—being suspended on the cross, nakedness, being pierced by nails, being nailed to

INCARNATION AND THE CROSS

the cross, crying out in solitude, and manifesting evil—draw upon the preceding chapters and converge in a singular, condensed event. They align with Irenaeus's and Tertullian's belief that Christ possessed a body like ours: not only having a lived body, but also skin and nerves, flesh and blood. Christ is even susceptible to our affects, including the darkest and most aversive affect of all—pain. The cross is where Christ is manifest as fully human, and thus serves as the preeminent revelation of the specific incarnation.

8

Embodied Hope

The death of Jesus must have been a catastrophic event for the first disciples. Without any divine intervention, all hopes for the new Messiah were extinguished. Remarkably, when God seems absent and all hope lost, the Gospels narrate a dramatic reversal as Christ rises on the third day. It was the resurrection that became the event which ignited faith and hope anew among the early believers. This renewed hope was firmly rooted in the Easter faith.[1] Regardless of one's interpretation, this does suggest some general structures of hope worth considering. According to the Christian narrative, hope does not negate loss and despair, but springs in a sense forth from them. In an ultimate sense, hope implies that death, the absolute boundary for human life, does not define the horizon of hope. Hope can extend beyond death, and, according to this narrative, the human body serves as the pivot between loss and hope, death and life.

However, this proposition might be problematic: it seems conceptually confused to assert that hope primarily arises in a situation of hopelessness. As for the body, it is no secret that it will eventually become a corpse and decay. The Platonic notion of the immortal soul is untroubled by this, but the conception of the resurrection of the body certainly is. Moreover, claiming that the body is integral to the concept of hope seems to contradict the nature of hope, since hope is not constrained by the body, its finite position, its states, or capabilities. What we hope for, it seems, is precisely what transcends our limitations within our bodily situation here and now. Nevertheless, I want to propose that hope—even the ultimate hope beyond death—is anchored in our incarnate state, that it emerges from hopelessness, and that the ultimate hope beyond death may encompass the body. Before elaborating on this position, let me suggest an outline of some aspects of temporality that is relevant for my analysis of hope.

Temporality of Everydayness, Pleasure, and Pain

Husserl's analysis of time consciousness distinguishes between different strata of temporality, such as the absolute streaming temporal conscious-

176

ness, constituted immanent time, and objective time. Within such stratification, Husserl provides complex analyses of how the three phases of past, present, and future intersect.[2] While Husserl's analyses have proved decisive for later phenomenological investigations of temporality, he does not deal with how shifting contexts of our life in the world shape different experiences of time. While Heidegger offers a novel understanding of the relationship between time and being in general, rooted in Dasein's care, his analysis of the temporality of everydayness is particularly relevant in my context, because it highlights how one mode of Dasein's existence corresponds to a specific experience of time. Since everydayness is the most common experience of time, it can also serve as a backdrop for understanding the temporality of pleasure and pain.

For Heidegger, everydayness denotes the mode in which we for the most part encounter the world. The notion of everydayness that runs through *Being and Time* seems to serve a double goal. On the one hand, it outlines the place where every phenomenological reflection can get started, namely in the pre-reflective engagements where things and others are given in average ways. On the other hand, Heidegger employs everydayness to show why phenomena not only reveal themselves as they are, but at the same time remain covered up.[3] This latter point is captured in the way everydayness signifies Dasein's tendency to become absorbed in the world to the point where it falls away from itself and loses itself in its occupations. Everydayness is the existential mode in which we live from day to day, according to repetitions and social conventions. In such inauthentic mode of existence, we lead our lives according to "the They" (*das Man*).[4]

Everydayness has its own characteristic temporality, which shapes the way the ecstasies of past, present, and future appear to us. Heidegger characterizes such time experience as "the monotony, the habit, the 'like yesterday, so today and tomorrow.'"[5] The unfolding of time itself is hardly taken notice of; it just moves on without ruptures or surprises. Even as this monotony leads us to take time for granted in its inauthentic mode, that time is conditioned by a deeper temporal structure that belongs to Dasein itself. Or as Heidegger continues the quote above: "the 'like yesterday, so today and tomorrow' and the 'for the most part' cannot be grasped without recourse to the 'temporal' stretching along of Dasein."[6] The inauthentic temporality of everydayness is thus a modification of Dasein's temporality that Heidegger deploys according to the basic structure of care.

One striking thing about Heidegger's everydayness is its lack of complexity and heterogeneity. It is as if nothing new or different comes to pass within ordinary life. But even if there is certainly more to say about

CHAPTER 8

the everyday, Heidegger has nonetheless elucidated one important aspect that belongs to everydayness, namely its inherent tendency to level out time experience into one monotonous and repetitive pattern. Now, both pain and pleasure can come to pass within the average everydayness, yet the more intense they get, the more they appear as breaking away from the duration of everydayness. How does the temporality of pain and pleasure relate to that of everydayness? Both intense pain and pleasure seem to diverge from the usual monotony of everydayness, albeit in distinct ways. Notably, their inherent temporality suggests that pain and pleasure should not be regarded as binary poles sharing the same phenomenological foundation, but instead must be treated as separate phenomena from the outset.

The experience of the present according to pleasure is not the presence of everydayness where each moment repeats a homogenous continuity, "like yesterday, so today and tomorrow." Pleasure makes the present grow and swell around itself, filled with its own satisfaction. Its temporal fullness is structurally like Husserl's living present: it is not punctual, as a pure transition, since it encompasses a halo of "not yet" and "not any longer." If the moment of pleasure swells, it does not freeze the experience of the passing of time, since the quality of the present stands out against the fact that it will inevitably slip away. This awareness of the slipping away of time enhances the intensity of the swollen moment, so that the melancholy over its transient character follows pleasure as its shadow. Nevertheless, the pleasures of food, wine, caresses, and erotic experience announce themselves with the imperative that they *must* last, for pleasure demands, as it were, its own perpetuation. This imperative of perpetuation inscribed in pleasure does not outline a goal, because, as Levinas has pointed out, pleasure seeks nothing further but the presence of pleasure itself.[7] Embodiment feels light even as it is intensified, life is suspended from its concerns, pleasure knows no plans, for pleasure is carefree—like the lilies and the birds (Matt. 6:26–29). And yet there is a future horizon peculiar to it. It is not directed toward the new, the different, or the surprising, but rather the opposite: just as the pleasure regrets the slipping into the past, its future is sketched out as its own prolongation. With regard to this temporal characteristic, Nietzsche is right in noting that "joy wants itself, wants eternity, wants recurrence, wants everything eternally the same."[8] We could even say that in enjoyment, an eternity is inscribed in its phenomenality: one wants it to repeat itself, in exactly the same way, to continue endlessly without breach. Even if it will not last, one can say that pleasure is anticipating the eternal now, even beyond time, as a foretaste of a state it demands to come.

The temporality of pain differs from the time of everydayness in another manner than pleasure does. Where pleasure lets the instant swell and lifts the embodied experience into weightlessness, pain violently breaks into the temporal flow and rivets the flesh to its bodily density and weight. The experience of pain, Husserl has said, is always localized. It fixes the body in pain to its inescapable "here." Likewise, time does not swell but shrinks into a fixed, immovable "now." Unlike the time of pleasure, there is no hint of melancholy over the slipping away of time; rather, what tortures the sufferer is that the lasting presence will *not* go away soon enough. Pleasure wants eternity, Nietzsche observes, but pain claims the opposite—"go away, refrain!"[9] It is because pain craves for escape from the present that the lingering time becomes an essential part of its suffering. Pain, however, does not go away, but stays. It makes all temporal escape in vain, as if pain entraps the sufferer in its present.

The ordinary streaming temporality is now experienced as frozen; the duration of time does not occur as passing or streaming but is brought to a standstill. This does not mean that there is no past and future to the pain experience, but that the way they are given is altered significantly. The past is no longer experienced as passing away from the present as a comet tail.[10] The past rather becomes uncoupled from the present, for it is no longer lived as an integral part of who one is. The saturated presence of pain has no place for the anticipation of a future, either. Pain cuts the sufferer off from the projects that filled his or her everydayness with directions and goals. The future does not lay ahead as an opportunity to carry on in the same or in a different way but becomes a wall behind which one cannot see. In this sense, pain is not structured by the rhythm of everydayness, not even by the existential care of which Heidegger speaks—it cannot care about what tomorrow brings. As Saulius Geniusas has pointed out: "To suffer from pain is to be stranded in the field of presence, which, at the level of explicit temporality, is lived as infinite sameness in that it is cut adrift from other temporal fields."[11] The future as well as the past are to some degree repressed beneath the weight of pain's intrusive force, and are no longer organically connected to the present. Such split-off temporal horizons will tend to appear as somewhat irreal—irreal because they simply do not matter to the living present.[12] To the extent that the sufferer nevertheless addresses the past and the future, it comes as an implicit or explicit revolt against it. It may come as in Job, cursing his birth and longing for death, that is, as the annihilation of time (Job 3:3, 21), or it may appear as a strange and stubborn hope, as if there must, despite the present, be something completely different to come.

CHAPTER 8

The Phenomenology of Hope

Before I explore the specific way in which pain can lead to hope, it is necessary to establish the outline of the phenomenology of hope. As its most salient character, hope has a specific temporal orientation toward the future. At the level of Husserl's analyses of immanent time, the imminent future announces itself as the protention that outlines things to come. Protention is itself part of the extended, lived presence and signifies how relatively empty intentions direct themselves to its expected fulfillment.[13] Such intentions are shaped on the basis of retentions, and according to the identity of the temporal object, the retentions are turned into anticipations of the coming phase. This holds true of more complex experiences as well: when I hear a sonata, I do not "hope" that the harmonic tension will resolve, but my expectations will implicitly anticipate it. Expectations are therefore markedly different from hope. I can, for instance, hope that a deadlocked personal conflict I am in will end in a reconciliation. In the latter case, there is no immediate expectation that anticipates an outcome according to the style of retentions, but instead there are mediate intentions that stretch beyond the lived presence toward the future as a separate field.[14]

Unlike memory, which reaches back to old intentions that have already been fulfilled, hope for the future is essentially unfulfilled. At the moment it is fulfilled (or disappointed), the future is turned into a present perception, and it is no longer hope. Saint Paul captures hope as essentially unfulfilled with precision when he writes that "hope that is seen is not hope. For who hopes for what is seen? But if we hope for what we do not see, we wait for it with patience" (Rom. 8:24–25). For the same reason, Augustine notes that in the life to come, love will flourish but faith and hope will no longer exist, since they will be fulfilled.[15] Even as hope is essentially unfulfilled, it does not lack direction toward what it hopes for. On the noetic pole, hope is lacking in fulfillment, yet its noematic pole, what it hopes for, must be outlined, even though it transgresses our expectations. Because of the excess over the factually given, hope is both unfulfilled and emphatically open.

Husserl does not say much about hope, but his analyses of expectations are relevant here. Expectations maintain an orientation to the future. These expectations are shaped by the content already given to us in retention, so we anticipate something similar based on the continuous style of previous occurrences.[16] The past thus shapes our expectations for the future. When our expectations are not fulfilled, the noema "explodes" and forces forth a revised perception. The fact that phenomena can turn out differently than expected attests to the relative openness of the horizon. But according to Husserl, such relative openness can only be conceived on the background of a fundamentally determined, familiar horizon, just as a surprise presupposes specific expectations. The primacy of the familiar horizon will in turn make the integration of the indeterminate or deviant possible and render it determinate.[17]

Like expectations, hope also implies an openness to the future, a future whose scope and direction are molded by the sedimentations of past experiences. The question remains whether the structures of expectation become too restrictive to capture the phenomenon of hope, both because expectations are shaped in similarity to the retentions, and because expectations tend to incorporate the anticipated within a stable, foreseeable horizon. Expectations, therefore, lack the radical openness of hope. Even if the hoped-for must be rooted positively or negatively in our familiar horizons, it is entirely possible to hope for something without predicting its fulfillment; one can even hope for something that conflicts with retentions and sedimentations. It is true that Husserl also speaks of the absolute horizon in terms of telos, at times identified as God.[18] But such a telos is less the open future correlated with hope than it is a principle of reason inscribed in the development of the sciences. If Husserl's analyses are applied to hope, it becomes clear that he leaves little room for hope for something absolutely new or a radical change. As Klaus Held has explained, the problem with Husserl's position is this:

> The "starting point" of such consciousness is already embedded in the retentional-protentional stream of consciousness, meaning that the "new" can always only occur as a response to certain prefigurations emerging from the retentional sedimentations of previous protentions and their fulfillment. There is no possibility that absolutely "new" events could emerge.[19]

In one respect, Husserl's account corresponds with Heidegger's everydayness: the streaming of time fundamentally affirms the already familiar and established: what holds for yesterday is true of today and tomorrow.

It is, however, this very homogeneity of the inauthentic mode that, according to Heidegger, is questioned in anxiety and the confrontation with death. Such experiences, Held argues, force us to "admit of the possibility of a future which radically surprises a human being."[20] Hope, at least in its radical sense, must hope for a future that is more than a prolongation of the now, or else it is a matter of expectation. Although it is true that hope must somehow be motivated by the familiarity of the lived present, its motivations tend to be negative. Satisfaction does not motivate hope, since it is happy with the present and does not yearn for any change to come. Hope, however, stretches out toward something different, a change, something that breaks with the present and past. In contrast, Husserl's expectations simply presuppose the unbroken relation between past, present, and future, relying on the continuous style of how things are.[21]

For hope to be something more than a blind leap, it must be projected from the lived present and motivated in a way that guides its direction. This motivation must stem from some form of lack of satisfaction; otherwise, hope would not stretch out toward something different and better. As Levinas points out: "What produces the thrust of hope is the gravity of the instant in which it occurs. The irreparable is its natural atmosphere."[22] It is this gravity—experienced as repressive, depressive, irreparable, or painful—that demands a future change that is beyond the "natural atmosphere" of the present situation. Gabriel Marcel sometimes speaks broadly of the experience of captivity as the soil of hope, where one is somehow prevented from fulfilling one's life and therefore turns to the hope of liberation. At times, Marcel invokes the metaphor of darkness and the hope for light: "As a matter of fact, the soul always turns to a light which it does not yet perceive, a light yet to be born, in the hope of being delivered from its present darkness, the darkness of waiting."[23] Across these different metaphors, two basic teachings are conveyed. First, hope wells up from the thrust of a situation, what Marcel calls imprisonment or darkness; and second, the hope that grows out of the darkness does not rely on something perceptually given (the light is not yet born) or on its expected fulfillment (as only darkness surrounds the one waiting).

An interesting account in this respect is Jonathan Lear's analysis of what he terms "radical hope." Plenty Coups, the last chief of the Crow nation in the United States, faced the prospect of the end of his tribe's form of life, which was indeed a situation of darkness. Lear is struck by how Plenty Coups nevertheless had hope. A dream convinced Plenty Coups that the form of life as they knew it would end, but that life would go on nonetheless, and more, that something good would come out of it. This, Lear points out, was not simply naive optimism, since Plenty Coups was not blind to the severe threats facing his people's cultural identity and form of life. What made his hope radical in Lear's sense is precisely the way it transcended the situation. There was nothing in its present state that supported any belief in a good future, and more importantly, what was hoped for went beyond any clear conception of the hope's fulfillment.[24] The hope's radicality departed from the ordinary conditions sedimented from the past and oriented itself toward a future that was clouded in uncertainties. Radical hope is therefore not a matter of expectation. Paradoxically, it seems that hope arises from situations that are precisely hopeless in the sense that a hoped-for outcome is not within the scope of what we can bring about.[25] Hope is therefore waiting for the hoped-for, patiently awaiting its deferred fulfillment that may or may not come to pass.

If a certain outcome is at my disposal, it merely depends on mustering strength, finding efficient ways to handle the situation, or finding the right means to that end. Hope first arises when the situation is out of my hands, not within the scope of "I can"; situations, that is, when I cannot bring the hoped-for about. In such cases, I implicitly or explicitly appeal to some otherness beyond me on which the hope depends.[26] Thus, when Plenty Coups hopes despite the probable destruction of the Crow nation's traditional way of life, without knowing what good can eventually come out of it, his hope is upheld by a deep trust in something beyond him. What is the nature of this "beyond" that supports hope despite everything?

Held has argued that Husserl's appeal to the basic trust in the world or *Urdoxa* can be taken as such a "beyond." However troubled my situation is, the world will always be there. Even when my expectations are disappointed, the world continues to open up new possibilities provided by horizons of expectation. These horizons can redirect our intentions, springing up from the world that is stable and constant. In this way, Held believes that Husserl's basic trust in the world will facilitate the motivational foundation of hope.[27] However, while it is true that hope takes some form of trust in something beyond myself, I have already expressed doubt about whether the closed circle of the familiar world can be the basis of hope's trust. The trust in the world does buttress a reliable continuity from the present to the future, but not toward something new or different. Interestingly, Held goes on to argue that there is something more to the "beyond" than just a trust in the world, since hope implies some kind of power that supports it even when it goes beyond any conceivable fulfillment or outstrips the compass of "I can." This insight was, according to Held, already known in Scholasticism, where the theological virtues of faith, love, and hope had the structure of gift, that is, something granted us independent of our achievements. As a contemporary manner of preserving this insight, Held suggests that hope appears as a basic mood (*Stimmung*), which is part of my factuality even while its power is not mine. Whether or not mood will capture the temporal dimension of hope, as fundamentally future-oriented, can be discussed.[28] But the point, for now, is that moods elucidate how hope implies a reference to something given to us, from beyond ourselves. In Held's version of it, hope does not have to be religiously conceived, yet he notes that such a conception corresponds with the biblical notion of grace.[29]

If hope cannot be upheld solely by my own powers, it corresponds to an acknowledgment of my finitude. The positive side of such acknowledgment, Anthony Steinbock argues, is that it refers to a dependence on an other-than-me that sustains hope. Steinbock distinguishes between two levels of hope: a concrete hope-act with specific content, and a ground for hope that makes the former possible. The latter need not be thematized; one does not first have to discover the ground in order to establish a hope-act. It is rather the other way around: through hoping for something specific, one can come to discover the other-than-me which sustains hope and makes it possible.[30] In a similar spirit to Held, Steinbock argues that such ground for hope need not be religiously conceived, but still it points to a religious dimension: "Even though hope does not have its only significance in the religious dimension of experience, hope takes on its full significance at this level."[31] In Marcel's analysis of hope, we find a more explicit religious horizon. In opposition to what Marcel terms the attitude of Having, which is characterized by a possessive attitude to oneself and one's surroundings, absolute hope concerns Being pure and simple. To Marcel, such Being suggests a religious significance. Absolute hope, Marcel writes,

> appears as a response of the creature to the infinite Being to whom it is conscious of owing everything that it has and upon whom it cannot impose any condition whatsoever without scandal. From the moment that I abase myself in some sense before the absolute Thou who in his infinite condescension has brought me forth out of nothingness, it seems as though I forbid myself ever again to despair.[32]

It may seem peculiar to prohibit oneself from despairing in the face of life's hardships, especially since Marcel has emphasized that human hope is triggered by imprisonment and darkness. Marcel also asserts that hope typically emerges through the cracks and openings of our otherwise possessive attitude of Having.[33] The point in the quote above, however, seems to articulate what Steinbock calls the grounds of hope, even in an idealized form, where the ego is not conceived in terms of self-mastery, but rather as finite and dependent on something beyond, or in this case a divine Thou to whom it owes everything. One of the upshots of Marcel's perspective on hope is that the trust of hope is decisively not anchored in a stable world, but refers to the divine creative power by which new and unforeseen possibilities arise. On such a ground, a radically open hope can be sustained.

Pain and Negative Hope

I previously outlined how the embodied sensations of pain and pleasure possess distinct temporal structures. I now want to propose that a phenomenology of pain can lead to an understanding of embodied hope. At first glance, searching for motivations for hope in pain appears futile, since I have noted how pain severs relations with others as well as with the religious Other and, in this sense, dismantles any trust in anything beyond. Moreover, I have argued that the temporal structure of pain uncouples the present from the past and future. Consequently, the temporality of pain appears utterly resistant to hope—and in one sense, it is. Pain nullifies the hope, or at least the expectation, of a direct path from the present to its future resolution, as it drives a wedge between the frozen present on the one hand and the past and future on the other. However, the past is not entirely obliterated, nor is the future. Cut off from his flowing temporal horizons, the only way the sufferer can reach out beyond his temporal imprisonment is by negating the ordinary future and past and projecting hope toward *another* horizon. While the one in pain is anchored to the body and confined to the present, a peculiar hope may arise, one that negates the current state and everything associated with it. This hope aspires to a radical change—overcoming pain, undoubtedly, but also the potential for the entirety of reality to unfold anew. Charles Bell captures this perspective, writing that to "imagine the absence of pain, is not only to imagine a new state of being but a change in the earth and all upon it."[34]

While they share significant structures, I want to differentiate radical hope, which concerns hope despite all probabilities, from what I will call "negative hope," which is hope motivated by bodily pain. The negation inherent in this term aims to express that negative hope opposes the sufferer's temporal and spatial situatedness, that is, the frozenness of time and the fixation on localization in the body. It is not sustained by a basic trust in the world or a reliance on its continuity. In its stubborn future orientation, negative hope turns to something beyond the given horizon, something other and unforeseen, indeed a "hope against hope" (Rom. 4:18). The Pauline hope against hope, "in spite of" everything, is correlated with a "how much more," which according to Ricoeur goes beyond the logic of equivalence toward a logic of surplus. The surplus of "how much more" transcends what seems possible and intimates another horizon beyond the horizon of expectations.[35]

In the absence of natural motivation and support, from where does such hope arise? It arises from the body, or more specifically, from pain's internal imperative. The imperative is already latent in Levinas's account of pain's urge to escape the inescapable, and even more succinctly in Nietzsche's observation that pain says: "go away, refrain!"[36] The imperative is given with pain and yet demands its own overcoming: from pain against pain. The manner in which this imperative turns into negative hope is by projecting it into the future. While the future of hope is open, negative hope gives it a particular direction: It entails that there must arrive a future radically different from the painful present. However, since pain is inescapable and fixed to the present, the imperative pushes beyond the future of everydayness, to another future that "must" arrive.

This point is nicely portrayed in the book of Job. As mentioned, Job's pain situates him in a state where the past makes no sense, and the future seems blocked (Job 3). But in the midst of Job's most fervent protests and despair, beams of hope break in, and he suddenly professes that his redeemer lives, even if he will first see Him after death (Job 19:25–26). From one perspective, this seems completely unmotivated, but from the perspective of negative hope, it becomes understandable. Job suddenly reaches out, beyond the horizon of expectation, and clings to a hope against all hope. And Job *must* do so, according to pain's imperative. The grammar of this "must" is not based on certainty and prediction, but is more aligned with Kant's categorical imperative, with the important difference that it is not imposed by the moral law but by the phenomenon of pain itself.[37] From this imperative, hope directs itself to the other future, both in reaching toward it and insisting on the imperative of its arrival.[38] This hoped-for arrival is, in Paul's lingo, "so much more" that must arrive at the "not yet" of hope. The hope against hope lives in this strange interval of time, between the frozen present, the lost past, and the unattainable future, and precisely from there, negative hope turns toward another future.

There might, however, be problems with my conception of negative hope. If such hope is not about an expected future, and is not based on the basic trust of the world, it is obviously not restricted to what we ordinarily think of as our reality. Hence, one might suspect that such hope is nothing but wishful thinking produced by our imagination. In a passage of his work on the imagination, Sartre distinguishes between a lived future based on protentions, and an imagined future which is detached from the lived situation and posited as that which is not yet. So far, the imagined future seems to account well for hope. However, Sartre's purpose is to underline the fact that imagination, unlike perception, lays no claim on the reality of the world, but employs our ability to posit irreality by annihilating the reality. Correspondingly, the imagined future isolates this "future and posits it for itself but by cutting it off from all reality and annihilating it, by *presentifying it as nothingness.*"[39]

It is easy to agree that imaginaries of the future do not posit a world as real as perception does, and for negative hope, it is apt to say that it annihilates the present in the sense that it transcends it. But since Sartre's account of the imagined future has nothing to do with perception or sensations, it does not arise from or respond to any perceptions or sensations either. Applied to hope, this will lead to the conclusion that hope is freely made up, nothing but wishful thinking or an irreal illusion, since it responds to no perceptual restraints. While there is no hard evidence against such a charge, since the radical openness cannot be verified or fulfilled from the standpoint of hope, I have, nevertheless, argued that negative hope has an inner sense of necessity following from the imperative of pain. If hope can well up from pain, it cannot be detached from its sensational content, and thus Sartre's imagined future fails to capture negative hope. Admittedly, hope can be populated with images and fantasies, but the free work of imagination is in this case secondary; fantasies can merely offer surrogates for the deferred fulfillment of hope, but not constitute it.

But then another problem arises: Does not the hoped-for state strangely repress the reality of the suffering, or at least cover over its reality in the face of a better future? Although Levinas supports the thought that hope can spring up from pain, he is nevertheless critical of the way in which hope is often taken to be part of an economy, where efforts lead to leisure, pain to release, and suffering to compensation. Alluding to Christianity, Levinas argues that by projecting a state in which all tears will be wiped away or death overcome in the life to come, the same economy is at stake: the future compensation is supposed to make up for the present suffering. However, the economy of compensation leads to a forgetfulness of the unforgivable and the irreparable undergone by the sufferer. For pain in the instant, writes Levinas, is not an object that can be exchanged for a future; rather, "the suffering of the present remains like a cry whose echo will resound forever in the eternity of space."[40]

This hyperbolic description makes at least one thing clear: a future compensation is no solution to the instant of pain. And yet, Levinas speaks of hope and salvation, but he does so by investing the hope in a new sense of the present. Hope must steadfastly be anchored in the presence of pain, a presence that in turn calls for another understanding of temporality—not the time of economy, but one located beneath it, on a more mysterious level. According to Levinas, such time is the constant resurrection within the instant, which is his version of messianic time. The death and resurrection unfolding in the present also bring a sense of future, a future that is nothing but the very resurrection and newness

CHAPTER 8

of the present.[41] By means of this notion of the future of the present, Levinas can interpret hope not as turning toward the distant, but as a response to the present: "All acuteness of hope in the midst of despair comes from the exigency that the very instant of despair [must] be redeemed. To understand the mystery of the work of time, we should start with the hope for the present, taken as a primary fact."[42]

However imperative it may be, isn't negative hope a false hope, a hope for compensation for a lived experience that cannot be altered by it? Is it not merely one of those ways we deceive ourselves in order to divert attention from our present suffering and despair? In the contested epilogue of the book of Job, after having endured immense suffering and losses, Job's estate, family members, wealth, and honor are suddenly restored to him (Job 42:10–15). Some commentators have found this happy ending even more intolerable than the trials Job underwent, as if they could simply be erased by such compensation.[43] However, alternative readings of this ending are possible. It can be seen as a mythical scenario, or more precisely, as an eschatological pointer that corresponds to the negative hope Job occasionally expresses. In this case, the ending is not so much about compensation as it is a mythical articulation of an impossible transformation beyond loss and pain, as glimpsed in negative hope.

Even if hope need not be considered as compensation for present suffering, Levinas remains cautious about any reference to a distant future that overshadows the present moment. But one could just as easily counter Levinas's argument, for it is difficult to see how hope could be hope unless it yearns for a radically different future. Insisting that hope feeds on the constant renewal of the present seems to be a distressing message to those who are immersed in the inescapable presence of pain. One might hope for the renewal of the present, but since that state has not presently arrived, it still seems to imply a future. Negative hope does not necessarily inscribe itself in the economy of exchange and compensation; it hopes for a radical change that figures on the horizon of a different future that remains radically open.

At first glance, one should expect the crucifixion of Christ to give rise to negative hope. But if Christ's last words are "My God, my God, why have you forsaken me?" there seems to be no suggestion of hope, but rather hopelessness or despair. Following Steinbock's analysis, a hopeless endeavor is specifically tied to a specific goal that one realizes cannot be attained. Nonetheless, the ground of hope is not thereby affected, just suspended for this occasion. If the hopelessness becomes global, however, then one despairs, for in despair one resigns not from a particular goal one is hoping to achieve, but from the very sustainability of hope itself.[44] This makes despair into the very reversal of hope, for it denies the very trust that sustains hope. Despair shares a futural orientation with hope, but it finds no support for hope in it. The one in despair does not necessarily deny that there are powers and dimensions beyond himself. It is just that they are outside that person's control and are turned against him or her. In despair, one no longer has trust in any way out, and as Steinbock puts it, despair "is the experience of abandonment as ultimate and decisive."[45]

Even in the darkest expressions of despair, even as pain tears Christ out of all relation, he addresses himself, as the Son, directly to his Father, as "my God." This seems to be little, almost nothing, and yet it means holding on to the fundamental trust, as if reaching out one last time to hope for something beyond the walls that imprison him. This dialectic inherent to negative hope is in fact part of the rhythm of the psalm that Jesus invokes. Right after the expression of abandonment, the psalm suddenly turns to hope, based on trust: "In you our ancestors trusted; they trusted, and you delivered them. To you they cried, and were saved; in you they trusted, and were not put to shame" (Psalm 22:4–5). The memory of the previous trust becomes the promise to hope for. Perhaps we could take such juxtaposition as the psalm's way of mirroring negative hope, which also resonates in Christ's last words.

Hope and Promise

My analysis of the embodied negative hope so far has appeared rather abstract. I have suggested that the imperative demands that things must change, but apart from that, little is said about the content of what is hoped for. In a way, this follows naturally from hope's excessive openness to the future, and there are dangers of being too specific when it comes to the content of hope. Ernst Bloch has criticized theological eschatologies for saying too much, erecting mythological depictions of the hoped-for state, and in so doing confusing hope with assurance. Moltmann agrees, claiming that there should be an iconoclasm of hope because hope is precisely invested in what is not seen.[46] Hope does have an intentional directedness, but since its fulfillment is kept in suspense, it is also open to the surprises of the future.

Theology tends to be quite specific about hope. Despite his invocation of iconoclasm, Moltmann takes for granted that all Christian hope is centered on Christ. This might be a problem if it means that the hope is somehow already fulfilled, say as the fulfillment of a promise. And indeed, Moltmann regards promises as indispensable for understanding hope and its role in the biblical tradition. He argues that promises and fulfillment are the central dynamics in the narrative axis of the Bible as a whole, and especially for understanding the resurrection of Christ as the ultimate fulfillment of all promises. But if promises guarantee a future outcome, how can they avoid making hope at best superfluous? Unfortunately, Moltmann is not always clear on this issue, but there are some basic tenets found in his theology that should make it possible to see how promise and hope do not necessarily eclipse one another.

In approaching the relation between promise and hope, it is helpful to pick up again Steinbock's distinction between hope-acts, which are directed to something hoped for, and the ground for hope, which supports it from beyond itself.[47] Accordingly, we could apply this to Moltmann by suggesting that God's promises should be regarded as belonging to the ground for hope, whereas the hope in the resurrection of the body, after the image of Christ's risen body, can be understood as a hope-act. Thus, while the present world leaves no doubt that all bodies will die and perish, the resurrection of Christ implies a trust in the promise that sustains the hope in a resurrection for all, despite everything we know. The promise issues a trust in a creative power beyond my reach, even beyond the present horizon. Even though Moltmann speaks, perhaps too unguardedly, about hope as anticipation of a future due to the promise, he holds that the future remains a hidden future. What makes hope in such a hidden future possible to maintain is the promise. In this sense, Moltmann locates the promise in between—in between knowing and not-knowing, between necessity and possibility, between what already is and what is to come. Hope sustained by promise is therefore oriented toward a future from the present, without any guaranteed outcome, as it remains "provisional, fragmentary, open, straining beyond itself."[48]

Given that the resurrection is the fulfillment of Old Testament promises, how can it instill hope since it is already fulfilled with Christ? The reason seems to be that fulfillment by the resurrection does not cancel hope, since the resurrection implies a double temporal structure, captured in the Pauline "already" and "not yet." The fulfillment of the promise is given, but with a surplus: the fulfillment that has "already" happened issues a new promise whose fulfillment is postponed and "not yet."[49] It suggests that there is an internal connection between Christ's resurrection, the first fruit, and the universal resurrection to come (1 Cor. 15:23). There is a temporal distinction implied in the order at stake, insofar as the first resurrection has already happened, while the latter is a promise suspended in an eschatological future. With reference to Moltmann, Ricoeur sums this up nicely:

> Resurrection, interpreted within a theology of promise, is not an event which closes, by fulfilling the promise, but an event which opens, because it adds to the promise by confirming it. . . . The meaning of the "Resurrection" is in suspense insofar as it is not fulfilled in a new creation, in a new totality of being. To recognize the Resurrection of Jesus Christ is to enter into the movement of hope in resurrection from the dead, to attain the new creation *ex nihilo*, that is, beyond death.[50]

The hope in the general resurrection is a radical hope, for life as we know it is determined to die. It rather exceeds our experiences, concepts, and expectations.

Whereas hope is oriented toward the future, promises imply a more complex temporal structure. To Moltmann, promise is not only at the heart of the overarching biblical narrative; it fundamentally shapes its sense of past, present, and future. Accordingly, the present lives from a promise of the past and is defined in contrast to the promised future.[51] It seems that promise, thus understood, must be interconnected with both memory and hope, of which Chrétien has provided an interesting analysis. According to Chrétien, memory implies an excess, partly because the past cannot be exhausted by memory, and partly because memory in the last analysis implies the immemorial and unforgettable, which is God. As immemorial, God exceeds the domain of human memory, yet insofar as we bear the imprint of God, being *imago Dei*, God is at the same time unforgettable. In a similar way, hope has its excess, for since hope cannot be an anticipation or a projection drawn from oneself in the way expectations are, it must somehow be given to us from elsewhere. It is this excess that Chrétien calls the unhoped-for. Such givenness from elsewhere is nothing else than the revelation that interrupts and cuts across our worldly concerns, in the instant. Chrétien argues that it is the promise, however, that holds the key to the interrelatedness of memory, hope, and revelation. By means of the promise, one can understand the weave of the temporality at work: the revelation in the present harks back to the promise from the past that it fulfills, and points onward to the excess of an outstanding future. In this way, the "correlation of the sudden, of what takes place once and for all, with the unforgettable and the unhoped-for characterizes all thoughts of the promise. It is at the heart of all biblical theology."[52]

What is it that makes the promise the knot that ties together revelation, memory, and hope, that is, present, past, and future? One important way Chrétien expounds this relation is by a reading of Paul's account of Abraham in the Epistle to the Romans. Despite Abraham's old body and Sarah's barrenness, Abraham maintains his confidence in God's announced promise: "Hoping against hope, he believed that he would become 'the father of many nations'" (Rom. 4:18). According to Chrétien, Paul does not suggest that such hope against hope is a human achievement, precisely because it is as unexpected and impossible as it is unhoped for. In fact, Abraham's first reaction is laughter, since the idea of begetting a child at their age appears ridiculous (Gen. 17:17). And yet, Abraham hung on to God's promise of the unhoped-for future.[53] Moreover, this promise was given in the suddenness of an instant that was not foreseen. The sudden revelation comes as a gift given in and through the human-divine encounter and radically opens memory and anticipations: "The instant of the gift brings together the unforgettable and the unhoped-for, in the gratuity of excess."[54]

According to Chrétien's reading, while Abraham's hope against hope responds to the revelation in the instant, it is made possible by God's promise given in the past. In other words, the promise of the future is only possible due to the recollection of the past. "Memory destines us," writes Chrétien, "it is the place of the promise because it remembers that which promises."[55] Note that Chrétien is not talking about human memory that stores the past or anticipated future as intentional correlates, but about memory and hope made possible by what exceeds them: the immemorial, the unforgettable, and the unhoped-for. While going beyond human power to contain them, this sense of memory and hope is made sustainable due to the promise.

The following passage sums up Chrétien's argument:

> God's promise unites the immemorial, unforgettable, and unhoped for. The genesis is immemorial, for we were not there when God founded the earth, and the origin is always already a past for us, forgotten without return. Through the word of God, this immemorial becomes unforgettable, for the sacred history that we must always remember begins with creation itself. This remembrance of the impossible is anticipation and this memory is hope, for in the Bible praise for the creator God is not separated from praise for the savior God. Recalling the origin belongs properly to hope tending toward the end.[56]

There is an unreachable dimension connected to both the origin as well as to the ultimate end, but we are not completely cut off from them. For there is also the unforgettable word of God and, along with it, the hope for the unhoped-for. It is the promise that ties the temporal dimensions together, from the immemorial to the unhoped-for, and sustains "hope in remembering and remember in hoping."[57] We find a similar conjunction of memory and hope in Ricoeur. In bridging the apparent gulf between Gadamer's hermeneutics and Habermas's critical theory, Ricoeur refers to the inheritance of exodus and resurrection as a dialectic between recollection and the anticipation of freedom. It is not, Ricoeur writes, necessary to "choose between reminiscence and hope! In theological terms, eschatology is nothing without the recitation of acts of deliverance from the past."[58] And I will add, the promise is what holds them together.

The past, reaching back to creation, and the hope pointing onward to the eschatological end, are the poles of what Chrétien calls the "sacred history" in the above quotation. Since he does not elaborate on his understanding of this notion, it is unclear what it entails. However, it seems to involve a tension, for while the creation and salvation remain immemorable and unforeseeable respectively, the notion of the sacred history suggests an overarching tendency in which both are enveloped. Apart from Chrétien's interpretation, sacred history can imply the history of salvation, as in Irenaeus's terms, or, more philosophically, it can overlap with the "wonderful teleology" that Husserl speaks of.[59] In any case, if the promise lies at the heart of such a grand history, one might suspect that it promises too much, because the origin and end seem to be already enclosed in the trajectory of the sacred history. If so, we are back at the problem where the promise cancels hope, leaving no place for the unhoped-for.

Ricoeur proposes a rather different understanding of the sacred history, or rather its reversal, focusing on the crucifixion. Discussing the foolishness of the cross (1 Cor. 1:18), and the outpouring (kenosis) of divinity in Christ (Phil. 2:5–8), Ricoeur argues that Paul emphatically opposes any assimilation of the crucifixion into sacred history.[60] Paul's Christ subverts the expectations of a mighty Messiah, culminating in the passion narrative. Far from being a royal road to triumph and glory, the passion narrative is the path to foolishness and nothingness. Not even the resurrection, Ricoeur argues, can be conceived as a transformation into power, but rather emphasizes and confirms that the way to resurrection passes through abandonment and humiliation. How can we recognize such nothingness and humility of Christ and believe that the sacred history's grand narrative will finally end well? Is there no promise of the resurrection? Ricoeur believes there is a promise and there is also a hope, but they are clearly not underpinned by knowledge and certainty. "If therefore the tie between foolishness and kenosis, on the one hand, and power and exaltation, on the other," Ricoeur writes, "it cannot be known through a rational account, and even cannot be recounted, inscribed in some grand narrative, it must be the object of a hope that respects the mystery."[61] The point I want to retain here is that promise cannot be

CHAPTER 8

divorced from the past and the unexpected future, but neither can it be derived from the teleology of the sacred history.

To sum up, the promise is neither identical with hope-acts, nor does it negate the radical openness of hope, as long as what it promises remains outside the scope of knowledge and anticipation. While one can have trust in the promise, it offers no guarantee and, therefore, allows hope to remain hope, even in the unhoped-for.

Hope and Resurrection

Since hope transcends the present, it can inspire beliefs in some form of life after death. This notion is central to various religious and philosophical systems. In the Christian tradition, that hope is specifically tied to the resurrection of the body, guided by Christ's resurrection, which was initially considered not as evidence of Christ's divinity, but as the inception of a new eschatological era. According to prevalent expectations of the time, one man's resurrection from the dead signifies the initiation of the end-times, in which all who belong to God will subsequently be resurrected.[62] This hope contradicts our knowledge of earthly bodies and their destinies. While all life must die, hope persists despite the seeming impossibility of life after death. Similarly, the body that I inhabit will inevitably decay and return to dust, yet the corresponding hope insists on the resurrection of the body. Hope connected to the body after death can only be a radical hope, which first acknowledges the absolute limit of death and yet maintains hope for a new beginning, in a changed yet recognizable incarnate life.

Can we conceive of a body after death? Confronted with this question, Paul offers a series of analogies, such as the seed and the plant, which all revolve around the strange combination of continuity and discontinuity through death and resurrection (1 Cor. 15:37).[63] Paul gestures in a direction, but does not provide much more. If we instead look for a model of the resurrection as prefigured in Christ as described in the Gospels, we encounter inconsistencies: on the one hand, a tangible body (John 20:27), and on the other, one that suddenly appears and disappears (Luke 24:30). What kind of body can this possibly be? Is it the objective, lived body, or perhaps flesh and blood? The answer remains unclear. However, since Christianity holds that Christ's resurrection provides direction for hope beyond death, it is worth pursuing the question further.

As noted earlier, Falque assumes that incarnation cannot simply mean having a flesh without material and animal dimensions. This would lead to the Gnostic "angelism" that Falque accuses Henry of advocating. Falque's view of incarnation might lead us to expect a strong emphasis on the material and animal dimension of the resurrected body as well, perhaps suggesting an alignment with Tertullian, whose theology Falque sympathizes with. However, this is not the case. Unlike Tertullian, who believes the whole point is the resurrection of the material human body, Falque rejects this option, because a "total identification of the *biological body* with the *resurrected body*, beyond the single case of incarnation, leads to major aberrations."[64] While Falque maintains that the incarnation involves God becoming an objective body (*Körper*), resurrection does not. Christ's resurrected body is a lived body (flesh, *Leib*), pure and simple.

This position conflicts with one strand of the Gospel, in which the risen Christ eats, touches, and is touched, and is essentially portrayed as materially present. Relying on the disciples' bewildered state in the face of an unprecedented phenomenon, Falque claims that "the disciples got things wrong, interpreting the body of flesh of Jesus as a simple molecular body."[65] The reason why Falque dismisses the account of the physical body is because it does not correspond to what we learn from the accounts otherwise. If Christ was not bodily transformed, why do the disciples not immediately recognize him? How can a body, bound by the restrictions of space and physical laws, move through closed doors? And how can a solid physical body suddenly disappear? "As long as the corporality remains substantial here (*Körper*)," Falque concludes, "we stay in the fairy story, even—to exaggerate little—in Walt Disney."[66] Such a position aligns with many theologians, most notably Rudolf Bultmann, who seeks to free the Gospels from mythological objectification and searches for more contemporary ways to understand the meaning of the resurrection. Rather than being a historical fact, the resurrection comes to pass in the preaching of the message, the kerygma.[67] Falque does not reduce the body to a word event; instead, he proposes a phenomenological conception of the risen body. This conception does not involve a dead body returning to life, but rather a transformation in which the same lived body and its unique subjective experience become present without its objective dimensions: "What was at stake along the way that Christ took was not simply showing people that he had a body like us—albeit that was what the argument with the Gnostics was about (incarnation)—but that he revealed 'in his flesh' a *certain way of living through his body*."[68]

In this way, Falque solves the difficulty connected with the objective body. Nevertheless, one may ask if his alternative replaces one difficulty with another. For good reasons, Falque has criticized Henry for proposing a flesh (*Leib*) without a body (*Körper*). As I see it, one of the advantages of Falque's notion of the spread body is to articulate a third sphere of the body, and thus move beyond the split between lived and objective body. Oddly, such a split seems to be taken for granted in Falque's account of the resurrected body. For his phenomenology of the risen Christ is precisely about a lived body; that is, a manner of living the body, appearing without any objective, material counterpart. But then, Falque seems to end up with a position of the risen Christ that he otherwise criticizes as "angelism." In a sense, Henry holds a less vulnerable position, as his auto-affecting flesh does not attempt to show itself in the world. However, that is precisely what Falque's risen body does. The complexity of Falque's position is not easy to grasp, as he can also write: "Not that the body of the resurrected Christ would be immaterial (which would imply angelism or Gnosticism), but simply that what is resurrected of him is his *way of living this materiality.*"[69] This assertion is bewildering, for having put much effort into combating the fairy tale of material, bodily resurrection, the material dimension now somehow returns as a constitutive part of the risen body.

The negative lesson to be drawn from this is that it is difficult to provide a precise phenomenological account of Christ's body, and consequently, so also of the general resurrection of bodies. Perhaps the Gospels do not even intend to account for the specific body of Christ at all, but rather express the disciples' state of confusion when confronted with a surprise they were unable to comprehend. Following Marion, all we can say is that the risen one appeared as a saturated phenomenon who exceeded all possible expectations and recognition.[70] This is why the resurrection narratives seem to raise questions that cannot be satisfactorily answered within philosophy. Perhaps this is also the position that Falque ultimately arrives at: "Is this to say that the body resurrected 'in the flesh' (*sarx*) and in bones (*ostea*) has in some way or another our molecular corporality, which would be as substantial as it is material (*Körper*)? Here we must be silent."[71]

The Body of Hope

If phenomenology cannot fully capture Christ's risen body, can it nevertheless say something about the general hope for an afterlife that it inspires? And if so, can it also make sense of a bodily afterlife? Max Scheler grapples with these questions in his analysis of the meaning of surviving death (*Fortleben*). He clarifies from the outset that it is beyond the scope of phenomenology to either prove that there is an afterlife or that no one survives death; all phenomenology can do is to describe the meaning of an afterlife in its essence and structure. Scheler assumes that if there is an afterlife, it must pertain to the notion of the spiritual person, not the corporeal body or states of mind. Scheler observes that most of our acts have a meaning that cannot be reduced to the body because they essentially exceed the boundaries of the body, which is fixed in time and space. He identifies various such surplus phenomena. The meaning of my love for my friend, or any other value of the same kind, will not come to an end the moment my body vanishes, since its meaning is not dependent on my corporeal existence. Scheler also notes how our perceptions always come with content and horizons that overflow my spatially delimited perspective. In a similar fashion, he also points out that our memory and expectations do always exceed the body's temporal limits.[72] Such considerations enable Scheler to draw two conclusions concerning the possibility of life after death. Negatively, the essence of the spiritual person is not restricted to the body in time and space. Positively, our basic acts extend beyond the body and therefore always point onward, with some even reaching toward eternity. In this sense, Scheler claims that the person already in this life experiences themself as living on beyond the border of death.[73]

Scheler's significant contribution lies in the way he identifies the tendencies within our experience here and now that indicate life after death. This is, after all, the only approach available to phenomenology. What is less satisfactory from my perspective is the way he sharply distinguishes spiritual or personal immortality from the mortal body. If our incarnation is taken seriously, the surplus and excess of our intentional acts need not lead to a separation from the lived body. That there are temporal and spatial horizons that go beyond the body's finite position, or its zero point of orientation, is hardly an argument against their embeddedness in our bodily constitution, whether conceived in spatial or temporal terms. However, Scheler surprisingly adds a precaution at the end of his essay, where he emphasizes that "a lived body belongs to a person."[74] He even states that any talk about the survival of a pure soul is nonsense. To him, the Christian belief in the resurrection of the flesh is "infinitely deeper and more meaningful than the modern teaching of the discarnated soul-substance."[75] Given his repeated emphasis on the non-bodily and purely spiritual nature of our acts, it is unclear how Scheler can consistently hold such a view. Indeed, he concedes that he cannot explicate the resurrection of the flesh further and that immortality will always remain beyond proof.

However inconclusive, I consider Scheler's approach suggestive: he does not invoke imaginaries or dogma, but grounds his analysis in sur-

CHAPTER 8

plus phenomena given to us. He makes it clear that this line of thought is not his invention but follows in the footsteps of Kant and Goethe: Kant speaks of how our duty makes demands on us beyond this short life, and Goethe speaks of how the power of the spirit which he feels overflows itself toward eternity.[76] In Scheler, Kant, and Goethe, there is an imperative for progress beyond this life that is already deeply grounded in that life. The question is whether such an imperative also includes the body. If that is to be the case, one cannot, like Scheler, start out from spiritual acts that are essentially independent of the body, but rather from experiences that are inalienably part of our incarnation.

I have previously pointed to such experiences, namely pain and pleasure. Like Scheler's examples, these come with an imperative that goes beyond this life, arguably including the body. Bodily pleasure, I have argued, comes with an internal demand that it must go on forever, it should not end, and it must renew itself eternally—a demand not added on to the phenomenon, but inscribed in its essence. This is, of course, no proof, logical or evidential, of a blissful eternity to come, but like Kant's moral imperative, its necessity is not dependent on its actual fulfillment but on its internal structure that prescribes its future horizon. Pain, I suggested, opposes the temporality of pleasure insofar as no one wants pain to last, but to cease and vanish. Although the temporal structures of pleasure and pain might be different, they converge as well. As Marion puts it: "Flesh and ultimate passivity (thus pain) manifest themselves in this way for the first time without restriction, or exception, in pleasure."[77] Both pain and pleasure stem from our incarnate being, and both have the power to manifest flesh. They not only converge in manifesting our incarnate state, but more interestingly, they do so according to their otherwise different temporal structures as well. Starting either from pleasure's imperative of the eternal return or pain's negative hope, both demand what is to come, negatively as free from pain and positively in everlasting enjoyment. If this is so, then we could at least say that there is a way in which phenomenology could provide the corresponding structure of the Christian promise of a life to come, or according to its imperative character, a life that *must* come.

It is no secret that death means the end of the body—its organic processes stop, the body stiffens, it slowly decays, and finally returns to earth. The most natural conclusion to draw is that if there will be an afterlife, then it must be discarnate, which, classically conceived, implies the immortality of the soul. Yet this is not, if I am right, what the phenomenological descrption suggests. Pain and pleasure cannot be conceived in the absence of our bodies; they do not so much occur in a body, informing some sort of a soul, as they are fully embodied experiences. Moreover, if the body encompasses my auto- and hetero-affections, sensations, and my entire perceptual relation to the world, it becomes difficult to single out the self or the soul in abstraction from its embodiment. In pain, the self is rather posited by the body and riveted to it. What then—is there not only hope for an afterlife, but also for a resurrection of the body? Whereas, at first sight, it seems that the notion of an immortal soul makes the most sense of the afterlife, the phenomenology of pain and pleasure strongly suggests the other way around. No knowledge or proof supports this, as Scheler is right to hold, and we can hardly flesh out the details of what is to come—and it is precisely therefore a matter of hope. Nevertheless, taking incarnation seriously will, I think, point in one direction of that hope, the direction that leads to Marion's tentative conclusion, namely that "if there must be an eternity, it will only be a resurrection of the body."[78]

Coda

As this book draws to a close, I wish to weave some of its central threads together, particularly those concerning pain, incarnation, and theology. The discourse on pain, or more precisely acute physical pain, has been central, not because of its cultural or existential significance, but because of its phenomenological function. Such pain possesses a unique power to disclose dimensions of our incarnation, distinguishing it both from the irritation of Sartre's eyes that manifests in his reading, and from chronic pain that, due to its lasting temporal character, colors the life-world as a mood. Whereas these may be said to disclose aspects of the world in certain ways, acute pain actively diverts us from the world, rendering it irrelevant, and throws us back on the inescapable nature of our concrete incarnation. It brings to light both the inherent familiarity and the foreignness of our body on its own terms, not through a phenomenological reduction or a reflexive return to experience, but rather through pain's unique capacity to make the body evident as inalienably ours. In short, pain offers us privileged phenomenological access into our incarnation.

This leads to a pivotal question posed by this book: How can we best understand this body that pain discloses to us? Does this experience of pain preclude the objective body, the body seen by others, and as I conceive it as mediated by others? Am I not also a part of this world, a thing among things? When pain affects me, it compels my focus away from the world shared with others, and consequently from my body as a worldly object. This, however, does not imply that my body suddenly vanishes from the world. The objective body is not a distinct ontological entity but, following Husserl, a particular perspective on the body that is seen as from a detached point of view and as intersubjectively available. Yet, subjective experience is not readily accessible from this third-person perspective, and thus pain, as essentially subjectively given, escapes the objective body. This is one of the reasons why Husserl insists on another notion, that of the lived body, where the body is given in the first-person perspective, as felt according to subjective experience. An incarnate subjectivity opens up to the world and can be aware of its bodily experiences.

Pain, as I have argued, is emphatically mine—it even reveals itself immediately at the location of my body where it is experienced. This notion of "mineness" does not suggest, as it is often expressed, that I

CODA

merely *have* a body, but that I *am* my body. However, it remains unclear whether Husserl contends that the transcendental ego—at least in its pure sense—can be completely identified with the lived body without compromising its constitutive function. Merleau-Ponty's approach appears less problematic; he conceptualizes subjectivity as evolving with the body, in a constant exchange with the perceptual world to which it responds and adapts. Such a incarnated subjectivity is part of the integrated unity of subjectivity, body, and world.

However, a question arises: Does Merleau-Ponty's unified notion of perceptual meaning allow for the disruptive sensation of pain? In his critique of Husserl's notion of *hyle*, Merleau-Ponty repeatedly points out that it is an abstraction that has never been perceived, because all we perceive, even the most "elementary event, is invested with meaning."[1] We always already see figures against a background, recognizing gestalt unities. And indeed, I believe this understanding aligns with the way the lived body ordinarily orients itself in the world. Yet, the ordinary is not homogeneous; from time to time it is irrupted by the extraordinary, in breakdown, illness, strangeness, and pain. Pain particularly resists easy integration into the world of meaning; it violently breaks it up and turns us, as it were, outside-in. To capture the body in pain, I have argued, we need to dig beneath the lived body and its world.

Despite the reservations I have made, I maintain that Henry's remarkable analysis of the flesh contributes a critical dimension to our understanding of the body in pain. While he does not reject the objective and the lived body, he does underscore that neither of them can account for our immediate sense of incarnation. As long as the lived body is modeled on intentionality, it establishes a distance between the intention and its noema, relegating the noema to an irreal correlate thrown in front of us. This separation severs the internal connection to the intending subject, preventing the phenomenon from revealing itself in immediate presence. Hence, Henry appeals to another dimension of our incarnation, namely, the flesh as the immanent site in which any impressions are revealed to themselves through auto-affection. When I no longer act, in cases of "I cannot," we can still feel our own flesh affecting itself upheld and made possible by the life we passively receive.

While Husserl and Merleau-Ponty do not invoke the passivity of life, one may wonder if they do not anticipate Henry's auto-affection in their elaboration of the two touching hands. In my exploration of the phenomenology of touch, it became clear that one of Husserl's points with the example of the touching hands is precisely that it constitutes the self-awareness of our embodiment. As Merleau-Ponty expands on this example, he notes an inherent ambiguity in this self-awareness: the self

CODA

as both the subject and object of touch. As a "subject-object," the body must retain its dual role where it both makes us perceive and yet remains a thing to be perceived.[2] If this is the case, however, we are no longer talking about the body in its immediate self-affection in Henry's strict sense, but a strange mix of hetero- and auto-affection. Unfortunately, Henry will not allow for this perspective, as his analysis of pain makes clear. It is not by chance that Henry invokes pain as one of his principal examples: pain is not intentionally directed towards the world but belongs to the immanence of flesh, where we feel the pain being crushed under its own weight, inseparable from us, offering no escape. So far, this analysis holds. However, there is a curious absence in Henry's analysis, which is what Levinas refers to as the "excess" of pain. Pain cannot, I have argued, be immediately given to itself in a closed auto-affective circuit because it presents itself as invasive, perpetually unwelcome, as a foreignness that resists integration into a homogenous immanence.

To account for the inner tension of the body in pain, we must introduce hetero-affection to complement the auto-affection feeling itself. Pain is incontestably mine, and yet, in a sense, it remains foreign. By the hetero-affection of pure pain, I am referring not to its external cause, but to the confrontation with another dimension of the body—the flesh and blood—that forcibly intrudes into my flesh. Flesh and blood refers to the expanse of our material density and visceral organs, which our conscious life presupposes but is only seldom aware of. In pain, the tension between auto- and hetero-affection is never resolved but constitutes the inherent dynamism of pain. We can therefore assert that the body in pain is both something we both *are* and *have*. Part of our difficulty to comprehend and communicate pain stems from a similar tension: a disparity between the excess of sensual matter and intelligible form that remains open in the experience of pain. There is an opaque core to pain that eludes comprehension and persists in what Adorno refers to as an addendum. Far from being a theoretical flaw, I argue that these tensions and contradictions are integral to the phenomenality of pain.

In my conceptualization of incarnation, I aim to preserve all four dimensions of the body: the objective body, the lived body, the flesh, and flesh and blood. If this can be consistently maintained, the question becomes how these aspects interrelate. The objective and lived bodies are not denied—I consider these to be the most adequate terms for the ordinary being in the world. Although the objective body is presupposed in many of the ways we interact with others, in medical practice and medical science, the objectification of the body is derived from the lived body. The lived body, through its practical and perceptual capacities, opens up and installs us in the world. We are for the most part actively involved

CODA

in the world—but not always. Illness, for instance, can disrupt the ordinary and lay bare the third notion, namely the passivity of our flesh that remains unthematic in the lived body. This is one of the contributions of Henry's notion of the flesh: it preserves a sense of life that is given in full passivity, prior to "I can." However, a problem arises when Henry uses the experience of the passivity of immanent life to account for our incarnation as such. The visible world, materiality, space and time—these are mere projections of irreal correlates according to Henry. Instead of seeing us as initially being-in-the-world, Henry seems to lapse back into some sort of idealist position concerning the world.

As I see it, the problem with Henry is that he generalizes the findings that only apply to a restricted mode of embodied experience. The passivity of life and the immanent auto-affection are important and do reveal themselves, but they do so exactly when our ordinary embodied modes are blocked, that is, in instances of "I cannot." When exhausted in a fever, I can feel my body affecting itself; yet, however revealing this auto-affection is, it remains an exceptional circumstance that must be understood against the backdrop of our ordinary embodied being-in-the-world. Instead of absolutizing the immanence as the original milieu and transcendental ground, it should be viewed as a dimension that reveals itself only in certain modes of our lives: we are ordinarily transcending towards things and others, being unaware of the deep self-awareness in our flesh. By contrast, illness removes us from the ordinary traffic and illuminates the important insight into passivity—and it can do so because it is extraordinary. Upon recovery, we return to our engagements.

This suggests that the flesh is not an immanence that must be split from our transcending, lived body, but names one of its dimensions that is discovered in specific situations. Yet, for Henry, there is no return to the lived body, no engagements to resume. Henry seems to insist precisely on the strict division of flesh and body, defining the flesh as "everything a body lacks, the flesh should not be confused with the body, but is instead, if one may say so, the exact opposite."[3] Yet, as Falque has repeatedly asked, does it make sense to speak of flesh without a body? Does any path lead from the flesh to the body?[4]

Building upon Falque's work, I posit that what is missing in the mentioned notions of the body (the objective body, the lived body, and the flesh) is the body's organic density and materiality. This fourth dimension, which Falque dubs the "stretched-out body" and I term "flesh and blood," allows us to account for the heaviness and opacity of our embodiment. Importantly, the materiality inherent in flesh and blood does not convert it into an objective body. Unlike the objective body, which encapsulates a third-person viewpoint, the flesh and blood dimension is essentially given to the first-person experience: without a conscious subject to feel and endure it, pain does not exist. In instances of pain, I perceive my organic matter as both mine and alien, like a hyletic non-I that is hetero-affecting my flesh from the inside.

Furthermore, the implications of flesh and blood might also have more substantial ramifications that could be far-reaching. While the objective and the lived body encapsulate third- and first-person perspectives on the body respectively, the unity of the body indicates that they stem from a shared dimension of the body. Flesh and blood, I argue, might serve as this common dimension due to its ambiguous nature: its materiality and weight pave the way for a detached inspection of the objective body while still being subjectively experienced, thereby grounding the lived body. Consequently, flesh and blood concerns the body prior to intentionality and the split between the lived and objective body.

In outlining these four dimensions of the body that constitute human incarnation, I invoke the theological concept of incarnation for two primary reasons. First, guided by the insights of Tertullian and Irenaeus, I emphasize Christ's body as part of creation. From this perspective, Christ's body is not special; instead, the meaning of the incarnation lies in God adopting a body similar to ours and thus participating entirely in created humanity. This is why Christ, like any human, is born of a woman, experiences various emotions, suffers, and dies. The dissonance this creates with Greek and later metaphysical notions of God only underscores the subversion that is entailed in the incarnation: as Merleau-Ponty asserts: "Incarnation changes everything."[5] Biblically speaking, Christ, like Adam—the symbol of all humanity—is made of the soil of the earth. This theological perspective carries phenomenological implications. To be incarnate, in general, is not sufficiently described as intentional, lived bodies. Incarnation delves deeper: it extends not just to the lived body or immanent flesh, but also to flesh and blood. This is made particularly clear on the cross: Christ suffers pain, as any human would have done, descending into the darkest corner of our incarnate state.

The second reason for invoking the theological concept of incarnation follows a reverse trajectory. It not only inspires phenomenology but necessitates it as a critical theological complement. If incarnation implicates the human body, we must clarify what that body signifies. However, phenomenology does not only serve as a neutral correlate for theology; it can also explore religious phenomena announced on the theological horizon. This book is my way of proposing a phenomenology of incarnation, crucifixion, and hope. It is this mutual reference, between the special incarnation of Christ and the general, human incarnation, between

CODA

theology and phenomenology, that has guided my dialogue between phenomenology and theology.

Naturally, there are numerous relevant aspects that have not been covered in the preceding chapters that could potentially stimulate further dialogues. The analyses of passivity and pain are significant for disability studies and the medical humanities; the cultural shaping of the lived body and the resistant flesh and blood could be explored within the purview of gender studies; and the organic and material dimension of our constitution could be expanded into enactivism's attempt to reconceive mind and nature, just to mention a few. At the end of this book, I wish to point to another potentially fruitful direction for future exploration. I am considering the notion of incarnation and its implications for our understanding of nature, encompassing both our living environment and the organic life sustaining us. The climate crisis and our ecological predicament necessitate a deeper understanding of our bodies, not only as a lens through which to perceive our surrounding nature but also, more critically, our participation in the nature that sustains us. Although this might seem trivial, it raises more profound inquiries about the nature of our bodies and the bodies within nature. To prevent an anthropomorphic projection of life onto nature, phenomenology must devise an adequate way to engage with nature.

If we are to be intentionally receptive to nature, we must first come to terms with how we understand living nature as distinct and more than inert things. Husserl noted that as lived, personal bodies, we express our souls. However, a similar expressiveness also characterizes nonhuman animals. When I see a cat playing, Husserl suggests, I perceive not just extension and movement, but an animated, lived body. The entire zoological field is given to me as lived bodies expressive of life.[6] This perspective, while accurate, seems restricted. While we can recognize animals' expressions through apperception due to their ensouled nature, similar to ours, what about plants, shellfish, and even more primitive organisms? Can phenomenology recognize them as living despite their lack of expressiveness? How far can we extend our empathy from our lived embodiment, and what criteria determine its applicability? At the very least, the lived human body does enable us to perceive nature outside. However, this perspective remains transcendental, illuminating one aspect of nature, specifically how nature appears to the incarnate subject. Yet, nature is not only out before us; it also underlies and infuses us, supporting the subject before any of its constitutive achievements.[7]

As bodies, we simultaneously exist as both subjects and organisms of nature. Merleau-Ponty asserts that we are both subjects and objects. The question then becomes how these "two leaves" of the body can connect us to nature beyond the subjective body. To make sense of this connection, Merleau-Ponty suggests in his later writings that we must turn to ontology, as signified by the concept of flesh. Far from only designating our own bodies, the flesh incorporates the visible and tangible world as such: the flesh designates their common being.[8] We are indeed made of the same "stuff" as nature, to which we belong, but in accordance with the chiasmatic structure, human perception is not entirely reduced to nature. A difference persists within the identity of the flesh.

Despite flesh's comprehensive ontological scope, it does not necessarily bring us closer to understanding nature as living. We still need to investigate the nature of various living organisms. Can we proceed phenomenologically from the bodies we are towards organisms, not merely through analogical transference, but by detailing how organic life operates on its own terms? Hans Jonas suggests that to understand the phenomenon of life, we need to start from the bodies that we are and expand to include all living organisms. According to Jonas, life intrinsically disrupts the dualism between the subjective mind and objective matter because it is structured by inseparable polarities. Organic life's core is shaped by the polarities between freedom and necessity, self and world, inwardness and outwardness, mind and organic nature. These polarities are not exclusively human but can be traced back to the simplest organisms. Jonas contends that "the organic even in its lowest forms prefigures mind, and that mind even on its highest reaches remains part of the organic."[9] Our embodiment is therefore inextricably intertwined with organic life. Although Jonas's argument ensures the continuity of life across humans and nonhumans, it raises further problems that need to be addressed. Does Jonas manage to transcend analogical transference or, worse, anthropomorphism? If the experience of life must first be given to us initially, how can we avoid projecting human traits onto nonhuman organisms? Is there any phenomenological evidence for the mind, the self, and freedom in an amoeba?

As previously noted, the problem of transference and anthropomorphism tends to recur in the literature, posing a challenge for phenomenology. While I do not attempt to solve this problem—at least not here—I want to conclude with a hint of how the concept of flesh and blood might contribute to our understanding of incarnation and nature. Merleau-Ponty suggests that nature can be viewed as the "brute" or "wild being" that eventually resists all reflective grasp. Though this resistance may seem like the end point of the investigation of nature, it could also

CODA

serve as a starting point, particularly if it somehow resonates with our own bodies. I have persistently argue that we occasionally have access to this resistant dimension of our bodies, namely as flesh and blood: the meat, bones, organs, and veins—which are simultaneously material and alive. Could this obscure region beneath our skin, often absent from our lived body, connect us to what the Bible terms dust and spirit? Does the organic life of my body bind me to living nature as such? If so, we are discussing not a correlation between lived body and life-world, but a correlation between flesh and blood and nature as earth. The earth lies beneath the life-world, yet it forms the soil that supports us, preceding all our intentional achievements. We should probe further into the nature of the relationship between flesh and blood and earth, and its significance. How does the correlation of flesh and blood and earth relate to that of the lived body and the life-world? Can we come to terms with nature, not just nature in front of us, but also inside and beneath us? Does nature's givenness correspond to the idea of a Creator? The answers to these questions and others await further exploration.

Notes

Introduction

1. Richard Kearney and Brian Treanor, eds., *Carnal Hermeneutics* (New York: Fordham University Press, 2015), 1.
2. Charles Taylor, *A Secular Age* (Cambridge, MA: Belknap Press of Harvard University Press, 2008), 554.
3. I have borrowed this notion from Drew Leder, *The Absent Body* (Chicago: University of Chicago Press, 1990), 65.
4. Shaun Gallagher and Dan Zahavi, *The Phenomenological Mind* (London: Routledge, 2012), 166.
5. Joel Michael Reynolds, *The Life Worth Living: Disability, Pain, and Morality* (Minneapolis: University of Minnesota Press, 2022), 22.
6. Maurice Merleau-Ponty, *Sense and Non-Sense*, trans. H. L. Dreyfus and P. A. Dreyfus (Evanston, IL: Northwestern University Press, 1964), 174.
7. Merleau-Ponty, *Sense and Non-Sense*, 175.
8. Dominique Janicaud, "The Theological Turn of French Phenomenology," in *Phenomenology and the "Theological Turn,"* trans. B.-G. Prusak (New York: Fordham University Press, 2000), 90–91, 98–103.
9. Bruce Ellis Benson and Norman Wirzba, *Words of Life: New Theological Turns in French Phenomenology* (New York: Fordham University Press, 2010), 4.
10. Paul Ricoeur, *The Conflict of Interpretations*, ed. D. Ihde (London: Continuum, 2004), 437.

Chapter 1

1. Gabriel Marcel, *Being and Having*, trans. K. Farrer (Westminster, UK: Dacre, 1949), 12, 84.
2. Jean-Paul Sartre, *Being and Nothingness: An Essay in Phenomenological Ontology*, trans. H. E. Barnes (London: Routledge, 2003), 329, 333.
3. Dan Zahavi, "Husserl's Phenomenology of the Body," *Études Phénoménologiques* 10 (1994): 69–70.
4. Gallagher and Zahavi, *The Phenomenological Mind*, 14.
5. Evan Thompson, *Mind in Life: Biology, Phenomenology, and the Sciences of Mind* (Cambridge, MA: Belknap Press of Harvard University Press, 2007), 235.

6. Helmuth Plessner, *Laughing and Crying: A Study of the Limits of Human Behavior*, trans. J. S. Churchill and M. Grene (Evanston, IL: Northwestern University Press, 2020), 32–36.

7. Edmund Husserl, *Cartesian Meditations: An Introduction to Phenomenology*, trans. D. Cairns (The Hague: Martinus Nijhoff, 1960), 97; Edmund Husserl, *The Crisis of European Sciences and Transcendental Phenomenology*, trans. D. Carr (Evanston, IL: Northwestern University Press, 1970), 107, 217–18.

8. For the most elaborate study of the complexity of the body according to *Ideas II*, see James Dodd, *Idealism and Corporeality: An Essay on the Problem of the Body in Husserl's Phenomenology* (Amsterdam: Springer, 1997).

9. Edmund Husserl, *Ideas Pertaining to a Pure Phenomenology and to a Phenomenological Philosophy, Second Book*, trans. R. Rojcewicz and A. Schuwer (Dordrecht: Kluwer Academic, 1989), 4–6; Paul Ricoeur, *Husserl: An Analysis of His Phenomenology*, trans. E. G. Ballard (Evanston, IL: Northwestern University Press, 1967), 37–38.

10. Husserl, *Cartesian Meditations*, 122–23.

11. Husserl, *Crisis of European Sciences*, 107.

12. Husserl, *Cartesian Meditations*, 97.

13. Husserl, *Ideas II*, 331–32.

14. Husserl, *Zur Phänomenologie der Intersubjektivität. Texte aus dem Nachlass. Erster Teil*, 1905–20, Husserliana 15, ed. I. Kern (The Hague: Martinus Nijhoff, 1973), 61–62.

15. Husserl, *Thing and Space: Lectures of 1907*, trans. R. Rojcewicz (Dordrecht: Springer, 1997), 241.

16. Husserl, *Cartesian Meditations*, 119.

17. Edmund Husserl, *Ideas II*, 166; see also 61–62.

18. Husserl, *Ideas II*, 158.

19. Husserl, *Ideas II*, 160.

20. Husserl, *Thing and Space*, 135–38.

21. Zahavi, "Husserl's Phenomenology of the Body," 67–68.

22. Husserl, *Crisis of the European Sciences*, 107.

23. Husserl, *Ideas II*, 159.

24. Husserl, *Ideas II*, 252.

25. Husserl, *Ideas II*, 260.

26. Husserl, *Ideas for a Pure Phenomenology and Phenomenological Philosophy, First Book,* trans. D. O. Dahlstrom (Indianapolis, IN: Hackett, 2014), 101.

27. Husserl, *Ideas I*, 105.

28. Zahavi, "Husserl's Phenomenology of the Body," 77. For Zahavi's defense of this notion of the ego, see his *Self-Awareness and Alterity* (Evanston, IL: Northwestern University Press, 1999), 148–52.

29. Husserl, *Ideas II*, 223.

30. Jean-Luc Marion, *Reduction and Givenness* (Evanston, IL: Northwestern University Press, 1998), 162.

31. Jacques Derrida, *Writing and Difference*, trans. A. Bass (London: Routledge, 2001), 154.

32. Husserl, *Ideas II*, 90.

NOTES TO PAGES 19-23

33. Taylor Carman, *Merleau-Ponty* (London: Routledge, 2008), 131.
34. Maurice Merleau-Ponty, *Phenomenology of Perception*, trans. C. Smith (London: Routledge, 1962), 408.
35. Merleau-Ponty, *Phenomenology of Perception*, 90. For a critical discussion of the split between the primordial and reflective body, see Richard Shusterman, *Body Consciousness: A Philosophy of Mindfulness and Somaesthetics* (Cambridge: Cambridge University Press, 2008), 66–73.
36. Maurice Merleau-Ponty, "A Prospectus of His Work," in *The Merleau-Ponty Reader*, ed. T. Toadvine and L. Lawlor (Evanston, IL: Northwestern University Press, 2007), 283.
37. Maurice Merleau-Ponty, "The Philosophy of Existence," in *Text and Context: On Philosophy, Politics, and Culture*, ed. H. J. Silverman and J. Berry Jr., trans. M. B. Smith et al. (New York: Humanity Books, 1992), 134.
38. Gabriel Marcel, *Creative Fidelity*, trans. R. Rosthal (New York: Fordham University Press, 2002), 16–21; Merleau-Ponty, *Phenomenology of Perception*, 150.
39. Merleau-Ponty, *Phenomenology of Perception*, 83.
40. Merleau-Ponty, "The Philosophy of Existence," 133.
41. Marcel, *Creative Fidelity*, 16–21.
42. See my "Preserving Wonder through the Reduction: Husserl, Marion, and Merleau-Ponty," in *The Problem of Religious Experience: Case Studies in Phenomenology, with Reflections and Commentaries*, ed. O. Louchakova-Schwartz (New York: Springer, 2020), 67–71.
43. Merleau-Ponty, *Phenomenology of Perception*, 138.
44. Merleau-Ponty, *Phenomenology of Perception*, 212.
45. Merleau-Ponty, *Phenomenology of Perception*, 350.
46. Merleau-Ponty, *Phenomenology of Perception*, 95. See also Martin C. Dillon, *Merleau-Ponty's Ontology* (Evanston, IL: Northwestern University Press, 1997), 143–44.
47. Merleau-Ponty, *Phenomenology of Perception*, xix.
48. Maurice Merleau-Ponty, *The Primacy of Perception and Other Essays* (Evanston, IL: Northwestern University Press, 1964), 12.
49. For gestalts and phenomena, see Renaud Barbaras, "A Phenomenology of Life," in *The Cambridge Companion to Merleau-Ponty*, ed. T. Carman and M. N. Hansen (Cambridge: Cambridge University Press, 2005), 218–19.
50. Dillon, *Merleau-Ponty's Ontology*, 147.
51. Merleau-Ponty, *Phenomenology of Perception*, 15, 24.
52. Merleau-Ponty, *Phenomenology of Perception*, 32.
53. Merleau-Ponty, *Phenomenology of Perception*, 52–53.
54. Merleau-Ponty, *Phenomenology of Perception*, 62. See also Maurice Merleau-Ponty, *The Visible and the Invisible*, trans. A. Lingis (Evanston, IL: Northwestern University Press, 1968), 4–5, 130.
55. Merleau-Ponty, *Phenomenology of Perception*, ix.
56. Merleau-Ponty, *Phenomenology of Perception*, 100. For the difference between body image and body schema, see Shaun Gallagher, "Body Image and Body Schema: A Conceptual Clarification," *Journal of Mind and Behavior* 7 (1986): 545–49.

57. Merleau-Ponty, *Phenomenology of Perception*, 150.
58. See also Donn Welton, "Biblical Bodies," in *Body and Flesh: A Philosophical Reader*, ed. D. Welton (Oxford: Blackwell, 1998), 235.
59. Merleau-Ponty, *Phenomenology of Perception*, 100.
60. Husserl, *Ideas I*, 78.
61. Husserl, *Ideas I*, 302.
62. Merleau-Ponty, *Phenomenology of Perception*, 67.
63. Maurice Merleau-Ponty, *In Praise of Philosophy and Other Essays*, trans. J. Wild et al. (Evanston, IL: Northwestern University Press, 1970), 45.
64. Merleau-Ponty, *Sense and Non-Sense*, 95. See also Merleau-Ponty, *In Praise of Philosophy*, 45.
65. Merleau-Ponty, *The Primacy of Perception*, 93.
66. Merleau-Ponty, *The Primacy of Perception*, 95.
67. Emmanuel Alloa, *Resistance of the Sensible World: An Introduction to Merleau-Ponty*, trans. J. M. Todd (New York: Fordham University Press, 2017), 17.
68. Edgar Orion, *Things Seen and Unseen: The Logic of Incarnation in Merleau-Ponty's Metaphysics of Flesh* (Eugene, OR: Wipf and Stock, 2016), 210–11.
69. Merleau-Ponty, *The Primacy of Perception*, 103.
70. Merleau-Ponty, *Sense and Non-Sense*, 97.
71. Merleau-Ponty, *Signs*, trans. R. C. McCleary (Evanston, IL: Northwestern University Press, 1964), 71.
72. Merleau-Ponty, *Signs*, 71.
73. Merleau-Ponty, *Sense and Non-Sense*, 177.
74. Hans Urs von Balthasar, *Mysterium Paschale: The Mystery of Easter*, trans. A. Nichols (San Francisco: Ignatius, 2000), 14.
75. See also Emmanuel Falque, *The Loving Struggle: Phenomenological and Theological Debates*, trans. B. B. Onishi and L. McCracken (London: Rowman and Littlefield, 2018), 71.
76. Merleau-Ponty, *Sense and Non-Sense*, 174.
77. Merleau-Ponty, *Sense and Non-Sense*, 175.
78. Merleau-Ponty, *The Primacy of Perception*, 103.
79. Merleau-Ponty, *Signs*, 180. See also Merleau-Ponty, *The Visible and the Invisible*, 178.
80. Merleau-Ponty, *The Visible and the Invisible*, 247.
81. Merleau-Ponty, *Sense and Non-Sense*, 175.
82. Merleau-Ponty, *Sense and Non-Sense*, 148–49, 175.
83. See Falque, *The Loving Struggle*, 74–75.
84. Merleau-Ponty, *Sense and Non-Sense*, 96.
85. Michel Henry, "Incarnation and the Problem of Touch," in *Carnal Hermeneutics*, ed. R. Kearney and B. Treanor (New York: Fordham University Press, 2015), 128.
86. Michel Henry, "Incarnation," in *The Michel Henry Reader*, ed. S. Davidson and F. Seyler (Evanston, IL: Northwestern University Press, 2019), 47–48.
87. Michel Henry, *The Essence of Manifestation*, trans. G. Etzkorn (The Hague: Martinus Nijhoff, 1973), 460–64.
88. Henry, *The Essence of Manifestation*, 54.

NOTES TO PAGES 30-39

89. See also Jean-Luc Marion, "The Invisible and the Phenomenon," in *Michel Henry: The Affects of Thought*, ed. J. Hanson and M. R. Kelly (London: Bloomsbury, 2012), 32–34.
90. Michel Henry, *Incarnation: A Philosophy of the Flesh*, trans. K. Hefty (Evanston, IL: Northwestern University Press, 2015), 4.
91. Henry, *Incarnation*, 112.
92. Husserl, *Ideas I*, 43.
93. Henry, *Incarnation*, 33.
94. Michel Henry, *Material Phenomenology*, trans. D. Scott (New York: Fordham University Press, 2008), 45–46.
95. Henry, *Incarnation*, 4.
96. Michel Henry, *Philosophy and Phenomenology of the Body*, trans. G. Etzkorn (The Hague: Martinus Nijhoff, 1975), 42–43.
97. Henry, *Incarnation*, 254.
98. Michel Henry, *I Am the Truth: Toward a Philosophy of Christianity* (Stanford, CA: Stanford University Press, 2003), 10.
99. Merleau-Ponty, *Sense and Non-Sense*, 174–75.
100. Henry, *I Am the Truth*, 26.
101. Henry, *I Am the Truth*, 27, 55.
102. Henry, *I Am the Truth*, 51.
103. Henry, *I Am the Truth*, 57.
104. Henry, *I Am the Truth*, 72.
105. Henry, *Incarnation*, 26.
106. Henry, *Incarnation*, 54.
107. Henry, "Incarnation and the Problem of Touch," 137.
108. Henry, "Incarnation and the Problem of Touch," 136.
109. Henry, *Incarnation*, 14.
110. Irenaeus, *Against Heresies*, in *Ante-Nicene Fathers, Volume 1*, ed. P. Schaff (Grand Rapids, MI: Eerdmans, 1979), III, 28.7.
111. Henry, *Incarnation*, 234.
112. Merleau-Ponty, *Phenomenology of Perception*, 376.
113. Husserl, *Ideas II*, 70. See also Rudolf Bernet, "The Subject in Nature: Reflections on Merleau-Ponty's *Phenomenology of Perception*," in *Merleau-Ponty in Contemporary Perspective*, ed. P. Burke and J. Van der Veken (Amsterdam: Kluwer Academic, 1993), 62.
114. Merleau-Ponty, *The Visible and the Invisible*, 183.
115. Leder, *The Absent Body*, 65.
116. Leder, *The Absent Body*, 65.
117. Merleau-Ponty, *The Visible and the Invisible*, 139.
118. Merleau-Ponty, *The Visible and the Invisible*, 137.
119. Maurice Merleau-Ponty, *Nature: Course Notes from the Collège de France*, trans. R. Vallier (Evanston, IL: Northwestern University Press, 2003), 218.
120. Ted Toadvine, *Merleau-Ponty's Philosophy of Nature* (Evanston, IL: Northwestern University Press, 2009), 65.
121. Henry, *Incarnation*, 3–4.
122. Jean-Luc Nancy holds the opposite view, as he believes the body is

exposed as an outside; Nancy, *Corpus*, trans. R. A. Rand (New York: Fordham University Press, 2008), 133–34.

123. Anthony Steinbock, "The Problem of Forgetfulness in Michel Henry," *Continental Philosophy Review* 32 (1999): 294.

124. Henry, *Incarnation*, 151.

125. Henry, *Incarnation*, 153.

126. Renaud Barbaras, "The Essence of Life: Drive or Desire?" in *Michel Henry: The Affects of Thought*, ed. J. Hanson and M. R. Kelly (London: Bloomsbury, 2012), 52–53.

127. Michel Henry, "Philosophy and Subjectivity," in *The Michel Henry Reader*, ed. S. Davidson and F. Seyler (Evanston, IL: Northwestern University Press, 2019), 101.

128. Henry, *Philosophy and Phenomenology of the Body*, 58.

129. Henry, *Philosophy and Phenomenology of the Body*, 59.

130. Barbaras, "The Essence of Life," 48.

131. Irenaeus, *Against Heresies*, III, xix.

132. Falque, *The Loving Struggle*, 169.

133. Joseph Rivera, *The Contemplative Self after Michel Henry* (Notre Dame, IN: University of Notre Dame Press, 2015), 183, 199.

134. Rivera, *The Contemplative Self*. See also Emmanuel Falque, *The Wedding Feast of the Lamb: Eros, the Body, and the Eucharist*, trans. G. Hughes (New York: Fordham University Press, 2016), 14.

135. Emmanuel Falque, *The Metamorphosis of Finitude: An Essay on Birth and Resurrection*, trans. G. Hughes (New York: Fordham University Press, 2012), 137.

136. Husserl, *Crisis of the European Sciences*, 107.

137. Merleau-Ponty, *Phenomenology of Perception*, 431. See also Shaun Gallagher, "Lived Body and Environment," *Research in Phenomenology* 16 (1986): 140–42.

138. Thompson, *Mind in Life*, 244.

139. In the end, Falque argues, the transcendental function of the flesh absorbes the objective body, turning the position into a "carnal monism." Emmanuel Falque, "Is There a Flesh without Body? A Debate with Michel Henry," *Journal of French and Francophone Philosophy* 24 (2016): 159.

140. See also Christian Grüny, *Zerstörte Erfarung: Eine Phänomenologie des Schmerzes* (Würzburg: Verlag Königshausen & Neumann, 2004), 236–38.

141. Leder, *The Absent Body*, 36–36, 66.

142. Falque, *The Wedding Feast of the Lamb*, 15.

143. Henry, *Incarnation*, 162.

144. Grüny, *Zerstörte Erfarung*, 251–52.

145. Shaun Gallagher, "Lived Body and Environment," *Research in Phenomenology* 16 (1986): 148–49.

146. Merleau-Ponty, *The Primacy of Perception*, 41; see also Merleau-Ponty, *Phenomenology of Perception*, 189.

147. Elisabeth A. Behnke, "Edmund Husserl's Contribution to Phenomenology of the Body in *Ideas II*," in *Issues in Husserl's Ideas II*, ed. T. Nenon and L. Embree (Dordrecht: Kluwer Academic, 1996), 139, n. 5.

NOTES TO PAGES 45-54

148. Falque, *The Wedding Feast and the Lamb*, 29.
149. Merleau-Ponty, *Signs*, 71.

Chapter 2

1. Judith Butler, *Bodies That Matter: On the Discursive Limits of Sex* (London: Routledge, 2011), xiv.
2. Butler, *Bodies That Matter*, xvi.
3. Husserl, *Zur Phänomenologie der Intersubjektivität. Erster Teil–*, 63.
4. Butler, *Bodies That Matter*, 9–10.
5. Butler, *Bodies That Matter*, xviii.
6. Butler, *Bodies That Matter*, 7.
7. Butler, *Bodies That Matter*, 13.
8. Butler, *Bodies That Matter*, 25.
9. Gill Jagger, *Judith Butler: Sexual Politics, Social Change, and the Power of the Performative* (London: Routledge, 2008), 78–82; Mayra Rivera, *Poetics of the Flesh* (Durham, NC: Duke University Press, 2015), 9, 149–50.
10. Butler, *Bodies That Matter*, 14.
11. See also Edmund Husserl, *Experience and Judgment*, trans. J. S. Churchill and K. Ameriks (Evanston, IL: Northwestern University Press, 1973), 77–78.
12. This movement has some overlapping interests with new realism and new materialism. Both movements want to revive the sense of real matter and things' agency. But where new materialism often moves into forms of process ontology, new realism pursues a more thing-oriented ontology. C. Keller and M. J. Rubenstein, eds., *Entangled Worlds: Religion, Science, and New Materialism* (New York: Fordham University Press, 2017), 2.
13. Quentin Meillassoux, *After Finitude: An Essay on the Necessity of Contingency* (London: Bloomsbury, 2008), 7.
14. Meillassoux, *After Finitude*, 5.
15. Husserl, *Crisis of the European Sciences*, 166; see also 159–60.
16. Graham Harman, *The Quadruple Object* (Winchester, UK: Zero Books, 2011), 60; see also 42–43.
17. Harman, *The Quadruple Object*, 64.
18. Dan Zahavi, *Husserl's Legacy: Phenomenology, Metaphysics & Transcendental Philosophy* (Oxford: Oxford University Press, 2017), 178.
19. Tom Sparrow, *The End of Phenomenology: Metaphysics and the New Realism* (Edinburgh: Edinburgh University Press, 2014), xi.
20. Sparrow, *The End of Phenomenology*, 26, 44.
21. Sparrow, *The End of Phenomenology*, 187.
22. Sparrow, *Plastic Bodies: Rebuilding Sensation after Phenomenology* (London: Open Humanities, 2015), 22.
23. Sparrow, *Plastic Bodies*, 22, 36.
24. Sparrow, *Plastic Bodies*, 38–39.
25. Sparrow, *Plastic Bodies*, 190–91.

26. Meillassoux, *After Finitude*, 26.
27. See also Renaud Barbaras, *Introduction to a Phenomenology of Life*, trans. L. Lawlor (Bloomington: Indiana University Press, 2021), 294–95.
28. Edmund Husserl, *Logical Investigations II*, trans. J. N. Findley (London: Routledge, 2001), 99.
29. For an analysis of the motivation behind this distinction and a critique of its idealist consequences, see Renaud Barbaras, *Desire and Distance: Introduction to a Phenomenology of Perception*, trans. P. B. Milan (Stanford, CA: Stanford University Press, 2006), 22–24.
30. Husserl, *Ideas I*, 166.
31. Husserl, *Ideas I*, 169.
32. Husserl, *Ideas I*, 165; Husserl, *Ideas II*, 346.
33. Husserl, *Ideas I*, 165.
34. In *Logical Investigations II*, the question of intentionality or nonintentionality of sensation feelings like pain is more complex; see 107–11.
35. Robert Sokolowski remarks that when time is taken into consideration, the distinction between form and matter dissolves. Sokolowski, *The Formation of Husserl's Concept of Constitution* (The Hague: Martinus Nijhoff, 1964), 142.
36. Husserl, *Ideas I*, 171.
37. Gurwitch, Sartre, and Merleau-Ponty are among the earliest critics. See also Shaun Gallagher, "Hyletic Experience and the Lived Body," *Husserl Studies* 3 (1986): 137–39.
38. Merleau-Ponty, *Phenomenology of Perception*, 241.
39. Merleau-Ponty, *Phenomenology of Perception*, 405.
40. Edmund Husserl, *Analyses concerning Passive Synthesis: Lectures on Transcendental Logic*, trans. A. Steinbock (Dordrecht: Kluwer Academic, 2001), 210.
41. Jean-Paul Sartre, *Being and Nothingness: An Essay on Phenomenological Ontology*, trans. H. E. Barnes (London: Routledge, 2003), 15.
42. Sartre, *Being and Nothingness*, 338.
43. Merleau-Ponty, *Phenomenology of Perception*, 5.
44. Gallagher, "Hyletic Experience and the Lived Body," 142.
45. Gallagher, "Hyletic Experience and the Lived Body," 10.
46. Edmund Husserl, *The Phenomenology of Internal Time-Consciousness*, trans. J. S. Churchill (Bloomington: Indiana University Press, 1964), 92, 131.
47. Henry, *Material Phenomenology*, 32–35.
48. Dan Zahavi, *Self-Awareness and Alterity: A Phenomenological Investigation* (Evanston, IL: Northwestern University Press, 1999), 121.
49. Husserl, *Experience and Judgment*, 72–74. See also Luis Roman Rabanaque, "Hyle, Genesis and Noema," *Husserl Studies* 19 (2003): 208–9.
50. Husserl, *Ideas I*, 165.
51. Husserl, *Ideas I*, 165.
52. Gallagher, "Hyletic Experience and the Lived Body," 141.
53. Husserl, *Ideas II*, 160. See also Didier Franck, *Flesh and Body: On the Phenomenology of Husserl*, trans. J. Rivera and S. Davidson (London: Bloomsbury, 2014), 163, 152.
54. Emmanuel Levinas, *Discovering Existence with Husserl*, trans. R. A. Cohen and M. B. Smith (Evanston, IL: Northwestern University Press, 1998), 145.

NOTES TO PAGES 61-71

55. Paul Ricoeur, *Oneself as Another*, trans. K. Blamey (Chicago: University of Chicago Press, 1992), 324.
56. Franck, *Flesh and Body*, 144–45.
57. Jacques Derrida, *On Touching—Jean-Luc Nancy*, trans. C. Irizarry (Stanford, CA: Stanford University Press, 2005), 142.
58. Husserl, *Ideas II*, 348; see also 329.
59. Husserl, *Ideas I*, 303–4.
60. Dorion Cairns, *Conversations with Husserl and Fink* (Dordrecht: Springer, 1976), 84.
61. Husserl, *Experience and Judgment*, 76.
62. Husserl, *Ideas II*, 346.
63. Though it is true that genetically, it leads to the analyses of time itself; see Husserl, *The Phenomenology of Internal Time-Consciousness*, 92.
64. See also Bernhard Waldenfels, *Das leibliche Selbst: Vorlesungen zur Phänomenologie des Leibes* (Frankfurt am Main: Suhrkamp, 2013), 200, 275.
65. Levinas, *Discovering Existence with Husserl*, 144.
66. See also Waldenfels, *Das leibliche Selbst*, 266.
67. Theodor W. Adorno, *Metaphysics: Concepts and Problems*, trans. E. Jephcott (Stanford, CA: Stanford University Press, 2001), 67, 78.
68. Adorno, *Metaphysics*, 117.
69. Plessner, *Laughing and Crying*, 34.

Chapter 3

1. Henry, *Philosophy and Phenomenology of the Body*, 57.
2. Immanuel Kant, *Critique of Pure Reason*, trans. Norman Kemp Smith (London: Macmillan, 1929), 152.
3. Merleau-Ponty, *Phenomenology of Perception*, 137.
4. Husserl, *Crisis of the European Sciences*, 106–7.
5. Husserl, *Ideas II*, 159–60.
6. Husserl, *Ideas II*, 269.
7. Leder, *The Absent Body*, 25–27.
8. Martin Heidegger, *Being and Time*, trans. J. Stambaugh (Albany: SUNY Press, 2010), 75.
9. Merleau-Ponty, *Phenomenology of Perception*, 100–101.
10. Merleau-Ponty, *Phenomenology of Perception*, 70–71.
11. Disability studies has shown that such a "normal" body is far from an innocent point of departure. Joel Michael Reynolds, *The Life Worth Living: Disability, Pain, and Morality* (Minneapolis: University of Minnesota Press, 2022), 18–19.
12. The most influential account that makes the active and pragmatic dimensions of *Being and Time* its central claim is Hubert L. Dreyfus, *Being-in-the-World: A Commentary on Heidegger's "Being and Time," Division I* (Cambridge, MA: MIT Press, 1991), 88–107. The contributions of more recent enactivism follow this approach to phenomenology, not least Merleau-Ponty's phenomenology. See

also Shaun Gallagher "A Well-Trodden Path: From Phenomenology to Enactivism," *Filosofisk Supplement* 3 (2018): 42–47.

13. Heidegger, *Being and Time*, 284–85.
14. See also Søren Overgaard, "Heidegger on Embodiment," *Journal of the British Society for Phenomenology* 35 (2004): 119–22.
15. Martin Heidegger, *Zollikoner Seminare*, ed. Medard Boss (Frankfurt am Main: Vittorio Klostermann, 1994), 111.
16. Heidegger, *Being and Time*, 72–76.
17. Heidegger, *Zollikoner Seminare*, 292–93.
18. Husserl, *Ideas II*, 270–71.
19. Husserl, *Ideas II*, 266.
20. Husserl, *Ideas II*, 266.
21. Jan Patocka, *Body, Community, Language, World*, trans. E. Kohak (Chicago: Open Court, 1998), 44.
22. Husserl, *Ideas II*, 266.
23. Merleau-Ponty, *Phenomenology of Perception*, 81–88.
24. Merleau-Ponty, *Phenomenology of Perception*, 110–11.
25. Merleau-Ponty, *Phenomenology of Perception*, 131.
26. Merleau-Ponty, *Phenomenology of Perception*, 107–8.
27. Grüny, *Zerstörte Erfahrung*, 91, 99.
28. Husserl, *Ideas II*, 72.
29. Gallagher and Zahavi, *The Phenomenological Mind*, 159.
30. Shusterman, *Body Consciousness*, 64.
31. Reynolds, *The Life Worth Living*, 4–5.
32. Reynolds, *The Life Worth Living*, 4–5.
33. Anthony Steinbock, *Home and Beyond: Generative Phenomenology after Husserl* (Evanston, IL: Northwestern University Press, 1995), 134–35, 144.
34. Maurice Merleau-Ponty, *The World of Perception* (London: Routledge, 2008), 54–55.
35. Merleau-Ponty, *The World of Perception*, 56.
36. S. Kay Toombs, "Illness and the Paradigm of the Lived Body," *Theoretical Medicine* 9 (1988): 207.
37. Toombs, "Illness," 208.
38. Toombs, "Illness," 211–13.
39. Heidegger, *Being and Time*, 139.
40. Heidegger, *Being and Time*, 252–53.
41. Heidegger, *Being and Time*, 266.
42. Havi Carel, *Illness: The Cry of the Flesh* (Durham, UK: Acumen, 2008), 80.
43. Carel, *Illness*, 83.
44. John A. T. Robinson, *The Body: A Study in Pauline Theology* (London: SCM, 1952), 9.
45. For a related analysis of mine, see "Weakness and Passivity: Phenomenology of the Body after Paul," in *Phenomenology of the Broken Body*, ed. E. Dahl, C. Falke, and T. E. Eriksen (London: Routledge, 2019), 22–26.
46. See also Candida R. Moss, "Christly Possession and Weakened Bodies: Reconsideration of the Function of Paul's Thorn in the Flesh," *Journal of Religion, Disability & Health* 16 (2012): 322–23.

NOTES TO PAGES 79–88

47. Ronald Russell, "Redemptive Suffering and Paul's Thorn in the Flesh," *Journal of Evangelical Theological Society* 39 (1996): 565–66.
48. Henry, *Incarnation*, 118.
49. Henry, *Philosophy and Phenomenology of the Body*, 56–60. In this early work, Henry does not yet speak of flesh (and its dependence on life), but, following Maine de Biran, of the "organic body," the "subjective" or "transcendental body."
50. Henry, *Incarnation*, 148.
51. Henry, *Philosophy and Phenomenology of the Body*, 73–75.
52. Henry, *Philosophy and Phenomenology of the Body*, 56.
53. Henry, *Philosophy and Phenomenology of the Body*, 158.
54. Henry, *Philosophy and Phenomenology of the Body*, 175.
55. Henry, *Philosophy and Phenomenology of the Body*, 167–68.
56. Husserl, *Ideas II*, 266.
57. Henry, *Incarnation*, 168. See also my "Mottageligheten og kroppens fenomenologi," in *Skapelsesnåde: Festskrift for Svein Aage Christoffersen*, ed. S. Holte, M. T. Mjaaland, and R. Jensen (Oslo: Novus, 2017), 46–50.
58. For a discussion of creation and generation, see Joseph Rivera, "Generation, Interiority, and the Phenomenology of Christianity in Michel Henry," *Continental Philosophy Review* 44 (2011): 219–21.
59. Henry, *Incarnation*, 177.
60. Henry, *Incarnation*, 173.
61. Henry, *Incarnation*, 173.
62. Henry, *Essence of Manifestation*, 226–27. Jean-Francois Lavigne argues that Henry succumbs to subjective idealism. Lavigne, "The Paradox and Limits of Michel Henry's Concept of Transcendence," *International Journal of Philosophical Studies* 17 (2009): 283.
63. Henry, *Incarnation*, 83.
64. Henry, *Incarnation*, 184.
65. Leder, *The Absent Body*, 4.
66. Leder, *The Absent Body*, 69.
67. Leder, *The Absent Body*, 81.
68. Jean-Louise Chrétien, *Call and Response*, trans. A. A. Davenport (New York: Fordham University Press, 2004), 123.
69. Chrétien, *Call and Response*, 120.
70. Henry, *Incarnation*, 184. See also Michel Henry, *Words of Christ*, trans. Christina M. Gschwandtner (Grand Rapids, MI: Eerdmans, 2012), 96–97.
71. Henry, *Incarnation*, 262.

Chapter 4

1. Aristotle, *On the Soul*, trans. J. Sachs (Santa Fe, NM: Green Lion, 2004), II.3.415a–a10.
2. See also Emmanuel Levinas, *Totality and Infinity*, trans. A. Lingis (Pittsburgh, PA: Duquesne University Press, 1969), 189–91; Henry, *I Am the Truth*, 14, 25–26.

3. Richard Kearney, *Touch: Recovering Our Most Vital Sense* (New York: Columbia University Press, 2021), 2–4.
4. Husserl, *Ideas II*, 152.
5. Husserl, *Ideas II*, 158.
6. Husserl, *Ideas II*, 154. See also Husserl, *Thing and Space*, 137–38.
7. See also Donn Welton, "Soft, Smooth Hands: Husserl's Phenomenology of the Lived Body," in *The Body: Classical and Contemporary Readings*, ed. D. Welton (Oxford: Blackwell, 1999), 45.
8. Husserl, *Ideas II*, 153.
9. Husserl, *Thing and Space*, 203–4.
10. Husserl, *Ideas II*, 155.
11. Husserl, *Ideas II*, 155.
12. Husserl, *Ideas II*, 158. While the constitution of the lived body as mine is central to Husserl's and Merleau-Ponty's interest in touch, Hans Jonas has argued that touch also makes up our fundamental sense of reality, experienced as resistance and force. Jonas, *The Phenomenology of Life: Toward a Philosophical Biology* (Evanston, IL: Northwestern University Press, 1966), 147–48.
13. Husserl, *Ideas II*, 47, 168.
14. Husserl, *Ideas II*, 158–59.
15. Augustine Serrano de Haro, "Is Pain an Intentional Experience?" *Phenomenology* 3 (2011): 394.
16. Saulius Geniusas, *The Phenomenology of Pain* (Athens: Ohio University Press, 2020), 136. Elaine Scarry points in the same direction when she claims that "touch, as is recognized in traditional descriptions of the senses, lies closer to pain than does vision." Scarry, *The Body in Pain: The Making and Unmaking of the World* (Oxford: Oxford University Press, 1985), 165.
17. Husserl, *Thing and Space*, 241.
18. Husserl, *Ideas II*, 160.
19. One can also make pain into a disease, observable for medical investigation. Sartre, *Being and Nothingness*, 379.
20. Sartre, *Being and Nothingness*, 357.
21. Merleau-Ponty, *Phenomenology of Perception*, 93.
22. Scarry, *The Body in Pain*, 164.
23. Constant irritation overlaps and is yet distinct from the "moods" of chronic pain. See Fredrik Svenaeus, "A Phenomenology of Chronic Pain: Embodiment and Alienation," *Continental Philosophy Review* 48 (2015): 115–18.
24. Husserl, *Logical Investigations II*, 109.
25. For a similar graduation of pain, see Shaun Gallagher, "Lived Body and Environment," *Research in Phenomenology* (1986): 151–52.
26. Husserl, *Ideas II*, 152. See also Husserl, *Thing and Space*, 137.
27. For a commentary, see Welton, "Soft, Smooth Hands," 44–48.
28. Merleau-Ponty, *The Visible and the Invisible*, 255.
29. Merleau-Ponty, *Phenomenology of Perception*, 93.
30. Merleau-Ponty, *The Visible and the Invisible*, 147–48.
31. Husserl, *Cartesian Meditations*, 95.
32. Husserl, *Cartesian Meditations*, 97.

NOTES TO PAGES 96–106

33. Franck, *Flesh and Body*, 144.
34. Franck, *Flesh and Body*, 144–45.
35. Franck, *Flesh and Body*, 145.
36. Derrida, *On Touching*, 192–93.
37. Derrida, *On Touching*, 179–81.
38. I have developed a version of this argument drawing on Stanley Cavell's engagements with Derrida in my "On Morality of Speech: Cavell's Critique of Derrida," *Continental Philosophical Review* 44 (2011): 81–101.
39. Kearney, *Touch*, 37.
40. See also Rudolf Bernet, "The Encounter with the Stranger," in *The Face of the Other and the Trace of God*, ed. J. Bloechl (New York: Fordham University Press, 2009), 46–47.
41. Jean-Louis Chrétien, *The Call and the Response*, trans. A. A. Davenport (New York: Fordham University Press), 86.
42. Chrétien, *The Call and the Response*, 87–88.
43. This is a Heideggerian understanding of phenomena. See Heidegger, *Being and Time*, 34.
44. Chrétien, *The Call and the Response*, 126–27.
45. Chrétien, *The Call and the Response*, 123.
46. Chrétien, *The Call and the Response*, 120–21.
47. Henry, *The Essence of Manifestation*, 501–3.
48. Henry, *Incarnation*, 163.
49. Husserl, *Ideas II*, 154.
50. Chrétien, *The Call and the Response*, 101.
51. Chrétien, *The Call and the Response*, 113.
52. Aristotle, *On the Soul*, II.3.414b.
53. For an affirmative interpretation of Husserl on this point, see Levinas, *Discovering Existence with Husserl*, 138–39, 145.
54. Levinas, *Totality and Infinity*, 188–91.
55. Levinas, *Totality and Infinity*, 129.
56. For a criticism of the implied view of the feminine in Levinas, see Luce Irigaray, *An Ethics of Sexual Difference*, trans. C. Burke and C. Gill (Ithaca, NY: Cornell University Press, 1993), 198–204.
57. Levinas, *Totality and Infinity*, 257.
58. Emmanuel Levinas, *Otherwise Than Being, or Beyond Essence*, trans. A. Lingis (Pittsburgh, PA: Duquesne University Press, 1998), 90.
59. Levinas, *Otherwise Than Being*, 63, 55.
60. Levinas, *Otherwise Than Being*, 51.
61. Levinas, *Time and the Other*, trans. R. A. Cohen (Pittsburgh, PA: Duquesne University Press, 1987), 69.
62. Irigaray, *An Ethics of Sexual Difference*, 162.
63. See also Derrida, *On Touching*, 250.
64. Chrétien, *The Call and the Response*, 128.
65. Chrétien, *The Call and the Response*, 129.
66. Chrétien, *The Call and the Response*, 130. For an interesting exploration of the divine as given within the human touch as such, see Judith Butler,

"Merleau-Ponty and the Touch of Malebranche," in *The Cambridge Companion to Merleau-Ponty*, ed. T. Carman and M. B. N. Hansen (Cambridge: Cambridge University Press, 2005), 195–97.

67. Derrida is among those who take notice of this; see also *On Touching*, 100.

68. Kearney, *Touch*, 75.

69. Elisabeth Moltmann-Wendel, *I Am My Body: A Theology of Embodiment*, trans. J. Bowden (New York: Continuum, 1995), x.

70. Tertullian, *Against Marcion*, in *Ante-Nicene Fathers, Volume 3*, ed. A. Roberts, J. Donaldson, and A. Cleveland Coxe (New York: Cosimo Classics, 2007), III, viii.

71. Tertullian, *Against Marcion*, 50.

Chapter 5

1. Drew Leder, *The Distressed Body: Rethinking Illness, Imprisonment, and Healing* (Chicago: University of Chicago Press, 2016), 25. For an earlier examination of evil, pain, and tensions, see my "The Inner Tension of Pain and the Phenomenology of Evil," *International Journal of Philosophy and Theology* 78 (2017): 396–406.

2. Husserl, *Logical Investigations II*, 107–9. For a discussion of how Husserl relates to Stumpf and Brentano on this point, see S. Geniusas, "The Origins of the Phenomenology of Pain: Brentano, Stumpf and Husserl," *Continental Philosophy Review* 47 (2014): 5–9.

3. Husserl, *Logical Investigations II*, 108.
4. Husserl, *Logical Investigations II*, 109–10.
5. Husserl, *Logical Investigations II*, 111.
6. Husserl, *Ideas I*, 165.
7. Edmund Husserl, *Phänomenologische Psychologie: Vorlesungen Sommersemester, 1925, Husserliana* 9, ed. W. Biemel (The Hague: Martinus Nijhoff, 1962), 163.
8. Henry, *The Essence of Manifestation*, 541.
9. Henry, *Incarnation*, 58.
10. Henry, *The Essence of Manifestation*, 463.
11. Henry, *Incarnation*, 58.
12. Henry, *Incarnation*, 59.
13. Henry, *Incarnation*, 60.
14. Henry, *Incarnation*, 61.
15. Henry, *The Essence of Manifestation*, 662.
16. Michel Henry, "Phenomenology of Life," *Angelaki: Journal of the Theoretical Humanities* 8 (2003): 106.
17. Henry, *I Am the Truth*, 204–5.
18. Paul Ricoeur, *Freedom and Nature: The Voluntary and the Involuntary*, trans. E. V. Kohak (Evanston, IL: Northwestern University Press, 1966), 105–7.
19. F. J. J. Buytendijk, *Pain*, trans. A. O'Shiel (London: Hutchinson, 1961), 27.

NOTES TO PAGES 115-122

20. Grüny, *Zerstörte Erfahrung*, 28–29.
21. Jean-Francois Lavigne, "Suffering and Ipseity in Michel Henry: The Problem of the Ego's Transcendental Identity," *Analectica Hermeneutica* 8 (2016): 76.
22. J. M. Bernstein, *Torture and Dignity: An Essay on Moral Injury* (Chicago: University of Chicago Press, 2015), 88.
23. Scarry, *The Body in Pain*, 162.
24. Emmanuel Levinas, "Useless Suffering," in *The Provocation of Levinas: Rethinking the Other* (London: Routledge, 2002), 156.
25. Levinas, *Time and the Other*, 69.
26. Levinas, "Useless Suffering," 156.
27. Buytendijk, *Pain*, 26.
28. Emmanuel Levinas, "Transcendence and Evil," in P. Nemo, *Job and the Excess of Evil*, trans. M. Kigel (Pittsburgh, PA: Duquesne University Press, 1998), 173.
29. de Haro, "Is Pain an Intentional Experience?" 395.
30. Friedrich Nietzsche, *Genealogy of Morals*, trans. H. B. Samuel (Edinburgh: Foulis, 1913), 210.
31. Levinas, "Useless Suffering," 157–58.
32. Levinas, "Transcendence and Evil," 173.
33. Levinas, "Useless Suffering," 157.
34. Levinas, "Useless Suffering," 156–57.
35. See also Leder, *The Absent Body*, 47.
36. Bernstein, *Torture and Dignity*, 88.
37. Jean Améry, *On Aging: Revolt and Resignation*, trans. J. D. Barlow (Bloomington: Indiana University Press, 1994), 43.
38. Husserl, *Ideas II*, 346.
39. Husserl, *Ideas II*, 348. See also Husserl, *The Phenomenology of Internal Time-Consciousness*, 92.
40. Buytendijk, *Pain*, 122.
41. Max Scheler, "Vom Sinn des Leidens," in *Max Scheler: Gesammelte Werke, Schriften zur Soziologie und Weltanschauungslehre*, vol. 6 (Munich: Francke Verlag, 1963), 39.
42. Husserl, *Ideas I*, 165.
43. Shaun Gallagher, "Hyletic Experience and the Lived Body," *Husserl Studies* 3 (1986): 148; see also 142.
44. David Bakan, *Disease, Pain, and Sacrifice: Toward a Psychology of Suffering* (Chicago: University of Chicago Press, 1968), 74.
45. Scarry, *The Body in Pain*, 52. For the alienation of one's own body, see Fredrik Svenaeus, *Phenomenological Bioethics: Medical Technologies, Human Suffering, and the Meaning of Being Alive* (London: Routledge, 2018), 37–42.
46. Henry, "Incarnation and the Problem of Touch," 132–33.
47. See also Barbaras, "The Essence of Life?" 41.
48. Michel Henry, "Theodicy from the Perspective of a Radical Phenomenology," in *The Michel Henry Reader*, ed. S. Davidson and F. Seyler (Evanston, IL: Northwestern University Press, 2019), 230, 232.

49. Grüny, *Zerstörte Erfahrung*, 251–52.
50. Falque, *The Metamorphosis of Finitude*, 77.
51. Emmanuel Falque, "This Is My Body: Contribution to a Philosophy of the Eucharist," in *Carnal Hermeneutics*, ed. R. Kearney and B. Treanor (New York: Fordham University Press, 2015), 282.
52. Emmanuel Falque, "Toward an Ethics of the Spread Body," in *Somatic Desire: Incorporating Desire in Contemporary Thought*, ed. S. Horton, S. Mendelsohn, C. Rojcewicz, and R. Kearney (London: Lexington Books, 2019), 101.
53. Geniusas, *The Phenomenology of Pain*, 137. It should be noted that Geniusas does not explore any regions beyond the lived and objective body, such as flesh and blood.
54. Milan Kundera, *Immortality* (New York: Grove Weidenfeld, 1991), 200.
55. Henry, *Philosophy and the Phenomenology of the Body*, 60.
56. Jean-Luc Marion, *In Excess: Studies of Saturated Phenomena*, trans. R. Horner (New York: Fordham University Press, 2002), 82.
57. Marion, *In Excess*, 86.
58. Marion, *In Excess*, 92–93.
59. Marion, *In Excess* 92. One might wonder where the more material dimension of being "earthed" goes in Marion's analysis—and insofar as he follows Henry closely in his conception of the flesh, a certain absence of materiality also recurs within Marion's account.
60. Falque, "Toward an Ethics of the Spread Body," 97.
61. Marion, *In Excess*, 98.
62. Buytendijk, *Pain*, 26–27.
63. See also Jean-Luc Marion, *Being Given: Toward a Phenomenology of Givenness*, trans. J. L. Kosky (Stanford, CA: Stanford University Press, 2002), 262–71.
64. Marion, *In Excess*, 99.
65. Marion, *In Excess*, 100.
66. Marion, *In Excess*, 101 (emphasis mine).
67. Bakan, *Disease, Pain, and Sacrifice*, 74.
68. Marion, *In Excess*, 92.
69. Leder, *The Absent Body*, 77.
70. Buytendijk, *Pain*, 26.
71. Sigmund Freud, *The Uncanny*, trans. D. McLintock (London: Penguin Books, 2003), 124.
72. Waldenfels, *Das leibliche Selbst*, 284 (my translation).

Chapter 6

1. Hannah Arendt, *The Human Condition* (Chicago: University of Chicago Press, 1958), 50–51.
2. Scarry, *The Body in Pain*, 4.
3. Lisa Folkmarson Käll, "Intercorporeality and the Sharability of Pain," in *Dimensions of Pain* (London: Routledge, 2017), 34–35, 38.

NOTES TO PAGES 130-137

4. Husserl, *Ideas II*, 249.
5. Husserl, *Ideas II*, 252.
6. Merleau-Ponty, *Phenomenology of Perception*, 189.
7. Merleau-Ponty, *Phenomenology of Perception*, 189. For the limitations of Merleau-Ponty's early view of language, see Alloa, *Resistance of the Sensible World*, 38–40.
8. Merleau-Ponty, *Phenomenology of Perception*, 184.
9. Merleau-Ponty, *Phenomenology of Perception*, 185.
10. Merleau-Ponty, *Phenomenology of Perception*, 296.
11. Merleau-Ponty, *Phenomenology of Perception*, 350.
12. Merleau-Ponty, *Phenomenology of Perception*, 359.
13. Merleau-Ponty, *Phenomenology of Perception*, 351.
14. Hanna Arendt, *The Human Condition*, 51.
15. Maurice Merleau-Ponty, *The Prose of the World*, trans. J. O'Neill (Evanston, IL: Northwestern University Press, 1973), 137.
16. Merleau-Ponty, *The Prose of the World*, 143.
17. Merleau-Ponty, *Phenomenology of Perception*, 196.
18. Arendt, *The Human Condition*, 114.
19. Bernstein, *Torture and Dignity*, 80–81.
20. For the claim to community and scepticism in general, I draw on my *Stanley Cavell, Religion, and Continental Philosophy* (Bloomington: Indiana University Press, 2014), 20, 37–48.
21. Scarry, *The Body in Pain*, 4.
22. Scarry, *The Body in Pain*, 5.
23. Scarry, *The Body in Pain*, 5; see also 162–64.
24. Talal Assad, "Agency and Pain: An Exploration," *Culture and Religion. An Interdisciplinary Journal* 1 (2000): 41–42; Mark D. Sullivan, "Pain in Language: From Sentience to Sapience," *Pain Forum* 4 (1995): 8–10; Elisabeth Dauphinée, "The Politics of *The Body in Pain*: Reading the Ethics of Imagery," *Security Dialogue* 38 (2007): 141, 150.
25. Ludwig Wittgenstein, *Philosophical Investigations*, trans. G. E. M. Anscombe, P. M. S. Hacker, and J. Schulte (Oxford: Wiley-Blackwell, 2009), §246.
26. P. M. S. Hacker, "Of Knowledge and of Knowing That Someone Is in Pain," in *Wittgenstein: The Philosopher and His Works*, ed. A. Pichler and S. Säätelä (Bergen: WAB, 2005), 204.
27. Wittgenstein, *Philosophical Investigations*, §§258, 261, 265. See also Norman Malcolm, "Wittgenstein's *Philosophical Investigations*," *Philosophical Review* 63 (1954): 532.
28. Scarry, *The Body in Pain*, 4; see also 54.
29. Wittgenstein, *Philosophical Investigations*, §244.
30. Merleau-Ponty, *Phenomenology of Perception*, 174.
31. Ludwig Wittgenstein, *Zettel*, ed. G. E. M. Anscombe and G. H. von Wright, trans. G. E. M. Anscombe (Oxford: Blackwell, 1967), §540 (emphasis mine).
32. Wittgenstein, *Philosophical Investigations*, §286.
33. Stanley Cavell, *Must We Mean What We Say? A Book of Essays* (Cambridge: Cambridge University Press, 1976), 263.

34. Wittgenstein, *Philosophical Investigations*, §287.
35. Wittgenstein, *Philosophical Investigations*, §307
36. Scarry, *The Body in Pain*, 53.
37. Wittgenstein, *Philosophical Investigations*, §§243–315.
38. Stanley Cavell, *The Claim of Reason: Wittgenstein, Skepticism, Morality, and Tragedy* (Oxford: Oxford University Press, 1981), 36.
39. Wittgenstein, *Philosophical Investigations*, §246.
40. Wittgenstein, *Philosophical Investigations*, §248.
41. Søren Overgaard has convincingly argued that this difference is as crucial to Wittgenstein as it is to the phenomenology of Husserl and Levinas. Overgaard, *Wittgenstein and Other Minds: Rethinking Subjectivity and Intersubjectivity with Wittgenstein, Levinas, and Husserl* (London: Routledge, 2007), 132–40.
42. Scarry, *The Body in Pain*, 56.
43. See my *The Problem of Job and the Problem of Evil* (Cambridge: Cambridge University Press, 2019), 8–13.
44. I have argued elsewhere that the central topics of the entire book of Job can be fruitfully read as motivated by physical pain; Dahl, "Job and the Problem of Physical Pain: A Phenomenological Reading," *Modern Theology* 32 (2016): 45–59.
45. David B. Morris, *The Culture of Pain* (Berkeley: University of California Press, 1991), 139.
46. Phillip Nemo, *Job and the Excess of Evil*, trans. M. Kigel (Pittsburgh, PA: Duquesne University Press, 1998), 31–34.
47. Paul Ricoeur, *Interpretation Theory: Discourse and the Surplus of Meaning* (Austin: University of Texas Press, 1976), 50–52. For metaphors and pain, see Scarry, *The Body in Pain*, 15–17.
48. Scarry, *The Body in Pain*, 15–19.
49. Donn Welton, "Biblical Bodies," in *Body and Flesh: A Philosophical Reader*, ed. D. Welton (Malden, MA: Blackwell, 1998), 246.
50. David Biro, "When Language Runs Dry: Pain, the Imagination, and Metaphor," in *Dimensions of Pain: Humanities and Social Science Perspectives*, ed. L. F. Käll (London: Routledge, 2012), 25.
51. See also David B. Burrell, *Deconstructing Theodicy: Why Job Has Nothing to Say to the Puzzle of Suffering* (Grand Rapids, MI: Brazos, 2008), 17, 109.
52. Wittgenstein, *Philosophical Investigations*, §248.
53. Nemo, *Job and the Excess of Evil*, 36.
54. Cavell, *Must We Mean What We Say*, 264.
55. Cavell, *Must We Mean What We Say*, 163.
56. See also Charles E. M. Dunlop, "Wittgenstein on Sensation and 'Seeing-As,'" *Synthese* 60 (1984): 354; Gordon Baker, *Wittgenstein's Method: Neglected Aspects*, ed. K. J. Morris (Oxford: Blackwell, 2004), 116.
57. Wittgenstein, *Philosophical Investigations*, §244.
58. Merleau-Ponty, *Phenomenology of Perception*, 179.
59. Ludwig Wittgenstein, *Last Writings on the Philosophy of Psychology*, vol. 1, ed. and trans. G. H. von Wright and Heikki Nyman (Oxford: Blackwell, 1992), §243.
60. Wittgenstein, *Philosophical Investigations*, II, §§192–95. (The paragraphs

NOTES TO PAGES 148–156

of the second part of the book, according to the present edition, will be marked by "II.")

61. Wittgenstein, *Zettel*, §220.
62. Wittgenstein, *Philosophical Investigations*, §285.
63. Merleau-Ponty, *Phenomenology of Perception*, 184.
64. Wittgenstein, *Philosophical Investigations*, II, §360.
65. Wittgenstein, *Philosophical Investigations*, §356.
66. Merleau-Ponty, *Phenomenology of Perception*, 187.
67. Scarry, *The Body in Pain*, 7–8.
68. For a critique of its rigidity, see Ariel Glucklich, *Sacred Pain: Hurting the Body for the Sake of the Soul* (Oxford: Oxford University Press, 2001), 75.
69. Cavell, *The Claim of Reason*, 32.
70. Wittgenstein, *Zettel*, §§532–33.
71. Wittgenstein, *Philosophical Investigations*, §§276, 261.
72. Stephen Mulhall, *Inheritance and Originality: Wittgenstein, Heidegger, Kierkegaard* (Oxford: Oxford University Press, 2001), 170–71.
73. Wittgenstein, *Philosophical Investigations*, II, §325.
74. Talal Asad, "Agency and Pain: An Exploration," *Culture and Religion. An Interdisciplinary Journal* 1 (2000): 42.
75. Wittgenstein, *Philosophical Investigations*, II, §365.
76. Wittgenstein, *Philosophical Investigations*, §242. See also Stanley Cavell, *This New Yet Unapproachable America: Lectures after Emerson after Wittgenstein* (Albuquerque, NM: Living Batch, 1989), 41.
77. Wittgenstein, *Philosophical Investigations*, §25.
78. See also Merleau-Ponty, *Phenomenology of Perception*, 189.
79. Wittgenstein, *Zettel*, §541.
80. Wittgenstein, *Zettel*, §541.
81. Wittgenstein, *Philosophical Investigations*, §261. For a discussion of the relationship between the conceptual and nonconceptual in the context of Wittgenstein's private language argument, see John McDowell, "One Strand of the Private Language Argument," in *Mind, Value, and Reality* (Cambridge, MA: Harvard University Press, 1998), 279–96.
82. Cavell, *The Claim of Reason*, 178.

Chapter 7

1. Merleau-Ponty, *Signs*, 71.
2. Henry, *Incarnation*, 136.
3. Majella Fanzmann, "Gnostic Portraits of Jesus," in *The Blackwell Companion to Jesus*, ed. D. Burkett (Oxford: Wiley-Blackwell, 2014), 160–75.
4. Ignatius, "Letter to the Smyrnaeans," VI.2, in *The Fathers of the Church I*, ed. and trans. F. X. Glimm, J. M. F. Mariquie, and G. G. Walsh (Washington, DC: Catholic University of America, 1947), 119.
5. Irenaeus, *Against Heresies*, V.17.1–2; see also Gustaf Wingren, "Skapelse,

Lagen och Inkarnationen enligt Ireneus," *Svensk Teologisk Kvartalskrift* 2 (1940): 139.

6. Irenaeus, *Against Heresies*, III.16.6.

7. Irenaeus, *Against Heresies*, V.14.2.

8. See also Thomas F. Torrance, *Space, Time and Resurrection* (London: T&T Clark, 2019), 86.

9. Irenaeus, *Against Heresies*, III.16.6.

10. Thomas G. Weinandy, "St. Irenaeus and the *Imago Dei*: The Importance of Being Human," *Logos* 6, no. 4 (2003): 18.

11. Emmanuel Falque, *God, the Flesh, and the Other*, trans. W. C. Hackett (Evanston, IL: Northwestern University Press, 2015), 143.

12. Tertullian, *On the Resurrection of the Flesh*, in *Ante-Nicene Fathers, Volume 3*, ed. A. Roberts, J. Donaldson, and A. Cleveland Coxe (New York: Cosimo Classics, 2007), IV.

13. Charlotte Radler, "The Dirty Physician: Necessary Dishonor and Fleshly Solidity in Tertullian's Writings," *Vigiliae Christianae* 63 (2009): 360–66

14. Tertullian, *On the Resurrection of the Flesh*, IX, V.

15. Tertullian, *On the Flesh of Christ*, in *Ante-Nicene Fathers, Volume 3*, V. Similar language is found in Irenaeus, *Against Heresies*, V.2.2.

16. Tertullian, *On the Flesh of Christ*, IX.

17. Tertullian, *On the Flesh of Christ*, IX. For similar points, see Irenaeus, *Against Heresies*, III.22.2.

18. Tertullian, *A Treatise on the Soul*, in *Ante-Nicene Fathers, Volume 3*, V.

19. Tertullian, *The Five Books against Marcion*, in *Ante-Nicene Fathers, Volume 3*, III.VIII.

20. Falque, *God, the Flesh, and the Other*, 151.

21. Henry, *Incarnation*, 14.

22. Tertullian, *On the Flesh of Christ*, XVII; Irenaeus, *Against Heresies*, III.XIX.

23. Henry, *Incarnation*, 14.

24. Henry, *Incarnation*, 17–18.

25. Tertullian, *On the Flesh of Christ*, V.

26. Henry, *Incarnation*, 129.

27. Tertullian, *On the Resurrection of the Flesh*, VII.

28. Henry, *Incarnation*, 17.

29. Henry, *Incarnation*, IV.

30. Henry, *I Am the Truth*, 59.

31. Henry, *Incarnation*, 121. See also Joseph M. Rivera, "Generation, Interiority, and Phenomenology of Christianity in Michel Henry," *Continental Philosophy Review* 44 (2011): 108–12.

32. Henry, "Incarnation and the Problem of Touch," 130.

33. Henry, "Incarnation and the Problem of Touch," 130.

34. Henry, *I Am the Truth*, 204.

35. Henry, *Incarnation*, 131–32.

36. Irenaeus, *Against Heresies*, V.3.3. The passage is quoted in Henry, *Incarnation*, 135.

37. Irenaeus, *Against Heresies*, V.3.2.

NOTES TO PAGES 163-170

38. Henry, *Incarnation*, 227–28.
39. Henry, *Incarnation*, 229.
40. Falque, *The Loving Struggle*, 143.
41. Kevin Hart, "Inward Life," in *Michel Henry: The Affects of Thought*, ed. J. Hanson and M. R. Kelly (London: Bloomsbury, 2012), 103–5; Rivera, *The Contemplative Self*, 199.
42. Hans Jonas, "The Gnostic Syndrome," in *Philosophical Essays: From Ancient Creed to Technological Man* (Chicago: University of Chicago Press, 1974), 267.
43. Rudolf Bernet, "Christianity and Philosophy," *Continental Philosophy Review* 32 (1999): 337.
44. Henry, *I Am the Truth*, 124.
45. Tertullian, *The Five Books against Marcion*, I.XIX.
46. Merleau-Ponty, *Sense and Non-Sense*, 174; Merleau-Ponty, *Signs*, 71.
47. Falque, "This Is My Body," 283.
48. Henry, *Incarnation*, 132.
49. Henry, *Incarnation*, 132.
50. Joseph Rivera, *Phenomenology and the Horizon of Experience: Spiritual Themes in Henry, Marion, and Lacoste* (Abingdon, UK: Routledge, 2022), 80.
51. Rivera, *Phenomenology*, 231.
52. Tertullian, *On the Flesh of Christ*, IX. See also Falque, *The Loving Struggle*, 170.
53. See also Falque, *The Metamorphosis of Finitude*, 19.
54. Scarry, *The Body in Pain*, 53.
55. Ola Sigurdsson, "Only Vulnerable Creatures Suffer," in *Phenomenology of the Broken Body*, ed. E. Dahl, C. Falke, and T. E. Eriksen (London: Routledge, 2019), 88.
56. Jürgen Moltmann, "The Passion of Christ and the Suffering of God," *Asbury Theological Journal* 48 (1993): 20.
57. Levinas, *Time and the Other*, 74. See also Emmanuel Falque, *Guide to Gethsemane*, 75.
58. Sartre, *Being and Nothingness*, 283–84.
59. Scarry, *The Body in Pain*, 53.
60. Jean Améry, *At the Mind's Limits: Contemplations by a Survivor on Auschwitz and Its Realities*, trans. S. Rosenfeld and S. P. Rosenfeld (Bloomington: Indiana University Press, 1980), 28.
61. Améry, *At the Mind's Limits*, 33.
62. Leder, *The Absent Body*, 75–76.
63. Simone Weil, *Gravity and Grace*, trans. E. Crawford and M. von der Ruhr (London: Routledge, 2002), 84.
64. Marcel, *Being and Having*, 85.
65. This inner tension of pain, Leder has pointed out, is similar to what anthropologists call "liminal phenomena." Leder, *The Distressed Body*, 40.
66. Scarry, *The Body in Pain*, 52.
67. Levinas, "Useless Suffering," 156.
68. Scarry, *The Body in Pain*, 53. See also Bernstein, *Torture and Dignity*, 88–89.

NOTES TO PAGES 171-180

69. Falque, *The Wedding Feast of the Lamb*, 14.
70. Emmanuel Falque, "The Discarnate Madman," *Journal for Continental Philosophy of Religion* 1 (2019): 102-3.
71. Henry, "Incarnation," in *The Michel Henry Reader*, 47.
72. Emmanuel Levinas, *On Escape*, trans. B. Bergo (Stanford, CA: Stanford University Press, 2003), 66.
73. Jürgen Moltmann, *The Crucified God*, trans. R. A. Wilson and J. Bowden (London: SCM, 2001), 155.
74. I have discussed the problems of theodicy in *The Problem of Job and the Problem of Evil*, 51-58.
75. Michel Henry, "Theodicy from the Perspective of a Radical Phenomenology," in *The Michel Henry Reader*, ed. S. Davidson and F. Seyler (Evanston, IL: Northwestern University Press, 2019), 228-30.
76. Falque, *Guide to Gethsemane*, 86.
77. Falque, *Guide to Gethsemane*, 88.
78. Falque, *Guide to Gethsemane*, 69.
79. Henry, "Theodicy," 233.
80. Henry, "Theodicy," 233.

Chapter 8

1. Gerhard Ebeling, *Word and Faith*, trans. J. W. Leitch (London: SCM, 1963), 301-2.
2. See also Geniusas, *The Phenomenology of Pain*, 100-105.
3. For the twofold sense of everydayness, see my "Augustine and Heidegger on Verticality and Everydayness," *Continental Philosophy Review* 56 (2023): 207-10.
4. Heidegger, *Being and Time*, 66-72, 169-74.
5. Heidegger, *Being and Time*, 353.
6. Heidegger, *Being and Time*, 353.
7. Levinas, *On Escape*, 61.
8. Friedrich Nietzsche, *Thus Spoke Zarathustra*, trans. A. del Caro (Cambridge: Cambridge University Press, 2006), 262.
9. Nietzsche, *Thus Spoke Zarathustra*, 184.
10. For Husserl's employment of the comet tail, see *The Phenomenology of Internal Time-Consciousness*, 52.
11. See also Geniusas, *The Phenomenology of Pain*, 111.
12. Geniusas, *The Phenomenology of Pain*, 112.
13. Husserl, *Analyses concerning Active and Passive Synthesis*, 44.
14. Edmund Husserl, *Die Bernauer Manuskripte Über das Zeitbewusstsein, Husserliana* 33, ed. R. Bernet and D. Lohmar (Dordrecht: Springer, 2001), 10.
15. Augustine, *On Christian Teaching*, trans. R. P. H. Green (Oxford: Oxford University Press, 1997), I.xxxvii.42.
16. Klaus Held, "Idee einer Phänomenologie der Hoffnung," in *Inter-

disziplinäre Perspektiven der Phänomenologie, ed. D. Lohmar and D. Fonfara (New York: Springer, 2006), 236.

17. Husserl, *Die Bernauer Manuskripte,* 11.

18. Husserl, *Crisis of the European Sciences,* 8–9; Husserl, *Ideas I,* 106–7. See also my *Phenomenology of the Holy: Religious Experience after Husserl* (London: SCM, 2010), 196–202.

19. Klaus Held, "The Phenomenology of 'Authentic Time' in Husserl and Heidegger," *International Journal of Philosophical Studies* 15 (2007): 337.

20. Held, "Phenomenology of 'Authentic Time,'" 338.

21. Anthony Steinbock, *Moral Emotions: Reclaiming the Evidence of the Heart* (Evvanston, IL: Northwestern University Press, 2014), 163.

22. Emmanuel Levinas, *Existence and Existents,* trans. A. Lingis (Pittsburgh, PA: Duquesne University Press, 2001), 91.

23. Gabriel Marcel, *Homo Viator: Introduction to a Metaphysics of Hope,* trans. E. Craufurd (Chicago: Henry Regnery, 1951), 31.

24. Jonathan Lear, *Radical Hope: Ethics in the Face of Cultural Devastation* (Cambridge, MA: Harvard University Press, 2006), 93–94, 103.

25. Steinbock, *Moral Emotions,* 164–66.

26. Steinbock, *Moral Emotions,* 167.

27. Held, "Idee einer Phänomenologie der Hoffnung," 131.

28. According to Heidegger, moods mark out the openness of the present, that is, thrownness and facticity, and not openness for the future. See also Heidegger, *Being and Time,* 131–33.

29. Held, "Idee einer Phänomenologie der Hoffnung," 134–35, 140.

30. Steinbock, *Moral Emotions,* 171.

31. Steinbock, *Moral Emotions,* 168–69.

32. Marcel, *Homo Viator,* 47.

33. Marcel, *Homo Viator,* 62.

34. Cited from *Dimensions of Pain: Humanities and Social Science Perspectives,* ed. L. Folkmarson Käll (London: Routledge, 2012), 1.

35. See also Paul Ricoeur, *The Conflict of Interpretations: Essays in Hermeneutics,* ed. and trans. D. Ihde (London: Continuum, 2004), 308–9, 404–5.

36. Nietzsche, *Thus Spoke Zarathustra,* 184.

37. The structure of negative hope also has some similarities with Kant's postulates of what we can hope for. To make sense of the present moral life, according to Kant, morality and happiness must be joined. Since this joining cannot be achieved in this life, we must postulate the immorality of the soul. As G. Greshake and J. Kremer rightly point out, the strength of such postulates of reason is their embeddedness in concrete experience, while their weakness is that they fail to prove anything and can only establish hope. I will rather suggest that hope only appears as weak if it is conflated with present knowledge. Greshake and Kremer, *Resurrection Mortuorum: Zum theologischen Verständnis der leiblichen Auferstehung* (Darmstadt: Wissenschaftliche Buchgesellschaft, 1986), 312–18.

38. For the arrival of the future, see Jürgen Moltmann, *The Coming of God: Christian Eschatology,* trans. M. Kohl (Minneapolis, MN: Fortress, 1996), 23–25.

39. Jean-Paul Sartre, *The Imaginary: A Phenomenological Analysis of the Imagination*, trans. J. Webber (London: Routledge, 2004), 182.
40. Levinas, *Existence and Existents*, 91.
41. Levinas, *Existence and Existents*, 94.
42. Levinas, *Existence and Existents*, 94.
43. I have in mind the readings of R. Girard, D. Sölle, E. Wiesel, and N. Verbin. See also my *The Problem of God and the Problem of Evil* (Cambridge: Cambridge University Press, 2019), 82–83.
44. Steinbock, *Moral Emotions*, 189.
45. Steinbock, *Moral Emotions*, 190.
46. Jürgen Moltmann, "'Das Prinzip Hoffnung' und die 'Theologie der Hoffnung,'" in *Theologie der Hoffnung: Untersuchungen zur Begründung und zu den Konsequenzen einer christilichen Eschatologie* (Munich: Gutersloher Verlagshaus, 1997), 331–34.
47. Steinbock, *Moral Emotions*, 171.
48. Jürgen Moltmann, *Theology of Hope: On the Ground and the Implications of a Christian Eschatology*, trans. J. W. Leitch (London: SCM, 1967), 189.
49. Devin Singh, "Resurrection as Surplus and Possibility: Moltmann and Ricoeur," *Scottish Journal of Theology* 61 (2008): 254.
50. Ricoeur, *The Conflict of Interpretations*, 401. See also Moltmann, *Theology of Hope*, 135.
51. Moltmann, *Theology of Hope*, 89–91.
52. Jean-Louis Chrétien, *The Unforgettable and the Unhoped For*, trans. J. Bloechl (New York: Fordham University Press, 2002), 114.
53. Chrétien, *The Unforgettable*, 107–8.
54. Chrétien, *The Unforgettable*, 113.
55. Chrétien, *The Unforgettable*, 88.
56. Chrétien, *The Unforgettable*, 117.
57. Chrétien, *The Unforgettable*, 118.
58. Paul Ricoeur, *Hermeneutics and the Human Sciences*, trans. J. B. Thompson (Cambridge: Cambridge University Press, 1981), 100. For a similar point, see also Moltmann, *Theology of Hope*, 107.
59. Husserl, *Ideas I*, 106.
60. Paul Ricoeur, *Hermeneutics*, trans. D. Pellauer (Cambridge: Polity, 2013), 165.
61. Ricoeur, *Hermeneutics*, 166.
62. Wolfhart Pannenberg, *Jesus—God and Man*, trans. L. L. Wilkins and D. A. Priebe (London: SCM, 2002), 74; Torrance, *Space, Time and Resurrection*, 36–37.
63. Ola Sigurdson, *Heavenly Bodies: Incarnation, the Gaze, and Embodiment in Christian Theology*, trans. C. Olsen (Grand Rapids, MI: Eerdmans, 2016), 245.
64. Falque, *The Metamorphosis of Finitude*, 137.
65. Falque, *The Metamorphosis of Finitude*, 138.
66. Falque, *The Metamorphosis of Finitude*, 141.
67. Rudolf Bultmann, "New Testament and Mythology," in *Kerygma and Myth*, ed. H. W. Bartsch (New York: Harper and Row, 1961), 39–41.

NOTES TO PAGES 195–206

68. Falque, *The Metamorphosis of Finitude*, 138.
69. Falque, *The Metamorphosis of Finitude*, 142.
70. Jean-Luc Marion, "They Recognized Him; and He Became Invisible to Them," *Modern Theology* 18 (2002): 146.
71. Falque, *The Metamorphosis of Finitude*, 143.
72. Max Scheler, "Tod und Fortleben," in *Schriften aus dem Nachlass,* vol. 1 (Bern: Franke Verlag, 1957), 43–45.
73. Scheler, "Tod und Fortleben," 47.
74. Scheler, "Tod und Fortleben," 49 (my translation).
75. Scheler, "Tod und Fortleben," 49 (my translation).
76. Scheler, "Tod und Fortleben," 50–51.
77. Marion, *In Excess*, 94.
78. Marion, *In Excess*, 98.

Coda

1. Merleau-Ponty, *Phenomenology of Perception*, 10.
2. Merleau-Ponty, *Signs*, 166; Merleau-Ponty, *The Visible and the Invisible*, 133.
3. Henry, *Incarnation*, 4.
4. Falque, "Is There a Flesh without a Body?"; see also 158.
5. Merleau-Ponty, *Sense and Non-Sense*, 172.
6. Husserl, *Ideas II*, 185.
7. Merleau-Ponty, *Nature*, 206.
8. Merleau-Ponty, *The Visible and the Invisible*, 138–39.
9. Toadvine, *Merleau-Ponty's Philosophy of Nature*, 58–59.

Bibliography

Adorno, Theodor W. *Metaphysics: Concepts and Problems.* Translated by E. Jephcott. Stanford, CA: Stanford University Press, 2001.
Alloa, Emmanuel. *Resistance of the Sensible World: An Introduction to Merleau-Ponty.* Translated by J. M. Todd. New York: Fordham University Press, 2017.
Améry, Jean. *At the Mind's Limits: Contemplations by a Survivor on Auschwitz and Its Realities.* Translated by S. Rosenfeld and S. P. Rosenfeld. Bloomington: Indiana University Press, 1980.
———. *On Aging: Revolt and Resignation.* Translated by J. D. Barlow. Bloomington: Indiana University Press, 1994.
Arendt, Hannah. *The Human Condition.* Chicago: University of Chicago Press, 1958.
Aristotle, *On the Soul.* Translated by J. Sachs. Santa Fe, NM: Green Lion, 2004.
Asad, Talal. "Agency and Pain: An Exploration." *Culture and Religion: An Interdisciplinary Journal* 1 (2000): 29–60.
Augustine, Saint. *On Christian Teaching.* Translated by R. P. H. Green. Oxford: Oxford University Press, 1997.
Bakan, David. *Disease, Pain, and Sacrifice: Toward a Psychology of Suffering.* Chicago: University of Chicago Press, 1968.
Baker, Gordon. *Wittgenstein's Method: Neglected Aspects.* Edited by K. J. Morris. Oxford: Blackwell, 2004.
Barbaras, Renaud. *Desire and Distance: Introduction to a Phenomenology of Perception.* Translated by P. B. Milan. Stanford, CA: Stanford University Press, 2006.
———. "The Essence of Life: Drive or Desire?" In *Michel Henry: The Affects of Thought,* edited by J. Hanson and M. R. Kelly, 37–56. London: Continuum, 2012.
———. *Introduction to a Phenomenology of Life.* Translated by L. Lawlor. Bloomington: Indiana University Press, 2021.
———. "A Phenomenology of Life." In *The Cambridge Companion to Merleau-Ponty,* edited by T. Carman and M. B. N. Hansen. Cambridge: Cambridge University Press, 2005.
Behnke, Elisabeth A. "Edmund Husserl's Contribution to Phenomenology of the Body in *Ideas II.*" In *Issues in Husserl's Ideas II,* edited by T. Nenon and L. Embree, 107–20. Dordrecht: Kluwer Academic, 1996.
Benson, Bruce Ellis, and Norman Wirzba, eds. *Words of Life: New Theological Turns in French Phenomenology.* New York: Fordham University Press, 2010.

BIBLIOGRAPHY

Bernet, Rudolf. "Christianity and Philosophy." *Continental Philosophy Review* 32 (1999): 325–42.

———. "The Encounter with the Stranger." In *The Face of the Other and the Trace of God*, edited by J. Bloechl, 46–47. New York: Fordham University Press, 2009.

———. "The Subject in Nature: Reflections on Merleau-Ponty's *Phenomenology of Perception*." In *Merleau-Ponty in Contemporary Perspective*, edited by P. Burke and J. Van der Veken, 9–20. Amsterdam: Kluwer Academic, 1993.

Bernstein, J. M. *Torture and Dignity: An Essay on Moral Injury*. Chicago: University of Chicago Press, 2015.

Biro, David. "When Language Runs Dry: Pain, the Imagination, and Metaphor." In *Dimensions of Pain: Humanities and Social Science Perspectives*, edited by L. F. Käll, 67–78. London: Routledge, 2012.

Bultmann, Rudolf. "New Testament and Mythology." In *Kerygma and Myth*, edited by H. W. Bartsch, 1–44. New York: Harper and Row, 1961.

Burrell, David B. *Deconstructing Theodicy: Why Job Has Nothing to Say to the Puzzle of Suffering*. Grand Rapids, MI: Brazos, 2008.

Butler, Judith. *Bodies That Matter: On the Discursive Limits of Sex*. London: Routledge, 2011.

———. "Merleau-Ponty and the Touch of Malebranche." In *The Cambridge Companion to Merleau-Ponty*, edited by T. Carman and M. B. N. Hansen, 181–205. Cambridge: Cambridge University Press, 2005.

Buytendijk, F. J. J. *Pain*. Translated by A. O'Shiel. London: Hutchinson, 1961.

Cairns, Dorion. *Conversations with Husserl and Fink*. Dordrecht: Springer, 1976.

Carel, Havi. *Illness: The Cry of the Flesh*. Durham, UK: Acumen, 2008.

Carman, Taylor. *Merleau-Ponty*. London: Routledge, 2008.

Cavell, Stanley. *The Claim of Reason: Wittgenstein, Skepticism, Morality, and Tragedy*. New York: Oxford University Press, 1979.

———. *Must We Mean What We Say? A Book of Essays*. Cambridge: Cambridge University Press, 1976.

———. *This New Yet Unapproachable America: Lectures after Emerson after Wittgenstein*. Albuquerque, NM: Living Batch, 1989.

Chrétien, Jean-Louise. *Call and Response*. Translated by A. A. Davenport. New York: Fordham University Press, 2004.

———. *The Unforgettable and the Unhoped For*. Translated by J. Bloechl. New York: Fordham University Press, 2002.

Dahl, Espen. "Augustine and Heidegger on Verticality and Everydayness." *Continental Philosophy Review* 56 (2023): 203–21.

———. "Inkarnasjon, kors og smertens fenomenologi." *Teologisk Tidsskrift* 4 (2015): 148–63.

———. "The Inner Tension of Pain and the Phenomenology of Evil." *International Journal of Philosophy and Theology* 78 (2017): 396–406.

———. "Job and the Problem of Physical Pain: A Phenomenological Reading." *Modern Theology* 32 (2016): 45–59.

———. "Mottageligheten og kroppens fenomenologi." In *Skapelsesnåde: Festskrift*

BIBLIOGRAPHY

for Svein Aage Christoffersen, edited by S. Holte, M. T. Mjaaland, and R. Jensen, 13–28. Oslo: Novus, 2017.

———. "On Morality of Speech: Cavell's Critique of Derrida." *Continental Philosophical Review* 44 (2011): 81–101.

———. *Phenomenology of the Holy: Religious Experience after Husserl.* London: SCM, 2010.

———. "Preserving Wonder through the Reduction: Husserl, Marion, and Merleau-Ponty." In *The Problem of Religious Experience: Case Studies in Phenomenology, with Reflections and Commentaries*, edited by O. Louchakova-Schwartz. New York: Springer, 2020.

———. *The Problem of Job and the Problem of Evil.* Cambridge: Cambridge University Press, 2019.

———. *Stanley Cavell, Religion, and Continental Philosophy.* Bloomington: Indiana University Press, 2014.

———. "Weakness and Passivity: Phenomenology of the Body after Paul." In *Phenomenology of the Broken Body*, edited by E. Dahl, C. Falke, and T. E. Eriksen, 36–50. London: Routledge, 2019.

Dauphinée, Elisabeth. "The Politics of the Body in Pain: Reading the Ethics of Imagery." *Security Dialogue* 38 (2007): 139–55.

de Haro, Augustine Serrano. "Is Pain an Intentional Experience?" *Phenomenology* 3 (2011): 386–95.

Derrida, Jacques. *On Touching—Jean-Luc Nancy.* Translated by C. Irizarry. Stanford, CA: Stanford University Press, 2005.

———. *Writing and Difference.* Translated by A. Bass. London: Routledge, 2001.

Dillon, Martin C. *Merleau-Ponty's Ontology.* Evanston, IL: Northwestern University Press, 1997.

Dodd, James. *Idealism and Corporeality: An Essay on the Problem of the Body in Husserl's Phenomenology.* Amsterdam: Springer, 1997.

Dunlop, Charles E. M. "Wittgenstein on Sensation and 'Seeing-As.'" *Synthese* 60 (1984): 349–67.

Dreyfus, Hubert L. *Being-in-the-World: A Commentary on Heidegger's "Being and Time," Division I.* Cambridge, MA: MIT Press, 1991.

Ebeling, Gerhard. *Word and Faith.* Translated by J. W. Leitch. London: SCM, 1963.

Falque, Emmanuel. "The Discarnate Madman." *Journal for Continental Philosophy of Religion* 1 (2019): 90–117.

———. *God, the Flesh, and the Other.* Translated by W. C. Hackett. Evanston, IL: Northwestern University Press, 2015.

———. "Is There a Flesh without Body? A Debate with Michel Henry." *Journal of French and Francophone Philosophy* 24 (2016): 139–66.

———. *The Loving Struggle: Phenomenological and Theological Debates.* Translated by B. B. Onishi and L. McCracken. London: Rowman and Littlefield, 2018.

———. *The Guide to Gethsemane: Anxiety, Suffering, Death.* Translated by G. Hughes. New York: Fordham University Press, 2019.

———. *The Metamorphosis of Finitude: An Essay on Birth and Resurrection.* Translated by G. Hughes. New York: Fordham University Press, 2012.

———. "This Is My Body: Contribution to the Philosophy of the Eucharist." In *Carnal Hermeneutics*, edited by R. Kearney and B. Treanor. New York: Fordham University Press, 2015.

———. "Toward an Ethics of the Spread Body." In *Somatic Desire: Incorporating Desire in Contemporary Thought*, edited by S. Horton, S. Mendelsohn, C. Rojcewicz, and R. Kearney. London: Lexington Books, 2019.

———. *The Wedding Feast of the Lamb: Eros, the Body, and the Eucharist*. Translated by G. Hughes. New York: Fordham University Press, 2016.

Fanzmann, Majella. "Gnostic Portraits of Jesus." In *The Blackwell Companion to Jesus*, edited by D. Burkett. Oxford: Wiley-Blackwell, 2014.

Franck, Didier. *Flesh and Body: On the Phenomenology of Husserl*. Translated by J. Rivera and S. Davidson. London: Bloomsbury 2014.

Freud, Sigmund. *The Uncanny*. Translated by D. McLintock. London: Penguin Books, 2003.

Gallagher, Shaun. "Body Image and Body Schema: A Conceptual Clarification." *Journal of Mind and Behavior* 7 (1986): 541–54.

———. "Hyletic Experience and the Lived Body." *Husserl Studies* 3 (1986): 131–66.

———. "Lived Body and Environment." *Research in Phenomenology* 16 (1986): 139–70.

———. "A Well-Trodden Path: From Phenomenology to Enactivism." *Filosofisk Supplement* 3 (2018).

Gallagher, Shaun, and Dan Zahavi. *The Phenomenological Mind*. London: Routledge, 2012.

Geniusas, Saulius. "The Origins of the Phenomenology of Pain: Brentano, Stumpf and Husserl." *Continental Philosophy Review* 47 (2014): 1–17.

———. *The Phenomenology of Pain*. Athens: Ohio University Press, 2020.

Glucklich, Ariel. *Sacred Pain: Hurting the Body for the Sake of the Soul*. Oxford: Oxford University Press, 2001.

Greshake, G., and J. Kremer. *Resurrection Mortuorum: Zum theologischen Verständnis der leiblichen Auferstehung*. Darmstadt: Wissenschaftliche Buchgesellschaft, 1986.

Grüny, Christian. *Zerstörte Erfarung: Eine Phänomenologie des Schmerzes*. Würzburg: Verlag Königshausen & Neumann, 2004.

Hacker, P. M. S. "Of Knowledge and of Knowing That Someone Is in Pain." In *Wittgenstein: The Philosopher and His Works*, edited by A. Pichler and S. Säätelä. Bergen: WAB, 2005.

Harman, Graham. *The Quadruple Object*. Winchester, UK: Zero Books, 2011.

Hart, Kevin. "Inward Life." In *Michel Henry: The Affects of Thought*, edited by J. Hanson and M. R. Kelly. London: Continuum, 2012.

Heidegger, Martin. *Being and Time*. Translated by J. Stambaugh. Albany: SUNY Press, 2010.

———. *Zollikoner Seminare*. Edited by M. Boss. Frankfurt am Main: Vittorio Klostermann, 1994.

Held, Klaus. "Idee einer Phänomenologie der Hoffnung." In *Interdisziplinäre Perspektiven der Phänomenologie*, edited by D. Lohmar and D. Fonfara. New York: Springer, 2006.

BIBLIOGRAPHY

———. "The Phenomenology of 'Authentic Time' in Husserl and Heidegger." *International Journal of Philosophical Studies* 15 (2007): 327–47.

Henry, Michel. *The Essence of Manifestation*. Translated by G. Etzkorn. The Hague: Martinus Nijhoff, 1973.

———. *I Am the Truth: Toward a Philosophy of Christianity*. Translated by S. Emmanuel. Stanford, CA: Stanford University Press, 2003.

———. "Incarnation." In *The Michel Henry Reader*, edited by S. Davidson and F. Seyler. Evanston, IL: Northwestern University Press, 2019.

———. *Incarnation: A Philosophy of the Flesh*. Translated by K. Hefty. Evanston, IL: Northwestern University Press, 2015.

———. "Incarnation and the Problem of Touch." In *Carnal Hermeneutics*, edited by R. Kearney and B. Treanor. New York: Fordham University Press, 2015.

———. *Material Phenomenology*. Translated by D. Scott. New York: Fordham University Press, 2008.

———. "Phenomenology of Life." *Angelaki: Journal of the Theoretical Humanities* 8 (2003): 97–110.

———. *Philosophy and Phenomenology of the Body*. Translated by G. Etzkorn. The Hague: Martinus Nijhoff, 1975.

———. "Philosophy and Subjectivity." In *The Michel Henry Reader*, edited by S. Davidson and F. Seyler. Evanston, IL: Northwestern University Press, 2019.

———. "Theodicy from the Perspective of a Radical Phenomenology." In *The Michel Henry Reader*, edited by S. Davidson and F. Seyler. Evanston, IL: Northwestern University Press, 2019.

———. *Words of Christ*. Translated by C. M. Gschwandtner. Grand Rapids, MI: Eerdmans, 2012.

Husserl, Edmund. *Analyses concerning Passive Synthesis: Lectures on Transcendental Logic*. Translated by A. Steinbock. Dordrecht: Kluwer Academic, 2001.

———. *Cartesian Meditations: An Introduction to Phenomenology*. Translated by D. Cairns. The Hague: Martinus Nijhoff, 1960.

———. *The Crisis of European Sciences and Transcendental Phenomenology*. Translated by D. Carr. Evanston, IL: Northwestern University Press, 1970.

———. *Die Bernauer Manuskripte über das Zeitbewusstsein*. Husserliana 33. Edited by R. Bernet and D. Lohmar. Dordrecht: Springer, 2001.

———. *Experience and Judgment*. Translated by J. S. Churchill and K. Ameriks. Evanston, IL: Northwestern University Press, 1973.

———. *Ideas for a Pure Phenomenology and Phenomenological Philosophy, First Book*. Translated by D. O. Dahlstrom. Indianapolis, IN: Hackett, 2014.

———. *Ideas Pertaining to a Pure Phenomenology and to a Phenomenological Philosophy, Second Book*. Translated by R. Rojcewicz and A. Schuwer. Dordrecht: Kluwer Academic, 1989.

———. *Logical Investigations II*. Translated by J. N. Findlay. London: Routledge, 2001.

———. *Phänomenologische Psychologie: Vorlesungen Sommersemester 1925*. Husserliana 9, edited by W. Biemel. The Hague: Martinus Nijhoff, 1962.

———. *The Phenomenology of Internal Time-Consciousness*. Translated by J. S. Churchill. Bloomington: Indiana University Press, 1964.

BIBLIOGRAPHY

———. *Thing and Space: Lectures of 1907*. Translated by R. Rojcewicz. Dordrecht: Springer, 1997.
———. *Zur Phänomenologie der Intersubjektivität. Texte aus dem Nachlass. Erster Teil, 1905–20, Husserliana 15*, edited by I. Kern. The Hague: Martinus Nijhoff, 1973.
Ignatius. "Letter to the Smyrnaeans." In *The Fathers of the Church I*, edited by F. X. Glimm, J. M. F. Mariquie, and G. G. Walsh. Washington, DC: Catholic University of America, 1947.
Irenaeus. *Against Heresies*. In *Ante-Nicene Fathers, Volume 1*, edited by P. Schaff. Grand Rapids, MI: Eerdmans, 1979.
Irigaray, Luce. *An Ethics of Sexual Difference*. Translated by C. Burke and C. Gill. Ithaca, NY: Cornell University Press, 1993.
Jagger, Gill. *Judith Butler: Sexual Politics, Social Change, and the Power of the Performative*. London: Routledge, 2008.
Janicaud, Dominique. "The Theological Turn of French Phenomenology." In *Phenomenology and the "Theological Turn*," translated by B.-G. Prusak. New York: Fordham University Press, 2000.
Jonas, Hans. "The Gnostic Syndrome." In *Philosophical Essays: From Ancient Creed to Technological Man*. Chicago: University of Chicago Press, 1974.
———. *The Phenomenology of Life: Toward a Philosophical Biology*. Evanston, IL: Northwestern University Press, 1966.
Käll, Lisa Folkmarson. "Intercorporeality and the Shareability of Pain." In *Dimensions of Pain*. London: Routledge, 2017.
Kant, Immanuel. *Critique of Pure Reason*. Translated by Norman Kemp Smith. London: Macmillan, 1929.
Kearney, Richard. *Touch: Recovering Our Most Vital Sense*. New York: Columbia University Press, 2021.
Kearney, Richard, and Brian Treanor, eds. *Carnal Hermeneutics*. New York: Fordham University Press, 2015.
Keller, C., and M. J. Rubenstein, eds. *Entangled Worlds: Religion, Science, and New Materialisms*. New York: Fordham University Press, 2017.
Kundera, Milan. *Immortality*. New York: Grove Weidenfeld, 1991.
Lavigne, Jean-Francois. "The Paradox and Limits of Michel Henry's Concept of Transcendence." *International Journal of Philosophical Studies* 17 (2009): 377–88.
———. "Suffering and Ipseity in Michel Henry: The Problem of the Ego's Transcendental Identity." *Analectica Hermeneutica* 8 (2016): 61–74.
Lear, Jonathan. *Radical Hope: Ethics in the Face of Cultural Devastation*. Cambridge, MA: Harvard University Press, 2006.
Leder, Drew. *The Absent Body*. Chicago: University of Chicago Press, 1990.
———. *The Distressed Body: Rethinking Illness, Imprisonment, and Healing*. Chicago: University of Chicago Press, 2016.
Levinas, Emmanuel. *Existence and Existents*. Translated by A. Lingis. Pittsburgh, PA: Duquesne University Press, 2001.
———. *Existence with Husserl*. Translated by R. A. Cohen and M. B. Smith. Evanston, IL: Northwestern University Press, 1998.

BIBLIOGRAPHY

———. *On Escape*. Translated by B. Bergo. Stanford, CA: Stanford University Press, 2003.
———. *Otherwise Than Being, or Beyond Essence*. Translated by A. Lingis. Pittsburgh, PA: Duquesne University Press, 1998.
———. *Time and the Other*. Translated by R. A. Cohen. Pittsburgh, PA: Duquesne University Press, 1987.
———. *Totality and Infinity*. Translated by A. Lingis. Pittsburgh, PA: Duquesne University Press, 1969.
———. "Transcendence and Evil." In P. Nemo, *Job and the Excess of Evil*, translated by M. Kigel. Pittsburgh, PA: Duquesne University Press, 1998.
———. "Useless Suffering." In *The Provocation of Levinas: Rethinking the Other*, edited by R. Bernasconi and D. Wood. London: Routledge, 2002.
Marcel, Gabriel. *Being and Having*. Translated by K. Farrer. Westminster, UK: Dacre, 1949.
———. *Creative Fidelity*. Translated by R. Rosthal. New York: Fordham University Press, 2002.
———. *Homo Viator: Introduction to a Metaphysics of Hope*. Translated by E. Craufurd. Chicago: Henry Regnery, 1951.
Marion, Jean-Luc. *Being Given: Toward a Phenomenology of Givenness*. Translated by J. L. Kosky. Stanford, CA: Stanford University Press, 2002.
———. *In Excess: Studies of Saturated Phenomena*. Translated by R. Horner. New York: Fordham University Press, 2002.
———. "The Invisible and the Phenomenon." In *Michel Henry: The Affects of Thought*, edited by J. Hanson and M. R. Kelly. London: Bloomsbury, 2012.
———. "They Recognized Him; and He Became Invisible to Them." *Modern Theology* 18 (2002): 145–52.
———. *Reduction and Givenness*. Evanston, IL: Northwestern University Press, 1998.
McDowell, John. "One Strand of the Private Language Argument." In *Mind, Value, and Reality*. Cambridge, MA: Harvard University Press, 1998.
Meillassoux, Quentin. *After Finitude: An Essay on the Necessity of Contingency*. London: Bloomsbury, 2008.
Merleau-Ponty, Maurice. *In Praise of Philosophy and Other Essays*. Translated by J. Wild et al. Evanston, IL: Northwestern University Press, 1970.
———. *Nature: Course Notes from the Collège de France*. Translated by R. Vallier. Evanston, IL: Northwestern University Press, 2003.
———. *Phenomenology of Perception*. Translated by C. Smith. London: Routledge, 1962.
———. "The Philosophy of Existence." In *Text and Context: On Philosophy, Politics, and Culture*, edited by H. J. Silverman and J. Berry Jr., translated by M. B. Smith et al. New York: Humanity Books, 1992.
———. *The Primacy of Perception and Other Essays*. Translated by J. M. Edie. Evanston, IL: Northwestern University Press, 1964.
———. *The Prose of the World*. Translated by J. O'Neill. Evanston, IL: Northwestern University Press, 1973.
———. "A Prospectus of His Work." In *The Merleau-Ponty Reader*, edited by

T. Toadvine and L. Lawlor. Evanston, IL: Northwestern University Press, 2007.

———. *Sense and Non-Sense.* Translated by H. L. Dreyfus and P. A. Dreyfus. Evanston, IL: Northwestern University Press, 1964.

———. *Signs.* Translated by R. C. McCleary. Evanston, IL: Northwestern University Press, 1964.

———. *The Visible and the Invisible.* Translated by A. Lingis. Evanston, IL: Northwestern University Press, 1968.

———. *The World of Perception.* Translated by O. Davis. London: Routledge, 2008.

Moltmann, Jürgen. *The Coming of God: Christian Eschatology.* Translated by M. Kohl. Minneapolis, MN: Fortress, 1996.

———. *The Crucified God.* Translated by R. A. Wilson and J. Bowden. London: SCM, 2001.

———. "'Das Prinzip Hoffnung' und die 'Theologie der Hoffnung.'" In *Theologie der Hoffnung: Untersuchungen zur Begründung und zu den Konsequenzen einer christilichen Eschatologie.* Munich: Gutersloher Verlagshaus, 1997.

———. "The Passion of Christ and the Suffering of God." *Asbury Theological Journal* 48 (1993): 19–28.

———. *Theology of Hope: On the Ground and the Implications of a Christian Eschatology.* Translated by J. W. Leitch. London: SCM, 1967.

Moltmann-Wendel, Elisabeth. *I Am My Body: A Theology of Embodiment.* Translated by J. Bowden. New York: Continuum, 1995.

Morris, David B. *The Culture of Pain.* Berkeley: University of California Press, 1991.

Moss, Candida R. "Christly Possession and Weakened Bodies: Reconsideration of the Function of Paul's Thorn in the Flesh." *Journal of Religion, Disability & Health* 16 (2012): 319–33.

Mulhall, Stephen. *Inheritance and Originality. Wittgenstein, Heidegger, Kierkegaard.* Oxford: Oxford University Press, 2001.

Nancy, Jean-Luc. *Corpus.* Translated by R. A. Rand. New York: Fordham University Press, 2008.

Nemo, Philippe. *Job and the Excess of Evil.* Translated by M. Kigel. Pittsburgh, PA: Duquesne University Press, 1998.

Nietzsche, Friedrich. *Genealogy of Morals.* Translated by H. B. Samuel. Edinburgh: Foulis, 1913.

———. *Thus Spoke Zarathustra.* Translated by A. del Caro. Cambridge: Cambridge University Press, 2006.

Orion, Edgar. *Things Seen and Unseen: The Logic of Incarnation in Merleau-Ponty's Metaphysics of Flesh.* Eugene, OR: Wipf and Stock, 2016.

Overgaard, Søren. "Heidegger on Embodiment." *Journal of the British Society for Phenomenology* 35 (2004): 116–31.

———. *Wittgenstein and Other Minds. Rethinking Subjectivity and Intersubjectivity with Wittgenstein, Levinas, and Husserl.* London: Routledge, 2007.

Pannenberg, Wolfhart. *Jesus—God and Man.* Translated by L. L. Wilkins and D. A. Priebe. London: SCM, 2002.

Patocka, Jan. *Body, Community, Language, World.* Translated by E. Kohak. Chicago: Open Court, 1998.

BIBLIOGRAPHY

Plessner, Helmuth. *Laughing and Crying: A Study of the Limits of Human Behavior.* Translated by J. S. Churchill and M. Grene. Evanston, IL: Northwestern University Press, 2020.

Rabanaque, Luis Roman. "Hyle, Genesis and Noema." *Husserl Studies* 19 (2003): 205–15.

Radler, Charlotte. "The Dirty Physician: Necessary Dishonor and Fleshly Solidity in Tertullian's Writings." *Vigiliae Christianae* 63 (2009): 345–68.

Reynolds, Joel Michael. *The Life Worth Living: Disability, Pain, and Morality.* Minneapolis: University of Minnesota Press, 2022.

Ricoeur, Paul. *The Conflict of Interpretations.* Edited by D. Ihde. London: Continuum, 2004.

———. *Freedom and Nature: The Voluntary and the Involuntary.* Translated by E. V. Kohak. Evanston, IL: Northwestern University Press, 1966.

———. *Hermeneutics and the Human Sciences.* Translated by J. B. Thompson. Cambridge: Cambridge University Press, 1981.

———. *Husserl: An Analysis of His Phenomenology.* Translated by E. G. Ballard. Evanston, IL: Northwestern University Press, 1967.

———. *Interpretation Theory: Discourse and the Surplus of Meaning.* Fort Worth: Texas Christian University Press, 1976.

———. *Oneself as Another.* Translated by K. Blamey. Chicago: University of Chicago Press, 1992.

Rivera, Joseph. *The Contemplative Self after Michel Henry.* Notre Dame, IN: University of Notre Dame Press, 2015.

———. "Generation, Interiority, and the Phenomenology of Christianity in Michel Henry." *Continental Philosophy Review* 44 (2011): 205–35.

———. *Phenomenology and the Horizon of Experience: Spiritual Themes in Henry, Marion, and Lacoste.* Abingdon, UK: Routledge, 2022.

Rivera, Mayra. *Poetics of the Flesh.* Durham, NC: Duke University Press, 2015.

Robinson, John A. T. *The Body: A Study in Pauline Theology.* London: SCM, 1952.

Russell, Ronald. "Redemptive Suffering and Paul's Thorn in the Flesh." *Journal of the Evangelical Theological Society* 39 (1996): 559–70.

Sartre, Jean-Paul. *Being and Nothingness: An Essay in Phenomenological Ontology.* Translated by H. E. Barnes. London: Routledge, 2003.

———. *The Imaginary: A Phenomenological Analysis of the Imagination.* Translated by J. Webber. London: Routledge, 2004.

Scarry, Elaine. *The Body in Pain: The Making and the Unmaking of the World.* Oxford: Oxford University Press, 1985.

Scheler, Max. "Tod und Fortleben." In *Schriften aus dem Nachlass*, vol. 1. Bern: Francke Verlag, 1957.

———. "Vom Sinn des Leidens." In *Max Scheler: Gesammelte Werke, Schriften zur Soziologie und Weltanschauungslehre*, vol. 6. Munich: Francke Verlag, 1963.

Shusterman, Richard. *Body Consciousness: A Philosophy of Mindfulness and Somaesthetics.* Cambridge: Cambridge University Press, 2008.

Sigurdson, Ola. *Heavenly Bodies: Incarnation, the Gaze, and Embodiment in Christian Theology.* Translated by C. Olsen. Grand Rapids, MI: Eerdmans, 2016.

———. "Only Vulnerable Creatures Suffer." In *Phenomenology of the Broken Body*, edited by E. Dahl, C. Falke, and T. E. Eriksen. London: Routledge, 2019.

Singh, Devin. "Resurrection as Surplus and Possibility: Moltmann and Ricoeur." *Scottish Journal of Theology* 61 (2008): 251–69.

Sokolowski, Robert. *The Formation of Husserl's Concept of Constitution*. The Hague: Martinus Nijhoff, 1964.

Sparrow, Tom. *The End of Phenomenology: Metaphysics and the New Realism*. Edinburgh: Edinburgh University Press, 2014.

———. *Plastic Bodies: Rebuilding Sensation after Phenomenology*. London: Open Humanities, 2015.

Steinbock, Anthony J. *Home and Beyond: Generative Phenomenology after Husserl*. Evanston, IL: Northwestern University Press, 1995.

———. *Moral Emotions: Reclaiming the Evidence of the Heart*. Evanston, IL: Northwestern University Press, 2014.

———. "The Problem of Forgetfulness in Michel Henry." *Continental Philosophy Review* 32 (1999): 271–302.

Sullivan, Mark D. "Pain in Language: From Sentience to Sapience." *Pain Forum* 4 (1995): 3–14.

Svenaeus, Fredrik. *Phenomenological Bioethics: Medical Technologies, Human Suffering, and the Meaning of Being Alive*. London: Routledge, 2018.

———. "A Phenomenology of Chronic Pain: Embodiment and Alienation." *Continental Philosophy Review* 48 (2015): 107–22.

Taylor, Charles. *A Secular Age*. Cambridge, MA: Belknap Press of Harvard University Press, 2008.

Tertullian, *Against Marcion*. In *Ante-Nicene Fathers, Volume 3*, edited by A. Roberts, J. Donaldson, and A. Cleveland Coxe. New York: Cosimo Classics, 2007.

———. *The Five Books against Marcion*. In *Ante-Nicene Fathers, Volume 3*, edited by A. Roberts, J. Donaldson, and A. Cleveland Coxe. New York: Cosimo Classics, 2007.

———. *On the Flesh of Christ*. In *Ante-Nicene Fathers, Volume 3*, edited by A. Roberts, J. Donaldson, and A. Cleveland Coxe. New York: Cosimo Classics, 2007.

———. *On the Resurrection of the Flesh*. In *Ante-Nicene Fathers, Volume 3*, edited by A. Roberts, J. Donaldson, and A. Cleveland Coxe. New York: Cosimo Classics, 2007.

———. *A Treatise on the Soul*. In *Ante-Nicene Fathers, Volume.3*, edited by A. Roberts, J. Donaldson, and A. Cleveland Coxe. New York: Cosimo Classics, 2007.

Thompson, Evan. *Mind in Life: Biology, Phenomenology, and the Sciences of Mind*. Cambridge, MA: Belknap Press of Harvard University Press, 2007.

Toadvine, Ted. *Merleau-Ponty's Philosophy of Nature*. Evanston, IL: Northwestern University Press, 2009.

Toombs, S. Key. "Illness and the Paradigm of the Lived Body." *Theoretical Medicine* 9 (1988): 201–26.

Torrance, Thomas F. *Space, Time and Resurrection*. London: T&T Clark, 2019.

von Balthasar, Hans Urs. *Mysterium Paschale: The Mystery of Easter*. Translated by A. Nichols. San Francisco: Ignatius, 2000.

BIBLIOGRAPHY

Waldenfels, Bernhard. *Das leibliche Selbst: Vorlesungen zur Phänomenologie des Leibes.* Frankfurt am Main: Suhrkamp, 2013.
Weil, Simone. *Gravity and Grace.* Translated by E. Crawford and M. von der Ruhr. London: Routledge, 2002.
Weinandy, Thomas G. "St. Irenaeus and the *Imago Dei*: The Importance of Being Human." *Logos* 6 (2003): 15–34.
Welton, Donn. "Biblical Bodies." In *Body and Flesh: A Philosophical Reader*, edited by D. Welton. Oxford: Blackwell, 1998.
———. "Soft, Smooth Hands: Husserl's Phenomenology of the Lived Body." In *The Body: Classical and Contemporary Readings*, edited by D. Welton. Oxford: Blackwell, 1999.
Wingren, Gustaf. "Skapelse, Lagen och Inkarnationen enligt Ireneus." *Svensk Teologisk Kvartalskrift* 2 (1940): 133–55.
Wittgenstein, Ludwig. *Last Writings on the Philosophy of Psychology*, vol. 1. Edited and translated by G. H. von Wright and Heikki Nyman. Oxford: Blackwell, 1992.
———. *Philosophical Investigations.* Translated by G. E. M. Anscombe, P. M. S. Hacker, and J. Schulte. Oxford: Wiley-Blackwell, 2009.
———. *Zettel.* Edited by G. E. M. Anscombe and G. H. von Wright, translated by G. E. M. Anscombe. Oxford: Blackwell, 1967.
Zahavi, Dan. *Husserl's Legacy: Phenomenology, Metaphysics & Transcendental Philosophy.* Oxford: Oxford University Press, 2017.
———. "Husserl's Phenomenology of the Body." *Études Phénoménologiques* 10 (1994): 63–84.
———. *Self-Awareness and Alterity: A Phenomenological Investigation.* Evanston, IL: Northwestern University Press, 1999.

Index

abnormality, 73–76, 102
Abraham, 191–93
absolute immediacy, 98–99
absolutes, 26, 28
abstraction, 14–15, 22, 26
access, philosophy of, 51, 52
Adam, 156, 157, 204
addendum (*das Hinzutretende*), 64–65, 66, 202
Adorno, Theodor, 64–65, 66, 202
affections, 158–59, 160, 166
affectivity, 62–63, 103–4, 160–61, 170. *See also* auto-affection; hetero-affection; self-affection
afterlife, 196–99
alienation, 164, 170
alter ego, 61, 97
alterity, 61–62, 64, 65, 77, 97–99, 122–23, 131–33
ambiguity, 22, 24, 25, 44; the body and, 65–66, 96; pain and, 109; preservation of, 7; self-awareness and, 201–2; skin and, 100, 104–5, 168–69
Améry, Jean, 119, 168–69
analogical apperception, 19, 89, 97–98, 149
analogical transference, 206
angelism, 195, 196
anthropomorphism, 206
appearances, vs. revelation, 34
arch-gnosis, 165
Arendt, Hannah, 129, 132, 133
Aristotle, 9, 10, 48–49, 50, 88, 89, 100, 103; Aristotelianism, 56, 64–65
Augustine, 180
auto-affection, 86–87, 97, 102, 112–13, 116, 118–19, 122–24, 126–27, 164–65, 170, 199, 201–3
autonomy of things, 51

backside of things, 28–29
Bakan, David, 126–27
Balthasar, Hans Urs von, 27
Barbaras, Renaud, 40, 55
Being, 33, 184; being-able-to-be (*Seinkönnen*), 77–78; being-for-itself, 92, 93; being-in-itself, 92, 93; being-toward-death, 80, 168
Bell, Charles, 185
belongingness, 103
Bernet, Rudolf, 164
Bernstein, Jay, 115, 119
biblical texts, 8. *See also specific texts*
Biro, David, 143
birth, 161, 163, 204
Bloch, Ernst, 189
body, the, 3–10, 32, 37–38, 78–81, 107–8, 161–62, 170; as absence, 86; affective, 157, 169–70; ambiguity and, 65–66; biological, 195; bodily appearance, 86–87; bodily gestures, 131; bodily presence (*leibhaften Wirklichkeit*), 21, 31; bodily reality, 46–47, 55; bodily reflexivity, 22; bodily self-transcendence, 31; breakdown of, 67–87; of Christ, 9, 29, 33–34, 44–45, 154–75, 204–5 (*see also* incarnation); concrete, 127; created, 155–59; different notions of, 42; double role of, 65; dysfunctional, 85–86; ecstatic, 38, 86; ego and, 81–82; empirical, 54; experience and, 3–4, 5, 6, 7; forgetfulness of, 70; between form and matter, 46–66; four dimensions of, 202–4 (*see also* flesh; flesh and blood; lived body [*Leib*]; objective body [*Körper*]); functional, 70; habitual, 54, 73, 86, 127; hope and, 176–99; *hyle* and, 60–66; immanence and, 38–39; immediate presence of, 89; imprisonment

247

INDEX

body, the (continued)
and, 104; incarnation and, 7, 46, 155–59, 204–5 (see also incarnation); intentionality and, 36–37, 38, 40, 65, 80–81, 86; interiority of, 39; Irenaeus and, 162; language and, 130–31; materiality and, 46–66, 169–70, 203–4; the mind and, 4, 7 (see also mind-body dualism); mortal, 169–70; mystery of, 20–21; natal, 169–70; "normal," 217n11; objectification of, 70; as object in the world, 4–7 (see also objective body [Körper]); organic density of, 203–4; ownership of, 19; pain and, 6–7, 92, 127–28; passivity of, 6, 67–87; phenomenality and, 32; philosophy and, 20–21; plasticity and, 53–54; primordial, 44–45; radical reduction and, 32; resistance and, 43–44, 207; resurrected, 195; self and, 76–77, 128; self-concealment and, 86; sensation and, 23–24; the soul and, 155, 160–61 (see also soul/body dualism); speculative realism and, 53–55; spirit and, 28; "spread body," 43–44; subjectivity and, 76–77, 201; as subject-object, 201–2; transcendence and, 39, 54; visceral, 38–39, 43, 85; visibility of worldly, 86–87; the world and, 37. See also embodiment
body-body problem, 42
body schema, 23
Brentano, Franz, 110
Bultmann, Rudolf, 195
Butler, Judith, 46, 47–50, 55; Bodies That Matter, 47
Buytendijk, F. J. J., 115, 120, 125, 128

Caputo, John, 27
Carel, Havi, 77–78
caress, 103–4, 108
Carman, Taylor, 19
categorical imperative, 186
catharsis, lack of, 173–74
Cavell, Stanley, 137, 138, 146–47
Chalcedon, 156
chiasms, 38
Chrétien, Jean-Louis, 8, 86–87, 100–102, 104, 105–7, 191–93
Christ, 7, 10–11, 28, 35, 156; abandonment of, 172–75, 189, 193; Adam and, 156, 157, 204; affections and, 158–59, 160, 166; birth of, 161, 204; the body of, 9, 29, 33–34, 44–45, 154–75, 204–5 (see also incarnation); death of, 171–72, 204; disciples of, 195, 196; Docetic view of body of, 155, 157; feeling and, 158–59; first disciples of, 176; flesh and blood and, 165–66; Gnosticism and, 164–65; healing of the sick and, 107; hope and, 189–90; humanity and, 154, 156; hung on the cross, 167, 174; incarnation and, 12, 13, 25–26, 29, 33–34, 44–45, 154–75, 204–5 (see also incarnation); isolation of, 172–73; last words of, 172, 189; lived body (Leib) of, 175; materiality and, 155, 157, 175, 195; as mediator, 36; nailed to the cross, 169–71, 174–75; nakedness and, 174; nakedness of, 168–69; pain and, 166–75; passion of, 167; resurrection of, 155, 194; revelation of, 28–29, 175; solitude of, 175; suffering and, 155, 157, 158–59, 160, 166–75, 171, 204
Christianity, 7–8, 187; the absolute and, 26; flesh and, 124; hope and, 189–90; incarnation and, 7, 12–13, 25–26, 40–44, 46, 154–75 (see also incarnation); lack of catharsis from pain, 173–74; metaphysics and, 26–27; pain and, 117; vertical transcendence and, 26. See also Christ
Christology, 41
Church Fathers, 36, 41. See also Augustine
cogito, 67–70, 73
communication: alterity and, 131–33; connectedness and, 131–34; Merleau-Ponty and, 130–33, 139, 148, 151; of pain, 140–53, 172; phenomenology of, 130–33; sensation(s) and, 135; sense and, 23; separateness and, 131–34; of suffering, 145–47; Wittgenstein and, 148–49, 150–53
community: with divinity, 19; intimate, 10; loss of, 172–73
compensation, 187–88
connectedness, communication and, 131–34
consciousness, 19, 31, 36–37, 51, 56–60, 68, 118, 176–77, 181; temporal, 176–77

INDEX

constructivism, 9, 46, 47–48, 49–50
correlationism, 51, 53, 54–56
creation, 162–65, 204
cross, the, 10–11, 193; incarnation and, 154–75; as manifestation of evil, 173; meaning of, 166–67; pain and, 166–75; as symbol of salvation, 173. *See also* crucifixion
Crow nation, 182–83
crucifixion, 10–11, 166–75, 193; as literalization of incarnation, 169–70; lived body (*Leib*) and, 172–73; negative hope and, 188–89; torture and, 167–69, 171–72
culture, vs. nature, 48

Dasein, 70, 71, 77–78, 177
death, 181; being-toward-death, 80, 168; of Christ, 171–72, 204; embodiment and, 198–99; of God, 26; hope beyond, 176; surviving (*Fortleben*), 196–99
Derrida, Jacques, 47, 62, 97–100, 102, 107
Descartes, René, 4, 39, 67–68, 124, 126, 127, 134
despair, 174, 176, 184, 188–89
difference, 98–99, 102
disabilities, 72, 85, 86, 205
disability studies, 205, 217n11
discourse, matter and, 49–50
discourses, normalizing, 48
disincarnation, touch as corrective to, 88
distanciation, 44, 119, 174; from pain, 174
divine touch, 105–7
Docetism, 155, 157
double sensation, 93–94, 95, 98, 102
double touch, 95
dualism, 155, 160, 163, 164–65, 206
dysfunction, 85–86

earth, 124–25, 207
Easter, 176
ecology, 205
effort, 40
ego, 4, 77, 131; the body and, 81–82; Cartesian, 67–68; embodiment and, 23; flesh and, 124–25; functional, 68–70, 71–72; Husserl and, 17–19, 68, 69, 73, 96; *hyle* and, 62–63; impressions and, 82; Kant and, 68; lived body (*Leib*) and, 201; normality and, 78; pain and, 109, 118, 126–27, 128; pleasure and, 105; practical, 68; spontaneous capability (*Urvermögen*) of, 69; transcendence and, 18, 19, 68, 201; transcendental, 68, 201
ek-stasis, 31
embodiment, 9, 17–18, 27, 40, 69–70, 179–99, 203; death and, 198–99; ego and, 23; experience and, 5, 7, 69; God and, 27–28; Henry and, 13, 37; hope and, 179–99; humanity and, 154; Husserl and, 37; Husserl on, 13–19; incarnation and, 46; lived body (*Leib*) vs. objective body (*Körber*) and, 61; Merleau-Ponty and, 13, 37; movement and, 69; organic life and, 206; pain and, 5–6, 198–99; pleasure and, 198–99; the self and, 76–77; self-awareness and, 201–2; suffering and, 104; touch and, 88. *See also* the body
Empfindnis, 89, 91
Empfindung, 89
enactivism, 205, 217–18n12
enjoyment, 103–4, 114–15, 178
escape, 174, 186
eschatologies, 189, 190, 193
essentialism, 46, 47–48, 49–50
eternity, 7, 24, 106, 156, 178, 179, 187, 197, 198, 199
everydayness, 176–79, 181
evil, 117, 173, 174–75
"excarnation," 4
existentialism, 20
expectations, 180–83, 185
experience, 3–4, 5, 6, 7, 62–64
exposure, pain and, 168
expressions, 130; facial, 148–49. *See also* communication; gestural meaning
exteriority, 6–7, 28, 104–5, 117–18
externality. *See* exteriority

Fall, the, 105
Falque, Emmanuel, 41–45, 122–23, 163, 165, 170–71, 173–74, 194–96, 203–4, 214n139
feeling, 158–59. *See also* affectivity; feeling-sensations (*Gefühlsempfindungen*)

feeling-sensations (*Gefühlsempfindungen*), 110–11, 115
"feminine, the": Levinas and, 103–4
feminism, 47–48, 49–50; performative, 46–47, 49–50, 55
finitude, 24, 25, 184
first-person perspective, 43, 203–4
flesh, 26, 32–33, 35–36, 39, 42, 46, 120–28, 160–66, 170–71, 202–4, 214n139; affectivity and, 36–37, 160–61, 165; auto-affection and, 36–37, 165; Christianity and, 124; derealization of, 39; forgetfulness of, 87; Henry and, 30, 121–22, 126, 170, 201, 203; immanence of, 86, 114; impressions and, 30, 121–22; incarnation and, 12; invisibility of, 43, 86–87; life and, 33; Marion and, 124–25; ontology and, 95, 206; pain and, 114, 127–28; Paul and, 78–81; phenomenality and, 32–33; thorn in, 79–80, 83; as withdrawal from the world, 85–87. *See also* flesh and blood
flesh and blood, 4–5, 7, 9, 13, 38–40, 43, 62, 64–66, 67, 154–55, 202–4; Christ and, 165–66; earth and, 207; givenness of, 46; pain and, 202
"flight reactions," 125
foreignness. *See* alterity
forgetfulness, 85–86, 87, 187
form (*morphe*), 9, 46, 55–60, 120; affectivity and, 170; Aristotelianism and, 64–65; Husserl and, 56–60, 110, 111; intelligibility and, 55; matter (*hyle*) and, 9, 46–66, 216n35
forms of life, 150–53
Foucault, Michel, 47, 48
Franck, Didier, 61, 96, 98; alterity and, 98–99; *Flesh and Body*, 96
Freud, Sigmund, 128
future, the, 182; expectations and, 180–81; hope and, 180, 188–89; imaginaries of, 186–87; openness to, 180–81; pain and, 179; of the present, 187–88; promise and, 193; Sartre and, 186–87

Gadamer, Hans Georg, 193
Gallagher, Shaun, 5–6, 60–61, 75, 121
Garden of Eden, 105
gender, vs. sex, 47–48

gender studies, 205
general incarnation, 12–13, 36; assessing the, 36–40; Henry on, 29–33; Merleau-Ponty on, 19–25. *See also* incarnation
generation, 162–63
Genesis, 163
Geniusas, Saulius, 91, 123, 179
Gestalt psychology, 22, 23, 58
givenness, modes of, 39, 102, 103
Gnosticism, 4, 41, 155–58, 160–62, 164–65, 195
Gnostics, 108, 195
God, 25, 41, 45; absence of, 172–73, 176, 189; as absolute Life, 33, 34; becoming flesh, 7; embodiment and, 27–28; externalization of, 164; Husserl's analysis of, 19; Merleau-Ponty's problematization of, 26–27, 29, 33; as metaphysical absolute, 26; Nietzsche on death of, 26; of the Old Testament, 105, 156; onto-theology and, 105; revelation of, 28, 33, 34; self-experience of, 34–35; as self-revelation that arrives in Christ, 33; telos and, 181; touch and, 105–6; vision and, 105; withdrawal of, 28
godforsakenness, 172–75, 176, 189. *See also* crucifixion; Job; suffering
God's-eye view, 24
Goethe, Johann Wolfgang von, 198
Gospel of John, 12, 33, 34, 155, 159–60, 161, 163, 172. *See also* Prologue of John
Gospel of Luke, 35, 161, 168, 172
Gospel of Mark, 168
Gospel of Matthew, 35, 161, 168
Gospels, 88, 107, 155, 167, 168, 174, 176, 195, 196. *See also specific Gospels*
grace, 184
Grünewald, Matthias, Isenheim altarpiece, 171–72
Grüny, Christian, 74, 115
Gurwitch, Aron, 121

Habermas, Jürgen, 193
hands, 89, 95, 97–98
haptics, 107. *See also* touch
Harman, Graham, 51–52, 55
healing narratives, 107–8
health, 85–86. *See also* illness
hearing, 89, 90, 105

INDEX

Heidegger, Martin, 33, 70, 74, 124, 179; *Being and Time*, 71, 177, 217–18n12; being-toward-death and 80, 168; Dasein and, 77–78, 177; everydayness and, 177–78, 181; indeterminacy and, 31; onto-theology and, 105; phenomenology of tools and, 51–52; "ready-to-hand" and, 51, 52, 69–70; temporality and, 177–78; tools and, 51–52, 55, 70

Held, Klaus, 181, 183–84

Henry, Michel, 8, 9, 19, 37, 42–43, 63, 68, 163–66, 195–96; affections and, 158–59; angelism and, 41, 195, 196; assessing, 163–66; auto-affection and, 112–13, 124, 201–2; creation and, 164–65; distinction between having and being a body, 31; dualism and, 164–65; embodiment and, 13, 37, 38–39; evil and, 173; flesh and, 39, 121–22, 126, 163–66, 170, 201, 203; forgetfulness and, 85–86; Gnosticism and, 164–65; on Husserl's distinction between *hyle* and *morphe*, 59, 61; *hyle* and, 46, 59, 61; "hyper-transcendentalism" of, 164; idealism and, 203, 219n62; the immanent body and, 38–39; impressional flesh and, 121–22; impressions and, 82, 112, 113–16, 121–22; *Incarnation*, 8, 87; incarnation and, 12, 13, 29–36, 40–41, 154–55, 159–63, 164–66; intentionality and, 30, 112, 201; Irenaeus and, 164; kinesthesis and, 40; Leibniz and, 173; lived body (*Leib*) and, 32, 37, 42–43, 85–86, 201, 203; objective body (*Körper*) and, 32, 37, 42–43, 85–86, 163, 166; pain and, 112, 113–16, 117, 118–19, 120, 122–23, 174; passivity and, 81–84, 203; "phenomenology of life" and, 32–33; radical passivity and, 83–84, 87; radical reduction and, 31, 32, 39, 86; resisting body and, 43–44; response to Irenaeus and Tertullian, 159–63; sensations and, 39–40; skin and, 101–2, 104; Tertullian and, 164; touch and, 101–2

hetero-affection, 112, 115, 116, 122–23, 126–27, 170, 199, 202, 204

heterogeneity, 98–99

heteronormative logic, 48–49

heterosexual logic, 48–49

Holocaust, 117

hope: beyond death, 176; the body and, 176–99; Christian, 189–90; darkness and, 182; despair as reversal of, 188–89; embodied, 179–99; excess and, 189, 191; the future and, 180, 188–89; levels of, 184; Levinas and, 182, 187; Marcel and, 184; memory and, 192–93; negative, 185–89, 231n37; pain and, 11, 185–89; phenomenology of, 180–84; promise and, 189–94; radical, 182–83, 185, 194; resurrection and, 176–99; temporal orientation toward the future, 180; theology and, 189–90

hope-acts, 184, 190, 194

hopelessness, 188–89

horizons, 25

horizontality, 26–27

humanity: Christ and, 154, 156; divinization of, 27

Husserl, Edmund, 3, 6, 8–10, 25, 29, 30, 43, 53, 68, 70, 78, 94, 226n41; on abnormality vs. normality, 75–76; alter ego and, 97; alterity, 97–98; analogical apperception and, 19, 89, 97–98, 149; basic trust in the world and, 183; bodily reflexivity and, 22; breakdown of the body and, 72–75, 76, 78, 80; *Cartesian Meditations*, 61, 96; consciousness and, 56, 57, 58, 68; contradictions of pain and, 119–20; disabilities and, 72, 85; distinction between *hyle* and *morphe*, 56–60, 61–66; double sensation and, 102; earth and, 124–25; ego and, 17–19, 68, 69, 71–72, 73, 96; embodiment and, 13–19, 37; expectations and, 180–82, 183; expressions and, 130; feeling-sensations (*Gefühlsempfindungen*) and, 110–11, 115; God and, 19; the hand and, 89; Henry and, 81–83; *hyle* and, 9, 46, 55–66, 82, 110–11, 119–20, 121, 201 (*see also* matter [*hyle*]); hyletic sensations and, 92; *Ideas*, 8, 14, 31, 37, 56, 96, 127; illness and, 72, 85; immanent time and, 180; impressions and, 62, 119–20; incarnation and, 12, 13; indeterminacy and, 31; intentionality and, 56; lived body (*Leib*) and, 29, 31, 36,

INDEX

Husserl, Edmund (*continued*) 37, 42, 61, 69, 200; living present and, 178; *Logical Investigations*, 51, 56–57, 110, 111, 216n34; Merleau-Ponty and, 57–58; model of acts and fulfillment, 117; *morphe* and, 9, 46, 56–60, 110, 111 (*see also* form [*morphe*]); nature and, 205; objective body (*Körper*) and, 29, 31, 36, 37, 42, 61, 163; pain and, 91, 93, 169, 179; passive synthesis and, 82; passivity and, 113, 118; philosophical activism and, 70, 71, 82–83, 84, 85; primacy of touch and, 100; primordial reduction and, 96; "principle of all principles" and, 42; sensation(s) and, 23, 110–11, 113; "sphere of ownness" and, 96; telos and, 181; time and, 176–77, 180; touch(ing) and, 88, 89, 91–92, 94–101, 201–2, 220n12; transcendental reduction of, 28; transition from "I think" to "I can," 81; *Urdoxa* and, 183; *Ursinnlichkeit* and, 113, 119; zero point of orientation and, 24

Husserl, Edmund and, time consciousness, 176–77

hyle. *See* matter (*hyle*)

hyletic experience, 65, 99

hyletic sensations, 92, 111

hylomorphism, 57–58

"I can," 67–70

"I cannot," 9–10, 71–78, 203

idealism, 51, 203, 219n62

Ignatius of Loyola, 155

illness, 72–76, 85, 86–87, 102, 107, 203

immanence, 18, 25, 27–28, 30, 36–40, 83, 85–86, 123, 177, 180, 203

immortality, 176, 196–99

impotence, 26–27

impressionality, 64, 113–16. *See also* impressions

impressions, 30, 32, 40, 46, 62, 63, 82, 163–64; ego and, 82; flesh and, 121–22; immanent givenness of, 112; knowledge and, 119–20; non-intentional, 112–16; self-impressions, 114

imprisonment, the body and, 104

incarnation, 4–9, 28, 54, 128, 194–95, 200–207; Christian idea of, 7, 12–13, 25–26, 40–44, 46, 154–75; the created body and, 155–59; the cross and, 154–75; divine touch and, 106–7; double revelation of, 154; embodiment and, 46; flesh and, 12; four dimensions of body and, 202–4; in France, 20; general, 12–13, 19–25, 29–33, 36–40; Henry and, 154–55, 159–66; Irenaeus and, 166; literalized in crucifixion, 169–70; materiality and, 40–45, 46; Merleau-Ponty and, 154, 156, 164, 204; nature and, 205–7; pain and, 91–92, 154–75; phenomenology and, 12–45, 204–5; resistance to verticality and, 26–27; revelation and, 35, 154–75; revolutionary impact of, 27; specific, 12–13, 25–29, 33–36; subjectivity and, 23, 200, 204; tactility and, 92; Tertullian and, 165, 166; touch and, 88–91

infinite, idea of, 28

intellectualism, 22, 68

intentionality, 30, 39, 56, 58, 60–61, 63, 65, 163–64, 180, 216n34; the body and, 36–37, 80–81; consciousness and, 31; Henry and, 112, 201; pain and, 110–11, 112, 117, 118, 135; phenomenality and, 31–32; vision and, 88

intercorporeality, 129

interiority, 28, 104–5, 118

intersubjectivity, 14–15, 44, 97, 129, 140–47. *See also* communication

intuition, 31, 42–43, 129

invisible, the, 26, 28

ipseity, 30, 34–35

Irenaeus, 8, 36, 41, 155–57, 158, 175, 204; anti-Gnostic argument of, 162, 164; the body and, 162; Henry and, 159–63, 164; incarnation and, 166; salvation and, 193

Irigaray, Luce, 105

irritation, chronic, 220n23

isolation, 10, 172

"I think," 67–70, 73

Janicaud, Dominique, 8

Jesus of Nazareth. *See* Christ

Job, book of, 10, 140–47, 150, 179, 186, 188, 226n44

Jonas, Hans, 27, 164, 206, 220n12

joy, 113, 114–15, 148–49. *See also* enjoyment; pleasure

INDEX

Kant, Immanuel, 65, 68; afterlife and, 198; categorical imperative and, 186; Copernican revolution of, 51; ego and, 68; hope and, 231n37; immoral responses to the Law and, 144–45
kenosis, 28, 41, 193
kerygma, 195
kinesthesis, 16–17, 30, 40, 68–69
knowledge: impressions and, 119–20; reflective, 23; sources of, 119–20
Kundera, Milan, 123

language: the body and, 130–31; pain and, 129–53; primitive reactions and, 152–53; resistance of, 135. *See also* communication
Lavigne, Jean-Francois, 115, 219n62
Lear, Jonathan, 182–83
Leder, Drew, 38, 43, 85–86, 109, 127
leibhaften Wirklichkeit, 21
leibhaft gegeben, 41, 42
Leibniz, Gottfried Wilhelm von, 24, 173
Levinas, Emmanuel, 8, 64, 168, 226n41; compensation and, 187–88; evil and, 117; excess of pain and, 170, 173, 202; "the feminine" and, 103–4; the future of the present and, 187–88; Holocaust and, 117; hope and, 182, 187; internal imperative of pain and, 185–86; nonintentional sensations and, 54; *Otherwise Than Being*, 104; pain and, 116–19, 123, 170, 171, 173; passivity and, 118; pleasure and, 178; resurrection and, 187–88; sensation(s) and, 103, 116–18, 120, 123; sensation(s) "in-spite-of-consciousness" and, 116–18, 120, 123; skin and, 103–4; suffering and, 171; time and, 187–88; *Totality and Infinity*, 103, 104; touch and, 103; vision and, 103
life, 206; flesh and, 33; forms of, 150–53; immanent, 203; passivity and, 203
limit, skin and, 100
lived body (*Leib*), 9, 13–18, 20, 24, 29, 31–32, 36–40, 46–47, 87, 202–4; of Christ, 175; crucifixion and, 172–73; ego and, 201; embodiment and, 61; gender studies and, 205; Henry and, 201, 203; Husserl and, 200; *hyle* and, 121; hyletic experience and, 64; incarnation and, 171; as mine, 13, 15, 17, 220n12 (see also mineness); objective body (*Körper*) and, 42–43, 44, 46, 47, 55, 61, 64, 85–86, 97, 102, 195–96; pain and, 109, 122, 127; passivity and, 69–70; primacy of, 163; "sphere of ownness" and, 96, 99; subjectivity and, 128; touch(ing) and, 89
localization, 90, 91; pain and, 92–93, 95, 120, 200–201; touch and, 92, 98
logos, 26, 35

Maine de Biran (François-Pierre-Gontier de Biran), 81–82, 83
Marcel, Gabriel, 3, 20–21, 31, 170, 182, 184
Marcion, 108, 156, 160
Marion, Jean-Luc, 8, 124–26, 196, 199
materiality, 9, 74, 165, 166; the body and, 46–66, 203–4; Christ and, 155, 157, 175, 195; experience and, 6; incarnation and, 40–45, 46; matter without, 47–50; phenomenology and, 46; signification and, 47–49
materialization, process of, 48–49, 50
matter, 9; discourse and, 49–50; vs. form, 48–50, 55; form and, 9, 46–66, 216n35; Husserl and, 9, 55–56; without materiality, 47–50
matter (*hyle*), 22, 32, 46, 55–60, 82, 91; affectivity and, 62–63, 170; Aristotelianism and, 64–65; the body and, 60–66; Husserl and, 56–60, 110, 111, 119–20, 121; lived body (*Leib*) and, 121; Merleau-Ponty and, 57–58, 121, 201; pain and, 63–64, 110–11, 119–20
McGuill Pain Questionnaire, 149
meaning, 58; of the cross, 166–67; gestural, 148, 151; pain and, 117–18, 146–51; perception and, 22–23, 201; perceptual, 201; production through power structures, 48, 65; reflection and, 22–23; Wittgenstein and, 135
meaninglessness, pain and, 117–18
mediation, 44, 47–48, 106–7
Meillassoux, Quentin, 51, 52, 54
Melzack, Ronald, 149
membrane, metaphor of, 102
memory, 180, 191–93. *See also* the past

Merleau-Ponty, Maurice, 3, 7, 9, 19, 37, 43, 70, 103, 217–18n12; abnormality and, 73–74, 76; ambiguity and, 44; ambiguity of the body and, 96; the body and, 13, 23, 31, 37–38, 54, 73–74, 76, 78, 80, 96; body schema and, 23; breakdown of the body and, 73–74, 76, 78, 80; case of Schneider, 73–74; chiasms and, 38; communication and, 130–31, 139, 148, 151; disabilities and, 85; distinction between having and being a body, 31; double touch and, 95; embodiment and, 13, 37–38; facial expressions and, 149; forgetfulness of bodily conditions and, 70; on general incarnation, 19–25, 36; God and, 45; habitual body and, 54; Henry and, 81–83; on Husserl's distinction between *hyle* and *morphe*, 57–58, 60, 61; *hyle* and, 57–58, 60, 61, 121, 201; illness and, 73, 74, 76, 85; incarnation and, 12, 13, 33, 40–41, 154, 156, 164, 204; intercorporeality and, 129; interlacing and, 38; lived body (*Leib*) vs. objective body (*Körber*) and, 37, 38; localization and, 93; nature and, 206–7; on normality, 76; objective body (*Körper*) and, 42; ontology and, 206; pain and, 93, 132; phantom limb and, 73; phenomenology and, 53; *Phenomenology of Perception*, 8, 37, 95; philosophical activism and, 70, 71, 82–83, 85; "The Primacy of Perception," 26; religion and, 25–26; skepticism and, 131–32; on specific incarnation, 25–29, 36; subjectivity and, 30, 201; subject-object and, 22; touch(ing) and, 95–96, 97–98, 101, 220n12; transcendental "I" and, 68; transition from "I think" to "I can," 81; zero point of orientation and, 24
metaphor, pain and, 150–51
metaphysics, 24; Christianity and, 26–27; metaphysical tradition, 88; of presence, 94–95; speculative, 8
mind, the: the body and, 4, 7 (*see also* mind-body dualism)
mind-body dualism, 42, 46, 124, 126
mineness, 5, 10, 43, 83, 96, 123, 125, 200
Moltmann, Jürgen, 27, 167, 172, 189–91
Moltmann-Wendell, Elisabeth, 107–8

mood (*Stimmung*), 183
morphe. *See* form (*morphe*)
mortality, 6
movement, 40, 68–69
mystics, divine touch and, 105–6

nakedness, 168–69, 174
nature: vs. culture, 48; flesh and blood and, 207; incarnation and, 205–7; resistance and, 206–7
negative hope, 185–89, 231n37
negativity, pain and, 115–16
Nemo, Philippe, 146
new materialism, 215n12
new realism, 215n12
New Testament, 156
Nicene Creed, 26
Nietzsche, Friedrich, 26, 117, 178, 186
noema, 56, 57, 58, 62, 64, 112, 201
normality, 75–76, 78, 102

object, subject and, 21–22, 23
objective body (*Körper*), 13–18, 20, 29, 31–32, 36, 41–44, 53–54, 62, 121–22, 157, 160–61, 163, 202–4; embodiment and, 61; Falque and, 195–96; vs. flesh, 161; Henry and, 32, 37, 42–43, 85–86, 166; hyletic experience and, 64; lived body (*Leib*) and, 42–43, 44, 46, 47, 55, 61, 64, 85–86, 97, 102, 195–96
objectivity, 4, 5, 6, 7, 21–22, 40, 43, 201–2
Old Testament, 156
omnipotence, 26–27
ontology, flesh and, 206
onto-theology, 105
organic life, embodiment and, 206
organisms, 205–6
Other, the, 118
otherness, 94–99. *See also* alterity
outer, inner and, 28

pain, 4–7, 44, 57, 64–65, 67, 74, 92, 104, 108, 127–28, 172, 200–207; acknowledgment of, 137, 139, 146; alienation and, 170; ambiguity and, 109; auto-affection and, 118–19, 122–23, 126–27, 170; aversiveness of, 118, 119, 120; Book of Job and, 140–47, 150; Christ and, 166–75; Christianity and, 117; communication of, 129–53, 172;

INDEX

consciousness and, 118; the cross and, 166–75; distanciation from, 44, 119, 168, 174; double movement of, 119; double sensation and, 93–94; ego and, 109, 118, 126–27, 128; embodiment and, 5–6, 198–99; escape from, 44, 174, 179, 186; evil and, 117, 173; excess of, 117–18, 119, 170, 173, 202; expectations and, 185; experience and, 6, 63–65; exposure and, 168; expressions of, 147–51; exteriority and, 104–5; flesh and, 114, 127–28; flesh and blood and, 202; foreignness of, 122–23, 127, 128, 170, 202; the future and, 179; grammar of, 136–37; Henry and, 112, 113–20, 122–23, 174; hetero-affection and, 126–27, 170; hope and, 11, 185–89; Husserl and, 91, 93, 169, 179; *hyle* and, 110, 111, 119–20; hyletic experience and, 63–64, 65, 99; hyletic givenness of, 94; hyletic sensations and, 111; immanence and, 114, 123; impressionality and, 113–16; inability to escape from, 6, 11, 92, 104, 112–13, 115–16, 118–19, 168, 170–71, 174, 179, 186, 200, 202; incarnation and, 91–92, 154–75; inner contradictions in, 118–20; inner contradictions of, 109–28; intentionality and, 110–11, 112, 117, 118, 135; internal imperative of, 185–86; intersubjectivity and, 129, 140–47; intuition and, 129; isolation and, 172; language and, 129–53; Levinas and, 116–19, 123, 170, 171, 173; lived body (*Leib*) and, 109; localization and, 92–93, 95, 120, 169–70, 179, 199, 200–201; loss of control and, 137–38, 168; loss of integrity and, 137–38, 168; meaning and, 117–18, 146–51; meaninglessness and, 117–18; Merleau-Ponty and, 93, 132; metaphor and, 150–51; negative hope and, 185–89; negativity and, 115–16; Nietzsche and, 186; pain behavior, 136–37; pain expression and secondary sense, 147–51; pain language, 153; passivity and, 113, 125, 167–68; the past and, 179; presence and, 179; the present and, 179; primitive reactions and, 150–53; primordial reduction and, 99; privacy of, 133–40; publicness of, 137–40, 145–46; resistance to language and, 129; Sartre and, 92–94, 111; self-affection and, 112–13; the self and, 123–28; self-identity and, 115, 116; sharing of, 129–53; skin and, 88, 103, 104–5; stoicism and, 112; subjectivity and, 123–28, 129, 140–47, 146; temporality of, 176–79, 179, 185–89, 198; torture and, 137–38; touch and, 88, 91–94; unacknowledged, 172; unsharability of, 129, 131–32, 151; Wittgenstein and, 135–36, 147–49, 150

pain behavior, 136–37
pain language, precariousness of, 153
paradox, 24, 25
passion narrative, 167, 168
passive synthesis, 82
passivity, 6, 9, 62, 63, 67–87, 102, 201; of Christ hung on the cross, 167–68; disabilities and, 205; Henry and, 81–84, 203; Husserl and, 113, 118; illness and, 203; of immanent life, 203; Levinas and, 118; life and, 203; Marion and, 125; pain and, 113, 125, 167–68; Paul and, 78–81; radical, 83–84, 87; as receptivity, 118
past, the, 182, 193; expectations and, 180–81; pain and, 179; promise and, 193; sedimentations of, 181
pathology, subjectivity and, 75
Patočka, Jan, 72
Paul, Saint, 180, 185, 186; crucifixion and, 193; Epistle to the Romans, 191–93; resurrection and, 194; Second Letter to the Corinthians, 79; thorn in the flesh and, 79–80; on weakness, 78–81
perception, 21, 24, 25, 59, 199; bodily, 21–22; meaning and, 22–23; perceptual meaning, 201; perspectival, 24–25. *See also specific senses*
performative feminism, 46–47, 55
perspective, 24–25, 30
phenomenality: the body and, 32; flesh and, 32–33; intentionality and, 31–32; visible and invisible modes of, 29–30
phenomenological activism, 9–10
phenomenology, 9, 51; the body and, 3–10; of communication, 130–33; correlationism and, 55–56; definition of, 31; in France, 20; of hope, 180–84; on *hyle*,

phenomenology (*continued*)
  55–60 (*see also* matter [*hyle*]); incarnation and, 12–45, 204–5; indeterminacy and, 31; intuition and, 43; materiality and, 46; on *morphe*, 55–60 (*see also* form [*morphe*]); speculative metaphysics and, 8; theology and, 7–8, 204–5; transcendental "I" and, 68
"phenomenology of life," 32–33
phenomenon (*phainesthai*), 30
philosophical activism, 70, 71, 78, 82–83, 85, 102
philosophy: of access, 51–52; the body and, 20–21; post-Cartesian, 46; post-Kantian, 51; theology and, 154–75
plasticity, the body and, 53–54
Plato, 48–49, 50
Platonism, 4
pleasure, 57, 113, 114–15, 178, 199; ego and, 105; embodiment and, 198–99; interiority and, 104–5; skin and, 103, 104–5; temporality of, 176–79, 198. *See also* enjoyment; joy
Plenty Coups, 182–83
Plessner, Helmuth, 3, 65
power, 26, 50; radical passivity and, 83–84; significance and, 48
powerlessness, stigma of, 83
presence, 21; intuitive, 42; metaphysics of, 75, 94–95; pain and, 179; touch and, 98–99
present, the, 182; experience of, 178; future of, 187–88; lived, 182; pain and, 179; promise and, 193
"present-at-hand," 52
primitive reactions, 142, 143, 146, 147–49, 150–53
primordial reduction, 98, 99
Prologue of John, 35, 155, 160, 166
promises: Christ as fulfillment of all, 190; hope-acts and, 194; hope and, 189–94; of resurrection, 190–91; temporal structure of, 191–93
protention, 180, 181
Psalm 22, 172, 189

radical hope, 182–83, 185, 194
radical passivity, 83–84, 87
radical reduction, 39, 86
reactions, primitive, 151–53

"ready-to-hand," 51, 52, 69–70
realism, 9, 50; new, 215n12; speculative, 46–47, 50–55, 65
reality, 51; bodily, 46–47, 55; without correlation, 50–55
reflection, meaning and, 22–23
repetition, enjoyment and, 178
resistance, 43–44; flesh and blood and, 207; nature and, 206–7
resurrection, 162, 172, 176, 187–88, 193, 196–99; abandonment and, 193; of Christ, 155, 190; as embodied hope, 176–99; Falque and, 194–96; as fulfillment of Old Testament promises, 190–91; hope and, 194–96; humiliation and, 193; Levinas and, 187–88
revelation, 28, 33, 39, 154–55; vs. appearances, 34; of Christ, 28–29, 175; as a circle, 35; double, 154; incarnation and, 35; truth and, 33–34
Reynolds, Joel Michael, 6, 75, 76
Ricoeur, Paul, 8, 27, 61, 62, 114–15, 185, 190–91, 193–94
Rivera, Joseph, 165

sacraments, 21
"sacred history," 192–94
salvation, 36, 173, 187, 193
Sartre, Jean-Paul, 58, 59, 60, 61, 92–94, 103, 111, 186, 200
"saturated phenomena," 125–26
Scarry, Elaine, 10, 93, 94, 115–16, 121, 129–30, 134; on communication of pain, 129–30, 134–37, 138–39, 142–43, 146, 151; on experience of pain, 170; primitive reactions and, 152–53; publicness of pain and, 137–38, 139–40; on torture, 137–38, 168; touch and, 220n16
Scheler, Max, 120, 196–99
Schusterman, Richard, 75, 76
self, the, 30, 34, 126–27, 199; the body and, 76–77, 128; embodiment and, 76–77; pain and, 123–28; suffering and, 161–62
self-affection. *See* auto-affection
self-awareness, 43; ambiguity and, 201–2; embodiment and, 201–2; touch(ing) and, 89–91, 201–2
self-concealment, 86

INDEX

self-givenness, 31, 121
self-revelation, touch and, 101
sensation(s), 16–17, 22, 23, 53, 57, 60, 63, 68–69, 116–18, 199; the body and, 23–24; communication and, 135; double sensation and, 89–91; dual meaning of, 89–91; *Empfindnisse*, 89; *Empfindung*, 89; feeling-sensations (*Gefühlsempfindungen*), 110–11, 113, 115; Henry and, 39–40; Husserl and, 23, 110–11, 113; impressions and, 30, 112–16; Levinas and, 103; non-intentional, 54; as non-intentional impressions, 54, 112–16; objective vs. subjective, 89; privacy of, 139; "in-spite-of-consciousness," 116–18, 120, 123. *See also* feeling-sensations (*Gefühlsempfindungen*); *specific senses*
sense(s), 21; communication and, 23; pain expression and, 147–51; secondary, 147–51; sense data, 22, 46, 56–57. *See also* perception; sensation(s); *specific senses*
sensibility, 69, 104
sensual content, 56–57
sensuous feelings, 16–17
separateness: communication and, 131–34 (*see also* separation)
separation, 98–99, 104. *See also* isolation; solipsism; solitude
Serrano de Haro, Augustin, 91, 117
sex, vs. gender, 47–48
shame, 168
signification: materiality and, 47–49, 50; power and, 48, 65
skepticism, 131–32, 134
skin, 6–7, 9, 10; affectivity and, 103–4; ambiguity and, 100, 102–3, 104–5, 168–69; Aristotle and, 103; Chrétien and, 104; double role of, 99–105, 108; exteriority and, 104; Henry and, 101–2, 104; Levinas and, 103–4; limit and, 100; as limit of invisible flesh, 102; nakedness and, 168–69; pain and, 88, 103, 104–5; pleasure and, 103, 104–5; separation and, 104; suffering and, 103; touch and, 88–108
Socrates, 75
Sokolowksi, Robert, 216n35
solipsism, 131–32

solitude, 131–32
soul, the, 199; the body and, 155, 160–61 (*see also* soul/body dualism); corporeal, 159; Platonic notion of immortal, 176
soul/body dualism, 160, 163
spacing, 98
Sparrow, Tom, 51, 52–54, 58; correlationism and, 53, 54; *Plastic Bodies*, 53
spatiality, 98; changes to, 77; spatial location, 30; spatial orientation, 3–4
"sphere of ownness," 96, 97, 98, 99
spirit, body and, 28
spiritualism, 33
"spread body," 43–44, 122–23, 170–71. *See also* flesh and blood
Steinbock, Anthony, 39, 184, 190
Stoicism, 112, 159
Stumpf, Carl Friedrich, 110
subject: incarnate, 19–20, 95; object and, 21–22, 23. *See also* subjectivity
subjectivity, 7, 20, 23, 40, 51, 126; the body and, 76–77, 201; correlationism and, 54–55; incarnation and, 23, 200; intersubjectivity (*see also* communication); lived body (*Leib*) and, 128; Merleau-Ponty and, 30, 201; objectivity and, 4, 5, 7, 21–22, 43, 201–2; pain and, 123–28, 129, 140–47; pathology and, 75; transcendental, 54–55; world and, 4, 5, 7, 28
suffering, 32, 87, 104, 114, 120, 123–24, 127–28, 187; Christ and, 155, 157, 158–59, 160, 166–75, 204; communication of, 145–47; embodiment and, 104; flesh and, 161–62; impressionality and, 113–14; in Job, 145–47; Levinas and, 171; self and, 161–62; skin and, 103; temporality and, 185; theodicy and, 173–74; why-questions and, 173–74. *See also* pain
synthesis, 69

tactility, 88–108; Husserl and, 91–92; incarnation and, 92; localization and, 90, 91, 92; pain as subcategory of, 169; self-awareness and, 89–91. *See also* touch(ing)
tangible, repression of the, 105
Taylor, Charles, 4

telos, 117, 181
temporality, 98, 216n35; changes to, 77; consciousness and, 176–77; of everydayness, 176–79; experiences of, 177–78; frozen, 179; Heidegger and, 177–78; immanent time, 177, 180; Levinas and, 187–88; messianic time, 187; objective, 177; of pain, 176–79, 185–89, 198; of pleasure, 176–79, 198; promises and, 191–93; suffering and, 185; temporal consciousness, 176–77
Tertullian, 8, 41, 108, 155–63, 170, 175, 195, 204; anti-Gnostic argument of, 160–62, 164; the body and, 161–62, 170; dualism and, 163; emphasis on birth, 161; Henry and, 159–63, 164; incarnation and, 165, 166; stoicism and, 159
theodicy, suffering and, 173–74
theological turn, 8
theology, 4–5, 7, 24, 200–207; the body and, 107–8; dialogue with, 8; hope and, 189–90; phenomenology and, 7–8, 204–5; philosophy and, 154–75
theosis, 27, 108
third-person perspective, 43, 203–4
Thomas Aquinas, 106
time. *See* temporality
tools, 51–52, 55, 70
Toombs, S. Kay, 76–77, 78
torture, 137–38, 167, 168–69; Améry's description of, 168–69; crucifixion and, 167–69, 171–72; loss of control and, 168; loss of integrity and, 168
touch(ing), 9, 10, 16, 22, 56, 89, 90, 220n12; alterity and, 97–98; auto-affection and, 97; Chrétien and, 100–102, 105–6; Derrida and, 97–98, 107; divine, 105–8; double role of, 108; double sensation and, 89–91, 95, 98; embodiment and, 88; God and, 105–6; Henry and, 101–2; Husserl and, 94–101, 201–2, 220n12; incarnation and, 88–91; intellectual, 106; Levinas and, 103; lived body (*Leib*) and, 89; localization and, 98; Merleau-Ponty and, 95–98, 220n12; otherness and, 94–99; pain and, 88, 91–94; presence and, 98–99; primacy of, 100, 105; Scarry on, 220n16; self-awareness and, 89, 201–2; self-revelation and, 101; skin and, 88–108; spiritual, 106; as transitive rather than reflexive, 101
transcendence, 25, 27–28, 39, 154, 203; consciousness as, 36–37; ego and, 18, 19; immanence and, 18, 85; vertical, 26–27
transparency, 25, 29
Trinity, 34–35, 41, 157
truth, 33–34, 40

uncanny, the, 128
Urdoxa, 183
Ursinnlichkeit, 113, 119

Valentinus, 41, 164–65
verticality, 26–27
virgin birth, story of, 35
visible, the, 26, 28
vision, 89; intentionality and, 88; Levinas and, 103; localization and, 90, 91; objectification and, 90; primacy of, 105; privilege granted to, 88
vulnerability, 6–7, 104

weakness, 27, 78–81
Weil, Simone, 169, 172–73
Welton, Donn, 143
why-questions, 173–74
Wittgenstein, Ludwig, 10, 130, 133, 226n41; communication and, 148–49, 150–53, 151; facial expressions and, 148–49; forms of life and, 150–53; grammar of pain and, 136–37, 146; grammatical illusions and, 138–39; meaning and, 135; pain and, 135–36, 147–49, 150; *Philosophical Investigations*, 138, 147–49; primitive reactions and, 136–37, 142, 143, 147–48, 150–53, 151–53; privacy and, 138–40; publicness of pain and, 137–38; subjective character of pain and, 146
Word (logos), 33, 35, 36, 41
world, the: the body and, 37; subjectivity and, 28; visible, 43
worldliness, 165

Zahavi, Dan, 5–6, 75
zero point of orientation, 24